Imperative Program Spe~~c~~ Approach Using ~~CLP~~

Julio C. Peralta and John P. Gallagher

University of Bristol, Dept. of Computer Science
Merchant Venturers Building, Woodland Rd
BS8 1UB Bristol, UK
{jperalta,john}@cs.bris.ac.uk

Abstract.
The semantics of an imperative programming language can be expressed as a program in a declarative constraint language. Not only does this render the semantics executable, but it opens up the possibility of applying to imperative languages the advances made in program analysis and transformation of declarative languages.

We propose a method for carrying out partial evaluation of imperative programs, using partial evaluation in a declarative language, but returning the results in the syntax of the imperative program which is to be partially evaluated. The approach uses a special form of the semantics and program points to aid partial evaluation. The partially evaluated semantics program is represented as a labelled directed graph. An algorithm for reconstructing an imperative program from the graph and the residual program is presented. Constraints provide a means through which information is propagated inside both branches of a conditional, the body of a loop, and along def-use chains in the program.

The method provides a framework for constructing a partial evaluator for any imperative programming language, by writing down its semantics as a declarative program (a constraint logic program, in the approach shown here).

1 Introduction

Program semantics have long been used as a formal basis for program manipulation. By this is meant that the formal semantics of a programming language is written down in some suitable mathematical notation, which is then used to establish program properties such as termination, correctness with respect to specifications, or the correctness of program transformations. Declarative languages are useful for representing aspects of program meanings [2]. In particular, formal operational semantics can be expressed conveniently as logic programs. Moreover, this connection opens up the possibility of applying well-developed techniques for transformation and analysis of declarative languages to imperative languages through semantics. We adopt this idea and show in [21] some analysis results. Here we shall discuss the use of partial evaluators in logic programs to obtain imperative program specialisation.

A. Bossi (Ed.): LOPSTR'99, LNCS 1817, pp. 102–117, 2000.
© Springer-Verlag Berlin Heidelberg 2000

A problem arises when we specialise semantics-based interpreters written as constraint logic programs. The result of specialisation is another constraint logic program. The problem to be overcome is to return the results in the syntax of the imperative language, otherwise the specialisation is less useful to the programmer who wrote the imperative program.

The experiments reported in this paper use logic programs, in particular constraint logic programs (CLP), for implementing the semantics of an imperative programming language. After specialising such a semantics with respect to an input imperative program, the result is, in effect, a translation of the imperative program into CLP. We can also specialise further with respect to some input data for the imperative program. However, it is not immediately clear how to relate the results of such specialisation and analysis back to the original program. In order to go back to a more readable form of the specialised semantics and thus a transformed version of the input imperative program we use program points to guide partial evaluation.

Section 2 considers the implementation of the operational semantics for a small imperative language. In Section 3 we describe the partial evaluation and give an example. Section 4 delves into extracting imperative programs from the residual programs generated by our partial evaluator. Section 5 discusses related work. Finally in Section 6 we state our final remarks and the scope of our framework as well as possibilities for extending to richer imperative languages.

2   From Operational Semantics to CLP

Here we describe briefly how we obtained a CLP program from operational semantics definitions, using constraint logic programs.

In [21] the relevance of *one-state small-step* operational semantics was noted. Also in that work program points were added to the semantics to obtain a specialised program where some predicates correspond to program points in the imperative program. We shall adopt a similar approach in order to obtain a systematic way of reconstructing the specialised imperative program from the specialised constraint logic program. We first illustrate the framework using a simple imperative language and then discuss how to extend it to more expressive languages.

Assume we have an imperative language L, such as the one used in [20], for assignments, with arithmetic expressions, while statements, if-then-else conditionals, and boolean expressions. Let S_1, S_2 be two nonempty sequences of syntactically correct statements in L. Let a_1, a_2 be arithmetic expressions in L, b a boolean expression, e a variable environment (mapping variable names to their value), and x a variable. For the semantics function $\Rightarrow$ giving meaning to statements in L, the meanings of an assignment, if-then-else statement and statement composition respectively, are:

$$\langle x := a, e \rangle \Rightarrow e[x \mapsto \mathcal{A}[\![a]\!]e]$$
$$\langle \textit{if } b \textit{ then } S_1 \textit{ else } S_2, e \rangle \Rightarrow \begin{cases} \langle S_1, e \rangle \text{ if } \mathcal{B}[\![b]\!]e = \mathbf{tt} \\ \langle S_2, e \rangle \text{ if } \mathcal{B}[\![b]\!]e = \mathbf{ff} \end{cases}$$

$$\langle S_1; S_2, e\rangle \Rightarrow \begin{cases} \langle S_1'; S_2, e'\rangle \text{ if } \langle S_1, e\rangle \Rightarrow \langle S_1', e'\rangle \\ \langle S_2, e'\rangle \quad \text{ if } \langle S_1, e\rangle \Rightarrow e' \end{cases}$$

where $\mathcal{A}$ is the semantics function for arithmetic expressions, and $\mathcal{B}$ is the semantics function for boolean expressions. Next we unfold the clause for composition using the clause for assignment and the clause for if-then-else and obtain[1]:

$$\langle x := a; S_2, e\rangle \Rightarrow \langle S_2, e[x \mapsto \mathcal{A}[\![a]\!]e]\rangle$$

$$\langle(if\ b\ then\ S_{11}\ else\ S_{12}); S_2,\ e\rangle \Rightarrow \begin{cases} \langle S_{11}; S_2, e\rangle \text{ if } \mathcal{B}[\![b]\!]e = \mathbf{tt} \\ \langle S_{12}; S_2, e\rangle \text{ if } \mathcal{B}[\![b]\!]e = \mathbf{ff} \end{cases}$$

The above semantic clauses can be implemented as follows, where assign (X,A) represents an assignment statement X := A. The term compose(S1,S2) denotes the composition of statement S1 with statement(s) S2.

```
statement(E1,compose(assign(X,Ae),S2)) <- a_expr(E1,Ae,V),
                                 update(E1,E2,X,V),
                                 statement(E2,S2)
statement(E,compose(if(B,S1,S2),S3)) <- append(S1,S3,S4),
                                 append(S2,S3,S5),
                                 ifte(E,B,_,S4,S5)
ifte(E,B,tt,S21,_) <- bool_e(E,B,tt), statement(E,S21)
ifte(E,B,ff,_,S22) <- bool_e(E,B,ff), statement(E,S22)
```

We assume that the observable semantics of an imperative program is the relation between the initial and final states in any computation. However, this relation is not included in the declarative meaning of the logic program capturing the one-state semantics. In fact statement(E1,P) holds holds if the execution of program P terminates for initial environment E1, which is obviously not expressive enough.

In order to capture the relation between initial and final states in the logic program, we add a statement halt to the language, which is placed at all the terminal points[2] of a program but has no effect on the environment. We also add a 'final state' argument to the statement predicate. Accordingly, the clause for the halt statement is

```
statement(E,halt,E) <- true
```

For the other clauses of predicate statement we simply copy the 'final state' argument from head to tail, as the following clause schema shows.

```
statement(E,S,Final) <- ...,

              ...,
              statement(E1,S1,Final)
```

---

[1] This is only an extract of the semantics.
[2] That is, points where the program exits execution.

The intended imperative semantics is that the program P maps the initial state E1 to the final state E2 exactly when the following clause is derivable from the logic program.

```
statement(E1,P,E2) <- true
```

The observable behaviour of the imperative program is thus included in the declarative semantics of the CLP program, and hence the correctness of partial evaluation and other transformations ensures that the imperative program semantics is preserved during specialisation. However for most practical analysis and specialisation applications the relation between the initial and final states is irrelevant. Hence, we avoid unfolding any atom of the form statement (E, halt, F) during specialisation. This prevents constraints linking E and F to be made explicit, which would increase the complexity of the specialised programs.

The constraint used to define the a_expr[3] predicate offers the possibility of enhancing partial evaluation of the interpreter derived from the semantics, when implemented as follows for addition of arithmetic expressions:

```
a_expr(E,plus(Ae1,Ae2),V) <- a_expr(E,Ae1,V1),
                              a_expr(E,Ae2,V2),
                              {V=V1+V2}
```

where the curly brackets are used to invoke the constraint solver. Furthermore, every term representing an imperative program statement is extended with an extra argument, further referred to as a program point. This extra argument will be used to guide partial evaluation as explained in the next section.

3   Partial Evaluation Using Constraints

Partial evaluation generates a *residual program* by *evaluating* a program with *part* of its input which is available at compile-time. The aim of partial evaluation is to gain speed by specialising the source program exploiting the input available. In our application the program to be specialised is the CLP program defining the semantics of an imperative language, while the partial input consists of a term representing the target imperative program, and a partially given environment[4], both of which appear as arguments of the semantics predicate.

The specialisation is designed to perform two somewhat conflicting functions. Firstly, it should yield a residual program which reflects the structure of the original imperative program; simultaneously it should propagate information through the successive environments generated by the semantics, so as to obtain the source code specialisations.

---

[3] A similar definition is given for boolean expressions.

[4] A *partially given environment* means that the variable names within scope are know but their contents may not be known.

Two main modifications of typical partial evaluation algorithms are employed. In order to keep track of the structure of the imperative program we decorate the semantics with information about program points, as described in [21]. These appear as an extra argument in the syntactic structures and can be used to control unfolding and polyvariance. Consider, for instance, the clause above defining an assignment statement

```
statement(E1,compose(assign(X,Ae),S2)) <- a_expr(E1,Ae,V),
                                          update(E1,E2,X,V),
                                          statement(E2,S2)
```

A statement S having program point label L is represented by p(L,S). As a result, the previous clause is rewritten as

```
statement(E1,compose(p(L,assign(X,Ae)),S2)) <- a_expr(E1,Ae,V),
                                               update(E1,E2,X,V),
                                               statement(E2,S2)
```

Given semantics definitions and imperative programs where statements are decorated by program points, the unfolding rule stops specialisation when a subgoal containing a program point is met. This is achieved by making the unfolding rule 'aware' of goals containing a program point, predicate statement here.

The second modification is the use of constraints to propagate information. The specialisation algorithm generates a set of constrained atoms (see Fig. 1), represented as atom-constraint pairs, instead of the set of atoms that is more typical of logic program partial evaluators [6]. A similar idea was developed for functional logic program specialisation by Lafave [16]. We use linear arithmetic constraints[5], though any available constraint domains could be used as well.

In spite of these modifications, the well-known correctness results of partial evaluation [17] may be carried over to this partial evaluator by considering constraints as an extension to logic programs [12]. In this sense, the partial evaluation algorithm below is a constraint extension of partial evaluation algorithm [7] and the definitions therein.

Constraints are generated by collecting the arithmetic expressions found during unfolding. The constraint component of each pair results from projecting the collected constraints onto the variables of the atom component of the pair. In order to ensure termination of partial evaluation, returning a finite set of atom-constraint pairs, an upper bound operation is needed. The upper bound incorporates *msg* on atoms and the convex hull and widening of constraints, as described in [24]. In the algorithm used (Fig. 1), the operation **generalise**(R, A_i) computes the upper bound between pairs in R and A_i.

The effect of these techniques is to give specialisations in which a different predicate is generated for each reachable program point in the source imperative program. Note that more than one predicate per program point may be generated if we use information (e.g. trace terms [8] or characteristic trees [6]) in addition to the program points for the **generalise** operation. This may lead to further

---

[5] Regular term constraints [24] were used in [9].

INPUT: a program P and goal $G = \{\leftarrow D\}$, and local control rule Cr.
OUTPUT: a set of pairs $\langle$atom, constraints$\rangle$

begin
$\quad\quad A_0 := \langle D, \mathsf{true}\rangle$
$\quad\quad i := 0$
$\quad\quad$ repeat
$\quad\quad\quad\quad P' :=$ a partial evaluation of A_i in P using Cr.
$\quad\quad\quad\quad R := \{ \langle p(\bar{t}), C_1\rangle \mid (B \leftarrow Q, p(\bar{t}), Q', C) \in P' \;\lor$
$\quad\quad\quad\quad\quad\quad\quad\quad\quad (B \leftarrow Q, \mathrm{not}(p(\bar{t})), Q', C) \in P' \;\land$
$\quad\quad\quad\quad\quad\quad\quad\quad\quad C_1$ is C projected onto $vars(\bar{t})$ $\}$
$\quad\quad\quad\quad A_{i+1} := \mathbf{generalise}(R, A_i)$
$\quad\quad\quad\quad i := i + 1$
$\quad\quad$ until $A_i = A_{i-1}$ (modulo variable renaming and constraint equivalence)
end

Fig. 1. The partial evaluation algorithm

specialisation: for example, loops can be unrolled yielding different versions of the loop body. Constraints that are unsatisfiable are used to prune code from if-then-else and while constructs and constraint solving performs constant propagation.

Global control is provided by the **generalise** operation (using trace terms) and local control by the unfolding rule Cr, using determinate unfolding. In particular, the generalisation operation computes the upper bound of two pairs having the same abstraction (a program point and/or a trace term). For instance, given the following two constrained atoms having the same abstraction (trace term)

$\langle$append([U,2],[T,4],[U,2,T,4]),C1$\rangle$
$\langle$append([a,B],[C,d],[a,B,C,d]),C2$\rangle$

their most specific generalisation is $\langle$append([X,Y],[Z,W],[X,Y,Z,W]), $\sqcup$(C1,C2)$\rangle$, where $\sqcup$(C1,C2) denotes an upper bound of C1 and C2. Convex polyhedra for linear arithmetic constraints serve this purpose.

Example. From the following imperative program by partial evaluation with respect to z=2 we obtain the constraint logic program (bottom).

```
1) while y<2 do
2)    x := x - 3*z;
3)    y := y + x
      endwhile;
4) w := y + 1;
5) if w<z then
6)    r := 1
   else
7)    r := -1
```

```
statement([R,W,X,Y,2]) <- while(1,[R,W,X,Y,2])
  while(1,[R,W,X,Y,2]) <- Y<2,
                          assign(2,[R,W,X,Y,2])
  while(1,[R,W,X,Y,2]) <- Y>=2,
                          assign(4,[R,W,X,Y,2])
 assign(2,[R,W,X,Y,2]) <- X1=X-6,
                          assign(3,[R,W,X1,Y,2])
 assign(3,[R,W,X,Y,2]) <- Y1=Y+X,
                          while(1,[R,W,X,Y1,2])
 assign(4,[R,W,X,Y,2]) <- W1=Y+1,
                          ifte(5,[R,W1,X,Y,2])
   ifte(5,[R,W,X,Y,2]) <- assign(7,[R,W,X,Y,2])
 assign(7,[R,W,X,Y,2]) <- R1=-1,
                          halt([R1,W,X,Y,2]).
     halt([R,W,X,Y,2]) <-
```

Note that, for conciseness, some information was omitted[6]. The missing information corresponds to the imperative program argument as well as the list of variable names[7]. Later on, this information is used to recover the associated imperative program. The first numeral argument to some predicates above denote the program point associated to that predicate. The list corresponds to half of the contents of the variable environment. The half not shown is [r,w,x,y,z].

From now on we may recover the specialised imperative program from this specialised logic program. We may assert that the residual programs generated by partial evaluation have a certain form as stated by the following definition.

Definition. A *flowgraph constraint logic program* is a constraint logic program with clauses of the following form:

- $H \leftarrow B$
- $H \leftarrow C, B$

where H and B are non-constraint atoms or true (B only), and C is a constraint atom.

Claim. Given an imperative program and an environment in which all variables used in the program are listed partial evaluation generates only flowgraph constraint logic programs.

---

[6] Also, statement predicates have been renamed to have the name of the first element (program construct) in their argument denoting the imperative program.

[7] We intentionally named the logic variables as their imperative counterpart for ease of reading.

Justification. Because the one-state small-step semantics yields a tail recursive program, for each clause in the semantics program the partial evaluator will be able to evaluate completely all subgoals (deterministic), leaving at most a single constraint (after elimination of local variables) and the last subgoal we chose not to expand so as to preserve the structure of the imperative program.

4   Imperative Program Extraction

In the following we shall show how to extract an imperative program from a constraint logic program. Notice that using a left to right top-down computation rule to execute flowgraph constraint logic programs closely resembles the execution of a program with tests, assignments and gotos. We will exploit this information to obtain the specialised imperative program from the residual constraint logic program.

Besides extracting some control information from the constraint logic program we need to know which logic variables are associated with which imperative variables. Partial evaluation is modified to record the correspondence of the filtered[8] atoms with the original atoms. Thus we obtain residual programs where each logic variable can be associated with its corresponding imperative variable using the structure of the variable environment (e.g. in variable environment `[[u,v,w],[X,Y,Z]]` logic variables X, Y and Z correspond to imperative variables u,v and w, respectively). In addition, some further manipulation of the constraints is necessary to enable the reconstruction of legal imperative assignments as well as to distinguish between assignments and equality tests (in CLP their syntax is the same). All this information is systematically extracted from the clause that contains the constraint.

Definition. The *callgraph* G of a flowgraph constraint logic program P is a set of nodes N and arcs A. There is a mapping from the atoms in P to N such that two atoms B_1 and B_2 map to the same node iff B_1, B_2 have a common instance. There is an arc, with no label, from node N_1 to node N_2 iff P contains clause $B_1 \leftarrow B_2$ and B_1, B_2 map to N_1, N_2 respectively; or P contains a clause $B_1 \leftarrow C', B_2$ and the arc is labelled by $C'\theta$, where substitution θ maps logic variables to imperative ones as determined by the structure of variable environments in B_1 and B_2.

Callgraphs so constructed have some arcs with no label. Those arcs only denote transfer of control, since their traversal does not depend on the variable environment contents. Hence it is suggested to eliminate them to obtain a smaller graph.

Definition. The *minimal callgraph* of callgraph G is graph G' obtained by removing from G every arc with no label along with its source node, provided the source node has no other directed-out arcs. All arcs entering the source node of such an arc are redirected to the target node of the arc removed.

---

[8] During partial evaluation a stage called *argument filtering* removes some ground terms from atoms.

Example (cont'd.) From the specialised program above construct its minimal callgraph, shown in Fig. 2a, using the atom mapping shown in 2b. There already exist techniques for constructing imperative programs from such callgraphs [19]. The name of the node denotes the statement and the label on the arc(s) coming out of it describe the command. From the graph we recover a while statement and four assignments which is the specialised imperative program, as shown in Fig. 3.

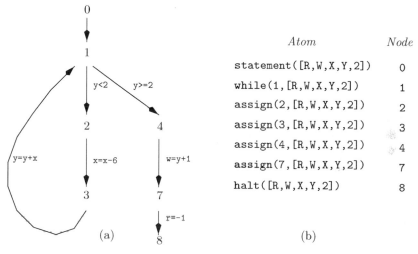

Atom	Node
statement([R,W,X,Y,2])	0
while(1,[R,W,X,Y,2])	1
assign(2,[R,W,X,Y,2])	2
assign(3,[R,W,X,Y,2])	3
assign(4,[R,W,X,Y,2])	4
assign(7,[R,W,X,Y,2])	7
halt([R,W,X,Y,2])	8

(a)   (b)

Fig. 2. Callgraph and atom mapping

```
while y<2 do
    x := x-6;
    y := y+x
endwhile;
w := y+1;
r := -1;
```

Fig. 3. Residual program

4.1   Reconstructing an Imperative Program

For the language shown here a combination of a method for structural analysis [19] with information from the flowgraph CLP program is enough to recover imperative programs. An algorithm is given in Fig. 4. In summary, structural analysis associates some graph shapes with program constructs. Because there is some overlapping between the graph shapes associated with different imperative program constructs, a common case arising in structural analysis, we use data contained in the source flowgraph CLP program. This information aids in resolving ambiguities by deciding which program construct corresponds to the (sub)graph considered. For instance, the following two clauses correspond to residual code for an if-then-else construct

```
ifte(1,[R,W,X,Y,2]) <- Y<2, assign(2,[R,W,X,Y,2])
ifte(1,[R,W,X,Y,2]) <- Y>=2, assign(4,[R,W,X,Y,2])
```

Recall that some arguments have been removed and added for presentation as well as during partial evaluation. Also, remember that this could be done automatically. In order to decide which assignment statement corresponds to the **then** branch and which corresponds to the **else** branch it is enough to see the non-filtered version of these two clauses. There the truth value given to each branch is shown. For instance, the head of the first clause could be

```
ifte(1,[[r,w,x,y,z],[R,W,X,Y,2]],le(y,2),tt,
                compose(p(2,assign(x,plus(x,2))),...),
                compose(p(4,assign(y,minus(y,1))),..))
```

where the given truth value is tt for true. Hence, the first clause corresponds to the **then** branch. The end of each branch is determined when they meet a common program point. A missing branch results in a transition of the callgraph whose associated program construct (if-then-else or while in the language considered) has been evaluated by the specialiser, thus yielding the kind of transitions eliminated when computing the minimal callgraph.

The algorithm of Fig. 4 describes the reconstruction of an abstract syntax tree from the residual program P and its associated minimal callgraph G. Function **subgraph** takes a directed graph and returns the smallest subgraph having a single entry and a single output nodes. It returns the same graph if the input graph has only one node/block with an input and an output edges only. The predicate **graph**(S,g) succeeds when S (a program statement) has graph representation g with the same edge and node labelings. Statement if-then-else is a generalisation of several forms of conditionals, hence predicate **graph** introduces the redundant information where appropriate (e.g, add skip to obtain an if-then statement). Replacing a subgraph by a single node is done by several functions depending on the case. **compress** takes a graph and replaces any non-branching sequence of nodes by a single node whose label is the sequential composition of the nodes compressed, returning another graph; **replace**(g,G,S) replaces subgraph g of G by a single node whose label is S; finally, **improper-region**(g_i,G_i,G_{i+1},P) recursively traverses the depth-first spanning tree of g_i bottom up until it finds an if-then-else or a while (through its program point and P) label on a node and replaces the appropriate subgraph of g_i (and G_i too) by the matched construct, until it reduces to a single node with an input and output edge only (graph G_{i+1}).

INPUT: A residual CLP program P and its associated minimal callgraph G
OUTPUT: An abstract syntax tree for an imperative program

$G_0 := \mathbf{compress}(G);$
$g_0 := \mathbf{subgraph}(G_0);$
$i := 0;$
repeat
      if $\mathbf{graph}($if B then S1 else S2, $g_i)$ then
         $G_{i+1} := \mathbf{replace}(g_i, G_i,$if B then S1 else S2$)$
      else
         if $\mathbf{graph}($while B do S, $g_i)$ then
            $G_{i+1} := \mathbf{replace}(g_i, G_i,$ while B do S$)$
         else
            $\mathbf{improper\text{-}region}(g_i, G_i, G_{i+1}, P)$
      $i := i + 2;$
      $G_i := \mathbf{compress}(G_{i-1});$
      $g_i := \mathbf{subgraph}(G_i)$
until $g_i = G_i$

Fig. 4. Imperative program recovery

4.2   Extending the Imperative Language

The imperative language specialised in this paper corresponds to the WHILE language of [20]. It contains if-then-else, while, and assignment constructs with simple arithmetic and boolean expressions over integers. We envisage three modifications to the current proposal to cope with extensions in the imperative language treated.

Compound data types. It is straightforward to extend the current semantics to include arrays and records yet preserving the one-state small-step operational semantics form. The ensuing modification to the specialiser is to allow flowgraph CLP programs to have a conjunction of constraints where there is only one constraint in the body of a clause. Such a conjunction of constraints includes atoms as well as arithmetic constraints. Arithmetic constraints are translated as explained above. The atoms in the conjunction represent unevaluated selector predicates for accessing parts of compound structures, e.g. a lookup in the variable environment. Those subgoals could be regarded as constraints on the logical variable representing the output of such an update. Recovering a variable name (array or record) is straightforward from the meaning of the selector predicate symbol according to the semantics.

Subroutines with parameters. The semantics would be modified in two ways in order to stay within the one-state small-step operational semantics form.

Firstly, the variable environment would be extended to have locations. Instead of the direct mapping from variable names to their contents there would be two mappings, one from variable names to locations and another one from locations to their contents. However, if parameters are passed by value locations are not needed. Locations open the possibility of having *pointers* in the language.

Secondly, the semantics predicate would include a third argument in addition to the variable environment and the program statements. This new argument would provide the functionality of the stack of activation records in traditional compiler implementations for imperative languages. A problem arises when computing the upper bound[9] of two atoms with the same program point but different stack of activation records. The partial evaluator, as presented here, needs to be modified. A promising solution is the use of regular approximations during generalisation in partial evaluation, as shown in [9]. A further extension is needed in order to propagate constraints as shown here. Similar techniques as those of [24] are being developed. Imperative program recovery remains the same as outlined for arrays and records above.

Other program constructs. Extending the language with `repeat-until`, `for`, `case` and other program constructs could be done with a price to pay in program recovery and preprocessing of the imperative program. It is well known that such program constructs could be expressed in terms of `while` and `if-then-else` constructs. As a result, their semantic definitions would have some overlapping with those of the basic program constructs (`while` and `if-then-else`). Hence, recovering the appropriate program statement raises potential problems of nondeterminism in reconstructing the imperative program. In addition, some contextual information is required to produce the appropriate abstract syntax trees for input to the semantics-based CLP program. For these reasons, such constructs are normally avoided for program analysis during partial evaluation, commonly regarded as "syntactic sugar" [10]. A possible solution is to allow the inclusion of the above program constructs at the expense of recovering programs where only `goto`, `while` and `if-then-else` constructs occur.

5   Related Work

Here we will consider work on partial evaluation of imperative languages. There has been important work [5,13] on the specialisation of imperative languages expressed as denotational definitions, to functional languages. Nevertheless we will only discuss some of the work which focuses on source-to-source specialisation of imperative languages.

In [18] a technique for partial evaluation of programs in a subset of the Pascal programming language is presented. Their specialisation method consists of a set of rules for transforming each construct in the language considered. It is a combination of off-line and on-line methods for specialisation. There is

---

[9] Within the **generalise** operation of Fig. 1.

no clear separation between the semantics representation (semantics-based interpretation/execution), and the partial evaluation. Using an on-line approach called *symbolic execution* Coen-Porisini et al. [4] present a method for specialising programs in a subset of the Ada programming language. Their method divides specialisation into two functions, whose definition is given for each program construct. One for symbolic execution and the other one for constructing the specialised program. The quality of the specialised code depends on the user helping the specialiser (e.g. providing invariants, helping the loop folder or helping the theorem prover). Both prototypes above were implemented in Lisp.

In [15] is described a partial evaluator for a subset of Fortran 77. Partial evaluation is a 4-step process: Translation from the Fortran program into a low level code (Core Fortran); monovariant binding-time analysis and annotation of the program statements as static or dynamic; specialisation of the annotated low level code; and translation into the source language, Fortran 77. The partial evaluator was written in Fortran. The monovariant binding-time analysis used results in little constant propagation.

Analysis and transformation of programs in ANSI C was the target of Andersen's work in [1], whose present form is briefly discussed in Glenstrup et al. [10]. The specialiser is automatic and generates generating extensions in C. The C program specialisation is achieved in several steps. Using a context-insensitive binding-time analysis the source C program is analysed. The analysed C program is transformed thus producing a generating extension program. Attaching the appropriate libraries and the partial input, the generating extension is executed. The output of such an execution is a specialised C program. A set of C libraries describe the transformations that the generated extension contains.

Recent work on specialisation of C programs is given in [11]. The specialiser handles a considerable subset of the C language. Their binding time analysis is polyvariant. Constraints haven't been integrated into their analysis phase though.

In a slightly different approach to partial evaluation Blazy et al. [3] adapt a partial evaluator for Fortran to aid program understanding through partial evaluation. A partial evaluator is modified so that loops are never unfolded neither procedure calls inlined thus residual programs preserve most of the structure of the source program. Through inference rules coded in Prolog the authors specify propagation of constants interprocedurally. Memoing allows them to obtain some control of polyvariance, however they fail to provide a terminating strategy for their online partial evaluator.

A similar approach to ours is presented by Ross [23]. Logical semantics provide definitions of imperative program constructs associating a relation with each program construct. Imperative program composition (sequencing) corresponds to the composition of relations. Thus, a logic program is derived from an imperative program by rewriting each program construct as a predicate, whose definition is made of Horn clauses, and composing such relations according to the control flow of the imperative program. Such a logic program describes the natural operational semantics of the imperative program with predicates denoting the input-output relation of variable values for each program construct. A preprocessing of the resulting logic program allows the removal of dead code in the presence of unconditional jumps (gotos). Later that logic program is partially evaluated and the resulting program analysed to reconstruct a partially evaluated imperative program. During reconstruction some literal reordering may be necessary in order to preserve the operational semantics of the residual imperative program. In contrast to their hand translation our approach uses program specialisation both for obtaining the logic program corresponding to an imperative program and for specialising the imperative program computation. Our framework is designed to be adaptable to any language for which operational semantics can be defined. Secondly, our use of one-state small-step semantics greatly reduces the complexity of the analysis of the specialised program as we discussed in [21].

Although most of the contributions are labelled as techniques for specialisation of imperative languages, only one language is explored in each paper, and it is not clear how to extend the techniques to other languages. Besides, we believe the methods above do not commit to a semantics-based approach. None of them take the semantics of the language studied as a basis for transforming the language programs, except [23]. Most of the methods above are off-line with the exception of [3,4,18,23]. Our method is based on an on-line partial evaluator which in principle allows greater specialisation, compared to off-line specialisation.

6   Concluding Remarks

Using a description of the operational semantics of a subset of an imperative language we implemented a logic program which mimics the semantics. With the help of a partial evaluator for constraint logic programs we can obtain program specialisation of imperative programs. Imperative programs so specialised end up as specialised logic programs, whereas what is needed is a specialised program in the imperative source language. We use a form of the semantics which is tail-recursive and aids the propagation of boolean tests into their program constructs. With the help of program points and some modifications to an on-line partial evaluator we can obtain constraint logic programs in a certain class where recovery of a specialised imperative program could be achieved automatically. As a result we obtain an on-line partial evaluator for single procedure imperative programs.

Not all imperative language constructs share a common semantics definition. There are subtle differences for each language, for each construct. Nonetheless, we believe that the technique proposed here can be generalised to more imperative languages, provided we had implemented the semantics definitions, for the desired language, in an adequate form to aid partial evaluation and imperative program extraction.

Scope and Extensibility of our results. In the experiments we have reported we used a single procedure imperative language with integer data types. Extension to imperative languages with procedures and other data types (records, arrays, pointers, etc.) is the subject of our current research. On the one side, we have extended the semantics above to include unidimensional arrays as shown in [21]. Handling of multidimensional arrays and records could be done in a similar way as above. Pointers may be represented using locations, and techniques from [22] could be used to increase the precision of the specialisation. On the other side, the semantics for a language with procedures and parameters by reference poses new problems to existing partial evaluation techniques. Similar problems have been successfully solved in [14,22] for program analysis, and recently in [9] for partial evaluation. Thus, we envisage success provided information is preserved upon generalisation. We are currently applying these techniques to the semantics of three languages (Pascal, Java and JVM) and generality of the results here shown should be drawn from the fact that these languages have different semantics but the partial evaluation techniques are the same (i.e. the same partial evaluator).

Acknowledgements. Julio C. Peralta is sponsored by a student grant from DGAPA, UNAM. Comments from the referees helped in improving the presentation of this work.

References

1. Lars Ole Andersen. *Program Analysis and Specialization for the C programming Language*. PhD thesis, DIKU, University of Copenhagen, Denmark, May 1994.
2. Andrew W. Appel. SSA is functional programming. *ACM SIGPLAN Notices*, 33(4):17–20, 1998.
3. Sandrine Blazy and Philippe Facon. An automatic interprocedural analysis for the understanding of scientific application programs. In O. Danvy, Robert Glück, and Peter Thieman, editors, *International Seminar on Partial Evaluation*, pages 1–16. Springer-Verlag, LNCS 1110, 1996.
4. Alberto Coen-Porisini, Flavio De Paoli, Carlo Ghezzi, and Dino Mandrioli. Software specialization via symbolic execution. *IEEE Transactions on Software Engineering*, 17(9):884–899, 1991.
5. Charles Consel and Olivier Danvy. Static and dymanic semantic processing. In ACM Press, editor, *Conference Record of the Eighteenth Annual ACM Symposium on Principles of Programming Languages*, pages 14–24, Orlando, Florida, 1991.
6. J. Gallagher and M. Bruynooghe. The derivation of an algorithm for program specialisation. *New Generation Computing*, 9(3&4):305–333, 1991.
7. John P. Gallagher. Tutorial on specialisation of logic programs. In *Proceedings of the ACM SIGPLAN Symposium on Partial Evaluation and Semantics-Based Program Manipulation*, pages 88–98, Copenhagen, Denmark, 1993. ACM Press.
8. John P. Gallagher and L. Lafave. Regular approximation of computation paths in logic and functional languages. In O. Danvy, R. Glück, and P. Thiemman, editors, *Partial Evaluation*, pages 115–136. Springer-Verlag, LNCS 1110, 1996.
9. John P. Gallagher and Julio C. Peralta. Using regular approximations for generalisation during partial evaluation. In *Workshop on Partial Evaluation and Program Manipulation*, pages 44–51. ACM Press, 2000. To appear in ACM SIGPLAN Notices.

10. Arne John Glenstrup, Henning Makholm, and Jens Peter Secher. C-mix: Specialization of C programs. Notes from the Partial Evaluation Summer School held at DIKU Copenhagen, Denmark, 1998.
11. Luke Hornof, Jaques Noyé, and Charles Consel. Effective specialization of realistic programs via use sensitivity. In Pascal Van Hentenryck, editor, *Static Analysis Symposium*, pages 293–318. Springer-Verlag, LNCS 1302, 1997.
12. Joxan Jaffar and Michael J. Maher. Constraint logic programming: A survey. *The Journal of Logic Programming*, 19(20):503–581, 1994.
13. Neil D. Jones, Carsten K. Gomard, and Peter Sestoft. *Partial Evaluation and Automatic Program Generation*. Prentice Hall International Series, 1993.
14. Neil D. Jones and Steven S. Muchnick. A flexible approach to interprocedural data flow analysis and programs with recursive data structures. In ACM Press, editor, *Conference Record of the Ninth Symposium on Principles of Programming Languages*, pages 66–74, 1982.
15. Paul Kleinrubatscher, Albert Kriegshaber, Robert Zöling, and Robert Glück. Fortran program specialization. *SIGPLAN Notices*, 30(4):61–70, 1995.
16. Laura Lafave. *A Constraint-based Partial Evaluator for Functional Logic Programs and its Application*. PhD thesis, University of Bristol, UK, 1999.
17. J. W. Lloyd and J. C. Shepherdson. Partial evaluation in logic programming. *The Journal of Logic Programming*, 11(3&4):217–242, 1991.
18. Uwe Meyer. Techniques for partial evaluation of imperative programs. In *Proceedings of the Symposium on Partial Evaluation and Semantics-Based Program Manipulation*, pages 94–115, New Haven, Conneticut, 1991. ACM Press.
19. Steven S. Muchnick. *Advanced Compiler Design and Implementation*. Morgan Kaufman, 1997.
20. Hanne Riis Nielson and Flemming Nielson. *Semantics with Applications*. John Wiley and Sons, 1992.
21. Julio C. Peralta, John P. Gallagher, and Hüseyin Sağlam. Analysis of imperative programs through analysis of constraint logic programs. In G. Levi, editor, *Static Analysis Symposium*, pages 246–261. Springer-Verlag, LNCS 1503, 1998.
22. Thomas Reps. Program analysis via graph reachability. Technical Report TR-1386, Computer Sciences Department, University of Wisconsin, August 1998. Extended version of invited paper in Proceedings of ILPS97.
23. Brian J. Ross. The partial evaluation of imperative programs using Prolog. In H. Abramson and M. H. Rogers, editors, *Meta-Programming in Logic Programming*, pages 341–363. MIT Press, 1989.
24. Hüseyin Sağlam and John P. Gallagher. Constrained regular approximations of logic programs. In N. Fuchs, editor, *LOPSTR'97*, pages 282–299. Springer-Verlag, LNCS 1463, 1997.

Proof Obligations of the B Formal Method: Local Proofs Ensure Global Consistency

Mireille Ducassé and Laurence Rozé

IRISA/INSA, Campus Universitaire de Beaulieu, F - 35042 Rennes Cedex, France
{ducasse, roze}@irisa.fr, http://www.irisa.fr/lande/ducasse/

Abstract. The B formal method has been successfully used in large projects and is not reserved to experts. The main correctness criterion of B is that every piece of code must preserve invariant properties. In this article, we briefly introduce the basic notions of B. We then concentrate on the proof obligations. After introducing them, we show how the sum of local proofs makes a global consistency. We believe that this strong modularity is essential for the tractability of the proofs.

1 Introduction

The B formal method is successfully used in the French industry of transportation. For example, the automatic train operating system of Météor, the first driver-less metro in the city of Paris, has been developed in B. Over 110 000 lines of B were written, generating 86 000 lines of ADA. More than 27 000 lemmas were proved, of which 92% could be proved automatically after some customizations of the tools; 2254 lemmas had to be proved interactively. No bugs were detected after the proofs, neither at the functional validation, at the integration validation, at on-site test, nor since the metro lines operate (October 1998). The people involved in the development enjoyed using the method and believe that it is not reserved to experts [3].

The B method is a mature synthesis of 30 years of software engineering research. Among the acknowledged sources are Floyd's initial work on proof obligations [7], Hoare's calculus [10], Parnas' specification modules [14], Dijkstra's weakest precondition [5], Gries' program development approach [8], as well as refinement theories of He and Hoare's [9], Morgan [13], Backhouse [2] and Jones [11].

This article is a followup to an invited presentation of the B formal method at LOPSTR'99. There already exist a number of introductions to the B method from the developer point of view (see for example [16] or [12]). Here we concentrate on the proof obligations of B. After introducing them, we show how the sum of local proofs makes a global consistency. As far as we know, this aspect is only implicit in the existing B publications. We believe, however, that it is one of the major strengths of the method and that it is worth being explicit. Indeed, local proofs, although not necessarily easy, are still tractable whereas global reasoning would be unbearable for both an automated prover and the person in charge of the interactive proving.

A. Bossi (Ed.): LOPSTR'99, LNCS 1817, pp. 10–29, 2000.

An exhaustive description of the method can be found in the B-Book from Jean-Raymond Abrial [1]. This article can be seen as an introduction to (or a discussion of) its chapters 4-6,11,12. These chapters cover more than 170 pages, we therefore cannot pretend to go here in all the formal details. In order to get an in-depth picture, interested readers are referred to the above mentioned chapters of the B-book.

In B, specification and code are structured into *abstract machines*. Abstract machines can be seen as classes without inheritance. An abstract machine encapsulates variables. Its main components are:

- an *invariant* (I) stating properties over variables which must always hold,
- *operations* or services (S_i) which are the only means to modify the encapsulated variables. Most services have a *precondition* (P_i), which states under which premises executing the services makes sense. Services are formalized by *substitutions*. A substitution can be the usual substitution (e.g., $x := 3$) or a *generalized substitution* introducing control in the services (e.g., IF $x < 0$ THEN $x := 3$ ELSE $x := x + 1$ END). All generalized substitutions are introduced in section 4.3.

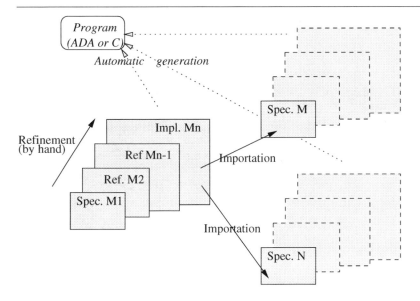

Fig. 1. The development steps of B machines: specification, refinements, implementation and importations, followed by the automatic generation of target implementation language code

As illustrated by Figure 1, when developing B software, one starts by a *specification* (its operations do not need to be executable), then one writes zero, one or several intermediate *refinement(s)*. The last refinement is called an *implementation*. It can call operations of other machines, this is called *importation*. Note that when importing a machine, one only deals with its specification. One does not need to know how the imported machine is refined and implemented. Once the B implementation machines are written, the compiler generates a program in a target implementation language (for example, Ada or C).

Correctness of a program only has a meaning with respect to correctness criteria. The main correctness criterion of B is that every abstract machine preserves invariant properties. At each step of the development, namely every time an abstract machine is added, a *proof obligation* (PO in the following) is created to ensure that all invariants hold.

Section 2 shows a small example of B source code. It gives a flavor of B and it is used afterwards to illustrate the proof obligations. Section 3 emphasizes that the keystone of the B method is the proof obligation of the specification which ensures that specified invariants are preserved. Section 4 lists the important features of B; in particular, Subsection 4.3 briefly introduces the central notion of *generalized substitution*. Section 5 describes most proof obligations of the B method and discusses how local proofs can ensure that invariants are globally preserved. Furthermore, it briefly emphasizes that termination and feasibility are also proved.

2   A Small Example of B Abstract Machines

This section presents a small example of B in order to give a flavor of B concepts. We are aware that this example may seem too trivial and artificial. However, as the given machines are used in the following to illustrate the proof obligations, it was important to keep them simple. For larger examples, see for example [17].

Figure 2 shows three abstract machines, *CALCULATOR*, *CALCULATOR_I*, and *SCALAR*. We describe and discuss them in turn in the following.

CALCULATOR encapsulates a single variable z. The invariant specifies that this variable must always be in the interval 0..100. It is initialized to 0. There is a single operation (service), **increment**, which has one parameter, a. At this stage it is only specified that the operation can replace z with any value between 0 and 100 (specified by the non-deterministic generalized substitution $z :\in 0..100$). The precondition tells that this is only valid if the parameter a of the operation belongs to the 0..100 interval and if $a + z$ also belongs to the same interval.

Basically, the specification pays attention to set the conditions under which it will make sense to add a to z, but it does not address the algorithm to achieve the addition. Whereas the machine is very small and may not seem very striking, for more sophisticated problems, one should appreciate the separation of concerns: one does not have to worry at the same time for preconditions and computation algorithms.

Note that non-deterministic specifications have no operational semantics. The target implementation languages are imperative and deterministic. The non-deterministic specifications can therefore be seen as "conception choice points". The developer can leave some possibilities open at specification time, and will make the choices later, at refinement and implementation times.

MACHINE
   $CALCULATOR$
VARIABLES
   z
INVARIANT
   $z \in 0..100$
INITIALIZATION
   $z := 0$
OPERATIONS
   increment(a) $\hat{=}$
     PRE
       $a \in 0..100$
       $\wedge\, a + z \in 0..100$
     THEN
       $z :\in 0..100$
     END
END

IMPLEMENTATION
   $CALCULATOR\_I$
REFINES
   $CALCULATOR$
IMPORTS
   $SCALAR(0)$
INVARIANT
   $x = z$
OPERATIONS
   increment(a) $\hat{=}$
     VAR v IN
       $v \leftarrow$ **value** ;
       $v := v + a$;
       modify(v)
     END
END

MACHINE
   $SCALAR(i)$
CONSTRAINTS
   $i \in NAT$
VARIABLES
   x
INVARIANT
   $x \in NAT$
INITIALIZATION
   $x := i$
OPERATIONS
   modify(v) $\hat{=}$
     PRE
       $v \in NAT$
     THEN
       $x := v$
     END ;
   $v \leftarrow$ **value** $\hat{=}$
     BEGIN $v := x$ END
END

Fig. 2. An example of B abstract machines

$CALCULATOR\_I$ refines and implements $CALCULATOR$. It has no variable of its own. It imports a basic machine $SCALAR$, with an initial value of 0, to delegate the management of its encapsulated variable. The invariant of CAL-$CULATOR\_I$ links the variable z of the refined machine ($CALCULATOR$) with the variable x of the imported machine ($SCALAR$). It states that at every moment the values of z and x should be equal. Note that the invariant is the only place where the two variables appear. Indeed, due to strong encapsulation, the only way to modify the variables of another machine is to use its operations. The **increment** operation uses a local variable v and calls the two operations of $SCALAR$, **modify** and **value**. The operation is no longer non-deterministic, this time we do perform an addition. Due to the precondition of the specification, we are sure that the result of the addition will always be within the proper interval.

$SCALAR$ is a *basic machine*, namely it has no refinement or implementation in B. It is directly implemented in the target implementation language (e.g., ADA or C). The basic machines are validated independently from the B method. Note, however, that these machines are so simple that it is relatively simple to validate them and to be convinced that this validation is in turn valid. $SCALAR$ has one parameter i which represents its initial value. The constraints tell that, in order to be called properly, i must be in NAT, namely an integer in $0..maxint$. $SCALAR$ encapsulates a variable x which is initialized by i. The two operations **modify** and **value** respectively replaces and gives the value of x.

3   The B Method Keystone

As mentioned in the introduction, the main correctness criterion of B is that every abstract machine preserves an invariant. The keystone of B is thus the (slightly simplified [1]) formula of the proof obligations for the abstract machine of a specification:

For all services i consisting of a precondition P_i and a substitution S_i,

$$\boxed{\ I \ \wedge \ P_i \ \Rightarrow \ [S_i]\, I\ }$$

This proof obligation means that for every service, we have to prove that if both the properties which have been specified in the invariant (I) and the precondition (P_i) of a given service hold, then after the execution of the substitution of this service (S_i) the invariant still holds.

More proof obligations exist, in particular for refinements and implementations (see section 5). Note, however, that the essence of B is contained in the above formula. Firstly, it contains the main components of an abstract machine, namely invariant, service and precondition. Secondly, it uses the central notion of generalized substitution (see section 4.3). Lastly, all the important notions of the B method and language follow from this particular formula (see next section).

4   Basic Stones

In this section we briefly introduce all the basic stones of the B method and language. As mentioned above, they are strongly connected to the proof obligation keystone. They are divided into two categories, theoretical foundations and abstract machine concepts. Generalized substitutions are such a central concept that they deserve a subsection by themselves.

4.1   Theoretical Foundations

First order logic. Proofs require some logics. In B, in general, only very stable pieces of theory are integrated, and the simpler the better. First order logic with equality is the first basic bloc.

Set theory. Predicates are fine to make proofs but they are not so well suited for specifications. Indeed, a very important aim of specifications is to be a basis for discussion. They therefore have to be easy to understand by a large community. It is mandatory that different people, not necessarily with a strong background in logic, can easily get convinced that they agree on their interpretation of the specification, namely on the reality which is modeled by the specification. Using first-oder logic alone for specification means that the formulae will quickly become complicated. Experience shows that people have difficulties to agree upon

---

[1] A complete formula is given in section 5.1

a common interpretation of formulae. A few connectors and quantifiers are sufficient to confuse most engineers. On the opposite, sets, relations and functions give a higher-level of abstraction which is much better understood by engineers, as constantly illustrated in our class. Since 1994, we give a B course to students preparing a software engineering degree [6]. No student has had real problems with specifying with sets, whereas approximatively half of them have major problems with plain logic. Thus, our experience sustains the design decision of the B method to keep first order logic mainly for proof mechanisms while people specify with sets.

Arithmetics and finite sequences. People do need arithmetics and lists, the latter therefore have been integrated in the B method. The usual fix point semantics with Tarsky theorems is the theoretical basis of this part.

4.2   Abstract Machine Concepts

Encapsulation. It is a common recommendation in software engineering to make modular software. Limiting the scope of identifiers and operations helps limiting the impact of possible errors; it also helps programmers understand each module. In B, the variables are encapsulated. They can only be modified by the services of their abstract machine. The internal structure of an abstract machine can therefore change but its interface remains the same. Encapsulation not only makes the software easier to maintain, it also makes proofs more tractable.

Precondition. A service of a given abstract machine can be used at different places. Its precondition tells the other abstract machines under which conditions this service can be used. Thus if an abstract machine calls this service, someone has to prove that its precondition is satisfied (see the proof obligation of the implementation and the discussion of section 5).

Note that, when a functionality is defined, there is no means to know how it will be used. Indeed, the calling code may not even be written. Hence, with a programming language without preconditions, a developer is left with the choice of either hoping that all calls to its functionalities will be proper, or making (possibly very costly) checkings at run-time. The first solution is definitely not a solution for critical softwares. The second solution may turn out too costly, for example for real-time systems. As, in B, preconditions are proved before execution, there is no need for run-time checkings. Preconditions therefore guarantee some safety without any cost at execution time.

Refinement. Refinements tune the algorithms to make them as operational and optimized as necessary. In particular, developers have to reduce the non-determinism and refine the data.

Specifications can be highly non-deterministic but, at the end of the refinement process, the produced implementation must be deterministic. It must implement one, and only one, of the possibilities stated in the specification. For example, the **increment** operation of the *CALCULATOR* machine of Figure 2 specifies that its result must be between 0 and 100. This is non-deterministic. The implementation of **increment** in $CALCULATOR\_I$ tells how to deterministically choose the value ($z := z + a$).

Data refinement is necessary when the refined algorithm used a different data structure. For example, a set of integers u can be refined into a single integer x if the sole purpose of the machine is to be able to return the maximum of u. At the abstract levels, entering a new integer does indeed add the integer to u; and returning the maximum does consider all the integers of u in turn to choose the max. At the refinement level, entering a new integer does compare the new integer with x and keeps the bigger one into x; and returning the maximum does simply return the value of x which is, indeed, the maximum of the integers entered so far.

The abstract and the refined substitutions have to be compared. As each machine encapsulates its own variables, the invariant of the refinement is mostly a *binding invariant* which tells how the variables of specification and refinement are related. For the previous example the binding invariant is $x = max(u \cup \{0\})$ (0 takes into account that u can be empty). For the implementation of Figure 2 the binding invariant is simply $x = z$ because there is no data refinement.

Between a high-level specification and an implementation, B allows several levels of refinements to take place. Indeed, B refinement is *transitive*:

$$\boxed{S \sqsubseteq T \wedge T \sqsubseteq U \Rightarrow S \sqsubseteq U}$$

If a specification S is refined by a refinement T, which in turn is refined by, say, an implementation U, then S is refined by U. The general idea of refinements is to go from high-level to machine level in an incremental way such that programmers understand what they are doing. Here again, splitting the concerns also helps to make proofs more tractable.

4.3   Generalized Substitutions

We have already mentioned that services are specified by substitutions. Beyond simple substitutions, programs require some control which is modeled by the generalized substitutions (e.g., IF $x < 0$ THEN $x := 3$ ELSE $x := x + 1$ END). Generalized substitutions extend the scope of the proof obligation without complexifying the formula. It remains $I \wedge P_i \Rightarrow [S_i]I$, however complicated S_i is.

Figure 3 gives the definition of all the generalized substitutions used in B. The first column gives the names of the substitutions, the second column gives the syntax(es). There are often two syntaxes: a concise one for proofs, and a more verbose one for programming. The third column gives the axiom which defines the semantics of $[S]I$ for the substitution. Generalized substitutions are based on Dijkstra weakest-precondition calculus [5]. They are defined as predicate transformers: $[S]I$ is the weakest condition which should hold before the substitution S takes place, in oder for S to establish I. In the following we comment each definition.

Substitution	Syntax(es)	Axiom
Simple	$x := E$	(As commonly known)
Multiple	$x, y := E, F$	$[x, y := E, F] R \Leftrightarrow$
	$x := E \parallel y := F$	$[z := F][x := E][y := z] R$
Empty	**skip**	$[\textbf{skip}] R \Leftrightarrow R$
Precondition	$P \mid S$	$[P \mid S] R \Leftrightarrow (P \wedge [S] R)$
	PRE P THEN S END	
Bounded	$S \, [] \, T$	$[S[]T]R \Leftrightarrow ([S]R \wedge [T]R)$
Choice	CHOICE S OR T END	
Guard	$Q \Longrightarrow S$	$[Q \Longrightarrow S]R \Leftrightarrow (Q \Rightarrow [S]R)$
	SELECT Q THEN S END	
Unbounded	$@x \cdot S$	$[@x \cdot S] R \Leftrightarrow \forall x \cdot [S] R$
Choice	ANY x S	$x \setminus R$
Sequence	$S \,; T$	$[S \,; T]R \Leftrightarrow [S][T]R$

Fig. 3. Definition of all B generalized substitutions where E and F are expressions; x, y and z are variables, S and T are substitutions (possibly generalized); P, Q and R are predicates; $x \setminus R$ means that x has no free occurrences in R; the substitution application is right associative.

The meaning of $[S]I$ for a simple substitution such as, for example, $x := 3$ is well known: all free occurrences of x in I are replaced by 3. The simple substitution is defined by induction on all the B constructs. For example, it has no effect if the variable to be substituted is already quantified in the predicate ($[x := 3]\forall x.P \Leftrightarrow \forall x.P$). Otherwise, it distributes over logical connectors and generalized substitution constructors. It is not affected by negation ($\neg[x := 3]I \Leftrightarrow [x := 3]\neg I$). The complete list of axioms can be found in [1, p755-756].

The multiple substitution is a sort of simultaneous substitution. For example, using the definition, one can easily see that $[x, y := y, x](x = y) \Leftrightarrow (y = x)$. Note that a multiple substitution has nothing to do with a sequence.

The empty substitution (**skip**) has no effect. This substitution preserves any invariant. It is convenient to specify operations which only have an operational semantics. For example, consider a system which has a top-level loop which simply reads entries and calls other machine operations to treat these entries; the corresponding abstract machine has no variable of its own, and the abstraction of the loop is **skip**. Another interesting example is an operation which simply writes a result. Its abstraction is again **skip**. Indeed, an output side effect only has an operational semantics to be specified at implementation time.

The precondition specifies which conditions must be true in order for the service to make sense and terminate.

The bounded choice leaves conception choice points. Further refinements will choose one possible branch. Whatever the chosen branch, the invariant must hold; therefore we have to prove that all possible branches preserve the invariant (hence the ∧ in the axiom).

The guard specifies which conditions must be true in order for the service to be feasible. Its primary purpose is to support the definition of the conditional substitution: IF G THEN S ELSE T END is defined by $(G \implies S) [] (\neg G \implies T)$ Note that if a guard G is always false the specification is not feasible but $[G \implies T]R$ will nevertheless hold for all R. The proof of the keystone PO therefore does not detect infeasible code, but we show in section 5.4 that the PO of refinement, if discharged, ensures feasibility.

The unbounded choice is another non-deterministic constructor. Further refinement will have to choose one particular s. Here again all the possibilities must preserve the invariant (hence the ∀ in the axiom). Note that this substitution is always used with a guard to type the variable: ANY x WHERE G THEN S END $(@x \cdot (G \implies S))$.

All the operations at specification level can be written using a combination of the above generalized substitutions. For example, the $z :\in U$ constructor used in the $CALCULATOR$ machine of Figure 2 is defined as $@y.(y \in U \implies z := y)$, z is non-deterministically substituted by any y belonging to U.

From an operational point of view, the sequence is the common sequence. For example, in sequence $(x, y := 6, 2 \; ; \; x := 1)$ the second valuation of x outdoes the first one. The final value of x is 1. The fact that the last substitution is the one which has the final impact at implementation level is modeled in the axiom. Indeed, the substitution application is right associative; in $[S][T]I$, T has the precedence over S. This is illustrated by the proof that sequence $(x, y := 6, 2 \; ; \; x := 1)$ preserves invariant $x + y < 4$:

$[x, y := 6, 2 \; ; \; x := 1](x + y < 4) \overset{sequence\ axiom}{\Leftrightarrow}$

$[x, y := 6, 2][x := 1](x + y < 4) \overset{right\ assoc.}{\Leftrightarrow}$

$[x, y := 6, 2](1 + y < 4) \overset{simple\ subst.}{\Leftrightarrow} (1 + 2 < 4) \Leftrightarrow (3 < 4)$

Note that the sequence is not allowed at specification level because it is too operational. It is, however, used in some of the proof obligations given in the following.

5   Local Proofs Ensure Global Consistency

The aim of the verification process is to prove a number of properties for the whole system. However, proving all the properties at the same time is not tractable. Instead, in B, at each step of the development, namely every time an abstract machine is added, a proof obligation is created. However, at the moment a PO is generated a number of properties cannot be proved and some of them are needed to discharge the PO. Provided that they are proved at some point, they can be used in the premises of the local PO thanks to the following theorem (which is straightforward to prove)

$(R \wedge W) \Leftrightarrow (R \wedge R \Rightarrow W)$.

For example, for a given machine, until the operations are actually called, we cannot know whether the preconditions of its operations hold. Thus, the precondition of an operation is in the premises of the PO of this operation. We will show that the precondition indeed holds at the times the operation is called.

When discussing the proof obligations, we systematically show that all the premises of all the PO are inductively proved in due times. The sum of the local proofs therefore ensures that the whole B code globally preserves all invariants.

Note that there are some mechanisms which weaken the strong encapsulation. For example, the *SEES* mechanism enables to get the values of machine variables without using machine operations. Extra care must be taken when combining it with importation [15].

In this section we present the proof obligation formulae. They are slightly simplified. In particular, they do not take into account output parameters and included machines. When machines are imported, parameter passing is implicit. We introduce two new kinds of properties: the *constraints on the calling parameters* (C) and the *properties on the constants and sets* (Q). In B all sets are finite. In the B-book formulae this is explicit. In the following formulae it is implicitly included in C and Q. These simplifications have no impact on what we want to demonstrate in this section.

5.1   Specification Proof Obligations

Figure 4 gives all the proof obligations for the specification machines of Figure 2, namely $CALCULATOR$ and $SCALAR$. Before we comment the figure, we give the PO formulae.

In abstract machines, services are specified by *operations*. The proof obligation of an operation $P_i \mid S_i$ is:

Proof Obligation 1 *(Operation of a specification)*

$$C \wedge Q \wedge I \wedge P_i \Rightarrow [S_i]\, I$$

This can be read as follows. If the constraints (C) on the calling parameters hold (i.e., the machine is called with proper parameters) and if the properties (Q) on the constants and sets hold (i.e., the implementation is done properly) and if the invariant (I) holds (ie, at the moment the operation is used, nothing has yet corrupted the state) and if the precondition (P_i) holds then we must prove that the substitution (S_i) preserves the invariant.

For example, in Figure 4, PO1 is the proof obligation for the **increment** operation of the $CALCULATOR$ machine. The machine has no parameters, no constants and no sets, there are therefore no constraints on parameters (i.e., no C) and no properties of constants and sets (i.e., no Q). The premises therefore consist only of the invariant and the two predicates of the operation precondition. The goal to prove is that if z is replaced by any value between 0 and 100, the resulting value will be between 0 and 100. The goal is trivially true. PO3 is the proof obligation for the **modify** operation of the $SCALAR$ machine. The

Proof obligations for the *CALCULA-TOR* machine

Proof obligations for the *SCALAR* machine

PO 1 increment *operation*

$$
\begin{array}{ll}
& \text{no Constraints} \\
& \text{no Properties} \\
z \in 0..100 & \text{Invariant} \\
\wedge\ a \in 0..100 & \text{Precondition (1)} \\
\wedge\ z + a \in 0..100 & \text{Precondition (2)} \\
\Rightarrow & \\
\quad [z : \in 0..100](z \in 0..100) &
\end{array}
$$

PO 2 *initialization*

$$
\begin{array}{ll}
& \text{no Constraints} \\
& \text{no Properties} \\
[z := 0](z \in 0..100) &
\end{array}
$$

PO 3 modify *operation*

$$
\begin{array}{ll}
i \in NAT & \text{Constraints} \\
& \text{no Properties} \\
x \in NAT & \text{Invariant} \\
\wedge\ v \in NAT & \text{Precondition} \\
\Rightarrow [x := v](x \in NAT) &
\end{array}
$$

PO 4 value *operation*

$$
\begin{array}{ll}
i \in NAT & \text{Constraints} \\
& \text{no Properties} \\
x \in NAT & \text{Invariant} \\
& \text{no Precondition} \\
\Rightarrow [v := x](x \in NAT) &
\end{array}
$$

PO 5 *initialization*

$$
\begin{array}{ll}
i \in NAT & \text{Constraints} \\
& \text{no Properties} \\
\Rightarrow [x := i](x \in NAT) &
\end{array}
$$

Fig. 4. Proof obligations for the specification machines of Figure 2

machine has one parameter, its constraints are that it must belong to NAT (C). The machine has no constants and no sets, there is therefore no Q. The goal to prove is that if x is replaced by v, the resulting value will belong to NAT. The goal is trivially true due to the third premise (the precondition). Note that if we had forgotten to specify the precondition, the PO would not be provable, and we therefore would have to check the specification and fix the bug. PO4 is the proof obligation for the **value** operation of the *SCALAR* machine. The premises are the same as in PO3 except for the precondition part, which is absent in this operation. Indeed, getting the value of the encapsulated variable is not a critical operation. The goal to prove is that if v is replaced by x, the value of x will belong to NAT. As x is not touched by the substitution, this is trivially true due to the second premise (the invariant).

Global consistency At the time of the specification, how the abstract machine will be used and how it will be implemented is unknown. The actual parameters as well as the actual constants and sets are undefined. It is, therefore, impossible to know whether the constraints over the actual parameters (C) and the properties over the constants and sets (Q) hold. In the same way, the calling context is unknown and there is no way to know at specification time whether the precondition will hold at calling time. We can only assume that they will be proved at some time. We show in the following that indeed proof obligations ask to prove C and P_i at importation time, and Q at implementation time.

The invariant I is also in the premisses. A proof obligation related to the initialization makes sure that it is safe to assume that initially the invariant holds.

Proof Obligation 2 *(Initialization of a specification)*

$$C \wedge Q \Rightarrow [S_{initialization}]I$$

This can be read as follows. If the constraints (C) on the calling parameters hold and if the properties (Q) on the constants and sets hold, then the initialization installs the invariant.

For example, in Figure 4, PO2 is the proof obligation for the initialization of the *CALCULATOR* machine. As for PO1, there are no constraints and no properties. The goal to prove is that if z is replaced by 0, the resulting value will be between 0 and 100. The goal is trivially true. PO5 is the proof obligation for the initialization of the *SCALAR* machine. As for PO3 and PO4, there is one constraint and no properties. The goal to prove is that if x is replaced by i, the resulting value belongs to NAT. This is trivially true thanks to the premise (the constraint).

Global consistency The initialization PO and the operation PO force the developer to prove that, provided that machine and services are called appropriately, the invariant is true after the initialization and after the application of each service. By induction, the invariant is therefore always true.

5.2 Refinement Proof Obligations

We have already mentioned that after a specification and before an implementation, the developer can write none or several intermediate refinements. In the following formulae exponents refer to abstract machines: 1 refers to the initial specification, 2 to $n-1$ refer to the previous refinements (if $n > 2$), and n refers to the refinement under proof.

The proof obligation for the operation specifying the nth refinement of a service $P_I \mid S_i$ is:

Proof Obligation 3 *(Operation of a refinement)*

$$C^1 \wedge Q^1 \wedge \ldots \wedge Q^n \wedge I^1 \wedge \ldots \wedge I^n \wedge P_i^1 \wedge \ldots P_i^{n-1}$$
$$\Rightarrow P^n \wedge [S_i^n] \neg [S_i^{n-1}] \neg I^n$$

This can be read as follows. If the contraints on the calling parameters of the specification (C^1) hold, if the properties on the constants and sets of the specification, the previous refinements and the current refinement ($Q^1 \wedge \ldots \wedge Q^n$) hold, if the invariants of the specification, the previous refinements and the current refinement ($I^1 \wedge \ldots \wedge I^n$) hold, and if the preconditions of the service in the specification and the previous refinements ($P_i \wedge \ldots P_i^{n-1}$) hold, then we must prove that the precondition P^n of the current refinement of the service holds and that the refined operation establishes the binding invariant for some of the functionalities of the abstract operation.

It is not our aim here to explain in depth where the proof obligations come from, but only to show their consistency. Let us simply underline that the double negation comes from the fact that while refining we may reduce the non-determinism. Intermediate refinements can take into account some of the possibilities of the specification and leave some of them apart. We want to prove that there exists part of the previous refinement (or specification if $n = 2$) which is encompassed in the refinement. Double negation is an elegant way to to formalize an existential proof.

In Subsection 5.3 we prove that the refinement of **increment** is valid and thus illustrate the use of the double negation on unbounded choice. Let us take here a simpler example. Assume that a machine M has a variable x and a service S^M which is $(x := 1 \,[\!]\, x := 2)$; assume that a machine N has a variable y, a service S^N which is $(y := 1)$, and an invariant I^N which is $(x = y)$. We want to prove that S^N refines S^M. This seems intuitively correct as it only reduces the non-determinism. Applying the above PO, we have to prove that

$$[y := 1]\neg[x := 1 \,[\!]\, x := 2])\neg(x = y)$$

which is equivalent to (see the axiom for the choice in section 4.3)

$$[y := 1]\neg([x := 1]\neg(x = y) \,\wedge\, [x := 2]\neg(x = y))$$

which in turn is equivalent to (due to the Morgan law)

$$[y := 1](\neg[x := 1]\neg(x = y) \,\vee\, \neg[x := 2]\neg(x = y))$$

which in turn is equivalent to (double negation has no influence on simple substitutions)

$$[y := 1]([x := 1](x = y) \,\vee\, [x := 2](x = y))$$

which in turn is equivalent to (substitution distributes over logical connectors)

$$[y := 1][x := 1](x = y) \,\vee\, [y := 1][x := 2](x = y)$$

Applying the substitutions the goal becomes

$$(1 = 1) \,\vee\, (2 = 1)$$

The second branch of the alternative cannot hold, but the first one does. The second branch means that $x := 2$ is not covered by the refinement, but this is valid because a refinement does not have to cope with the whole of a specification. Without the double negation we would have ended with $(1 = 1) \wedge (2 = 1)$ which does not hold, and does not have to.

Global consistency Coming back to the global consistency of the proof obligations, the discussion for the validity of the C^1, Q^1, I^1, and P_i^1 premisses is identical to the one of proof obligation 1 (see above). Constants and sets introduced in the previous and current refinements will be all instanciated in the implementation; they are unknown at the moment of the nth refinement; $Q^2, ..., Q^n$ will therefore be proved at implementation time together with Q^1. All the PO of the previous refinements must have been proved using this very proof obligation formula (Proof obligation 3); by induction, all their invariants $(I^2, ..., I^{n-1})$ and all their preconditions $(P_i^2, ..., P_i^{n-1})$ hold. As for I^n, with the following proof obligation related to initialization and by induction on all the proof obligations of all the service refinements of the current abstract machine, it is always true.

The proof obligation of the initialization of a refinement is as follows.

Proof Obligation 4 *(Initialization of a refinement)*

$$C^1 \wedge Q^1 \wedge \ldots \wedge Q^n \Rightarrow [S_{init}^n]\neg[S_{init}^{n-1}]\neg I^n$$

This can be read as follows. If the contraints on the calling parameters of the specification (C^1) hold, if the properties on the constants and sets of the specification, the previous refinements and the current refinement ($Q^1 \wedge \ldots \wedge Q^n$) hold, then we must prove that the refined initialization S_{init}^n copes with part of the functionalities of the abstract initialisation S_{init}^{n-1}.

5.3 Implementation Proof Obligations

The last refinement of an abstract machine is called an implementation. As already mentioned, besides the usual features of a refinement, an implementation instanciates constants and sets, and can call other machine services. The latter machines are said *imported*.

In the following, the convention for the exponents is the same as in the previous subsection: 1 refers to the initial specification, 2 to $n-1$ to the previous refinements (if $n > 2$), and n to the implementation under proof. Items without exponents refer to the imported machine(s).

Figure 5 gives all the proof obligations for *CALCULATOR_I*, the implementation machine of Figure 2. Before we comment the figure, we give the PO formulae: for the operations, for the initialization, for constant and set properties and for parameter passing.

The proof obligation of the implementation of a service is very similar to the PO for operations of refinements.

Proof Obligation 5 *(Operation of an implementation)*

$$C^1 \wedge Q^1 \wedge \ldots \wedge Q^n \wedge I^1 \wedge \ldots \wedge I^n \wedge P_i^1 \wedge \ldots P_i^{n-1} \wedge Q$$
$$\Rightarrow P^n \wedge [S_i^n]\neg[S_i^{n-1}]\neg I^n$$

The only difference is that we have to assume that the constants and sets of the imported machines satisfy their requested properties (Q). Indeed, when importing a machine, the developers only have to consider its specification. They do not have to cope for the refinements and implementation. The proof of Q is done when the imported machine is implemented.

For example, in Figure 5, PO6 is the proof obligation for the **increment** operation of the *CALCULATOR_I* machine. The specification machine, namely *CALCULATOR* has no parameters, and both specification and implementation have no constants and no sets; there are therefore no constraints on parameters (i.e., no C) and no properties of constants and sets (i.e., no Q). The premises therefore consist only of the invariant of the specification machine, the invariant

PO 6 increment *operation*

$$\begin{array}{ll} & \text{no Constraints for } CALCULATOR \\ & \text{no Properties for any machine} \\ z \in 0..100 & I^1 \quad \text{Invariant of } CALCULATOR \\ x = z & I^2 \quad \text{Invariant of } CALCULATOR\_I \\ \wedge \ a \in 0..100 & P_1^1 \quad \text{Precondition (1)} \\ \wedge \ z + a \in 0..100 & P_1^1 \quad \text{Precondition (2)} \\ \Rightarrow & \\ & \text{no precondition in } CALCULATOR\_I \end{array}$$

$[\text{VAR } v \text{ IN } v \leftarrow \textbf{value} \ ; \ v := v + a \ ; \ \textbf{modify}(v) \text{ END}] \neg [z :\in 0..100] \neg (x = z)$

PO 7 *initialization of* CALCULATOR_I

$$\begin{array}{l} \text{no Constraints for } CALCULATOR \\ \text{no Properties for any machine} \end{array}$$

$[x := 0] \neg [z := 0] \neg (x = z)$

PO 8 *NO PO about properties of constants and sets (there are no constants and no sets).*

PO 9 *parameter passing*

$$\begin{array}{l} \text{no Constraints for } CALCULATOR \\ \text{no Properties for any machine} \end{array}$$

$[i := 0](i \in NAT)$

Fig. 5. PO for the $CALCULATOR\_I$ implementation machine of Figure 2

of the implementation machine and the two predicates of the precondition of the specification. As the implementation has no precondition of its own, the goal to prove is "only":

$[\text{VAR } v \text{ IN } v \leftarrow \textbf{value} \ ; \ v := v + a \ ; \ \textbf{modify}(v) \text{ END}] \neg [z :\in 0..100] \neg (x = z)$

As this is the first goal of our examples not to be trivially true, let us show its proof. Firstly, VAR and $:\in$ are only syntactic variations of the unbounded substitution (see Section 4.3), the goal is therefore of the form

$[@v.(S_1; S_2; S_3)] \neg [@y.(G \implies z := y)] \neg (x = z)$

where S_1 is $v \leftarrow \textbf{value}$, S_2 is $v := v + a$, S_3 is $\textbf{modify}(v)$, G is $y \in 0..100$.

The goal is equivalent to (due to the axioms of the unbounded substitution, the guard and the sequence)

$$\forall v.([S_1][S_2][S_3]\neg(\forall y.(G \Rightarrow [z := y]\neg(x = z)))).$$

which is equivalent to (definition of $\exists$, definition of $\vee$, Morgan law)

$$\forall v.([S_1][S_2][S_3](\exists y.(G \wedge (\neg[z := y]\neg(x = z))))).$$

As v does not occur in the premises we can use the (usual) generalization rule and eliminate the quantification. We can also eliminate the double negation as it is around a simple substitution, and apply the substitution, namely replace z by y. We then have to prove:

$$[v \leftarrow \textbf{value}]\ [v := v + a]\ [\textbf{modify}(v)]\ (\exists y.(y \in 0..100 \wedge x = y))$$

We have to replace the called operations by their actual code.

$$[v := x][v := v + a][(v \in NAT)\ |\ x := v](\exists y.(y \in 0..100 \wedge (x = y)))$$

This is equivalent to (axiom of precondition and distribution of substitution)

$$[v := x][v := v + a](v \in NAT)$$
$$\wedge\ [v := x][v := v + a][x := v](\exists y.(y \in 0..100 \wedge (x = y)))$$

After applying the substitution (it is right associative), the first subgoal becomes
  $x + a \in NAT$
This is true because the premises state that $x = z$ and $z + a \in 0..100$. Note that we have just proved that the precondition of the called **modify** operation hold. The second subgoal becomes
  $\exists y.(y \in 0..100 \wedge (x + a = y))$
This is true because the premises state that $x = z$ and $z + a \in 0..100$; we have to choose $y = z + a$. PO6 is thus discharged.

Global consistency The inductive proof mechanism requires, once more, to prove the consistency of the initialization. Furthermore, implementation is the moment where a number of delayed proofs can be made. Indeed, constants and sets are instanciated, and operations are called.

  The PO for the initialization of the implementation also includes Q in the premisses. Besides, the initialization of the implementation only makes sense if the imported machine is also initialized. Therefore, the corresponding substitution in the following formula is $[S_{init}\ ;\ S_{init}^n]$ which is the sequence of the initializations of the imported machine and of the implementation.

Proof Obligation 6 *(Initialization of an implementation)*

$$C^1 \wedge Q^1 \wedge ... \wedge Q^n \wedge Q \Rightarrow [S_{init}\ ;\ S_{init}^n]\neg[S_{init}^{n-1}]\neg I^n$$

For example, in Figure 5, PO7 is the proof obligation for the initialization of the $CALCULATOR\_I$ machine. As for PO6, there are no constraints and no properties. The goal to prove is that if we replace z and x by 0 then $x = z$. This is trivially true.

For all the other PO, we have mentioned that the properties of the constants and sets could not be verified because their values were not known. Implementation is the time where constants and sets get their values; it is therefore the time where these verifications are done.

Proof Obligation 7 *(Constant and set properties at implementation time)*

$$Q \ \Rightarrow \ [actual\ constant\ and\ set\ substitution](Q_1 \ \wedge \ ... \ \wedge \ Q_n)$$

This can be read: if the properties of the constants and sets of the imported machines hold, then we must prove that the properties of the constants and sets of the specification, previous refinements and current implementation hold.

In Figure 5, PO8 states that there is no PO related to constants and sets because there are no constants and no sets in both $CALCULATOR$ and $CAL\text{-}CULATOR\_1$.

We have also mentioned that, at the time of the other PO, we could not prove that the constraints of the parameters hold because we did not know how the proved machines would be called. At implementation time, we call some services, and we import some machines. It is therefore the time to prove that the callling parameters satisfy their constraints:

Proof Obligation 8 *(Parameter constraints at importation time)*

$$C^1 \ \wedge \ Q^1 \ \wedge \ ... \ \wedge \ Q^n \ \Rightarrow \ [actual\ parameter\ substitution]\ C$$

This can be read: if the constraints of the parameters of the specification hold, and if the properties of the specification, previous refinements and implementation hold, then the actual calling parameters of the imported machines satisfy their respective constraints.

For example, in Figure 5, PO9 is the proof obligation related to the parameter passing of the actual importation of the $SCALAR$ machine. There are no constraints for the specification of the importing machine (no C). There are no properties for any machine (no Q^j). The goal to prove is that if i is replaced by 0 then the resulting value belongs to NAT. This is trivially true.

There is a last thing that we said could only be proved at importation time, namely the precondition of the services of a specification (the preconditions of refinements and implementation are encompassed in the PO of refinement and implementation). There is however, no dedicated PO for that proof. Indeed, let us assume that an operation S_i^n of the implemention calls an operation $P \mid S$ of an imported machine. In the PO of the implementation

$$[S_i^n]\neg[S_i^{n-1}]\neg I^n$$

will be replaced by

$$[P \mid S]\neg[S_i^{n-1}]\neg I^n$$

which is equivalent to (see the axiom of the precondition in section 4.3)

$$P \ \wedge \ [S]\neg[S_i^{n-1}]\neg I^n$$

Thus, the very first thing that the PO of the implementation makes us prove is that the preconditions of the imported operations hold.

5.4 Termination and Feasibility

The PO defined in the previous subsections are designed in order to make sure that the specified invariants always hold. There are, moreover, two very important properties which are proved at no extra costs: termination and feasibility. In the following we briefly explain how this is the case.

A preliminary note is that every substitution can be put into a normalized form. The normalized form of a generalized substitution S, which acts upon variable x, is $P \mid @x'.(G \implies x := x')$.

Termination. The formula to ensure termination is as follows.

$$term(S) \Leftrightarrow [S](x = x)$$

If the service S terminates then the trivially true predicate $x = x$ holds after the service has been applied. Conversely, if S does not terminate, we are not able to prove that $[S](x = x)$ holds.

It is proved that, if S is in normalized form: $P \mid @x'.(G \implies x := x')$, then the termination property is exactly equivalent to the precondition:

$$term(S) \Leftrightarrow P$$

We have shown in the previous section that the precondition is systematically proved if one discharges all the PO related to the importation of a given machine. Therefore, one free extra result is that, if we have made all the machine importation proofs, we also have proved that this machine will terminate. This, to our point of view, is a very strong result.

Feasibility. The formula to ensure feasibility is as follows.

$$fis(S) \Leftrightarrow \neg[S](x \neq x)$$

If the service S is feasible then we cannot prove the miracle of making $x \neq x$ true. Conversely, if S is not feasible then we can prove the miracle $[S](x \neq x)$.

It is proved that, if S is in normalized form: $P \mid @x'.(G \implies x := x')$, then the feasibility property is exactly equivalent to the precondition implying that there is a way to make the guard true:

$$fis(S) \Leftrightarrow (P \implies \exists x'.G)$$

The PO of the specification does not enforce to prove $\exists x'.G$. An existential proof is always a potential problem for a theorem prover. However, at the moment of the refinement we do have to prove that the refinement makes the guard true. Let us assume that the service of a specification is of the form $G \implies S$, and that it is refined by a service S^2, the goal of the refinement PO will be

$$[S^2]\neg[G \implies S]\neg I^2$$

which is equivalent to (axiom of the guard)

$$[S^2]\neg(G \Rightarrow [S]\neg I^2)$$

which in turn is equivalent to (definition of the implication)
$$[S^2]\neg(\neg G \vee [S]\neg I^2)$$
which in turn is equivalent to (Morgan law)
$$[S^2](G \wedge \neg[S]\neg I^2)$$
which in turn is equivalent to (distribution of substitution)
$$[S^2]G \wedge [S^2]\neg[S]\neg I^2$$
The first part makes us prove that the refinement has picked a substitution which makes the guard true. Hence, for every refinement, we prove that S is not miraculous if $S2$ is in turn not miraculous. The language used for implementation[2] is by construction not miraculous. Therefore, if the refinement proofs are made, by induction the abstract machines are proved feasible. This is another strong result.

Moreover, by delaying the feasibility proof to the refinements, the prover no longer has to make a difficult existential proof, the developer has somehow done the job for it.

6 Conclusion

We have presented the keystone of the B method: the proof obligation that all operations of a specification preserve the invariant. We have listed the theoretical foundations: first order logic, set theory and fix point theory. We have also presented the basic concepts: encapsulation, precondition, refinement and generalized substitutions. We have detailed the proof obligations of specifications, refinements and implementations. We have shown that the sum of local proofs indeed ensures that the invariants always hold. We believe that this strong modularity is essential for the tractability of the proofs. Last but not least, we have emphasized that these proof obligations also ensure termination and feasibility.

Acknowledgements. We thank Jean-Raymond Abrial and Daniel Herman for enlightening discussions. Jean-Raymond Abrial, the anonymous referees and Erwan Jahier made very helpful comments on earlier versions of this article.

References

1. J.-R. Abrial. *The B Book: Assigning programs to meanings.* Cambridge University Press, 1996.
2. R.C. Backhouse. *Program construction and verification.* International Series in Computer Science. Prentice Hall, 1986. ISBN : 0-937291-46-3.
3. P. Behm, P. Benoit, A. Faivre, and J.-M. Meynadier. Météor: A successful application of B in a large project. In J. Wing et al., editor, *FM'99, World Congress on Formal Methods in the Development of Computing Systems*, pages 369–387. Springer, Lecture Notes in Computer Science 1708, September 1999.
4. D. Bert, editor. *B'98: Recent Advances in the Development and Use of the B Method.* Springer, Lecture Notes in Computer Science 1393, April 1998.

---

[2] This language is a traditional imperative language without pointers.

5. E.W. Dijkstra. *A discipline of programming*. Automatic Computation. Prentice-Hall, 1976. ISBN: 0-13-215871-X.
6. M. Ducassé. Teaching B at a technical university is possible and rewarding. In H. Habrias and S. E. Dunn, editors, *B'98, Proceedings of the Educational Session*. APCB : http://www.sciences.univ-nantes.fr/asso/APCB/, avril 1998. ISBN: 2-9512461-0-2.
7. R. W. Floyd. Assigning meaning to programs. In J. T. Schwartz, editor, *Mathematical aspects of computer science: Proc. American Mathematics Soc. symposia*, volume 19, pages 19–31, Providence RI, 1967. American Mathematical Society.
8. D. Gries. *The Science of Programming*. Text and Monographs in Computer Science. Springer-Verlag, 1981.
9. J. He, C.A.R. Hoare, and J.W. Sanders. Data refinement refined. In B. Robinet and R. Wilhelm, editors, *ESOP 86, European Symposium on Programming*, volume 213 of *Lecture Notes in Computer Science*, pages 187–196. Springer-Verlag, 1986.
10. C. A. R. Hoare. An axiomatic basis for computer programming. *Communications of the ACM*, 12(10):576–580, October 1969.
11. C.B. Jones. *Systematic software development using VDM*. International Series in Computer Science. Prentice-Hall, 1986. ISBN : 0-13-880725-6.
12. K. Lano. *The B Language and Method*. Formal Approaches to Computing and Information Technology. Springer, 1996. ISBN 3-540-76033-4.
13. C. Morgan. *Programming from specifications, 2nd edition*. International Series in Computer Science. Prentice Hall, 1994. ISBN 0-13-123274-6.
14. D.L. Parnas. A technique for software module specification with examples. *CACM*, 15(5):330–336, May 1972.
15. M.-L. Potet and Y. Rouzaud. Composition and refinement in the B-Method. In Bert [4], pages 46–65.
16. K.A. Robinson. Introduction to the B method. In Sekerinski and Sere [17], chapter 1, pages 3–37. ISBN 1-85233-053-8.
17. E. Sekerinski and K. Sere, editors. *Program development by refinement, Case studies using the B method*. Formal Approaches to Computing and Information Technology. Springer, 1999. ISBN 1-85233-053-8.

Specialising Finite Domain Programs Using Polyhedra

Jacob M. Howe and Andy King

Computing Laboratory
University of Kent, Canterbury, CT2 7NF, UK
email{J.M.Howe, A.M.King}@ukc.ac.uk

Abstract. A procedure is described for tightening domain constraints of finite domain logic programs by applying a static analysis based on convex polyhedra. Individual finite domain constraints are over-approximated by polyhedra to describe the solution space over n integer variables as an n dimensional polyhedron. This polyhedron is then approximated, using projection, as an n dimensional bounding box that can be used to specialise and improve the domain constraints. The analysis can be implemented straightforwardly and an empirical evaluation of the specialisation technique is given.

1 Introduction

Finite domain constraint logic programs classically have two components: a constraint component and a generate component. The constraint component posts to the store constraints which characterise the problem and define the search space. The generate component systematically enumerates the search space with a labelling strategy (such as fail first). Tightening the constraints, for example the domain constraints that bound the values of the variables, reduces the search space and thereby speeds up the program.

In order to reduce the search space, finite domain constraint solvers propagate constraints on the values that can be taken by the variables. Constraint propagation does not necessarily have to be applied with labelling and many solvers, for example the ECL^iPS^e and SICStus finite domain solvers, can prune the values of variables before any labelling is applied. This paper describes in detail and empirically evaluates one technique for performing constraint propagation at compiletime through program specialisation.

The analysis in this paper is founded on classic work on polyhedral approximation [5], [6]. Finite domain constraints are interpreted as relations over sets of points. These constraints are over approximated and represented as a (possibly unbounded) polyhedron. The intersection of polyhedra corresponds to composing constraints. Projection onto an integer grid gives (low-valency) domain constraints that can be added to the program without compromising efficiency. The main technique for propagating constraints in finite domain solvers is by bound propagation. This involves substituting known variable bounds into linear constraints to give new variable bounds. The polyhedral analysis described here is

A. Bossi (Ed.): LOPSTR'99, LNCS 1817, pp. 118–135, 2000.

a stronger compiletime technique than bound propagation; compiletime bound propagation over linear finite domain constraints is subsumed by the technique described in this paper. The example in Figure 1 illustrates that polyhedral analysis can give considerably tighter approximations than those resulting from bound propagation. In this example, projection onto each of the variables gives

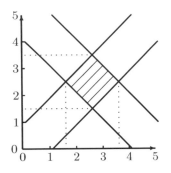

```
:- use_module(library(clpfd)).
main:-
    domain([X, Y], 0, 6),
    Y#>=X-1,
    Y#=<X+1,
    Y#>=4-X,
    Y#=<6-X.
```

Fig. 1. The polyhedron represented by $\{y \geq x - 1, y \leq x + 1, y \geq 4 - x, y \leq 6 - x\}$ with variable domains $x \in [0, 6], y \in [0, 6]$.

bounds $3/2 \leq x \leq 7/2, 3/2 \leq y \leq 7/2$. Tightening to integers defines the finite domain solution set $x \in [2, 3], y \in [2, 3]$, which can be used to specialise the domain constraints of the original program to domain([X, Y], 2, 3). Bound propagation does not tighten the variable bounds at all.

The polyhedral analysis described in this paper develops the static analysis of constraint logic programs outlined in [14]. However, the analysis in this paper is specifically tailored to specialise finite domain programs. In particular, the analysis is designed to complement runtime constraint propagation techniques. As the example above illustrates, polyhedra capture deep inter-variable relationships which cannot always be traced in bound propagation. Note, however, that the technique is, to a certain extent, dependent on the data being present in the program – a static analysis cannot reason about runtime data. This paper makes the following contributions:

- it presents a deterministic algorithm (not involving labelling) based on polyhedra for refining domain constraints and it shows that the analysis can be easily implemented using constraint solving machinery;
- it shows how interval and polyhedral approximating techniques can be combined to reason about non-linear constraints;
- the analysis and the associated program transformation are shown to be correct;
- an empirical study and evaluation of the technique applied to SICStus finite domain programs is given. The analysis can significantly improve the speed of programs (sometimes by several orders of magnitude);
- applying the analysis through specialisation means that the solver does not need to be modified. Specialisation never impedes built-in constraint propa-

gation techniques and comes with a no slow down guarantee. Moreover, the improved domain constraints often interact with built-in constraint propagation techniques resulting in further pruning. Interestingly, the analysis can be interpreted as a compiletime solution to combining constraint solvers.

The structure of the paper is as follows: section 2 works through an example program to illustrate the way in which the analysis works and its power; section 3 formalises the analysis in terms of abstract interpretation; section 4 describes the various mathematical techniques utilised in the analysis; section 5 compares the approach taken by this paper with bound propagation; section 6 works through another example program to illustrate all of the techniques introduced in the paper; section 7 describes the implementation of the analysis and gives the results of its application to some benchmark programs; section 8 reviews related work; section 9 concludes and outlines future work.

2   Example: Magic Square

This example illustrates the approach taken by this analysis, as well as its power relative to compiletime bound propagation.

The magic square puzzle takes a three by three grid and the numbers one to nine and sets the challenge of placing the numbers in the grid so that all of the rows, columns and diagonals sum to the same number. The solutions are ordered so as to reduce the number of solutions identical up to symmetry which can be found. A SICStus finite domain program to solve this problem is:

```
:- use_module(library(clpfd)).
square(A, B, C, D, E, F, G, H, I):-
         domain([A, B, C, D, E, F, G, H, I], 1, 9),
         all_different([A, B, C, D, E, F, G, H, I]),
         A#<C, A#<G, A#<I, %symmetry constraints
         A+B+C #= D+E+F, A+B+C #= G+H+I,
         A+B+C #= A+D+G, A+B+C #= B+E+H, A+B+C #= C+F+I,
         A+B+C #= A+E+I, A+B+C #= C+E+G,
         labeling([], [A, B, C, D, E, F, G, H, I]).
```

(In SICStus, domain(List, Inf, Sup) abbreviates Inf#=<X, X#=<Sup, for each variable X in List.) The finite domain constraints in this program are approximated by a polyhedron (each constraint is interpreted as a non-strict inequality with rational coefficients, these inequalities define the polyhedron). The all_different constraint cannot be captured in an informative way by a polyhedron, hence is ignored. The finite domain constraints are abstracted to the polyhedron defined by the following linear inequalities (an equality can be understood as a pair of inequalities):

$$1 \leq A, B, C, D, E, F, G, H, I \leq 9$$

$$A \leq C - 1 \qquad\qquad A \leq G - 1 \qquad\qquad\qquad A \leq I - 1$$
$$A + B + C = D + E + F \qquad A + B + C = G + H + I$$
$$A + B + C = A + D + G \qquad A + B + C = B + E + H$$
$$A + B + C = C + F + I \qquad A + B + C = A + E + I$$
$$A + B + C = C + E + G$$

The above inequalities define a polyhedron in nine (the number of variables) dimensional rational space. Projection onto each variable will give rational bounds on those variables. The result of this is as follows:

$$3/2 \leq A \leq 11/2 \qquad 4 \leq B \leq 8 \qquad 7/2 \leq C \leq 15/2$$
$$5 \leq D \leq 9 \qquad 3 \leq E \leq 7 \qquad 1 \leq F \leq 5$$
$$5/2 \leq G \leq 13/2 \qquad 2 \leq H \leq 6 \qquad 9/2 \leq I \leq 17/2$$

A specialised finite domain program is obtained by reinterpreting these new rational bounds as finite domain bounds, by tightening to integer values. The constraint domain([A, ..., I], 0, 9) is replaced in the program by the finite domain constraints given below. The bounds in the left column below are those obtained by the above procedure, those on the right are those that SICStus finds by bound propagation.

%Polyhedral	%Bound Propagation
2 #=< A, A #=< 5,	1 #=< A, A #=< 8,
4 #=< B, B #=< 8,	1 #=< B, B #=< 8,
4 #=< C, C #=< 7,	2 #=< C, C #=< 9,
5 #=< D, D #=< 9,	2 #=< D, D #=< 9,
3 #=< E, E #=< 7,	1 #=< E, E #=< 9,
1 #=< F, F #=< 5,	1 #=< F, F #=< 9,
3 #=< G, G #=< 6,	2 #=< G, G #=< 9,
2 #=< H, H #=< 6,	1 #=< H, H #=< 9,
5 #=< I, I #=< 8,	2 #=< I, I #=< 9,

Notice that the propagation of constraints by the polyhedral method is better than that of bound propagation. That the improvement is a large one can be seen by calculating the number of points in each of the search spaces. The finite domain which results from the polyhedral analysis has 8×10^5 points, whereas the domain resulting from bounds propagation has approximately 1.9×10^8 points, nearly 240 times larger a search space.

3   Formalised Analysis

This section formalises both the analysis and the program transformation described in this paper, then states their correctness. Details and proofs can be found in [9].

3.1   Polyhedral Analysis

In order to have confidence in the analysis a mathematical justification is essential. The formalisation is an application of the s-approach detailed in [4] and is fairly dense and complicated. Thus, before giving the formal analysis, an informal overview of the remainder of the section is given, indicating where the operations described in section 4 are required. Abstract interpretation is used to connect a (concrete) ground semantics for finite domain constraint programs [11], [12] to an (abstract) s-semantics [4]. A Galois insertion links the concrete domain (the set of ground interpretations) and the abstract domain (the set of interpretations over constrained unit clauses). The concrete semantics is essentially the set of solutions for a given program. The abstract semantics (formulated in terms of a fixpoint) is an over-approximation of this set of solutions, with each predicate constrained by the conjunction of the constraints on its body atoms. The abstract operator approximates non-linear constraints as linear constraints. In order that the formalised analysis is the same as that implemented, the number of unit clauses is kept small by over-approximation in the form of a convex hull calculation. The termination of the fixpoint calculation is ensured by the use of a widening. The analysis is proved to be correct, as is the program transformation (which involves the use of projection with the fixpoint).

Concrete Domain. For a (finite domain) program P, let Π denote the set of predicate symbols that occur in P and let Σ denote the set of integer ($\mathbb{Z}$) and function symbols that occur in P. Let D_{FD} be the set of finite trees over the signature Σ. Let R_{FD} be the set of constraint predicates. Let V be a countable set of variables. C_{FD} is the system of finite domain constraints generated from D_{FD}, R_{FD}, V and the function symbols. Elements of C_{FD} are regarded modulo logical equivalence and C_{FD} is ordered by entailment, $\models_{FD}$. $(C_{FD}, \models_{FD}, \wedge)$ is a (bounded) meet-semilattice with bottom and top elements $true$ and $false$. C_{FD} is closed under variable elimination and $\exists\{x_1, ..., x_n\}c$ (projection out) abbreviates $\exists x_1 \ldots \exists x_n.c$. $\bar{\exists}Xc$ (projection onto) is used as a shorthand for $\exists(var(c)\backslash X)c$, where $var(o)$ denotes the set of variables occurring in the syntactic object o. The interpretation base for P is $B_{FD} = \{p(\bar{t}) \mid p \in \Pi, \bar{t} \in (D_{FD})^n\}$. The concrete domain is $(\mathcal{P}(B_{FD}), \subseteq, \cap, \cup)$, a complete lattice.

Abstract Domain. Let D_{Lin} be the set of rational numbers, $\mathbb{Q}$. Let C_{Lin} be the system of linear constraints over D_{Lin}, V, the set of constraint predicates R_{Lin} and the function symbols. C_{Lin} is quotiented by equivalence and ordered by entailment, $\models_{Lin}$. $(C_{Lin}, \models_{Lin}, \wedge)$ is a (bounded) meet-semilattice and is closed under projection out, $\exists$, and projection onto, $\bar{\exists}$. Unit clauses have the form $p(\bar{x}) \leftarrow c$ where $c \in C_{Lin}$. Equivalence on clauses, $\equiv$, is defined as follows: $(p(\bar{x}) \leftarrow c) \equiv (p(\bar{x}') \leftarrow c')$ iff $\bar{\exists}var(\bar{x})c = \bar{\exists}var(\bar{x})(c' \wedge (\bar{x} = \bar{x}'))$. The interpretation base for program P is $B_{Lin} = \{[p(\bar{x}) \leftarrow c]_{\equiv} | p \in \Pi, c \in C_{Lin}\}$. Entailment induces an order relation, $\sqsubseteq$, on $\mathcal{P}(B_{Lin})$ as follows: $I \sqsubseteq I'$ iff $\forall [p(\bar{x}) \leftarrow c]_{\equiv} \in I.\exists [p(\bar{x}) \leftarrow c']_{\equiv} \in I'.c \models_{Lin} c'$. $\mathcal{P}(B_{Lin})$ ordered by $\sqsubseteq$ is a preorder. Quotienting by equivalence, $\equiv$, gives the abstract domain $(\mathcal{P}(B_{Lin})/\equiv, \sqsubseteq, \sqcup)$, a complete join-semilattice, where $\sqcup_{i=1}^{\infty}[I_i]_{\equiv} = [\cup_{i=1}^{\infty}I_i]_{\equiv}$.

Concretisation. The concretisation map $\gamma : C_{Lin} \to C_{FD}$, interprets a linear constraint over the rationals as a finite domain constraint as follows:

$$\gamma \left(\sum_{i=1}^{m} \frac{n_i}{d_i} x_i \leq \frac{n}{d} \right) = \sum_{i=1}^{m} \frac{D.n_i}{d_i} x_i \leq \frac{D.n}{d}, \text{ where } D = d. \prod_{i=1}^{m} d_i$$

Note that the coefficients of $\gamma(c_{Lin})$ are in $\mathbb{Z}$. The abstraction map, $\alpha : C_{FD} \to C_{Lin}$ can be defined in terms of γ by $\alpha(c_{FD}) = \wedge\{c_{Lin}|c_{FD} \models_{FD} \gamma(c_{Lin})\}$. Observe that α, γ form a Galois insertion.

The concretisation map $\gamma : \mathcal{P}(B_{Lin})/\equiv \to \mathcal{P}(B_{FD})$ on interpretations is defined in terms of the concretisation map for constraints:

$$\gamma([I]_\equiv) = \{p(\bar{\mathbf{t}})|[p(\bar{\mathbf{x}}) \leftarrow c]_\equiv \in I, (\bar{\mathbf{x}} = \bar{\mathbf{t}}) \models_{FD} \gamma(c)\}.$$

The abstraction map $\alpha : \mathcal{P}(B_{FD}) \to \mathcal{P}(B_{Lin})/\equiv$ is defined as follows:

$$\alpha(J) = [\{[p(\bar{\mathbf{x}}) \leftarrow c]_\equiv | p(\bar{\mathbf{t}}) \in J, \alpha(\bar{\mathbf{x}} = \bar{\mathbf{t}}) = c\}]_\equiv$$

Proposition 1 α, γ *on interpretations form a Galois insertion.*

Concrete Semantics. The fixpoint semantics, $\mathcal{F}_{FD}$, is defined in terms of an immediate consequences operator $T_P^g : \mathcal{P}(B_{FD}) \to \mathcal{P}(B_{FD})$, defined by

$$T_P^g(I) = \left\{ p(\bar{\mathbf{t}}) \; \middle| \; \begin{array}{l} w \in P, w = p(\bar{\mathbf{x}}) \leftarrow c, p_1(\bar{\mathbf{x}}_1), ..., p_n(\bar{\mathbf{x}}_n), \\ p_i(\bar{\mathbf{t}}_i) \in I, (\bar{\mathbf{x}} = \bar{\mathbf{t}}) \models_{FD} \exists var(\bar{\mathbf{x}})(\wedge_{i=1}^{n}(\bar{\mathbf{x}}_i = \bar{\mathbf{t}}_i) \wedge c) \end{array} \right\}$$

T_P^g is continuous, thus the least fixpoint exists and $\mathcal{F}_{FD}[\![P]\!] = lfp(T_P^g)$.

Abstract Semantics. To define the immediate consequences operator for the abstract semantics, a special conjunction operator $\wedge_{FL} : C_{FD} \times C_{Lin} \to C_{Lin}$ is introduced. The operator $\wedge_{FL}$ is assumed to satisfy the property $c_{FD} \wedge \gamma(c_{Lin}) \models_{FD} \gamma(c_{FD} \wedge_{FL} c_{Lin})$. This operator allows the approximation of non-linear finite domain constraints.

The fixpoint semantics, $\mathcal{F}_{Lin}$, is defined in terms of an immediate consequences operator, $T_P^s : \mathcal{P}(B_{Lin})/\equiv \to \mathcal{P}(B_{Lin})/\equiv$, defined by $T_P^s([I]_\equiv) = [J]_\equiv$, where

$$J = \left\{ [p(\bar{\mathbf{x}}) \leftarrow c]_\equiv \; \middle| \; \begin{array}{l} w \in P, w = p(\bar{\mathbf{x}}) \leftarrow c', p_1(\bar{\mathbf{x}}_1), ..., p_n(\bar{\mathbf{x}}_n), \\ [w_i]_\equiv \in I, w_i = p_i(\bar{\mathbf{y}}_i) \leftarrow c_i, \\ \forall i.(var(w) \cap var(w_i) = \phi), \\ \forall i \neq j.(var(w_i) \cap var(w_j) = \phi), \\ c = c' \wedge_{FL} (\wedge_{i=1}^{n}((\bar{\mathbf{x}}_i = \bar{\mathbf{y}}_i) \wedge c_i)) \end{array} \right\}$$

T_P^s is continuous, thus $lfp(T_P^s)$ exists. Since $\mathcal{P}(B_{Lin})/\equiv$ is a complete partial order, Kleene iteration [5] can be used to compute $\mathcal{F}_{Lin}[\![P]\!] = lfp(T_P^s) = \sqcup_{i=1}^{\infty} T_P^s \uparrow i$, where $T_P^s \uparrow 0 = \phi$ and $T_P^s \uparrow i + 1 = T_P^s(T_P^s \uparrow i)$.

Space-Efficient Over-Approximation. To keep the number of unit clauses in $T^s_P \uparrow k$ small, hence the fixpoint calculation manageable, $T^s_P \uparrow k$ is over-approximated by an interpretation I (that is, $T^s_P \uparrow k \sqsubseteq I$) containing at most one unit clause for each predicate symbol.

The join for the domain of linear constraints, $\vee : C_{Lin} \times C_{Lin} \to C_{Lin}$, is defined by $c_1 \vee c_2 = \wedge \{c \in C_{Lin} | c_1 \models_{Lin} c, c_2 \models_{Lin} c\}$. When the constraints are interpreted as defining polyhedra, the meet corresponds to the closure of the convex hull. The operator is lifted in stages to an operator on the abstract domain. First it is lifted to the interpretation base, $\vee : B^\perp_{Lin} \times B^\perp_{Lin} \to B^\perp_{Lin}$, where $B^\perp_{Lin} = B_{Lin} \cup \{\perp\}$, as follows:

$$
\begin{aligned}
[p(\overline{\mathbf{x}}) \leftarrow c_1]_\equiv \vee [p(\overline{\mathbf{x}}) \leftarrow c_2]_\equiv &= [p(\overline{\mathbf{x}}) \leftarrow c_1 \vee c_2]_\equiv \\
[p(\overline{\mathbf{x}}) \leftarrow c_1]_\equiv \vee [q(\overline{\mathbf{y}}) \leftarrow c_2]_\equiv &= \perp \qquad \text{if } p \neq q \\
[p(\overline{\mathbf{x}}) \leftarrow c]_\equiv \vee \perp &= [p(\overline{\mathbf{x}}) \leftarrow c]_\equiv \\
\perp \vee [p(\overline{\mathbf{x}}) \leftarrow c]_\equiv &= [p(\overline{\mathbf{x}}) \leftarrow c]_\equiv
\end{aligned}
$$

This in turn defines the unary function, $\vee : \mathcal{P}(B_{Lin})/\equiv \to \mathcal{P}(B_{Lin})/\equiv$, on the abstract domain given by $\vee([I]_\equiv) = [\cup_{w \in I} \{\vee_{u \in I}(w \vee u)\}]_\equiv$. Since for every $I \in \mathcal{P}(B_{Lin})/\equiv$, $T^s_P(I) \sqsubseteq \vee \circ T^s_P(I)$, it follows that $lfp(T^s_P) \sqsubseteq lfp(\vee \circ T^s_P)$. Hence $\vee$ does not compromise safety.

Termination of the Polyhedral Analysis. As before, Kleene iteration can be used to compute $lfp(\vee \circ T^s_P)$. However, the chain of iterates $\vee \circ T^s_P \uparrow k$ may not stabilise in a finite number of steps. In order to obtain convergence, widening (a fixpoint acceleration technique) [5], is applied.

Given a standard widening on polyhedra [3], [5], [6] (or equivalently, on linear constraints), $\nabla : C_{Lin} \times C_{Lin} \to C_{Lin}$, a widening, $\nabla : B^\perp_{Lin} \times B^\perp_{Lin} \to B^\perp_{Lin}$, (where $B^\perp_{Lin} = B_{Lin} \cup \{\perp\}$) on the interpretation base is induced as follows:

$$
\begin{aligned}
[p(\overline{\mathbf{x}}) \leftarrow c_1]_\equiv \nabla [p(\overline{\mathbf{x}}) \leftarrow c_2]_\equiv &= [p(\overline{\mathbf{x}}) \leftarrow c_1 \nabla c_2]_\equiv \\
[p(\overline{\mathbf{x}}) \leftarrow c_1]_\equiv \nabla [q(\overline{\mathbf{y}}) \leftarrow c_2]_\equiv &= \perp \qquad \text{if } p \neq q \\
[p(\overline{\mathbf{x}}) \leftarrow c]_\equiv \nabla \perp &= [p(\overline{\mathbf{x}}) \leftarrow c]_\equiv \\
\perp \nabla [p(\overline{\mathbf{x}}) \leftarrow c]_\equiv &= [p(\overline{\mathbf{x}}) \leftarrow c]_\equiv
\end{aligned}
$$

This lifts to the abstract domain, $\nabla : \mathcal{P}(B_{Lin})/\equiv \times \mathcal{P}(B_{Lin})/\equiv \to \mathcal{P}(B_{Lin})/\equiv$

$$
[I_1]_\equiv \nabla [I_2]_\equiv = [\cup_{w \in I_2} \{\vee_{u \in I_1}(w \nabla u)\}]_\equiv
$$

3.2   Correctness of the Polyhedral Analysis

This section states the correctness of the analysis. That is, upward iteration of $\vee \circ T^s_P$, with widening, stabilises at an interpretation I with $lfp(T^g_P) \sqsubseteq \gamma(I)$. The result is a corollary of Proposition 13 in [5].

Proposition 2 *The upward iteration sequence of $\vee \circ T^s_P$ with widening ∇ is ultimately stable with limit I and I is safe, that is, $\vee \circ T^s_P(I) \sqsubseteq I$ and $lfp(T^g_P) \sqsubseteq \gamma(I)$.*

3.3   Program Transformation and Its Correctness

Once an upper approximation to $\mathcal{F}_{FD}[\![P]\!]$ is computed, it can be used to transform the program. This is done by projecting the convex polyhedron resulting from the fixpoint calculation onto each variable in turn, tightening this interval constraint to integer values and adding it to the initial program. The following theorem details the transformation and also asserts safety.

An auxiliary (partial) map, $\cdot^t : C_{Lin} \to C_{Lin}$, is defined in order to tighten bounds on variables to integer values, as follows: $c^t = u(c) \wedge l(c)$ where

$$u(c) = \begin{cases} x \leq \lfloor q \rfloor & \text{if } (x \leq q) = c \\ true & \text{otherwise} \end{cases}, \quad l(c) = \begin{cases} x \geq \lceil q \rceil & \text{if } (x \geq q) = c \\ true & \text{otherwise} \end{cases}.$$

Theorem 1 *If $lfp(T_P^g) \subseteq \gamma([I]_{\equiv})$, then $\mathcal{F}_{FD}[\![P]\!] = \mathcal{F}_{FD}[\![P']\!]$, where*

$$P' = \left\{ w' \left| \begin{array}{l} w \in P, w = p(\overline{\mathbf{x}}) \leftarrow c, p_1(\overline{\mathbf{x}}_1), ..., p_n(\overline{\mathbf{x}}_n), \\ [w_i]_{\equiv} \in I, w_i = p_i(\overline{\mathbf{y}}_i) \leftarrow c_i, \\ \forall i.(var(w) \cap var(w_i) = \phi), \\ \forall i \neq j.(var(w_i) \cap var(w_j) = \phi), \\ c' = c \wedge (\wedge_{y \in var(w)} \gamma((\overline{\exists} y \wedge_{i=1}^n ((\overline{\mathbf{x}}_i = \overline{\mathbf{y}}_i) \wedge c_i))^t)), \\ w' = p(\overline{\mathbf{x}}) \leftarrow c', p_1(\overline{\mathbf{x}}_1), ..., p_n(\overline{\mathbf{x}}_n) \end{array} \right. \right\}$$

4   Computational Techniques

The analysis and program transformation strategy is parameterised by the operators $\wedge_{FL}$ and ∇. In this section instances of these operators are specified and algorithms for computing other operations, such as $\vee$ and $\overline{\exists}$, are presented.

In particular this section reviews some computational techniques for: calculating the convex hull of two n dimensional polyhedra; projecting an n dimensional polyhedra onto an m dimension space where $m < n$; widening chains of polyhedra; approximating non-linear constraints by polyhedra.

4.1   Projection

The analysis described in this paper requires a projection that takes as input a set of inequalities in n variables and outputs a set of inequalities in a subset of these variables. The output is such that all solutions of the original set of inequalities can be specialised to a solution of the new, and all solutions of the new set of inequalities represent partial solutions of the original. Less formally, projection is the calculation of the shadow cast by the polyhedron represented by the inequalities onto the space defined by the subset of variables. For example, the projection of a two dimension polyhedron onto the variable x is the shadow cast onto the x-axis when the polyhedron is lit from above.

In the implementation of the analysis given in this paper, projection is performed using Fourier-Motzkin variable elimination (see, for example, [10], [12],

[13], [18]), as this is the algorithm used by SICStus. Fourier-Motzkin variable elimination takes a set of linear inequalities and eliminates variables one at a time until the only variable occurrences left are of those variables being projected onto. Inequalities are arranged so that the variable to be eliminated is on the lesser side of all inequalities in which it occurs. It will either have a positive or negative polarity. All possible ways of eliminating the variable from a pair of inequalities are explored, giving a new set of inequalities with one variable fewer. This is illustrated with the following simple example, projecting onto the single variable z:

$$
\begin{array}{l} x+y\leq 4 \\ x-y\geq 6 \\ z\leq y \end{array} \overset{\text{shuffle}}{\rightsquigarrow} \begin{array}{l} x\leq 4-y \\ -x\leq -6-y \\ z\leq y \end{array} \overset{\text{eliminate}}{\rightsquigarrow} \begin{array}{l} 0\leq -2-2y \\ z\leq y \end{array} \overset{\text{shuffle}}{\rightsquigarrow} \begin{array}{l} y\leq -1 \\ -y\leq -z \end{array} \overset{\text{eliminate}}{\rightsquigarrow} z\leq -1
$$

4.2 Convex Hull

The convex hull of two polyhedra is the smallest polyhedron containing both polyhedra. The convex hull calculations are performed as in [3]. Polyhedra are represented as a set of linear inequalities. The convex hull, P_C, of two polyhedra, P_1 and P_2, is given by the following (where $\overline{\mathbf{x}}$ is a vector and A_i, B_i are matrices, together giving the linear inequalities that define the polyhedra):

$$
P_1 = \{\overline{\mathbf{x}}_1 \in \mathbb{Q}^n | A_1\overline{\mathbf{x}}_1 \leq B_1\}, \qquad P_2 = \{\overline{\mathbf{x}}_2 \in \mathbb{Q}^n | A_2\overline{\mathbf{x}}_2 \leq B_2\}
$$

$$
P_C = \left\{\overline{\mathbf{x}} \in \mathbb{Q}^n \middle| \begin{array}{l} \overline{\mathbf{x}} = \overline{\mathbf{y}}_1 + \overline{\mathbf{y}}_2 \ \wedge \ A_1\overline{\mathbf{y}}_1 \leq \sigma_1 B_1 \ \wedge \ A_2\overline{\mathbf{y}}_2 \leq \sigma_2 B_2 \\ \wedge \ \sigma_1 + \sigma_2 = 1 \ \wedge \ -\sigma_1 \leq 0 \ \wedge \ -\sigma_2 \leq 0 \end{array} \right\}
$$

By projecting out $\sigma_1, \sigma_2, \overline{\mathbf{y}}_1, \overline{\mathbf{y}}_2$, that is, projecting onto $\overline{\mathbf{x}}$, the linear inequalities for the convex hull can be found. In this way, the convex hull calculation is reduced to variable elimination.

Example 1. Figure 2 lists a program giving rise to polyhedra that are a square and triangle. The triangle P_T and the square P_S are described below:

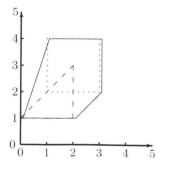

```
:- use_module(library(clpfd)).
p(X, Y):-
        -X+Y#=<1,
        X#=<2,
        1#=<Y
p(X, Y):-
        1#=<X, X#=<3,
        2#=<Y, Y#=<4.
```

Fig. 2. The Convex Hull of triangle P_T and square P_S

$$P_T = \left\{ \begin{pmatrix} x \\ y \end{pmatrix} \middle| \begin{pmatrix} -1 & 1 \\ 1 & 0 \\ 0 & -1 \end{pmatrix} \begin{pmatrix} x \\ y \end{pmatrix} \le \begin{pmatrix} 1 \\ 2 \\ -1 \end{pmatrix} \right\}, \quad P_S = \left\{ \begin{pmatrix} x \\ y \end{pmatrix} \middle| \begin{pmatrix} -1 & 0 \\ 1 & 0 \\ 0 & -1 \\ 0 & 1 \end{pmatrix} \begin{pmatrix} x \\ y \end{pmatrix} \le \begin{pmatrix} -1 \\ 3 \\ -2 \\ 4 \end{pmatrix} \right\}$$

Putting these together as in the definition, and then projecting out $\sigma_1, \sigma_2, \overline{y}_1, \overline{y}_2$, the convex hull, P_C, is found to be

$$P_C = \left\{ \begin{pmatrix} x \\ y \end{pmatrix} \middle| \begin{pmatrix} 0 & -1 \\ 1 & -1 \\ 1 & 0 \\ 0 & 1 \\ -3 & 1 \end{pmatrix} \begin{pmatrix} x \\ y \end{pmatrix} \le \begin{pmatrix} -1 \\ 1 \\ 3 \\ 4 \\ 1 \end{pmatrix} \right\}$$

Observe that P_C describes the convex hull: a pentagon.

4.3   Approximating Non-linear Constraints

A non-linear inequality cannot be accurately approximated by polyhedra. However, suppose that the non-linear inequality I describes a region R and that P is a polyhedron. The intersection $R \cap P$ can sometimes be approximated by a polyhedron P' such that $P' \subset P$. This problem arises in the analysis of finite domain programs that contain non-linear constraints. This section describes an algorithm for computing such a P' given non-linear inequality I and polyhedron P.

The following approximation technique arose from bound propagation algorithms for non-linear inequalities [13] and is outlined below:

1. I is rewritten to $(\wedge_{i=1}^{n} \prod X_i \le \prod Y_i) \wedge (\wedge_{j=1}^{m} \sum Z_j \le c_j)$ where X_i, Y_i, Z_j are variable multisets and c_j is a constant. For brevity the rewrite rules are omitted, instead a simple illustrative example is given. The non-linear inequality $z \le x \times (u + v) \times y$ is rewritten to $z \le x \times a \times y, a - u - v \le 0, u + v - a \le 0$, where a is a fresh variable.
2. In each product $\prod W_i$, where $W_i = \{w_1, ..., w_n\}$, every variable w_i has an upper bound, u_i, and a lower bound, l_i, which can be calculated by projecting P onto that variable (where $l_i, u_i \in \mathbb{Q} \cup \{+\infty, -\infty\}$). For every $k \in \{1, ..., n\}$, upper and lower bounds for the product $\prod W_i$ are computed by $w_k^u = w_k \cdot \prod_{i \in S} u_i$ and $w_k^l = w_k \cdot \prod_{i \in S} l_i$, where $S = \{1, ..., n\} - \{k\}$.
3. The upper and lower bounds on the products generate the following linear constraint for each non-linear inequality $\prod X_i \le \prod Y_i$, where $X_i = \{x_1, ..., x_n\}, Y_i = \{y_1, ..., y_m\}$:

$$L_i = \wedge\{x_k^l \le y_j^u \mid k \in \{1, ..., n\}, j \in \{1, ..., m\}\}$$

4. Finally the region $R \cap P$ is approximated by the polyhedron $P' = R' \cap P$ where R' is the polyhedron represented by

$$(\wedge_{i=1}^{n} L_i) \wedge (\wedge_{j=1}^{m} \sum Z_j \le c_j)$$

Example 2. Consider the region $R = \{(x, y, z)|z \leq x \times y\}$ and the polyhedron $P = \{(x, y, z)|1 \leq x, 2 \leq y \leq 4\}$. The region $R \cap P$ is approximated by a polyhedron P'. The non-linear inequality does not need to be rewritten as it is already in the required form. Projecting P onto x and y gives $1 \leq x \leq \infty$ and $2 \leq y \leq 4$. Then, $x \times y$ has upper bounds ∞, $4x$ and lower bounds y, $2x$. z has itself as upper and lower bounds. These generate the following linear inequalities $z \leq \infty, y \leq z, z \leq 4x, 2x \leq z$. Call the region generated by these inequalities R'. Then $P' = R' \cap P$.

The inequalities that arise assume the form $c_1 x \leq c_2 y$ rather than $c_1 x \leq c_2$. This is because if a tighter bound on x (or y) is later found, then the inequality $c_1 x \leq c_2 y$ can potentially tighten y (or x). This can only improve accuracy.

The analysis of non-linear constraints given here is an instance of the special conjunction operation, $\wedge_{FL}$, given in section 3: $R \wedge_{FL} P = P'$.

4.4   Widening

Widening is required to ensure that the fixpoint calculation will stabilise, that is, the polyhedra in the final two iterates coincide. Widenings for polyhedra can be found in [3], [5] and [6]. To keep the exposition reasonably self-contained, the [5] widening is detailed here.

Polyhedra are represented by sets of linear inequalities. If the previous iteration has produced polyhedron $P_k = \{\overline{x} \in \mathbb{Q}^n | \wedge S_k\}$, where $S_k = \{I_1, ..., I_l\}$ and the current iteration has given polyhedron $P_{k+1} = \{\overline{x} \in \mathbb{Q}^n | \wedge S_{k+1}\}$, where $S_{k+1} = \{J_1, ..., J_m\}$ (I_i and J_j are linear inequalities), then applying the widening results in the polyhedron given by the following set of linear inequalities:

$$\{I \in S_k | \wedge S_{k+1} \models I\} \cup \{J \in S_{k+1} | \exists I \in S_k. \wedge ((S_k - \{I\}) \cup \{J\}) = \wedge S_k\}.$$

Example 3. A smaller triangle $P_1 = \{(x, y)|y \leq x, x \leq 1, y \geq 0\}$, and a larger triangle $P_2 = \{(x, y)|y \leq 2x, x \leq 1, y \geq 0\}$ are widened to give the region $P_1 \triangledown P_2 = \{(x, y)|x \leq 1, y \geq 0\}$. The inequality $y \leq x$ from P_1 is not satisfied by all points in P_2 and the other inequalities in P_1 are. The inequality $y \leq 2x$ from P_2 does not satisfy the swapping condition, and the other inequalities describing P_2 do.

5   Comparison with Bound Propagation

As noted above, the polyhedral analysis described in this paper subsumes compiletime bound propagation. Bound propagation is used in finite domain systems, such as ECL^iPS^e and SICStus. Good expositions of bound propagation can be found in [1] and [13]. A brief outline of the technique is given here.

Given any inequality, the known bounds for each of the variables occurring in the inequality are used to find possibly tighter bounds for these variables. One variable is chosen and the upper and lower bounds for the other variables are used to find a possible upper or lower bound for this chosen variable. If the bound calculated in this way is tighter than the previous known bound for that variable, this bound is adopted in place of the older, weaker one. This process can be repeated for each variable in the inequality. An equality can be treated as two inequalities. To give a very simple illustrative example consider the following two variable case:

$$y = x + 7, 0 \leq x \leq 3, 0 \leq y \leq 12.$$

Propagating the bounds on x into the inequalities involving x and y it is found that $7 \leq y \leq 10$, tighter bounds than previously.

Bound propagation can give good tightening of constraints. For example, bound propagation in the send more money problem (one of the example programs, see Table 1) actually gives the same results as the polyhedral analysis! However, there are many examples where the polyhedral analysis improves on bound propagation, for example the program in Figure 1 of the introduction. Improvement can also be seen in the program `alpha` (see Table 1). Improvements over bound propagation can occur in any program with more than one inequality containing more than one variable. In bound propagation, individual constraints interact with the domain constraints in the store, but are unable to interact with each other. The power of the polyhedral analysis comes from allowing this interaction between constraints in order to achieve better propagation.

It can be seen that the polyhedral method subsumes bound propagation for linear constraints, when both are applied as static analyses. This follows since bound propagation can be viewed as performing Fourier-Motzkin variable elimination on a subset of the inequalities comprising the problem: a subset containing only the bounds from the store and a single inequality with more than one variable. Therefore, as extra information can only lead to tighter bounds, variables will be bounded at least as tightly after Fourier-Motzkin variable elimination for the full problem.

6   Example: Calculating Factorials

This section works through a more complicated example. Performing the analysis automatically on arbitrary (recursive) programs requires machinery which includes, among other things: convex hulls, projection, and widening. These operations are illustrated by the example in this section. The example program calculates factorials. The objective again is to infer bounds on the variables. Usually this reduces searching, but in this case it simply tightens one of the constraints – the point of the example being illustrative. The program (in SICStus syntax) is as follows:

```
:- use_module(library(clpfd)).
fac(0, 1).
fac(N, NewF):-
          N#>=0, NewF#>=0,
          NewF#=N*F,
          M #= N-1,
          fac(M, F).
```

The clause `fac(0,1).` is the first considered. The arguments are described by the polyhedron $P_1 = \{(x,y)|x = 0, y = 1\}$. Next, the second clause is considered. The problem here is to compute a two dimensional polyhedron that describes the coordinate space (N, `NewF`). First observe that `fac(M, F)` can be described by the polyhedron $\{(N, NewF, M, F)|M = 0, F = 1\}$. Note too, that the constraints `M #= N - 1`, `N#>=0`, `NewF#>=0` are represented by the polyhedron $\{(N, NewF, M, F)|M = N - 1, N \geq 0, NewF \geq 0\}$. The intersection of these two polyhedra, $\{(N, NewF, M, F)|M = 0, F = 1, M = N - 1, N \geq 0, NewF \geq 0\}$, represents the conjunction of the four constraints. The non-linear constraint `NewF#=N*F` cannot, by itself, be accurately represented by a polyhedron. Note, however, that the polyhedron $\{(N, NewF, M, F)|NewF = N, M = 0, F = 1, M = N - 1, N \geq 0, NewF \geq 0\}$ accurately describes all the constraints. Projecting the four dimensional polyhedron onto the coordinate space (N, `NewF`) gives the polyhedron $\{(N, NewF)|NewF = N, 0 = N - 1\}$, equivalently $P_2' = \{(x,y)|x = 1, y = 1\}$.

To avoid representing disjunctive information, the solution set $P_1 \cup P_2'$ is over approximated by its convex hull, $P_2'' = \{(x,y)|0 \leq x \leq 1, y = 1\}$. The bound information extracted from the convex hull by projection is exactly the same as that extracted from the union of the original pair of polyhedra by projection. The convex hull gives the second iterate. Continuing in this fashion will give a sequence of increasing polyhedra which does not stabilise. A fixpoint acceleration technique, widening, is therefore used to enforce convergence (albeit at the expense of precision). The widening essentially finds stable bounds on the sequence of polyhedra. P_1 is widened with P_2'' to give the polyhedron $P_2 = \{(x,y)|0 \leq x, y = 1\}$. $P_2 \neq P_1$, and so the fixpoint stability check fails and thus the next iteration is calculated. This results in the polyhedra $P_3' = \{(x,y)|x \geq 1, y \geq 1\}$, $P_3'' = \{(x,y)|x \geq 0, y \geq 1\}$ and $P_3 = \{(x,y)|x \geq 0, y \geq 1\}$. $P_2 \neq P_3$ and stability has still not been reached. However, $P_3 = P_4$, and the fixpoint is found. Projecting P_3 onto the first and second arguments gives the bounds $x \geq 0, y \geq 1$.

Specialising the program by adding these bounds results in the following:

```
:- use_module(library(clpfd)).
fac(0, 1):-
          0#>=0, 1#>=1.
fac(N, NewF):-
          N#>=0, NewF#>=1,
          NewF#=N*F,
          M #= N-1,
          fac(M, F).
```

The redundant constraints in the first clause can be removed. The second clause has one of its domain constraint trivially tightened. The specialisation will always preserve the set of computed answer substitutions.

7   Implementation and Experimental Results

The analysis has been implemented in SICStus Prolog 3.8. The analyser uses rational constraints rather than real constraints as problematic rounding errors occur with the CLP($\mathcal{R}$) package. The call_residue built-in that comes as part of the SICStus CLP($\mathcal{Q}$) package is used for projection in this implementation. Other parts of the analyser, such as the convex hull machinery, are taken from [3]. The analyser uses a semi-naïve iteration strategy.

The prototype analyser was tested on a selection of programs from the benchmarks suite that comes with the SICStus release of the CLP($\mathcal{FD}$) package. The programs were chosen for their compatibility with the parser: those programs which passed through the prototype front-end (abstractor) without giving error messages were used.

Bound propagation is applied by the finite domain solver at runtime. To demonstrate that the polyhedral analysis is doing more than shifting some of the work done by bound propagation from runtime to compiletime, experiments were also carried out with bound propagation applied as a compiletime analysis and program transformation.

The programs alpha, crypta, donald and smm are all cryptoarithmetic problems. Letters are assigned digits or numbers and equations involving these letters are given. The solution is an assignment of numbers/digits to letters so that the equations are satisfied. The programs eq10 and eq20 find solutions to sets of linear equations in seven variables. The program fac calculated factorials (in this case 10!). The program magic finds magic squares (up to equivalence). The program five is a version of the zebra problem, where five lists of five elements are assigned the numbers one to five so that certain relational properties hold. The program pythagor calculates Pythagorean triples (in this case with individual values up to one thousand).

The results of the analysis can be seen in Table 1. Vars is the sum of the arities of the predicates that occur in the program; T. Vars is the number of these argument positions tightened by the analysis; Time is the runtime of the original program (in milliseconds); T. Time is the runtime of the specialised program (in milliseconds); Bound Prop. is the runtime of the program when specialised by the values obtained by bound propagation (in milliseconds); Fixpoint is the time taken to calculate the fixpoint (in milliseconds); Fix and Proj. is the runtime of the analysis including the final projection stage (in milliseconds). Note that all times are averages taken over one hundred runs. The experiments were conducted using a PC with a 366MHz Pentium processor and 128Mb of RAM, running Red Hat Linux 6.1.

All but one of the example programs have at least one predicate position tightened by the analysis, indicating that the analysis can be widely applied. No specialised program runs slower than before. After specialisation, the programs alpha, eq10, eq20 and magic run significantly quicker than both the original programs and the programs specialised by adding the results of bound propagation. This indicates that the analysis can significantly prune the search space. The fixpoint analysis times are reasonable considering that the analyser is a

Table 1. Test Results

Program	Vars	T. Vars	Time	T. Time	Bound Prop.	Fixpoint	Fix. and Proj.
alpha	26	25	2390	4	2390	280	2100
crypta	10	3	6	6	6	460	59430
donald	10	3	47	47	47	80	490
eq10	7	7	13	0.7	13	100	110
eq20	7	7	20	0.2	19	130	140
fac^{10}	2	2	0.8	1.0	0.8	260	260
five	25	3	1.8	1.8	1.8	100	190
magic	9	9	6.5	3.2	6.4	100	230
smm	8	3	0.9	0.9	0.9	60	340
pythagor^{1000}	3	0	155	154	154	180	190

prototype in an early stage of development. In particular, the iteration technique can be improved. Amongst the more expensive fixpoint times are those for fac and pythagor. These programs are recursive, and although the analyser has been designed to deal with all programs, it is expected that most finite domain programs are not recursive. Notice that the most significant factor in analysing many of the programs is the cost of the final projection stage. The analyser currently uses the projection technique that comes with SICStus. It is to be expected that the use of a projection technique tailored to the specific task of projecting onto a single variable would give significantly improved performance.

8   Related Work

The use of convex polyhedra to describe the constraints in constraint logic programs over the reals has been outlined in [14]. The paper does not describe an implementation and does not directly address the analysis and specialisation of finite domain programs.

The analysis in this paper has its foundations in classic work on polyhedral approximation [5], [6]. Polyhedral approximation has been applied in areas as diverse as: argument size analysis [3]; compiletime array bounds analysis [6]; termination of deductive databases [21]; off-line partial deduction [15]; parallelisation of imperative languages [19]; control generation for logic programs [16]; memory management of symbolic languages based on cdr-coding of lists [8]. The work in this paper directly builds on the work of Benoy and King ([3]) to show how a finite domain program specialiser can be built with off-the-shelf linear constraint solving machinery.

Static analysis of finite domain constraint logic programs is not a new idea. Bagnara [2] proposes an interval analysis for refining domain constraints. The critical observation in this paper is that a finite domain solver will usually perform constraint propagation at runtime, for example through indexical based propagation. The static analysis presented in this paper is designed to complement a runtime constraint analysis: polyhedra capture deep inter-variable relationships which cannot always be traced in bound propagation.

The current work could be viewed as a compiletime approach to the collaboration of constraint solvers. There are many recent papers on collaboration of constraint solvers, such as [17], [20]. Different kinds of constraint solvers will propagate information in different ways, and mixing technologies often gives the best framework for solving a problem. Using a variety of solvers can give propagation that cannot be achieved in a single solver. The approach taken here is attractive because it uses off the shelf technologies and combines their use, but this has the drawback that the propagation is not as intelligent as it might be.

Another compilation technique based on projection arises in providing predictable time-critical user interfaces, [7]. There, however, the objective is to remove runtime constraint solving altogether.

9   Conclusions and Future Work

Analysis of finite domain constraint logic programs using polyhedra promises to be a powerful compiletime technique for reducing the search space of finite domain constraint logic programs. This analysis can extract more information than bound propagation alone. By using program specialisation, other methods of domain reduction can still be applied at runtime. The analysis is safe in two senses: the specialised program is never incorrect; it never runs more slowly that the original. The analysis can be implemented straightforwardly using a rational constraint solver.

The results show that the analysis will tighten the domains of many of the variables in programs – indeed, the analysis completely solves the problems in eq10 and eq20. The timing values in the results table, in particular those for the program alpha (where the analysis time plus the tightened time is less than the original time), indicate that polyhedral analysis can give a significant speed up. As a compiletime technique, some extra cost is not prohibitive, however, it is expected that further development will lead to a significant speedup of analysis. The analysis can therefore be considered practical. However, the analysis is not as powerful when data is input at runtime: clearly, in this situation no compiletime specialisation procedure will be effective. The programs with which the analyser has been used have all had the data built into the programs. A wider study of finite domain programs is needed before the significance of this drawback can be assessed.

Future work will focus on developing the analyser. Beyond improving the convex hull and projection calculations, there are several areas where work is in progress. The use of widening could be delayed to improve precision and non-linear constraints could be better approximated. The analyser will also be extended to support other finite domain solvers. It would be an interesting to investigate whether or not it is practical to exploit the extra propagation gained by reanalysing the specialised programs.

Acknowledgements. The work of both authors is supported by EPSRC grant number GR/MO8769. The authors would like to thank Florence Benoy, Pat Hill, Jon Martin and Barbara Smith for their helpful comments and suggestions.

References

1. K. R. Apt. A Proof Theoretic View of Constraint Programming. *Fundamenta Informaticae*, 33:1–27, 1998.
2. R. Bagnara. *Data-flow Analysis for Constraint Logic-based Languages*. PhD thesis, Università di Pisa, 1997. TD-1/97.
3. F. Benoy and A. King. Inferring Argument Size Relationships with CLP($\mathcal{R}$). In J. Gallagher, editor, *Logic Program Synthesis and Transformation*, volume 1207 of *Lecture Notes in Computer Science*, pages 204–224. Springer, 1996.
4. A. Bossi, M. Gabbrielli, G. Levi, and M. Martelli. The *s*-semantics Approach: Theory and Applications. *Journal of Logic Programming*, 19-20:149–197, 1994.
5. P. Cousot and R. Cousot. Comparing the Galois Connection and Widening/Narrowing Approaches to Abstract Interpretation. Technical Report LIENS-92-16, Laboratoire d'Informatique de l'Ecole Normal Superiéure, 1992.
6. P. Cousot and N. Halbwachs. Automatic Discovery of Restraints among Variables of a Program. In *Proceedings of the Fifth Annual ACM Symposium on Principles of Programming Languages*, pages 84–97, 1978.
7. H. Harvey, P. J. Stuckey, and A. Borning. Compiling Constraint Solving Using Projection. In *Proceedings of Principles and Practice of Constraint Programming*, volume 1330 of *Lecture Notes in Computer Science*, pages 491–505. Springer, 1997.
8. R. N. Horspool. Analyzing List Usage in Prolog Code. University of Victoria, 1990.
9. J. M. Howe and A. King. A Semantic Basis for Specialising Domain Constraints. Technical Report 21-99, University of Kent, 1999.
10. T. Huynh, C. Lassez, and J.-L. Lassez. Practical Issues on the Projection of Polyhedral Sets. *Annals of Mathematics and Artificial Intelligence*, 6:295–316, 1992.
11. J. Jaffar and J.-L. Lassez. Constraint Logic Programming. In *Proceedings of the Symposium on Principles of Programming Languages*, pages 111–119. ACM Press, 1987.
12. J. Jaffar and M. J. Maher. Constraint Logic Programming: A Survey. *Journal of Logic Programming*, 19-20:503–582, 1994.
13. K. Marriot and P. J. Stuckey. *Programming With Constraints*. MIT Press, Cambridge, MA., 1998.
14. K. Marriott and P. J. Stuckey. The 3 R's of Optimizing Constraint Logic Programs: Refinement, Removal and Reordering. In *Proceedings of the Twentieth Annual ACM Symposium on Principles of Programming Languages*, pages 334–344. ACM Press, 1993.
15. J. C. Martin. *Judgement Day: Terminating Logic Programs*. PhD thesis, University of Southampton, 1999.
16. J. C. Martin and A. King. Generating Efficient, Terminating Logic Programs. In *Proceedings of the Seventh International Joint Conference on Theory and Practice of Software Development*, volume 1214 of *Lecture Notes in Computer Science*, pages 273–284, Lille, France, 1997. Springer.

17. E. Monfroy. An Environment for Designing/Executing Constraint Solver Collaborations. *Electronic Notes in Theoretical Computer Science*, 16(1), 1998.
18. K. G. Murty. *Linear Programming*. Wiley, 1983.
19. W. Pugh. The Omega Test: a Fast and Practical Integer Programming Algorithm for Dependency Analysis. *Communications of the ACM*, pages 102–114, August 1992.
20. R. Rodošek and M. Wallace. A Generic Model and Hybrid Algorithm for Hoist Scheduling Problems. In *Proceedings of the 4th International Conference on Principals and Practice of Constraint Programming*, volume 1520 of *Lecture Notes in Computer Science*, pages 385–399. Springer, 1998.
21. A. van Gelder. Deriving Constraints Amongst Argument Sizes in Logic Programs. *Annals of Mathematics and Artificial Intelligence*, 3(2-4), 1991.

Roles of Program Extension [*]

Ralf Lämmel[1], Günter Riedewald[2], and Wolfgang Lohmann[2]

[1] CWI, P.O. Box 94079, NL-1090 GB Amsterdam
[2] Universität Rostock, Fachbereich Informatik, D-18051 Rostock

Abstract. A formal and effective approach to the extension of the computational behaviour of logic programs is presented. The approach builds upon the following concepts. The extension of computational behaviour is modelled by semantics-preserving program transformations. Several basic roles involved in such transformations are identified. Every transformation defined solely in terms of the basic roles will be semantics-preserving by definition. Functional meta-programs on logic object programs are used to specify the basic roles and to derive programming techniques in the style of stepwise enhancement. Thus, the process of extending the computational behaviour of logic programs is regarded as disciplined meta-programming.

1 Introduction

This paper is about adding functionality to declarative programs. We present a rigorous approach which relies on program transformation concepts and meta-programming technology. Transformations are used to model the enhancement of programs, i.e., the extension by computational behaviour. The approach is spelled out in this paper for logic programs (definite clause programs), but it is also applicable to several other declarative languages such as attribute grammars and algebraic specifications as discussed to some extent in [14,15,16]. The paper identifies the following basic roles involved in semantics-preserving transformations facilitating the extension of computational behaviour:

- adding parameters,
- applying substitutions,
- renaming symbols,
- inserting literals in bodies of clauses,
- adding definitions for predicate symbols.

The basic roles will be defined in terms of functional meta-programs. They also will be illustrated by deriving programming techniques in the style of stepwise enhancement [26,13,11].

[*] This work was supported, in part, by *DFG*, in the project *Komposition beweisbarkorrekter Sprachbausteine*, and by *NWO*, in the project *Generation of Program Transformation Systems*.

A. Bossi (Ed.): LOPSTR'99, LNCS 1817, pp. 136–155, 2000.

Example 1. The following example has been adopted from [10]. Let us start with a very simple program for traversing *AND-OR* trees:[1]

$traverse(\downarrow \text{tree}(\text{OP}, \text{NODE}, \text{TREE}^*_{child})) \Leftarrow traverse\_list(\downarrow \text{TREE}^*_{child}).$
$traverse\_list(\downarrow [\,]).$
$traverse\_list(\downarrow [\text{TREE}|\text{TREE}^*]) \Leftarrow traverse(\downarrow \text{TREE}), traverse\_list(\downarrow \text{TREE}^*).$

An enhancement of this simple program is the following version which additionally computes labels for each node. A node is labelled with true or false according to the conventions of an *AND-OR* tree, i.e., all *AND* leaf-nodes are considered as successful and all *OR* leaf-nodes are considered as failed:

$label(\downarrow \text{tree}(\text{OP}, \text{NODE}, \text{TREE}^*_{child}), \boxed{\uparrow \text{LABEL}}) \Leftarrow$
   $\boxed{init\_label(\downarrow \text{OP}, \uparrow \text{LABEL}_{init}),}$
   $label\_list(\downarrow \text{TREE}^*_{child}, \boxed{\downarrow \text{OP}, \downarrow \text{LABEL}_{init}, \uparrow \text{LABEL}}).$

$label\_list(\downarrow [\,], \boxed{\downarrow \text{OP}, \downarrow \text{LABEL}, \uparrow \text{LABEL}}).$

$label\_list(\downarrow [\text{TREE}|\text{TREE}^*], \boxed{\downarrow \text{OP}, \downarrow \text{LABEL}_{in}, \uparrow \text{LABEL}_{out}}) \Leftarrow$
   $label(\downarrow \text{TREE}, \boxed{\uparrow \text{LABEL}}),$
   $\boxed{and\_or(\downarrow \text{OP}, \downarrow \text{LABEL}_{in}, \downarrow \text{LABEL}, \uparrow \text{LABEL}_{temp}),}$
   $label\_list(\downarrow \text{TREE}^*, \boxed{\downarrow \text{OP}, \downarrow \text{LABEL}_{temp}, \uparrow \text{LABEL}_{out}}).$

$\boxed{\begin{array}{l} init\_label(\downarrow \text{and}, \uparrow \text{true}). \\ init\_label(\downarrow \text{or}, \uparrow \text{false}). \end{array}}$

$\boxed{\begin{array}{l} and\_or(\downarrow \text{and}, \downarrow \text{false}, \downarrow \text{false}, \uparrow \text{false}). \\ and\_or(\downarrow \text{and}, \downarrow \text{false}, \downarrow \text{true}, \uparrow \text{false}). \\ \ldots \end{array}}$

The label computed, for example, for the *AND-OR* tree

$$\text{tree}(\text{and}, n_1, [\text{tree}(\text{and}, n_2, []), \text{tree}(\text{or}, n_3, [])])$$

is false, where n_1, n_2 and n_3 are some values at the nodes. Note that the boxed clauses, literals and parameters had to be projected away in order to derive the basic program from the enhanced program. Moreover, renaming is involved in the sense that the symbols *traverse* and *traverse_list* used in the basic program are called *label* and *label_list* resp. in the enhanced version.

The rest of the paper is structured as follows.

- In Section 2, a general meta-programming framework for specifying and executing program transformations is developed. The framework is not yet tuned towards the particular kind of semantics-preserving transformations we have in mind. Transformations are represented as functional programs in this framework. There is an abstract data type for object programs, i.e., logic programs.

---

[1] The arrows $\downarrow$ and $\uparrow$ are used in the logic programs in this paper to indicate the mode of the positions (input versus output).

- Section 3 is the central part of the paper. First, the basic roles listed above are investigated more carefully with emphasis on semantics-preservation. Second, the basic roles are specified in the meta-programming framework from the previous section. Third, the operators are shown to be useful to derive common programming techniques such as accumulators.
- In Section 4, related work is discussed, results are summarized and some topics for future work are indicated.

2   The Underlying Meta-programming Framework

The meta-programming framework used to specify program transformations in this paper can be characterized as follows:

- Program transformations are regarded as functions and finally represented as *pure functional programs* in *Haskell*.[2]
- *Monads* [19,28,7] are used to model two effects involved in meta-programs, namely errors and a state for generating fresh symbols and other entities.
- Meta-programs do not operate on concrete representations of object programs. Construction and destruction of object programs are supported by a corresponding abstract data type. Thereby, well-formedness / well-typedness can be enforced for constructed object programs.
- Parameter positions are associated with *modes* and *types*. These annotations can be used in order to enforce a certain type system of the object language. Modes and types are also used to control meta-programs. This role is also sensible for untyped object languages.
- While modes and types support more conceptual addressing methods, internally unambiguous *selectors* are used at several levels of addressing.

To the best of our knowledge, this setting is unique. Some of the characteristics are explained in detail in the subsequent subsections. The framework is discussed in more detail in [17].

2.1   The Effect Space

In our setting, meta-programs need to cope with two global effects, that is to say propagating errors and generating fresh symbols, variables and others.

Errors It is an inherent property of program transformations to be partially defined. Usually, transformations are only applicable if certain preconditions are satisfied. If a precondition for a meta-program is not satisfied, it should fail. Meta-programs are functions. Thus, the functions used in a meta-program return an error value to encode failure.

---

[2] We assume familiarity with functional programming (in *Haskell*), in particular with curried functions, standard higher-order functions like *map* and *foldr*, and monads. We do not rely on lazy evaluation. Other typed functional languages, e.g., languages from the *SML* family, would be applicable, too.

States It is also very common for program transformations to require fresh entities, e.g., fresh variables in Example 1. Thus, we need to keep track of entities
in use and we need a scheme to generate fresh entities.

Assuming a pure style of functional meta-programming, monads [19,28,7]
seem to be most appropriate to deal with effects. Consequently, the functions
in the meta-programming framework are supposed to be computed in an effect
space; refer to Figure 1[3] for an illustration and a definition of the type constructors of the relevant monads. The error monad $\mathcal{E}$ is adopted to deal with errors
and especially strict error handling (propagation). The state monad $\mathcal{S}$ hides states used for the generation of fresh symbols, variables and others. $\mathcal{ES}$ denotes
the composed monad.[4] $\mathcal{M}$ is used in the text whenever an explanation applies
to an arbitrary monad.

$$\mathcal{S}\ \alpha = \mathsf{State} \rightarrow (\mathsf{State} \times \alpha)$$
$$\mathcal{E}\ \alpha = \alpha + \{error\}$$
$$\mathcal{ES}\ \alpha = \mathsf{State} \rightarrow ((\mathsf{State} \times \alpha) + \{error\})$$

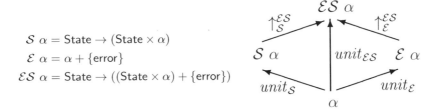

Fig. 1. The Effect Space

For convenience, we recall some facts on monads. A monad can be regar-
ded as a triple $\langle \mathcal{M}, unit_{\mathcal{M}}, \ggg_{\mathcal{M}} \rangle$, where $\mathcal{M}$ is a type constructor, and $unit_{\mathcal{M}}$
(sometimes also called *return*) and $\ggg_{\mathcal{M}}$ (usually called *bind*) are polymorphic
functions with the following types:

$$unit_{\mathcal{M}} : \alpha \rightarrow \mathcal{M}\ \alpha$$
$$\ggg_{\mathcal{M}} : \mathcal{M}\ \alpha \rightarrow (\alpha \rightarrow \mathcal{M}\ \beta) \rightarrow \mathcal{M}\ \beta$$

The type constructor $\mathcal{M}$ models "computations" for a certain effect. It takes a
type — the type of "values" — and returns the corresponding type of compu-
tations. $unit_{\mathcal{M}}$ lifts a simple value to a computation in $\mathcal{M}$. The infix operator
$\ggg_{\mathcal{M}}$ is used to sequence computations and to pass intermediate results. $unit_{\mathcal{M}}$
and $\ggg_{\mathcal{M}}$ have to obey the common monad laws. In the effect space in Figure 1,
the functions $\uparrow_{\mathcal{S}}^{\mathcal{ES}}$ and $\uparrow_{\mathcal{E}}^{\mathcal{ES}}$ are used to lift computations in $\mathcal{S}$ resp. $\mathcal{E}$ to $\mathcal{ES}$. The
definitions are straightforward; refer to [19,28,7] for similar definitions.

---

[3] We only use *Haskell*-notation in *Haskell*-code. Otherwise, we use mathematical notation: $\times$ for products; $+$ for disjoint unions; * and $^{+}$ for list types; $\mathcal{P}$ for power
sets; $\langle$ and $\rangle$ to enclose tuples and sequences; $\pi_1, \pi_2, \ldots$ for projection operators, i.e.,
$\pi_i\ \langle d_1, \ldots, d_n \rangle = d_i$; $\#s$ for the length of the sequence s; $+\!\!\!+$ for list concatenation.
[4] Monad transformers could be used in order to derive $\mathcal{ES}$ in a more modular way.

2.2   Object Programs

Logic programs are regarded as object programs in the meta-programming framework. Actually, the terminology used below will occasionally deviate from logic programming terminology because the framework is more generic in the sense that it also supports other declarative languages as discussed in [14,17]. Object programs are modelled by an abstract data type whose interface is defined in Figure 2.

Sorts of object program fragments

Program		-- complete programs
Definition		-- groups of rules
Rule		-- tagged rules consisting of LHS and RHS
Literal		-- parameterized operators
Parameter		-- variables and compound parameters
Variable		-- variables
Term		-- compound parameters
Operator		-- symbols used in literals
Constructor		-- symbols used in terms
Selector		-- selectors for addressing
Type		-- object type expressions
Mode	$= \{\downarrow, \uparrow, \ldots\}$	-- parameter modes

Functions to construct object programs

$program$: $\mathsf{Definition}^* \to \mathcal{E}$ $\mathsf{Program}$
$definition$: $\mathsf{Rule}^+ \to \mathcal{E}$ $\mathsf{Definition}$
$rule$: $\mathsf{Selector} \to \mathsf{Literal} \to (\mathsf{Selector} \times \mathsf{Literal})^* \to \mathcal{E}$ Rule
$literal$: $\mathsf{Operator} \to (\mathsf{Selector} \times \mathsf{Mode} \times \mathsf{Parameter})^* \to \mathcal{E}$ $\mathsf{Literal}$
$term$: $\mathsf{Constructor} \to (\mathsf{Selector} \times \mathsf{Parameter})^* \to \mathsf{Type} \to \mathcal{E}$ $\mathsf{Parameter}$
$fresh_{\mathsf{Variable}}$: $\mathsf{Type} \to \mathcal{S}$ $\mathsf{Parameter}$
$fresh_\alpha$: $\mathcal{S}$ α for $\alpha = $ $\mathsf{Selector}, \mathsf{Operator}, \mathsf{Constructor}$

Functions to destruct object programs

$definitions$: $\mathsf{Program} \to \mathsf{Definition}^*$
$defines$: $\mathsf{Definition} \to \mathsf{Operator}$
$rules$: $\mathsf{Definition} \to \mathsf{Rule}^+$
tag : $\mathsf{Rule} \to \mathsf{Selector}$
lhs : $\mathsf{Rule} \to \mathsf{Literal}$
rhs : $\mathsf{Rule} \to (\mathsf{Selector} \times \mathsf{Literal})^*$
$operator$: $\mathsf{Literal} \to \mathsf{Operator}$
$parameterization$: $\mathsf{Literal} \to (\mathsf{Selector} \times \mathsf{Mode} \times \mathsf{Parameter})^*$
$typeOf$: $\mathsf{Parameter} \to \mathsf{Type}$
$descend$: $(\mathsf{Variable} \to \alpha) \to (\mathsf{Constructor} \to (\mathsf{Selector} \times \mathsf{Parameter})^* \to \alpha) \to \mathsf{Parameter} \to \alpha$

Fig. 2. Interface of the Abstract Data Type for Object Programs

The structure of object programs can be best understood by looking at the types of the constructor functions in Figure 2.[5] A complete program consists of a number of definitions, that is to say groups of rules. The rules in such a group are meant to define one "operator" corresponding to the definite clauses for a certain predicate symbol in logic programming. A rule consists of a kind of tag,

---

[5] We should mention that some uses of * or $^+$ versus $\mathcal{P}$ are debatable. We prefer lists rather than power sets for minor implementational reasons.

a LHS (left-hand side; the head in a definite clause) and a RHS (right-hand side; the body in a definite clause). A LHS is just a literal, whereas a RHS is a list of literals each qualified with a selector to facilitate addressing. A literal, in turn, is a parameterized operator (say, predicate symbol). Each parameter of a literal is associated with a selector and a mode. Finally, parameters are either variables or compound terms and they are associated with a type.

Example 2. The initial program in Example 1 consists of two definitions, one for *traverse* and another for *traverse_list*. The definition of *traverse_list* consists of two rules. There are only parameters with the mode ↓. The program is not explicitly annotated with selectors.

It is an important observation that most constructor functions in Figure 2 are computations in $\mathcal{E}$, i.e., it is assumed that the construction of object program fragments might fail. That is indeed necessary because the framework has to prevent meta-programs from constructing and observing improper object program fragments as constrained by straightforward notions of well-formedness and well-typedness. The attempt to construct an ill-typed logic program must result in an error. The *fresh*-constructors in Figure 2 are computations rather in $\mathcal{S}$ than in $\mathcal{E}$. These constructors serve for the generation of certain kinds of entities.

Example 3. Consider a list of definitions. To qualify it as a proper program, the constructor *program* has to be used. The application of the constructor might fail for two reasons. Either the types of the symbols involved in the different definitions are not compatible, or there are two or more definitions for the same symbol.

There are no effects involved in the destruction of object programs. The destructor functions should be self-explanatory by their types. *descend* is a kind of case construct on parameters. Two functions need to be supplied to *descend*, one to handle variables, another one for compound parameters.

Consequently, program transformations are modelled as functions of type Trafo = Program → $\mathcal{ES}$ Program. By now, the utility of monads should also be clear. They enforce some discipline of meta-programming, and they facilitate reasoning about meta-programs. Without encapsulating the error effect, the strict propagation of errors could not be guaranteed. Without encapsulating the state effect, freshness of entities could hardly be ensured. Besides, meta-programs get tangled if they had to deal with the effects explicitly.

2.3   Types at the Object Level

Types (including modes of parameter positions) at the object level are relevant in the meta-programming framework in two important ways:

1. Types are regarded as annotations of object programs useful to provide more information about the sorts of data and the data flow. Types can be used to address, for example, parameter positions. This conceptual role of types is used to control meta-programs.

2. If the object language is typed, e.g., Gödel [9], the type system should be respected by the meta-programming framework in the sense that well-typedness is enforced. For untyped languages like Prolog, still a kind of "conceptual" well-typedness in the sense of 1. should be enforced.

The notion of typing we use corresponds, essentially, to many-sorted (like in Gödel [9]) directional [4] types. Note however, that the framework is not restricted to typed logic programs as explained above. Technically, a type of a program or some fragment is just a collection of profiles for the symbols in the program as modelled by Sigma:

$$\text{Sigma} = \mathcal{P}\,(\text{Operator} \times (\text{Selector} \times \text{Mode} \times \text{Type})^{\star})$$
$$\times\, \mathcal{P}\,(\text{Constructor} \times (\text{Selector} \times \text{Type})^{\star} \times \text{Type})$$

It is assumed that overloading is not supported, i.e., $\forall \Sigma \in \text{Sigma} : \forall p, p' \in \pi_i(\Sigma) : \pi_1(p) = \pi_1(p') \Rightarrow p = p'$, where $i = 1, 2$. $\mathcal{TYPE}(P) \in \text{Sigma}$ denotes the type of a program $P \in \text{Program}$. It is easily defined by traversing P and accumulating the profiles of the operators and constructors.

Example 4. Using some standard notation for profiles, the predicate symbols for the enhanced program in Example 1 are of the following types:

$$label : \text{TREE} \rightarrow \text{LABEL}$$
$$label\_list : \text{TREE}^{\star} \times \text{OP} \times \text{LABEL} \rightarrow \text{LABEL}$$
$$init\_label : \text{OP} \rightarrow \text{LABEL}$$
$$and\_or : \text{OP} \times \text{LABEL} \times \text{LABEL} \rightarrow \text{LABEL}$$

Based on modes, parameter positions can be subdivided into *applied* and *defining* positions. LHS positions with mode ↑ and RHS positions with mode ↓ are called applied positions; complementary for defining positions. The intuition behind these terms is that variables on applied positions are expected to be "computed" in terms of variables on defining positions. These terms are actually used in much the same way in extended attribute grammars [29]. The concept of applied and defining positions is relevant for meta-programming, for example, if certain positions need to be computed from other positions according to some scheme like accumulation or reduction.

2.4   Addressing Fragments

It is clear that fragments of object programs need to be addressed during meta-programming. We should discuss all the various ways to address fragments. At the top level, a certain definition in a program can be addressed by the symbol on the LHS which have all the rules in a definition in common. At the next level, a certain rule in a definition can be addressed by its tag. At the level of a rule, first, either the LHS or the RHS has to be selected. For RHSs, a certain literal can be addressed using a selector. Finally, a possibly nested parameter position can be addressed by a non-empty selector sequence. Conceptually, it is maybe more convenient to use modes and types instead of selectors.

Example 5. Let us consider the first rule in the enhanced program in Example 1. The additional computational behaviour as manifested by new parameter positions of *label* and *label_list*, and the new literal *init_label*(...) refers to some variables of the initial program. Thus, a transformation performing the enhancement would have to address these variables. Using an ad hoc notation for references, the variable *OP*, for example, can be addressed by LHS $\rightarrow$ $\downarrow$TREE $\rightarrow$ tree.OP, i.e., first, the LHS of the rule is addressed, then the input position of type TREE is selected, and, finally, the nested parameter of type OP rooted by the constructor *tree* is selected.

It is debatable if there should be different kinds of selectors (rule tags, selectors for RHS literals, etc.). Of course, it is a basic well-formedness requirement that selectors are pairwise distinct at any level of addressing. Moreover, selectors also contribute to "conceptual" well-typedness in a straightforward sense. The selectors used for the parameter positions of literals, for example, have to be the same for all literals with a certain symbol in a program. Note also that object programs do not necessarily need to define selectors explicitly. Selectors might be generated automatically during the construction of the internal representation so that they can be observed by meta-programs traversing object programs.

deref	: Reference $\rightarrow$ Rule $\rightarrow$ $\mathcal{E}$ Parameter	-- dereferencing
references	: Rule $\rightarrow$ Reference*	-- return all references
lhsOrRhs	: $\alpha \rightarrow$ (Selector $\rightarrow \alpha$) $\rightarrow$ Reference $\rightarrow \alpha$	-- handle LHS/RHS reference
operator	: Reference $\rightarrow$ Operator	-- referenced operator
typeOf	: Reference $\rightarrow$ Type	-- type of the reference
refersToAP	: Reference $\rightarrow$ Bool	-- applied position
refersToDP	: Reference $\rightarrow$ Bool	-- defining position
leq	: Reference $\rightarrow$ Reference $\rightarrow$ Rule $\rightarrow$ $\mathcal{E}$ Bool	-- $\leq$ on Reference
rightmost	: Reference* $\rightarrow$ Rule $\rightarrow$ $\mathcal{E}$ Reference	-- maximum on Reference

Fig. 3. Interface of the Abstract Data Type for Addressing

The interface of a corresponding abstract data type for addressing is shown in part in Figure 3. The central type is Reference modelling references to a literal within a rule and in turn to a parameter in a literal. *deref* returns the parameter according to a reference. If a meta-program has to iterate on the parameters of a rule, all the references can be accumulated with *references*. The function *lhsOrRhs* provides a case construct on references to process LHS resp. RHS references differently. References have a type which can be selected with *typeOf*. The remaining functions in Figure 3 deal with data flow issues. *refersToAP* and *refersToDP* check if a given reference refers to an applied or a defining position. The operation *leq* defines a left-to-right total order on Reference. LHS input positions are the smallest positions. The order on the RHS respects the order of the literals where input positions of a literal are smaller than the output positions of the same literal. The LHS output positions are the greatest positions. This order is useful in order to enforce a certain data flow from left to right (or vice versa), e.g., in accumulation.

3   Extending Computational Behaviour

In Subsection 3.1, the basic roles listed in the introduction will be reviewed w.r.t. semantics-preservation. In Subsection 3.2, a core calculus supporting these roles is defined in the meta-programming framework. In Subsection 3.3, the core calculus is completed to get transformation operators operating at the level of complete object programs. Finally, it is illustrated in Subsection 3.4 that the developed calculus is useful to derive common programming techniques.

3.1   Semantics-Preservation

When extending a program, a crucial question is whether the computational behaviour is preserved. Kirschbaum, Sterling and Jain have shown in [12] that program maps, which capture most transformations derivable in our framework, preserve the computational behaviour of a logic program, if it is assumed that behaviour is manifested by the (SLD-) computations of the program. In contrast, we will discuss here in an informal way why the roles identified by us are semantics-preserving. Given a logic program P and an enhancement P', the discussion of the correctness of the transformation will be based on the proof-tree semantics for P and P'.[6] We should point out that we have correctness but not completeness, i.e., each proof tree for P' can be projected onto a proof tree of P, but not vice versa.

Adding parameters Correctness holds because the new parameters in P' can also be projected away in its proof trees. Completeness does not hold in general because the new parameters might constrain variables from P too much or the unification involved in unfolding fails in the new parameter positions. Several schemes to add parameters can be proved to imply completeness.

Applying substitutions Correctness holds because the substitution can also be applied to proof trees of P. Completeness does not hold because a substitution might instantiate variables, and thereby certain unfolding steps are not possible any longer.

Renaming symbols It is clear that a proper renaming is performed consistently. It is very common to require that a renaming does not confuse symbols. In this case, correctness and completeness follows trivially. We also consider renamings, where the parameters of an open program might be confused with each other or with symbols already defined by the program. This is a sensible design decision for open programs.

Inserting literals Proof trees in P' will contain additional subtrees which can be projected away to obtain P. Completeness cannot be ensured because a proof subtree for a new literal might not exist, or variables of P might be constrained by all possible proof subtrees for the new literal too much.

---

[6] Our arguments for the correctness of the roles do not rely on certain technical conditions assumed for the rigorous proof in [12].

Adding definitions The extension of a definition for a symbol by new rules needs to be forbidden. Providing definitions for a symbol s previously not defined by P is correct. There are two cases. If s has not been used in P, then the proof-tree semantics for P and P' are equivalent. Otherwise, P is an open program with parameter s. Providing a definition is sensible.

3.2 A Core Calculus

In defining transformation operators corresponding to the basic roles, less complex types of object program fragments are preferably chosen, and the state effect is ignored whenever possible. Renaming predicates, for example, can essentially be defined at the literal level, and indeed the state effect is not relevant for renaming. The resulting core calculus is completed in the next subsection by lifting all the operators to the type $\mathsf{Trafo} = \mathsf{Program} \to \mathcal{ES}\ \mathsf{Program}$ in a simple and natural way.

The definition of the core calculus is presented in Figure 4. States are only involved in adding parameters ($\underline{\mathbf{add}}_0$). Note that it is not possible to abstract from errors at all because all operators construct object program fragments, i.e., the operators are inherently partial. Adding parameters ($\underline{\mathbf{add}}_0$) and renaming operators ($\underline{\mathbf{rename}}_0$) can be defined at the Literal level. Substitution ($\underline{\mathbf{substitute}}_0$) can even be defined at the Parameter level. On the other hand, inserting literals ($\underline{\mathbf{insert}}_0$) must be defined at the Rule level and the definition of operators ($\underline{\mathbf{define}}_0$) has even to be defined at the top level, i.e., at the Program level.

There is the following rationale for the definition of $\underline{\mathbf{add}}_0$ intended to add positions to literals. If the given literal lit has an operator which is different from op, the whole literal is preserved. Otherwise, first a fresh variable of type t is generated. Then, the given literal is reconstructed preserving the operator and extending the list of parameters by the new parameter associating it with the given selector sel and mode m. Generating fresh variables is performed in the state monad $\mathcal{S}$, whereas fragment construction is performed in the error monad $\mathcal{E}$. To compose these computations, they are lifted to $\mathcal{ES}$ by $\uparrow_{\mathcal{S}}^{\mathcal{ES}}$ and $\uparrow_{\mathcal{E}}^{\mathcal{ES}}$.

The definition of $\underline{\mathbf{substitute}}_0$ uses the function $descend$ to destruct parameters. Consequently, there are two cases corresponding to the functions sv and st. Variables are replaced by the term according to the supplied substitution $subst$. The auxiliary function $apply$ performs the required table lookup and it behaves like identity if there is no entry for v. The monadic map for lists defined in Figure 5 is used for the traversal of nested parameters.

We should comment on the design of the $\underline{\mathbf{insert}}_0$ operator. For reasons of orthogonality, the inserted literal carries an empty list of parameters because parameters can be added subsequently by $\underline{\mathbf{add}}_0$. There should be some way to define the actual target position on the RHS of a rule. Note that the order of the RHS literals may be significant for the data-flow or control-flow in the object program, or for the performance of subsequent transformations. References are a suitable abstract means of specifying a RHS position. The idea is that the literal is inserted $next$ to the literal referred to by the reference passed to $\underline{\mathbf{insert}}_0$, also using the concept of applied and defining positions.

$\textbf{add}_0$: Operator → Selector → Mode → Type → Literal → $\mathcal{ES}$ Literal
$\textbf{substitute}_0$: Substitution → Parameter → $\mathcal{E}$ Parameter
$\textbf{rename}_0$: Operator → Operator → Literal → $\mathcal{E}$ Literal
$\textbf{insert}_0$: Reference → Selector → Operator → Rule → $\mathcal{E}$ Rule
$\textbf{define}_0$: Definition → Program → $\mathcal{E}$ Program

$\textbf{add}_0$ op sel m t $lit =$
  $\textbf{if}$ $(operator\ lit) \neq op$
    $\textbf{then}$ $unit_{\mathcal{ES}}$ lit
    $\textbf{else}$ $\uparrow_S^{\mathcal{ES}} (fresh_{\text{Variable}}\ t) \ggeq_{\mathcal{ES}} \lambda p \rightarrow$
        $\uparrow_{\mathcal{E}}^{\mathcal{ES}} (literal\ (operator\ lit)\ ((parameterization\ lit) + \!\!+ [(sel, m, p)]))$

$\textbf{substitute}_0$ $subst$ $p = descend$ sv st p
  $\textbf{where}$
    $sv\ v = apply\ subst\ v\ (typeOf\ p)$
    $st\ sym\ paras = mmap\ f\ paras \ggeq_{\mathcal{E}} \lambda paras' \rightarrow term\ sym\ paras'\ (typeOf\ p)$
    $f\ (sel, p) = \textbf{substitute}_0\ subst\ p \ggeq_{\mathcal{E}} \lambda p' \rightarrow unit_{\mathcal{E}}\ (sel, p')$

$\textbf{rename}_0$ op op' $lit =$
  $literal$ $(\textbf{if}\ (operator\ lit) \neq op\ \textbf{then}\ (operator\ lit)\ \textbf{else}\ op')\ (parameterization\ lit)$

$\textbf{insert}_0$ ref sel op $r =$
  $deref\ ref\ r \ggeq_{\mathcal{E}} \lambda\_ \rightarrow$
  $literal\ op\ [\,] \ggeq_{\mathcal{E}} \lambda lit_0 \rightarrow$
  $rule\ (tag\ r)\ (lhs\ r)\ (f\ (sel, lit_0))$
  $\textbf{where}$
    $f\ new = lhsOrRhs\ il\ ir\ ref$
      $\textbf{where}$
        $il = \textbf{if}\ refersToAP\ ref\ \textbf{then}\ new : (rhs\ r)\ \textbf{else}\ (rhs\ r) + \!\!+ [new]$
        $ir\ sel' = g\ (rhs\ r)$
          $\textbf{where}$
            $g\ (qlit@(sel'', lit) : qlits) =$
            $\textbf{if}\ and[sel' == sel'', (operator\ ref) == (operator\ lit)]$
              $\textbf{then if}\ refersToAP\ ref\ \textbf{then}\ [new, qlit] + \!\!+ qlits\ \textbf{else}\ [qlit, new] + \!\!+ qlits$
              $\textbf{else}\ qlit : (g\ qlits)$

$\textbf{define}_0$ d $p = program\ (definitions\ p + \!\!+ [d])$

Fig. 4. The Core Calculus

3.3   Completion of the Core Calculus

The core calculus is completed by lifting the operators from the previous subs-ection to Trafo. Lifting means here that a function defined on a certain fragment type α is lifted to a more complex type α' and finally to Program — the type of complete object programs. To model that kind of lifting, generalized and mona-dic *maps* [18] are useful.[7] The meta-programming framework provides monadic

---

[7] The adjective *generalized* means other types than just α and α^* are associated. The adjective *monadic* means that computations in a monad can be involved, i.e., a function $f : \tau \rightarrow \mathcal{M}\ \sigma$ (rather than $f : \tau \rightarrow \sigma$) is lifted to a function $f' : \tau' \rightarrow \mathcal{M}\ \sigma'$ (rather than $f' : \tau' \rightarrow \sigma'$).

$$mfoldr : (\alpha \to \beta \to \mathcal{M}\ \beta) \to \beta \to \alpha^\star \to \mathcal{M}\ \beta$$
$$mfoldr\ f\ e\ l = foldr\ g\ (unit_{\mathcal{M}}\ e)\ l\ \textbf{where}\ g\ x\ c = c \ggg_{\mathcal{M}} \lambda v \to f\ x\ v$$

$$mmap : (\alpha \to \mathcal{M}\ \beta) \to \alpha^\star \to \mathcal{M}\ \beta^\star$$
$$mmap\ f = mfoldr\ g\ [\ ]\ \textbf{where}\ g\ x\ l = f\ x \ggg_{\mathcal{M}} \lambda x' \to unit_{\mathcal{M}}\ (x' : l)$$

Fig. 5. Monadic foldr/map on Lists

maps for all the fragment types of object programs. The symbol *mmap* is overloaded to denote all monadic map functions, including the common monadic map for lists as defined in Figure 5. In Figure 6, all the types related to each other by *mmap* are illustrated. The figure also defines an instance of *mmap*, namely the instance for lifting functions on literals to functions on rules.

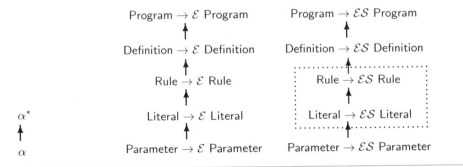

$$mmap : (\text{Literal} \to \mathcal{ES}\ \text{Literal}) \to \text{Rule} \to \mathcal{ES}\ \text{Rule}$$
$$mmap\ f\ r =$$
$$f\ (lhs\ r) \ggg_{\mathcal{ES}} \lambda lhs' \to mmap\ g\ (rhs\ r) \ggg_{\mathcal{ES}} \lambda rhs' \to \uparrow_{\mathcal{E}}^{\mathcal{ES}} (rule\ (tag\ r)\ lhs'\ rhs')$$
$$\textbf{where}\ g\ (sel, lit) = f\ lit \ggg_{\mathcal{ES}} \lambda lit' \to unit_{\mathcal{ES}}\ (sel, lit')$$

Fig. 6. Lifting by *mmap*

Figure 7 lifts the basic transformation operators in Figure 4 up to Trafo. The specification of **add**, **rename** and **define** should be self-explanatory since only *mmap* and the operation $\uparrow_{\mathcal{E}}^{\mathcal{ES}}$ lifting computations in $\mathcal{E}$ to $\mathcal{ES}$ are involved. The specification of **substitute** is slightly more complex. The actual substitution to be performed is not passed to **substitute** as a parameter but more indirectly as a function from Rule to $\mathcal{ES}$ Substitution. This is a sensible design because there is no sense in applying a single substitution to all rules in a program. The specification of **insert** exploits a similar trick. The first parameter is a boolean function intented to control if for a given rule a literal has to be included, e.g., based on the rule's tag.

Example 6. The enhanced program in Example 1 is derived in the following atomic steps. For readability, we use a semi-formal style. For brevity, we omit the steps which are specific to the second and the third rule.

add   : Operator → Selector → Mode → Type → Trafo
substitute : (Rule → $\mathcal{ES}$ Substitution) → Trafo
rename   : Operator → Operator → Trafo
insert   : (Rule → $\mathcal{ES}$ Bool) → Reference → Selector → Operator → Trafo
define   : Definition → Trafo

add $op\ sel\ m\ t = mmap\ (mmap\ (mmap\ (\textbf{add}_0\ op\ sel\ m\ t)))$

substitute $f = mmap\ (mmap\ g)$
  where
    $g\ r = f\ r \ggeq_\varepsilon \lambda subst \to mmap\ (mmap\ (\lambda p \to \uparrow_\varepsilon^{\mathcal{ES}}\ (\textbf{substitute}_0\ subst\ p)))\ r$

rename $op_1\ op_2\ p = \uparrow_\varepsilon^{\mathcal{ES}}\ (mmap\ (mmap\ (mmap\ (\textbf{rename}_0\ op_1\ op_2)))\ p)$

insert $f\ ref\ sel\ op = mmap\ (mmap\ g)$
  where
    $g\ r = f\ r \ggeq_\varepsilon \lambda b \to$
        if b **then** $\uparrow_\varepsilon^{\mathcal{ES}}\ (\textbf{insert}_0\ ref\ sel\ op\ r)$ **else** $unit_{\mathcal{ES}}\ r$

define $d\ p = \uparrow_\varepsilon^{\mathcal{ES}}\ (\textbf{define}_0\ d\ p)$

Fig. 7. The Completed Calculus

1. Rename *traverse* resp. *traverse_list* to *label* resp. *label_list*.
2. Add an output position of type LABEL to *label*.
3. Add an input position of type OP to *label_list*.
4. Add an input position of type LABEL to *label_list*.
5. Add an output position of type LABEL to *label_list*.
6. Focus on the first rule
   a) Insert *init_label* before *label_list*'s input position of type LABEL.
   b) Add an input position of type OP to *init_label*.
   c) Add an output position of type LABEL to *init_label*.
   d) Apply a substitution unifying the positions for the variable OP.
   e) Apply a substitution unifying the positions for the variable LABEL_{init}.
   f) Apply a substitution unifying the positions for the variable LABEL.
7. Focus on the second rule ...
8. Focus on the third rule ...
9. Add the definitions for *init_label* and *and_or*.

It is relatively easy to see that the defined operators actually implement the intended roles. We do not attempt a proper verification here, but a few arguments regarding the correctness of the implementations should be provided. Let us consider, for example, the operator **add**:

- The output program has the same shape as the input program (number of definitions, number of rules in a definition, tags of rules, number of RHS literals, selectors on RHSs) because it is obtained by just transforming at the Literal level. This property is implied by simple properties of *mmap*.
- The operator of each literal is preserved. This is implied by standard laws of destruction and construction.
- The list of parameters of a literal is either completely preserved or extended by another parameter as implied again by laws of destruction, construction.

From the above arguments it follows that **add** only extends the relevant parameter lists without changing any other part of the input program. For **substitute** and **rename** one has to show that the simple concepts substitution and consistent renaming resp. are actually specified. The correctness of **define** follows from the fact that all definitions from the input program are preserved in the output program. We skip the discussion of **insert**.

3.4   Techniques

The operators defined above are useful to derive high-level abstractions of common adaptations of programs — techniques in the terminology of stepwise enhancement [26,13,11], e.g., the *accumulate* technique can be derived from **add** and **substitute**, whereas *calculate* techniques also require **insert**.

Figure 8 presents the operator **l2r** capturing certain data flow oriented techniques. One important way to use the operator is to simulate the *accumulate* technique. Note that **l2r** it more flexible. The operator unifies parameters of a given type in a way to establish a data-flow from left to right. To introduce an accumulator with **l2r**, first all the relevant symbols had to be extended by two parameter positions of the given type, one of mode $\downarrow$, another of mode $\uparrow$. The operator **l2r** is based on the operator **copy** also shown in Figure 8. **copy** inserts a "copy rule" (using attribute grammar jargon) by means of **substitute**. Its first argument is — as in the case of **insert** — a function to decide which rule should be adapted. The remaining two arguments refer to the parameters which should be unified. *solve* is assumed to compute the most general unifier for a list of equations on parameters according to Robinson's algorithm.

Example 7. We cannot use **l2r** for the enhancement in Example 1 because an *accumulate-calculate* rather than a pure *accumulate* technique would be needed. To illustrate **l2r**, an enhancement of the initial program to support an accumulator is derived:

$$traverse(\downarrow tree(OP, NODE, TREE^\star_{child}), \boxed{\downarrow ACC_0, \uparrow ACC_1}) \Leftarrow$$
$$traverse\_list(\downarrow TREE^\star_{child}, \boxed{\downarrow ACC_0, \uparrow ACC_1}).$$
$$traverse\_list(\downarrow [\,], \boxed{\downarrow ACC, \uparrow ACC}).$$
$$traverse\_list(\downarrow [TREE|TREE^\star], \boxed{\downarrow ACC_0, \uparrow ACC_2}) \Leftarrow$$
$$traverse(\downarrow TREE, \boxed{\downarrow ACC_0, \uparrow ACC_1}),$$
$$traverse\_list(\downarrow TREE^\star, \boxed{\downarrow ACC_1, \uparrow ACC_2}).$$

This enhancement is derived by adding the parameter positions of type ACC with the operator **add** and performing **l2r** ACC afterwards.

In [14,16], we consider other techniques based on similar operator suites, e.g., a reduction technique, where the intermediate results computed by some predicates are combined in a pairwise manner. The technology developed in [14] is also sufficient to support the kind of higher-order reconstruction of stepwise enhancement proposed in [20]. A proper catalogue of techniques covering all the common techniques in stepwise enhancement is a subject for further work.

l2r : Type $\rightarrow$ Trafo
l2r t p $=$ $\uparrow_{\mathcal{E}}^{\mathcal{ES}}$ $(mfoldr\ f\ e\ (definitions\ p))$ $\ggg_{\mathcal{ES}}$ $\lambda\ trafo \rightarrow trafo\ p$
where
-- identity
e : Trafo
e $=$ $\lambda p \rightarrow unit_{\mathcal{ES}}\ p$
-- transform definitions
f : Definition $\rightarrow$ Trafo $\rightarrow \mathcal{E}$ Trafo
$f\ d\ e$ $=$ $mfoldr\ g\ e\ (rules\ d)$
-- transform rules
g : Rule $\rightarrow$ Trafo $\rightarrow \mathcal{E}$ Trafo
$g\ r\ e$ $=$ $mfoldr\ h\ e\ to$
  where
  -- accumulate all relevant references
  $from$ $=$ $[x|x \in references\ r, typeOf\ x == t, refersToDP\ x]$
  to $=$ $[x|x \in references\ r, typeOf\ x == t, refersToAP\ x]$
  -- iterate applied references
  h : Reference $\rightarrow$ Trafo $\rightarrow \mathcal{E}$ Trafo
  $h\ x\ e$ $=$ $mfoldr\ before\ [\ ]\ from$ $\ggg_{\mathcal{E}}$ $\lambda from' \rightarrow$
       $rightmost\ from'\ r$ $\ggg_{\mathcal{E}}$ $\lambda y \rightarrow$
       $unit_{\mathcal{E}}\ (\lambda p \rightarrow e\ p$ $\ggg_{\mathcal{ES}}$ **copy** $(\lambda r' \rightarrow unit_{\mathcal{ES}}(tag\ r\ == \ tag\ r'))\ y\ x)$
    where
    -- find all defining references smaller than x
    $before$: Reference $\rightarrow$ Reference* $\rightarrow \mathcal{E}$ Reference*
    $before\ y\ ys$ $=$ $leq\ y\ x\ r$ $\ggg_{\mathcal{E}}$ $\lambda b \rightarrow unit_{\mathcal{E}}$ (**if** b **then** $(y : ys)$ **else** ys)

copy : (Rule $\rightarrow \mathcal{ES}$ Bool) $\rightarrow$ Reference $\rightarrow$ Reference $\rightarrow$ Trafo
copy $cond\ ref\ ref'$ $=$ **substitute** f
where
$f\ r$ $=$ $cond\ r$ $\ggg_{\mathcal{ES}}$ $\lambda b \rightarrow$ **if** b
  then $\uparrow_{\mathcal{E}}^{\mathcal{ES}}$ $(deref\ ref\ r$ $\ggg_{\mathcal{E}}$ $\lambda p \rightarrow deref\ ref'\ r$ $\ggg_{\mathcal{E}}$ $\lambda p' \rightarrow solve\ [(p, p')])$
  else $unit_{\mathcal{ES}}\ empty$

Fig. 8. Technique for Accumulation

4   Concluding Remarks

In Subsection 4.1, related work will be discussed to some extent with emphasis on stepwise enhancement. In Subsection 4.2, the main results of the paper are concluded. Finally, in Subsection 4.3, a perspective for future work is provided.

4.1   Related Work

Research in the field of program transformation for logic programs traditionally focuses on optimization rather than support for reusability and extensibility. Fold/unfold strategies provide the basic mechanism; refer, e.g., to [21,23]. It is a common point of view to regard techniques in stepwise enhancement [26,13,11] as transformations but this is the first paper which presents an effective calculus to describe the corresponding transformations.

Related notions for relations on programs have been defined in the stepwise enhancement community [22,12,10]. Our roles can be captured by a kind of projection notion which is similar to the program maps in [12] and symbol mappings in [10]. The former preserve computational behaviour. However, substitution is involved neither in program maps nor in symbol mappings. Another important difference is that modes, selectors and types are used in our setting. Symbol mappings are slightly more general than program maps because many-1 rather than 1-1 predicate symbol mappings are used. Many-1 symbol mappings may not preserve computational behaviour when symbols get unified. Our role of renaming facilitates unification in a safe way. Unification is only possible for the symbols which are not defined by a program, i.e., parameters of an open program can be unified. It is easy to see that our renaming operator does not support general (i.e., unsafe) many-1 symbol mappings, since a corresponding unification of symbols results in a non-well-formed object program with multiple definitions for one symbol and thus in an error. In [22], a more general notion of enhancement is sketched. It includes modulations and mutations, i.e., programs equivalent under fold/unfold transformations, and programs obtained by structural alterations of the control flow. However, [22] formalizes only extensions in the sense of program maps [12].

The Appendix contains the definition of a projection notion underlying the roles in the paper. The idea is that for all transformation operators defined in the paper, an input program P and the corresponding output program P' are related according to the projection notion.

Stepwise enhancement has been integrated with programming environments [13,3,24]. Such environments focus on tool support for applying techniques, whereas our framework is intended as a solid basis for defining and executing techniques. It is a subject for future work to develop a transformational programming environment based on the framework. In [30], Whittle et al. describe an ML editor based on the proof-as-programs idea. Programs are created incrementally using a collection of correctness-preserving editing commands. Such an approach might also be sensible for our roles and techniques derived from them.

In [5], Brogi et al. describe a related meta-programming framework. The approach is based on a special language LML which can be regarded as another approach to integrate functional and logic programming in a certain way. LML also is intended for the construction of knowledge based systems. Logic programming is supported by means of a data type of theories at the level of functional programming. Our intentions are different. We just want to provide a solid framework for general and typeful meta-programming. Our approach is entirely different from multi-stage programming [27], where code and functions on code facilitate different binding times but not enhancement of given object programs. The selection of *Haskell* to implement the framework is in line with Bowers [2]. Typed and modular functional languages like *Haskell* provide an excellent basis for meta-programming.

Our work on extending computational behaviour is related to modularity, composition and decomposition. Modularity concepts such as [6] are well-suited for functional decomposition but they do not facilitate the introduction of additional functionality if it had to be weaved into the program in a systematic way as facilitated by the developed transformation operators. There are notions of composition which go beyond the limit of modularity in the common sense, e.g., Sterling et al. suggest in [25] the composition of programs having some basic skeleton in common. Related proposals can be found elsewhere based on terms like superposition, partitioning and tupling. This perspective on composition merely emphasizes that we can compose different extensions of the same underlying program by a kind of descriptional composition. In contrast, our paper is concerned with the actual specification of extensions.

There are certain techniques in the sense of stepwise enhancement which have some counterpart in actual attribute grammar specification languages. We study such constructs in [16].

4.2   Results

This paper addressed the following questions and provided the following answers:

1. What are the *basic roles* needed for the development of transformations to extend the computational behaviour of programs. We identified five roles, e.g., adding parameters and performing substitutions. These roles can be specified in separation and they can effectively be used to derive interesting program transformations.
2. How can the basic roles and the derived techniques be *formalized* and *implemented*? We developed a formal and operational framework supporting functional (and thus *declarative*) meta-programming. The framework employs a number of powerful concepts such as monads, abstract data types and generalized maps. The actual language *Haskell* has been chosen to implement the framework.

We believe that the results from research in stepwise enhancement in general, and our new results on extending computational behaviour in particular, provide a solid ground for contributions to a more formal and technical understanding of notions in mainstream programming like adaptive and aspect-oriented programming. In [15], the first author presents a proposal for declarative aspect-oriented programming including a form of weaving by means of meta-programming.

4.3   Future Work

The class of semantics-preserving transformations should be enriched to cover modulations and mutations as suggested (but not formalized) in [22].

The static analysis of meta-programs has to be improved based on further formal properties of transformations. We should be able, for example, to provide sufficient criteria for a transformation to be defined, or to associate a transformation with a kind of type constructor modelling the effect of the transformation regarding object types. It is a demanding experiment to investigate the utility of dependent types [1,31] in order to model such properties in the meta-programming framework.

A speculative topic for future work concerns the generalization of the chosen object language. There is some evidence that other rather different languages (e.g., higher-order functional languages, object-oriented languages) and formalisms (e.g., syntax definition formalisms) are sensible for similar roles of transformation. There are related notions like superposition and refinement in several frameworks. Any contribution to the unification of some of these concepts had to be regarded as a progress in programming theory.

Acknowledgement. The first author is indebted to Isabelle Attali and Paul Klint for their remarks on material used in this paper, to Leon Sterling for valuable comments he sent by email, to Jan Heering for discussions, to Jan Kort and Joost Visser for proofreading. We also thank the anonymous LOPSTR'99 referees for good advices.

References

1. L. Augustsson. Cayenne – A Language with Dependent Types. In S. D. Swierstra, P. R. Henriques, and J. N. Oliveira, editors, *Advanced Functional Programming, Third International School, AFP '98*, volume 1608 of *LNCS*, pages 240–267, Braga, Portugal, Sept. 1999. Springer-Verlag.
2. A. Bowers. *Effective Meta-programming in Declarative Languages*. PhD thesis, Department of Computer Science, University of Bristol, Jan. 1998.
3. A. Bowles, D. Robertson, W. Vasconcelos, V. M. Vargas, and D. Bental. Applying Prolog Programming Techniques. *International Journal of Human-Computer Studies*, 41(3):329–350, Sept. 1994.
4. J. Boye and J. Maluszynski. Directional Types and the Annotation Method. *Journal of Logic Programming*, 33(3):179–220, Dec. 1997.
5. A. Brogi, P. Mancarella, D. Pedreschi, and F. Turini. Logic Programming within a Functional Framework. In P. Deransart and J. Małuszyński, editors, *Proceedings of Programming Language Implementation and Logic Programming*, number 456 in LNCS, pages 372–386. Springer-Verlag, Aug. 1990.
6. A. Brogi, P. Mancarella, D. Pedreschi, and F. Turini. Modular Logic Programming. *ACM Transactions on Programming Languages and Systems*, 16(3):225–237, 1994.
7. D. A. Espinosa. *Semantic Lego*. PhD thesis, Graduate School of Arts and Sciences, Columbia University, 1995.
8. N. E. Fuchs, editor. *Logic program synthesis and transformation: 7th international workshop, LOPSTR'97, Leuven, Belgium, July 10–12, 1997: proceedings*, volume 1463 of *Lecture Notes in Computer Science*, New York, NY, USA, 1998. Springer-Verlag Inc.
9. P. Hill and J. Lloyd. *The Gödel Programming Language*. MIT Press, 1994.
10. A. Jain. Projections of Logic Programs using Symbol Mappings. In L. Sterling, editor, *Logic Programming, Proceedings of the Twelfth International Conference on Logic Programming, June 13-16, 1995, Tokyo, Japan*. MIT Press, June 1995.

11. M. Kirschenbaum, S. Michaylov, and L. Sterling. Skeletons and Techniques as a Normative Approach to Program Development in Logic-Based Languages. In *Proceedings ACSC'96, Australian Computer Science Communications, 18(1)*, pages 516–524, 1996.
12. M. Kirschenbaum, L. Sterling, and A. Jain. Relating logic programs via program maps. In *Annals of Mathematics and Artifical Intelligence, 8(III-IV)*, pages 229–246, 1993.
13. A. Lakhotia. *A Workbench for Developing Logic Programs by Stepwise Enhancement*. PhD thesis, Case Western Reserve University, 1989.
14. R. Lämmel. *Functional meta-programs towards reusability in the declarative paradigm*. PhD thesis, University of Rostock, Department of Computer Science, 1998. Published by Shaker Verlag, ISBN 3-8265-6042-6.
15. R. Lämmel. Declarative aspect-oriented programming. In O. Danvy, editor, *Proceedings PEPM'99, 1999 ACM SIGPLAN Workshop on Partial Evaluation and Semantics-Based Program Manipulation PEPM'99, San Antonio (Texas), BRICS Notes Series NS-99-1*, pages 131–146, Jan. 1999.
16. R. Lämmel and G. Riedewald. Reconstruction of paradigm shifts. In *Second Workshop on Attribute Grammars and their Applications*, pages 37–56, Mar. 1999. reviewed version submitted to Informatica.
17. W. Lohmann. Ein Rahmenwerk für höherfunktionale Meta-Programmierung. Master's thesis, University of Rostock, Department of Computer Science, Oct. 1999.
18. E. Meijer and J. Jeuring. Merging Maps and Folds for Functional Programming. In J. Jeuring and E. Meijer, editors, *Advanced Functional Programming*, volume 925 of *LNCS*, pages 228–266. Springer-Verlag, 1995.
19. E. Moggi. Notions of computation and monads. *Information and Computation*, 93(1):55–92, July 1991.
20. L. Naish and L. Sterling. A Higher Order Reconstruction of Stepwise Enhancement. In Fuchs [8].
21. A. Pettorossi and M. Proietti. Rules and Strategies for Transforming Functional and Logic Programs. *ACM Computing Surveys*, 28(2):360–414, June 1996.
22. A. Power and L. Sterling. A notion of Map Between Logic Programs. In D. H. D. Warren and P. Szeredi, editors, *Proceedings 7th International Conference on Logic Programming*, pages 390–404. The MIT Press, 1990.
23. J. Richardson and N. Fuchs. Development of Correct Transformation Schemata for Prolog Programs. In Fuchs [8].
24. D. Robertson. An Empirical Study of the LSS specification Toolkit in Use. In *8th International Conference on Software Engineering and Knowledge Engineering, June 10-12, 1996, Hyatt Regency, Lake Tahoe, Nevada, USA*, June 1996.
25. L. Sterling, A. Jain, and M. Kirschenbaum. Composition Based on Skeletons and Techniques. In *ILPS '93 post conference workshop on Methodologies for Composing Logic Programs, Vancouver*, Oct. 1993.
26. L. Sterling and E. Shapiro. *The Art of Prolog*. MIT Press, 1994. 2nd edition.
27. W. Taha and T. Sheard. Multi-stage programming with explicit annotations. In *Proceedings of the ACM SIGPLAN Symposium on Partial Evaluation and Semantics-Based Program Manipulation (PEPM-97)*, volume 32, 12 of *ACM SIGPLAN Notices*, pages 203–217, New York, June 12–13 1997. ACM Press.
28. P. Wadler. The essence of functional programming. In *Conference Record of the Nineteenth Annual ACM SIGPLAN-SIGACT Symposium on Principles of Programming Languages*, pages 1–14, Albequerque, New Mexico, Jan. 1992.
29. D. Watt and O. Madsen. Extended attribute grammars. Technical Report no. 10, University of Glasgow, July 1977.

30. J. Whittle, A. Bundy, R. Boulton, and H. Lowe. An ML Editor Based on Proofs-as-Programs. In R. Hall and E. Tyugu, editors, *Proceedings of ASE-99: The 14th IEEE Conference on Automated Software Engineering*, Cocoa Beach, Florida, Oct. 1999. IEEE CS Press.
31. H. Xi and F. Pfenning. Dependent types in practical programming. In *Conference Record of POPL '99: The 26th ACM SIGPLAN-SIGACT Symposium on Principles of Programming Languages*, San Antonio, Texas, pages 214–227, New York, N.Y., Jan. 1999. ACM.

A   A Notion of Projections of Programs

The class of transformations covered by the paper can be captured by a kind of projection notion as follows. A *projection* P of a program P', denoted by $P \rhd P'$, is a program where some of the functionality of P', i.e., some of its definitions, RHS literals, parameters, have been projected away. Moreover, substitution, renaming and permutation may be involved. The relation $\rhd$ is formalized in the meta-programming framework as follows. Given $P, P' \in \mathsf{Program}$, $P \rhd P'$ if $\exists \sigma : \mathsf{Operator} \to \mathsf{Operator}$:

1. $\forall p \in \pi_1\ \mathcal{TYPE}(P)$: $\exists p' \in \pi_1\ \mathcal{TYPE}(P')$: $\sigma\ (\pi_1\ p) = \pi_1\ p' \wedge \pi_2\ p \subseteq \pi_2\ p'$
2. $\pi_2\ \mathcal{TYPE}(P) \subseteq \pi_2\ \mathcal{TYPE}(P')$
3. $\forall d \in \mathit{definitions}\ P$: $\exists d' \in \mathit{definitions}\ P'$:
   a) $\sigma\ (\mathit{defines}\ d) = \mathit{defines}\ d'$ and $\#(\mathit{rules}\ d) = \#(\mathit{rules}\ d')$
   b) $\forall r \in \mathit{rules}\ d$: $\exists r' \in \mathit{rules}\ d'$:
      $\exists \theta : \mathsf{Variable} \to \mathsf{Parameter}$: $\exists w_1, \ldots, w_n \in \{1, \ldots, n'\}$:
      i. $\mathit{tag}\ r = \mathit{tag}\ r'$
      ii. $\sigma\ (\mathit{operator}\ l_0) = \mathit{operator}\ l_0'$
      iii. $\theta\ (\mathit{parameterization}\ l_0) \subseteq \mathit{parameterization}\ l_0'$
      iv. $w_1 < \cdots < w_n$
      v. $s_i = s_{w_i}'$ for $i = 1, \ldots, n$
      vi. $\sigma\ (\mathit{operator}\ l_i) = \mathit{operator}\ l_{w_i}'$ for $i = 1, \ldots, n$
      vii. $\theta\ (\mathit{parameterization}\ l_i) \subseteq \mathit{parameterization}\ l_{w_i}'$ for $i = 1, \ldots, n$
      where
      – $\mathit{lhs}\ r = l_0$, $\mathit{rhs}\ r = \langle\langle s_1, l_1 \rangle, \ldots, \langle s_n, l_n \rangle\rangle$,
      – $\mathit{lhs}\ r' = l_0'$, $\mathit{rhs}\ r' = \langle\langle s_1', l_1' \rangle, \ldots, \langle s_{n'}', l_{n'}' \rangle\rangle$.

We assume that $\subseteq$ is defined on sequences by regarding them as sets.

The definition can be read as follows. σ is a function which renames (or substitutes) operators. (1.) constrains types of operators by saying that the types of P' should cover the types of P, where an operator in P' might have more positions than the corresponding operator in P. (2.) says that the constructors of P' should cover the constructors of P. (3.) formalizes the actual projection on rules. P' might provide more definitions than P. θ is a substitution. Tags and LHS operators (modulo renaming) must be the same for the matching rules from P and P'. The rule in P' might have more literals on the RHS. The literals originating from P are indexed by the w_i. The relative order of the literals from P must be preserved in P' (refer to 3.*iv.*). Regarding related literals, the literal in P' might have more parameters than in P. Substitution is involved in relating the parameters (refer to 3.*vii.*).

The definition is restricted in the sense that constructors and selectors cannot be renamed, and permutation and projection is not performed for nested parameters. It is straightforward to remove these restrictions.

Transformation of Left Terminating Programs

Annalisa Bossi[1], Nicoletta Cocco[1], and Sandro Etalle[2]

[1] Dip. di Informatica, Università di Venezia-Ca' Foscari - Italy
{bossi,cocco}@dsi.unive.it
[2] Dept. of Computer Science, University of Maastricht - The Netherlands
etalle@cs.unimaas.nl

Abstract. We propose an unfold-fold transformation system which preserves left termination for definite programs besides its declarative semantics. The system extends our previous proposal in [BCE95] by allowing to switch the atoms in the clause bodies when a specific applicability condition is satisfied. The applicability condition is very simple to verify, yet very common in practice. We also discuss how to verify such condition by exploiting mode information.

1 Introduction

Tamaki and Sato [TS84] proposed an elegant framework for the transformation of logic programs based on unfold/fold rules which is the main reference point in the literature of transformations of logic programs.

However Tamaki-Sato's method often cannot be applied "as it is" to pure Prolog programs, as it does not preserve *left-termination*, i.e., termination wrt the leftmost selection rule. In other words, it can happen that a left-terminating program (a program whose derivations starting in a ground query are all finite under the leftmost selection rule) be transformed into a non-terminating one.

In this paper we present a new transformation system for definite logic programs which preserves left termination.

As we already remarked in [BCE95], in order to maintain transformation properties, a transformation system has to take into account the order of the atoms in the clause bodies. Moreover, in order to achieve a reasonable degree of flexibility, the system should provide special operations for *reordering* them. These special operations are critical as they can easily spoil termination.For this, the system we propose is provided with a *switch* operation, together with suitable applicability conditions, which are very simple to verify, yet rather common in practice. These conditions are particularly powerful in the case that the transformed programs are *well-moded*.

The present system extends the one we proposed in [BCE95], we also show how the two methods can be profitably combined together.

Structure of the Paper. Section 2 contains the notation and the preliminaries on left terminating programs. In Section 3 we define the basic unfold/fold

A. Bossi (Ed.): LOPSTR'99, LNCS 1817, pp. 156–175, 2000.

transformation system. In Section 4 we introduce the reordering problem and the applicability condition for switching atoms in the bodies. The transformation system extended with such "allowed switch" can be proved to preserve left termination. In Section 5 we consider well-moded programs and extend the condition for allowed switching to such programs. Such extended transformation system for well-moded programs preserves left termination and it is applicable to most practical cases, as discussed in Section 6. Conclusions and some discussion on related papers follow in Section 7.

2   Preliminaries

In what follows we study definite logic programs executed by means of *LD-resolution*, namely SLD-resolution with the leftmost selection rule (the Prolog selection rule).

We use bold characters (es. **B**) to indicate sequences of objects, typically **B** indicates a sequence of atoms, $B_1, \ldots, B_n$, **t** indicates a sequence of terms, $t_1, \ldots, t_n$, and **x** denotes a sequence of variables, $x_1, \ldots, x_n$.

We work with *queries* that is *sequences* of atoms, $B_1, \ldots, B_n$, instead of *goals*. Apart from this, we use the standard notation of Lloyd [Llo87] and Apt [Apt97]. In particular, given a syntactic construct E (so for example, a term, an atom or a set of equations) we denote by $Var(E)$ the set of the variables appearing in E. Given a substitution $\theta = \{x_1/t_1, \ldots, x_n/t_n\}$ we denote by $Dom(\theta)$ the set of variables $\{x_1, \ldots, x_n\}$, and by $Ran(\theta)$ the set of variables appearing in $\{t_1, \ldots, t_n\}$. Finally, we define $Var(\theta) = Dom(\theta) \cup Ran(\theta)$.

A substitution θ is called *grounding* if $Ran(\theta)$ is empty, and it is called a *renaming* if it is a permutation of the variables in $Dom(\theta)$. Given a substitution θ and a set (sequence) of variables **v**, we denote by $\theta_{|\mathbf{v}}$ the substitution obtained from θ by restricting its domain to **v**. By $Pred(E)$ we denote the set of predicate symbols occurring in the expression E.

We use the notation introduced in [AP93,Apt97], and we say that a predicate p *is defined in the program* P iff there is a clause in P that uses p in its head. Given two relations p, q in $Pred(P)$, we say that p *refers to* q *in* P if there is a clause in P that uses p in its head and q in its body. We say that p *depends on* q *in* P, if (p, q) is in the reflexive, transitive closure of the relation *refers to*.

Let P, Q be programs which define different predicates, we say that P *extends* Q, $P \sqsupset Q$, if there is no $q \in Pred(Q)$ which refers (in Q) to a predicate p defined in P. Notice that $\sqsupset$ is a well-founded ordering. We harmlessly extend this notation to atoms and programs. Let B be an atom, by $P|_B$ we denote the set of clauses of P that define the predicates which the predicate of B depends on. Similarly by $P|_p$ we denote the set of clauses of P that define a predicate p and all the predicates which it depends on.

2.1   Acceptable and Left Terminating Programs

The class of left terminating definite logic program has been characterized by Apt and Pedreschi in [AP90]. This is done by using the definition of *acceptable programs*. We briefly restate the results of [AP90].

Definition 1 (Left Terminating Program). *A program P is called* left terminating *if all LD-derivations of P starting in a ground query are finite.*   □

The basic tool used to prove (and characterize) that a program is left terminating is the concept of *level mapping* originally due to Bezem [Bez93] and Cavedon [Cav89]. A *level mapping for a program P* is a function $| \ | : \mathbf{B}_P \to \mathbb{N}$, from the ground atoms of the Herbrand base of P to natural numbers. We call $|B|$ the *norm of B* wrt the level mapping $| \ |$. We omit the reference to P when the choice of the language does not play a significant role.

We can now provide the central definition of [AP90].

Definition 2 (Acceptable Program). *Let P be a program, $| \ |$ a level mapping for P and I a (not necessarily Herbrand) interpretation of P.*

- *A clause of P is* acceptable *with respect to $| \ |$ and I if I is a model of P and for every ground instance $H \leftarrow B_1, \ldots, B_m$ of the clause, the following implication holds:*

$$ if \ I \models B_1, \ldots, B_{i-1} \ then \ |H| > |B_i|. $$

- *P is* acceptable *with respect to $| \ |$ and I if all its clauses are.*
- *P is called* acceptable *if it is acceptable with respect to some level mapping and interpretation of P.*   □

The use of acceptable programs is motivated by the following result of Apt and Pedreschi [AP93]

Theorem 3. *A definite program is left terminating iff it is acceptable.*

Here, we also need a new definition for a stronger termination property.

Definition 4 (Always-Left-Terminating Program). *A program P is called* always-left-terminating *if all LD-derivations of P starting in any query are finite.*   □

In an always-left-terminating program, no computation can diverge. They are generally defined by clauses which are not recursive or by built-ins and used to perform some checks. Clearly an always-left-terminating program is also left terminating.

2.2   Modes, Well-Moded Programs, and Termination

The transformation system we propose is provided with special applicability conditions for the case in which the considered programs are *well-moded*. We now give the basic definitions we refer to in the sequel.

Modes are extensively used in the literature on logic programs, usually they indicate how the arguments of a relation should be used.

Definition 5 (Mode). *Consider an n-ary predicate symbol p. By a* mode *for p we mean a function m_p from $\{1, \ldots, n\}$ to the set $\{+, -\}$. If $m_p(i) = $ '$+$', we call i an* input position *of p and if $m_p(i) = $ '$-$', we call i an* output position *of p (both w.r.t. m_p).* ☐

Most predicates have a natural moding, which reflects their intended use. For example, the natural moding for the usual program append, when used for concatenating two lists, is app(+,+,-); the natural moding for the predicates in Example 10 are: path(+,-), arc(+,-), goodlist(+) goodpath(+,-).

We say that a program is moded if each predicate symbol has a mode associated to it. Multiple modes may be obtained by simply renaming the predicates. When every considered predicate has a mode associated with it, we can talk about input positions and output positions of an atom.

The concept of well-moded program is essentially due to Dembinski and Maluszynski [DM85]. To simplify the notation, when writing an atom as $p(\mathbf{u}, \mathbf{v})$, we are indicating with $\mathbf{u}$ the sequence of terms filling in the input positions of p and with $\mathbf{v}$ the sequence of terms filling in the output positions of p.

Definition 6 (Well-Moded Query, Program). *A* clause $p_0(\mathbf{t}_0, \mathbf{s}_{n+1}) \leftarrow p_1(\mathbf{s}_1, \mathbf{t}_1), \ldots, p_n(\mathbf{s}_n, \mathbf{t}_n)$ *is called* well-moded *if for $i \in [1, n+1]$*

$$Var(\mathbf{s}_i) \subseteq \bigcup_{j=0}^{i-1} Var(\mathbf{t}_j)$$

A query $\mathbf{A}$ is called well-moded *if the clause $q \leftarrow \mathbf{A}$ is well-moded, where q is any (dummy) atom of zero arity.*

A program is called well-moded *if every clause of it is well-moded.* ☐

Note that the first atom of a well-moded query is ground in its input positions and a variant of a well-moded clause is well-moded. The following lemma, due to [AM94], shows the "persistence" of the notion of well-modedness.

Lemma 7. *An LD-resolvent of a well-moded query and a well-moded clause with no variable in common, is well-moded.* ☐

The relevance of both modes and well-moding for termination is studied in [EBC99]. Where the following concept of *well-terminating* program is defined as follows:

Definition 8 (Well-Terminating Program). *A program is called* well-ter-minating *iff all its LD-derivations starting in a well-moded goal are finite.*   □

Clearly a well-terminating program is also left terminating. In [EBC99] it is also shown that if a well-moded program is acceptable wrt a moded level mapping, namely a level mapping which depends only on the terms filling in input positi-ons, then it is well-terminating (Actually, in [EBC99] it is shown that this holds also when employing the much weaker definition of weakly acceptable program).

3   An Unfold/Fold Transformation System

In this section we introduce a new unfold/fold transformation system. We start from the requirements on the *initial* program which we assume to be divisible into a hierarchy of modules. Here and in the sequel, standardization apart is always assumed.

Definition 9 (Initial Program). *We call a definite program P_0 an* initial program *if it can be partitioned into three programs P_{new}, P_{old} and P_{base}, such that the following conditions are satisfied:*

(I1) $P_{new} \sqsupset (P_{old} \cup P_{base})$ and $P_{old} \sqsupset P_{base}$.
(I2) P_{new} is not recursive.
(I3) all the atoms in the bodies of the clauses of P_{old} are labelled "f", with the exception of atoms defined in P_{base}; no other atom of the initial program is labelled.   □

Predicate (atoms) defined in P_{new} are called *new* predicates (atoms), those defined in P_{old} are called the *old* ones, while those defined in P_{base} are called the *base* predicates. The reason of this partition into modules will be clear in the sequel of the paper. Notice that the combination of **I1** and **I2** guarantees that all the predicates which are defined in P_{new} occur neither in $P_{old} \cup P_{base}$ nor in the bodies of the clauses in P_{new}, which is similar to the condition on the initial program provided in [TS84]. We label with "f" (for fold-allowing) only *old* atoms in the bodies of P_{old}.

The new element of this definition w.r.t. its predecessors ([TS84,Sek93,EG96]) lies in the use of the labelling and in the fact that we distinguish P_{base}, which is the part of the initial program which is not modified by the transformation. These elements will be needed to guarantee the preservation of left termination.

The following example is inspired by the one in [Sek93].

Example 10. Let P_0 contain the following clauses

```
c1:   path(X,X,[X]).
c2:   path(X,Z,[X|Xs]) ← arc(X,Y), path(Y,Z,Xs)ᶠ.

c3:   goodlist([]).
c4:   goodlist([X|Xs]) ← good(X), goodlist(Xs)ᶠ.

c5:   goodpath(X,Z,Xs) ← path(X,Z,Xs),goodlist(Xs).
```

where $P_{old} = \{c1, \ldots, c4\}$ and $P_{new} = \{c5\}$, thus goodpath is the only new predicate, while the predicates arc and good are defined in P_{base} by facts.

The query goodpath(X,Z,Xs) can be employed for finding a path Xs starting in the node X and ending in the node Z which contains exclusively "good" nodes. Under the assumption that the graph described by the predicate arc is acyclic, this program is left terminating. goodpath works on a "generate and test" basis. We can obtain an efficiency improvement via an unfold/fold transformation. □

According to a well-established transformation strategy, the first operation we apply is unfold. Unfold is the fundamental operation for partial evaluation [LS91] and consists in applying a resolution step to a selected atom using all possible resolving clauses. Here – as opposed to the definition adopted in [TS84] and in most of the literature – the *order of the atoms in the queries and in the bodies of the clauses is relevant*. This is natural, since we are dealing with *LD*-resolution.

Definition 11 (Unfold). *Let* $cl : H \leftarrow \mathbf{J}, A, \mathbf{K}.$ *be a clause of a program* P, *and* $\{A_1 \leftarrow \mathbf{B}_1., \ldots, A_n \leftarrow \mathbf{B}_n.\}$ *be the set of clauses of* P *whose heads unify with* A, *by mgu's* $\{\theta_1, \ldots, \theta_n\}$.

- *Unfolding A in cl consists of substituting cl by* $\{cl'_1, \ldots, cl'_n\}$,
  where, for each i, $cl'_i = (H \leftarrow \mathbf{J}, \mathbf{B}_i, \mathbf{K})\theta_i.$ □

The unfold operation doesn't modify the labels of the atoms, no matter if the unfolded atom itself is labelled or not. Notice that unfold propagates the labels inside the clauses in the obvious way, as shown by the following example.

Example 10 (part 2). By unfolding the atom path(X, Z, Xs) in the body of c5, we obtain

```
c6:   goodpath(X,X,[X])  ← goodlist([X]).
c7:   goodpath(X,Z,[X|Xs])  ← arc(X,Y),
         path(Y,Z,Xs)ᶠ,
         goodlist([X|Xs]).
```

In the above clauses we can unfold goodlist([X]) and goodlist([X|Xs]) The resulting clauses, after a further unfolding of goodlist([]) in the clause obtained from c6, are

```
c8:   goodpath(X,X,[X])  ← good(X).
c9:   goodpath(X,Z,[X|Xs])  ← arc(X,Y),
         path(Y,Z,Xs)ᶠ,
         good(X),
         goodlist(Xs)ᶠ.
```

□

Thanks to its correspondence to a resolution step, the unfold operation preserves basically all the declarative semantics available for logic programs. It has also already been proven in [BC94] that it preserves universal termination of a query, namely any query with a finite LD-tree in a program P has a finite LD-tree also in a program obtained by unfolding P. Hence unfold preserves also the property of being left terminating.

Now we have reached a crucial step in the transformation: in order to be able to perform the fold operation, we need to permute the atoms $\text{path}(Y, Xs)^f$ and $\text{good}(X)$ in c9. For this, we introduce the switch operation.

Definition 12 (Switch). *Let* $cl : H \leftarrow \mathbf{J}, A, B, \mathbf{K}.$ *be a clause of a program* P. *Switching A with B in cl* *consists of replacing cl by* $cl' : H \leftarrow \mathbf{J}, B, A, \mathbf{K}.$ □

Example 10 (part 3). By permuting $\text{path}(Y, Z, Xs)^f$ with $\text{good}(X)$ in c9 we obtain the following clause:

```
c10:  goodpath(X,Z,[X|Xs])  ← arc(X,Y),
          good(X),
          path(Y,Z,Xs)ᶠ,
          goodlist(Xs)ᶠ.
```

□

Fold is the inverse of unfold (when one single clause unifies with the atom to be unfolded). This operation is used in all the transformation systems in order to fold back unfolded clauses and to introduce direct recursion on the definitions. As in Tamaki and Sato [TS84], the transformation sequence and the fold operation are defined in terms of each other.

Definition 13 (Transformation Sequence). *A* transformation sequence *is a sequence of programs* $P_0, \ldots, P_n$, $n \geq 0$, *such that each program* P_{i+1}, $0 \leq i < n$, *is obtained from* P_i *by applying an unfold, a switch, or a fold operation to a clause of* $P_i \backslash P_{base}$. □

Definition 14 (Fold). *Let* $P_0, \ldots, P_i$, $i \geq 0$, *be a transformation sequence,* $cl : H \leftarrow \mathbf{J}, \mathbf{B}, \mathbf{K}.$ *be a clause in* $P_i \backslash P_{base}$, *and* $d : D \leftarrow \mathbf{B}'.$ *be a clause in* P_{new}. *Folding* $\mathbf{B}$ *in cl via* τ *consists of replacing cl by* $cl' : H \leftarrow \mathbf{J}, D\tau, \mathbf{K}$, *provided that* τ *is a substitution such that* $Dom(\tau) = Var(d)$ *and such that the following conditions hold:*

(F1) d *is the only clause in* P_{new} *whose head is unifiable with* $D\tau$;
(F2) If we unfold $D\tau$ *in cl', then the result of the operation is a variant (obtained by renaming) of cl;*
(F3) one of the atoms in $\mathbf{J}$, *or the leftmost of the atoms in* $\mathbf{B}$ *is labelled "f".* □

The conjunction of conditions **F1** and **F2** corresponds to the conjunction of the conditions 1...3 of [TS84]. Therefore, apart from the fact that we take into consideration the order of the atoms in the bodies of the clauses, what distinguishes this fold definition from the one in [TS84] is the further condition **F3**. Note that condition **F3** is less restrictive than the similar one introduced by

Seki [Sek91] to preserve finite failures[1]. The label "f" indicates that a previous unfolding step of an *old* atom has occurred in the transformation sequence and this is used to ensure that a fold operation cannot introduce loops. Notice that fold eliminates the labels in the folded part of the body.

Example 10 (part 4). We can now fold $path(Y, Z, Xs)^f, goodlist(Xs)^f$ in c10. The resulting new definition of goodpath is

```
c8:   goodpath(X,X,[X])  ← good(X).
c11:  goodpath(X,Z,[X|Xs])  ← arc(X,Y),
        good(X),
        goodpath(Y,Z,Xs).
```

Notice that the definition of goodpath is now recursive and it checks the "goodness" of the path while generating the path itself.   □

Correctness Result, Declarative Viewpoint. Of course, it is of primary importance ensuring the correctness of the system from a declarative point of view. In the case of our system, the applicability conditions are more restrictive than those used by Tamaki-Sato in [TS84] (which, on the other hand, does not guarantee the preservation of left termination). For this reason, all the correctness results for the declarative semantics that hold for the system of [TS84] are valid for our system as well and we have the following.

Remark 15. Let $P_0, \ldots, P_n$ be a transformation sequence.

- [TS84] The least Herbrand models of the initial and final programs coincide.
- [KK90] The computed answers substitution semantics of the initial and final programs coincide.   □

4   Preservation of Left Termination

The system presented in the previous section does not preserve left-termination yet. This is because the switching operation is *unrestricted*: It has no special applicability conditions.

In this section we first analyze the reasons why in general an unfold/fold transformation system does not preserve termination, then we provide a simple condition on the switch operation that will ensure the preservation of the left termination property.

The Reordering Problem. As already explained in the introduction, the rearrangement of the atoms in the body of a clause is a typical operation which does not preserve left termination. For instance if we take the program

```
p ← q, p.
```

---

[1] Seki's system requires that all folded atoms be the result of a previous unfolding, moreover it partitions the initial program in P_{new} and P_{old} only.

We have that at the moment the program is terminating (q fails), however, if we swap the two atoms in the body of the clause, we get a program which is not terminating. Another typical situation is the one in which we have in the body of a clause a combination such as ...p(X,Y), q(Y,Z)... , where the rightmost atom uses Y as input variable; in this case, bringing q(Y,Z) to the left of p(X,Y) can easily introduce non-termination, as q(Y,Z) might be called with its arguments not sufficiently instantiated.

In the context of an unfold/fold transformation system, this situation is further complicated by the presence of the other operations, in particular of fold which may introduce recursion and hence non-termination. Consider the following example taken from [BCE95].

Example 16. Let P_0 be the program

```
c1:   z ← p, r.
c2:   p ← q^f, r.
c3:   q ← r, p^f.
```

Where $P_{new} = \{c1\}$, $P_{old} = \{c2, c3\}$ and r is a *base* predicate which fails. Notice that this program is left terminating. By unfolding p in c1 we obtain the following clause:

```
c4:   z ← q^f, r, r.
```

By further unfolding q in c4 we obtain:

```
c5:   z ← r, p^f, r, r.
```

Now if we permute the first two atoms, we get:

```
c6:   z ← p^f, r, r, r.
```

Notice that this switch operation *does preserve left termination*. However, if we now fold the first two atoms, using clause c1 for folding, we obtain the following:

```
c7:   z ← z, r, r.
```

which is obviously not left terminating.   □

In this example the fold operation satisfies our applicability conditions and the applicability conditions of both Tamaki-Sato's [TS84] and Seki's [Sek91] systems. This shows the need of introducing extra applicability conditions for the switch operation. In the above example the switch operation does preserve left termination, while left termination is subsequently spoiled by the application of the fold operation.

Now, we present a new applicability condition for switching. This condition is extremely simple, yet rather common in practice. We call this operation an *allowed switch* since, when P_{base} has an appropriate termination property, it guarantees the preservation of left termination in a transformation sequence, namely also after folding.

Definition 17 (Allowed Switching, (Condition SW1)). *Let $P_0, \ldots, P_n$ be a transformation sequence. Suppose that, for some i, P_{i+1} is obtained from P_i by switching A with B in the clause $cl : H \leftarrow \mathbf{J}, A, B, \mathbf{K}$. This operation is allowed if B is a base atom.* □

Condition SW1 allows us to prove the following.

Theorem 18 (Main). *Let $P_0, \ldots, P_n$ be a transformation sequence. If P_{base} is always-left-terminating, P_0 is left terminating and every switch operation performed in $P_0, \ldots, P_n$ satisfies condition SW1, then P_n is left terminating.* □

The intuition behind the above result is that if the base atoms cannot diverge (P_{base} always-left-terminating), then one is allowed to move them to the left (condition SW1) in the body of a clause. The fact that P_{base} cannot be modified by the transformation sequence further guarantees that the transformation does not spoil its own applicability condition by making base atoms non always-left-terminating.

The situation described by Theorem 18 is quite common when we transform programs via an unfold/fold transformation: The atoms we need to move leftward often perform some checking. Therefore they are usually defined by built-ins or by sets of unit clauses. Notice that it applies for instance to the transformation of Example 10: In it, the base predicates `arc` and `good` are defined by facts, and therefore P_{base} is always-terminating; moreover, the switch operation consists in shifting a base atom to the left.

The proof of Theorem 18 can be given by cases, since we have to consider each possible transformation operation. By induction on i, $i \in [0, n]$, we can prove that each P_i is acceptable wrt to a level mapping derived from the one of P_0. Moreover, we need to apply the following modularity result in order to guarantee that P_i is left terminating for $i \in [0, n]$.

Proposition 19. *Let P and Q be two programs such that P extends Q. Let M be a model of $P \cup Q$ such that M is a model of $Comp(P \cup Q)$. Suppose that*

(i) Q is always-left-terminating,
(ii) P is acceptable wrt M (and a level mapping $| \ |_P$).

Then $P \cup Q$ is left terminating. □

This result is based on the intuition that, given a ground query G in $P \cup Q$, we can "ignore" the atoms defined in Q in the LD-derivations of G, since they always terminate. Namely we can substitute the atoms in Q by the results of their finite LD-trees.

Finally, since for left terminating programs the Finite Failure set coincides with the complement of the least Herbrand model, we also have the following.

Corollary 20 (Preservation of finite failure). *If the conditions of Theorem 18 are satisfied then the finite failure set of P_n coincides with the one of P_0.* □

The following is a simple example of transformation making use of such an allowed switch.

Example 21. Let P_{old} be the left terminating program

```
c1:   prefix(Xs,[]).
c2:   prefix([X|Xs], [X|Ys]) ← prefix(Xs, Ys)ᶠ.

c3:   eqTo([], N).
c4:   eqTo([N|Xs], N) ← eqTo(Xs, N)ᶠ.

c5:   pos([]).
c6:   pos([X|Xs]) ← X>0, pos(Xs)ᶠ.

c7:   pre(Ls, N, Ss) ← prefix(Ls, Ss)ᶠ, eqTo(Ss, N)ᶠ, pos(Ss)ᶠ.
```

where the predicate > is a built-in and then in P_{base}.
pre(Ls, N, Ss) states the property of Ss of being a prefix of Ls composed of elements which are all of value N and positive. In order to avoid scanning the list Ls many times, we can apply the following transformation sequence.
We introduce a *new* predicate

```
d:    scan(N, Ss) ← eqTo(Ss, N), pos(Ss).
```

Hence $P_0 = \{d, c1, \ldots, c7\}$. We unfold both atoms in the body of d

```
d1:   scan(N, []).
d2:   scan(N, [N|Xs]) ← eqTo(Xs, N)ᶠ, N>0, pos(Xs)ᶠ.
```

In order to fold back in d2 with the definition d, we need to switch eqTo(Xs, N)ᶠ and N>0. Condition SW1 holds, hence we may safely perform the switch

```
d3:   scan(N, [N|Xs]) ← N>0, eqTo(Xs, N)ᶠ, pos(Xs)ᶠ.
```

and then fold with definition d both in d3 and in c7. The resulting program P contains $\{c3, \ldots, c6\}$ and

```
c1:   prefix(Xs,[]).
c2:   prefix([X|Xs], [X|Ys]) ← prefix(Xs, Ys)ᶠ.
c8:   pre(Ls, N, Ss) ← prefix(Ls, Ss)ᶠ, scan(N, Ss).
d1:   scan(N, []).
d4:   scan(N, [N|Xs]) ← N>0, scan(N, Xs).
```

where $\{c3, \ldots, c6\}$ are no more in $P|_{pre}$.

We can continue the manipulation of the program through another transformation sequence. Now P_0 is the final program $P|_{pre}$ and we want to further simplify it. The only *base* atom is N > 0 as before, so $P_{old} = \{c1, c2, d1, d4\}$, while the predicate pre is now in P_{new}. In accordance with this choice, we have to modify the labelling in d4 and c8. This means that we add the label "f" to scan(N, Ss) in the body of d4 while we cancel it to pre(Ls, N, Ss) in the body of c8.

Let us unfold both the atoms in the body of c8.

e1:   pre(Ls, N, []).
e2:   pre([N|Ls'], N, [N|Ss']) ← prefix(Ls', Ss')^f, N>0,
           scan(N, Ss')^f.

In order to fold back in P_{new} with the definition in c8, we need to switch
prefix(Ls', Ss')^f and N > 0. SW1 is trivially verified. Hence we can perform
the switch

e3:   pre([X|Ls'], N, [X|Ss']) ← N>0, prefix(Ls', Ss')^f,
           scan(N, Ss')^f.

and then fold with c8.

e1:   pre(Ls, N, []).
e4:   pre([N|Ls'], N, [N|Ss']) ← N>0, pre(Ls', N, Ss').

Let the final program be P', no other clause is in $P'|_{pre}$.

In this case, Theorem 18 guarantees that the final program is left-terminating.
Notice that checking this is trivial: One has to check that the atom shifted to
the left is a *base* atom with P_{base} always-left-terminating. This can be trivially
guaranteed by the fact that P_{base} is not recursively defined or that it contains
only built-ins.   □

One might wonder why in the definition of initial program we do not allow
base atoms to be labeled "f". Our condition SW1 for allowed switch always
admits to move *base* atoms to the left. As a consequence, if *base* atoms would
be labelled, condition **F3** in fold definition would often be trivially satisfied,
yielding to unsound applicability conditions. The following example shows it.

Example 22. Let P_0 be the program

c1:   p ← q, r(X).
c2:   r(g(X)) ← r(X)^f, s^f.
c3:   s.

where $P_{new} = \{c1\}$, $P_{old} = \{c2\}$, $P_{base} = \{c3\}$. Notice that P_0 is left terminating
and P_{base} is always terminating. Here we have labeled "f" the *base* atom s in
the second clause. By unfolding r(X) in c1 we obtain the following clause

c4:   p ← q, r(Y)^f, s^f.

Now, since s is a *base* atom, by condition **SW1**, we are allowed to move it
leftward. By doing this twice, we obtain the clause

c5:   p ← s^f, q, r(Y)^f.

Now, the presence of the labeled atom s^f allows us – by condition **F3** – to fold
q, r(Y)^f with c1 in c5, the resulting program is $\{c2, c3\}$ plus the clause

c6:   p ← s^f, p.

which is obviously not left terminating.   □

5   Transformation of Well-Moded Programs

In this section we introduce an extension of Theorem 18. By referring to *moded* programs, we can partially lift the requirement that P_{base} has to be always-terminating. In this setting, it is sufficient that it is *well-terminating*, i.e. that it terminates for every *well-moded* query. This enlarges considerably the application of our techniques: Most well-moded programs are in fact well-terminating; in particular a well-terminating programs might well be recursive, which is usually not the case for *always-terminating* ones.

Theorem 23 (Main for Well-Moded Programs). *Let P_0 be a well-moded definite program and $P_0, \ldots, P_n$ a transformation sequence of well-moded programs. If P_{base} is well-terminating, P_0 is left terminating and every switch operation performed in $P_0, \ldots, P_n$ satisfies condition **SW1**, then P_n is left terminating.* ☐

The proof is similar to the one of Theorem 18, but we need to apply the following modularity result.

Proposition 24. *Let P and Q be two well-moded programs such that P extends Q. Let M be a model of $P \cup Q$. Suppose that*

(i) Q is well-terminating,
(ii) P is acceptable wrt M and a level mapping $| \; |_P$.

Then $P \cup Q$ is left terminating. ☐

Due to the lack of space the proof is omitted. The intuition is the following. Since a ground query is well-moded and LD-resolution preserves well-moding, see Lemma 7, then any LD-resolvent of a ground query is also well-moded. As a consequence, when the leftmost atom in an LD-resolvent is in Q, it is well-moded as well and then terminating.

Example 25. Let us consider the following simple program which counts the elements in a list of natural numbers and computes their sum.

```
d:    p(Ls, S, N)  ← sumList(Ls, S), count(Ls, N).

c1:   sumList([], 0).
c2:   sumList([H|Ts], S)  ← sumList(Ts, S')ᶠ, sum(S', H, S).

c3:   sum(0, Y, Y).
c4:   sum(s(X), Y, s(Z))  ← sum(X, Y, Z).

c5:   count([], 0).
c6:   count([H|Ts], s(N))  ← count(Ts, N).
```

Let us consider the following modes: p(+,-,-), sumList(+,-), sum(+,+,-) and count(+,-). p is the only *new* predicate and count and sum are *base* predicates. Note that P_0 is well-moded and P_{base} is well-terminating for the given modes. p scans the list three times; this can be fixed via an unfold/fold transformation sequence. As usual, our first step consists in some unfold operations. Let us unfold all the atoms in the body of d

```
d1:   p([], 0, 0).
d2:   p([H|Ts], S, s(N')) ← sumList(Ts, S')ᶠ,
         sum(S', H, S), count(Ts, N').
```

Now we need to move count(Ts, N') to the left of sum(S', H, S). This is allowed by SW1 since count(Ts, N') is in P_{base} After the switch operation we obtain the following clause:

```
d3:   p([H|Ts], S, s(N')) ← sumList(Ts, S')ᶠ,
         count(Ts, N'), sum(S', H, S).
```

We can now apply the fold operation, and fold sumList(Ts, S')ᶠ, count(Ts, N') with definition d in the body of d3. After this operation the final program is given by {c1, ..., c6} plus

```
d1:   p([], 0, 0).
d4:   p([H|Ts], S, s(N')) ← p(Ts, S', N'), sum(S', H, S).
```

Now p has a recursive definition which scans the list only once.   □

6   On the Applicability of Condition SW1

In this Section we intend to discuss the applicability of condition **SW1** for switching and to relate it to our previous proposal in [BCE95].

In our experience, in presence of modes, Theorem 23 allows one to perform almost any switch. The requirement that P_{base} be well-terminating is not a real restriction: As we already mentioned, in presence of modes most terminating programs are well-terminating as well. Thus in practice there remain two main situations in which Theorem 23 is not applicable: The first one is when the switching spoils the well-modedness of the clause. This is a very reasonable limitation: Since we apply our transformation sequence to well-moded programs, we want to preserve the well-modedness property and this clearly restricts the applicability of transformation operations. The second case is when the atom we want to shift leftward cannot be a *base* atom because it is either defined in that part of the program which is being modified by the transformation, or because we need to label it in order to apply the folding operation (condition **(F3)**). In this case we can usually apply another condition for switching, namely the one we already defined in [BCE95]. We briefly recall here such condition.

Given a moded atom A, we denote by $In(A)$ and $Out(A)$ the sequence of terms filling in, respectively, the input and the output positions of A. Moreover we denote by $VarIn(A)$ (resp. $VarOut(A)$) the set of variables occurring in the input (resp. output) positions of A. A similar notation is used for sequences of atoms.

Definition 26 (Non-Failing Atom). *Let P be a moded definite program, M_P its least Herbrand model and $cl : H \leftarrow \mathbf{J}, A, \mathbf{K}$. be a clause in P. We say that A is non-failing in cl if for each grounding θ, such that $Dom(\theta) = Var(In(H), \mathbf{J}, In(A))$ and $M_P \models \mathbf{J}\theta$, there exists γ such that $M_P \models A\theta\gamma$.*   □

The reason why we called such an atom "non-failing" is the following: Suppose that cl is used in the resolution process, and that the unification only binds the variables in the input positions of H, then, if A will eventually be selected by the leftmost selection rule, the computation of the subgoal A will eventually succeed.

Definition 27 (Allowed Switching, (Condition SW2)). *Let* $cl : H \leftarrow J, A, B, \mathbf{K}$. *be a clause of a moded program* P, *and let* P' *be the result of* switching A with B in cl. *The switch is* allowed *if the following three conditions are satisfied*

- *A is an* old *atom,*
- $VarOut(A) \cap VarIn(B) = \emptyset$, *and*
- *A is non-failing in cl.*   □

Requiring that $VarOut(A) \cap VarIn(B) = \emptyset$ ensures that the input of B does not depend on the output of A, and this is a natural requirement when transforming moded programs. On the other hand, the requirement that A is non-failing in cl intuitively forbids the possibility that left termination holds by failure of A, even if B is non-terminating; in such a case, moving A rightward would result in the introduction of a loop.

We give now an example where it is necessary to apply condition **SW2** for switching two atoms.

Example 28. Let P_0 be the program

```
c1:   diff(Ls, I1, I2, N) ←
          count(Ls, I1, N1)ᶠ, count(Ls, I2, N2)ᶠ, (N is N1-N2).

c2:   count([], I, 0).
c3:   count([H|Ts], I, M) ←
          member(H, I, yes), count(Ts, I, M1)ᶠ, (M is M1+1).
c4:   count([H|Ts], I, M) ← member(H, I, no), count(Ts, I, M)ᶠ.

c5:   member(X, [], no).
c6:   member(X, [X|Xs], yes).
c7:   member(X, [Y|Xs], R) ← X ≠ Y, member(X, Xs, R).

d:    p(Ls, I1, I2, N1, N2) ←
          count(Ls, I1, N1), count(Ls, I2, N2).
```

together with the following modes: $diff(+,+,+,-)$, $count(+,+,-)$, member $(+,+,-)$, $is(-,+)$, $\neq (+,+)$ and $p(+,+,+,-,-)$.

p is the only *new* predicate. member, $\neq$ and is are *base* predicates. member is well-terminating, $\neq$ and is are built-ins, hence trivially well-terminating. P_0 is well-moded.

The predicate p is meant to improve the efficiency of predicate diff. Given a list Ls and two check-lists I1 and I2, p determines how many elements of Ls are in each check-list. In order to scan Ls only once, we apply the transformation sequence of well-moded programs.

Let us unfold both the atoms in the body of d

```
d1:  p([], I1, I2, 0, 0).
d2:  p([H|Ts], I1, I2, N1, N2) ←
         member(H, I1, yes), count(Ts, I1, N1'), (N1 is N1'+1),
         member(H, I2, yes), count(Ts, I2, N2')ᶠ, (N2 is N2'+1).
d3:  p([H|Ts], I1, I2, N1, N2) ←
         member(H, I1, no), count(Ts, I1, N1)ᶠ,
         member(H, I2, yes), count(Ts, I2, N2')ᶠ, (N2 is N2'+1).
d4:  p([H|Ts], I1, I2, N1, N2) ←
         member(H, I1, yes), count(Ts, I1, N1')ᶠ, (N1 is N1'+1),
         member(H, I2, no), count(Ts, I2, N2)ᶠ.
d5:  p([H|Ts], I1, I2, N1, N2) ←
         member(H, I1, no), count(Ts, I1, N1)ᶠ,
         member(H, I2, no), count(Ts, I2, N2)ᶠ.
```

In order to fold back with definition d we need to reorder the atoms in all the clauses {d2, ..., d5}. First we switch the third and the fourth atoms and then the fourth and the fifth ones in clauses d2, d4. The first switch is allowed for the condition **SW1** since the fourth atom, member, is a *base* one.

The second switch can be allowed only by condition **SW2**. In fact the fifth atom, count, is not a *base* atom. Such atom cannot be in P_{base}, otherwise the final folding with d would be forbidden because condition **(F3)** in fold definition cannot be satisfied.

Hence we have to verify condition **SW2**, namely to prove that (N1 is N1'+1) is non-failing in d2.

These switches move the *is* atom two positions to the right

```
d1:  p([], I1, I2, 0, 0).
d6:  p([H|Ts], I1, I2, N1, N2) ←
         member(H, I1, yes), count(Ts, I1, N1')ᶠ,
         member(H, I2, yes), count(Ts, I2, N2')ᶠ,
         (N1 is N1'+1), (N2 is N2'+1).
d3:  p([H|Ts], I1, I2, N1, N2) ←
         member(H, I1, no), count(Ts, I1, N1)ᶠ,
         member(H, I2, yes), count(Ts, I2, N2')ᶠ, (N2 is N2'+1).
d7:  p([H|Ts], I1, I2, N1, N2) ←
         member(H, I1, yes), count(Ts, I1, N1')ᶠ,
         member(H, I2, no), count(Ts, I2, N2)ᶠ, (N1 is N1'+1).
d5:  p([H|Ts], I1, I2, N1, N2) ←
         member(H, I1, no), count(Ts, I1, N1)ᶠ,
         member(H, I2, no), count(Ts, I2, N2)ᶠ.
```

Now we switch the second and the third atom in all the clauses {d6, d3, d7, d5}. This is allowed by condition **SW1** since member is a *base* atom.

```
d1:  p([], I1, I2, 0, 0).
e2:  p([H|Ts], I1, I2, N1, N2) ←
        member(H, I1, yes), member(H, I2, yes),
        count(Ts, I1, N1')ᶠ, count(Ts, I2, N2')ᶠ,
        (N1 is N1'+1), (N2 is N2'+1).
e3:  p([H|Ts], I1, I2, N1, N2) ←
        member(H, I1, no), member(H, I2, yes),
        count(Ts, I1, N1)ᶠ, count(Ts, I2, N2')ᶠ, (N2 is N2'+1).
e4:  p([H|Ts], I1, I2, N1, N2) ←
        member(H, I1, yes), member(H, I2, no),
        count(Ts, I1, N1')ᶠ, count(Ts, I2, N2)ᶠ, (N1 is N1'+1).
e5:  p([H|Ts], I1, I2, N1, N2) ←
        member(H, I1, no), member(H, I2, no),
        count(Ts, I1, N1)ᶠ, count(Ts, I2, N2)ᶠ.
```

Now fold is possible and we obtain the final program which is given by $\{c5,\ c6,\ c7\}$ plus

```
f1:  diff(Ls, I1, I2, N) ←
        p(Ls, I1, I2, N1, N2), (N is N1-N2).

d1:  p([], I1, I2, 0, 0).
f2:  p([H|Ts], I1, I2, N1, N2) ←
        member(H, I1, yes), member(H, I2, yes),
        p(Ts, I1, I2, N1', N2'), (N1 is N1'+1), (N2 is N2'+1).
f3:  p([H|Ts], I1, I2, N1, N2) ←
        member(H, I1, no), member(H, I2, yes),
        p(Ts, I1, I2, N1, N2'), (N2 is N2'+1).
f4:  p([H|Ts], I1, I2, N1, N2) ←
        member(H, I1, yes), member(H, I2, no),
        p(Ts, I1, I2, N1', N2), (N1 is N1'+1).
f5:  p([H|Ts], I1, I2, N1, N2) ←
        member(H, I1, no), member(H, I2, no),
        p(Ts, I1, I2, N1, N2).
```

$\{c1,\ \dots,\ c4\}$ are no more in $P|_{\texttt{diff}}$.   □

The proof of Theorem 23 can be extended to include also switches allowed by condition **SW2**. In fact this switch is compatible with our transformation system and it allows one to move an atom to the right when it is an *old non-failing* atom, whose output cannot influence the input of the atom to its right This applicability condition, differently from **SW1**, is not trivial at all to verify. In fact being *non-failing* is a semantic requirement and in general not computable. Nevertheless, if we have more information on the initial program P_0 and on the transformation sequence, such verification becomes feasible. In fact in [BC98] we have defined the class of *noFD programs and queries* which cannot have finitely failing *LD*-derivations and in [BC99] we have defined a larger class of *successful programs* which, for terminating noFD queries, are guaranteed to have at least one successful derivation. Often the noFD and the successful properties for terminating programs are easy to verify and they are sufficient to guarantee the *non-failing* property.

7   Conclusions and Related Work

This paper extends our previous work in [BCE95] and proposes an unfold-fold transformation system able to preserve left termination besides declarative semantics. The system introduce a new applicability condition for the *switching operation*. This condition is simple to verify, yet common in practice. We have also considered separately the situation in which the transformed program is *well-mode*. For this case the applicability condition of the switching operation are particularly mild. This proposal can also integrated with our previous one for switching, given in [BCE95], for solving the few cases in which SW1 is not applicable.

Summarizing, in order to preserve left termination, we have modified Tamaki-Sato's system by

- adopting a definition of unfold and fold which takes into account the order of the atoms in the bodies of the clauses;
- introducing the possibility of reordering – under appropriate applicability conditions – atoms in the bodies by allowed switches;
- adopting a labelling rule and a new applicability condition for the folding operation which is slightly more restrictive than the one of [TS84].

Our system is based on a modularization of the program which distinguishes the part which can be transformed and guides the transformation.

Other approaches to preserving termination properties, while transforming a program, can be found in [PP91,CG94,BE94,BC94,BC97].

The work of Proietti and Pettorossi in [PP91] made an important step forward in the direction of the preservation of left termination. They proposed a transformation system which is more restrictive than the ordered version of [TS84] since only unfolding the leftmost atom or a deterministic atom is allowed. They proved that such a system preserves the "sequence of answer substitution semantics" (a semantics for Prolog programs, defined in [JM84,Bau89]). This guarantees also that if the initial program is left terminating, then the resulting program is left terminating as well. They do not allow any reordering of atoms.

In [BE94] we proved that Tamaki-Sato's transformation system preserves the property of being *acyclic* [AB90]. This has to do with the preservation of termination, in fact a definite program P is *acyclic* if and only if all its derivations starting in a ground goal are finite *whichever is the selection rule employed*. Moreover, the tools used in [BE94] are quite similar to the ones used here. Unfortunately, as pointed out in [AP93], the class of acyclic programs is quite restrictive, and there are many natural programs which are left terminating but not acyclic.

The preservation of universal termination of a query with *LD-resolution* was also studied in [BC94], where we defined an appropriate operational semantics and split the equivalence condition to be satisfied into two complementary conditions: a "completeness" condition and the condition of being "non-increasing". The validity of this second condition, which is very operational, ensures us that a transformation cannot introduce infinite derivations. Again, however, the allowed transformations are seriously restricted by the impossibility of reordering atoms in the bodies. Hence in [BC97] the transformation system was extended by introducing a *replacement* transformation operation, a very powerful operation which includes switch as a particular case. The major problem in this proposal is how to verify in practice the applicability conditions necessary for preserving universal termination which are semantic conditions and operational in style.

More difficult is a comparison with [CG94] since they define a transformation system based only on unfold and replacement operations. In [CG94]the preservation of termination is considered but no condition for it is given and the verification is "a posteriori".

Acknowledgements. This work was supported partly by Italian MURST with the National Research Project 9701248444-004 on "Tecniche formali per la specifica, l'analisi, la verifica, la sintesi e la trasformazione di sistemi software".

References

AB90.   K. R. Apt and M. Bezem. Acyclic programs. In D. H. D. Warren and P. Szeredi, editors, *Proceedings of the Seventh International Conference on Logic Programming*, pages 617–633. The MIT Press, 1990.

AM94.   K.R. Apt and E. Marchiori. Reasoning about Prolog programs: from Modes through Types to Assertions. *Formal Aspects of Computing*, 6(6A):743–765, 1994.

AP90.   K. R. Apt and D. Pedreschi. Studies in pure Prolog: termination. In J.W. Lloyd, editor, *Symposium on Computional Logic*, pages 150–176, Berlin, 1990. Springer-Verlag.

AP93.   K. R. Apt and D. Pedreschi. Reasoning about termination of pure Prolog programs. *Information and Computation*, 106(1):109–157, 1993.

Apt97.   K. R. Apt. *From Logic Programming to Prolog*. Prentice Hall, 1997.

Bau89.   M. Baudinet. *Logic Programming Semantics: Techniques and Applications*. PhD thesis, Stanford University, Stanford, California, 1989.

BC94.   A. Bossi and N. Cocco. Preserving universal termination through unfold/fold. In G. Levi and M. Rodríguez-Artalejo, editors, *Proc. Fourth Int'l Conf. on Algebraic and Logic Programming*, volume 850 of *Lecture Notes in Computer Science*, pages 269–286. Springer-Verlag, Berlin, 1994.

BC97.   A. Bossi and N. Cocco. Replacement Can Preserve Termination. In J. Gallagher, editor, *Proceedings LOPSTR'96*, volume 1207 of *Lecture Notes in Computer Science*, pages 104–129. Springer-Verlag, Berlin, 1997.

BC98.   A. Bossi and N. Cocco. Programs without Failures. In N. Fuchs, editor, *Proceedings LOPSTR'97*, volume 1463 of *Lecture Notes in Computer Science*, pages 28–48. Springer-Verlag, Berlin, 1998.

BC99.   A. Bossi and N. Cocco. Successes in Logic Programs. In P. Flener, editor, *Proceedings LOPSTR'98*, volume 1559 of *Lecture Notes in Computer Science*, pages 219–239. Springer-Verlag, Berlin, 1999.

BCE95.   A. Bossi, N. Cocco, and S. Etalle. Transformation of Left Terminating Programs: the Reordering Problem. In M. Proietti, editor, *LOPSTR95 – Fifth International Workshop on Logic Program Synthesis and Transformation*, number 1048 in LNCS, pages 33–45. Springer-Verlag, 1995.

BE94.   A. Bossi and S. Etalle. Transforming Acyclic Programs. *ACM Transactions on Programming Languages and Systems*, 16(4):1081–1096, July 1994.

Bez93.   M. Bezem. Strong termination of logic programs. *Journal of Logic Programming*, 15(1&2):79–97, 1993.

Cav89.   L. Cavedon. Continuity, consistency and completeness properties for logic programs. In G. Levi and M. Martelli, editors, *6 International Conference on Logic Programming*, pages 571–584. MIT press, 1989.

CG94.   J. Cook and J.P. Gallagher. A transformation system for definite programs based on termination analysis. In F. Turini, editor, *Proc. Fourth Workshop on Logic Program Synthesis and Transformation*. Springer-Verlag, 1994.

DM85.   P. Dembinski and J. Maluszynski. AND-parallelism with intelligent backtracking for annotated logic programs. In *Proceedings of the International Symposium on Logic Programming*, pages 29–38, Boston, 1985.

EBC99.   S. Etalle, A. Bossi, and N. Cocco. Termination of Well-Moded Programs. *Journal of Logic Programming*, 38(2):243–257, 1999.

EG96.   S. Etalle and M. Gabbrielli. Transformations of CLP modules. *Theoretical Computer Science*, 166(1):101–146, 1996.

JM84.   N. Jones and A. Mycroft. Stepwise Development of Operational and Denotational Semantics for Prolog. In Sten-Åke Tärnlund, editor, *Proc. Second Int'l Conf. on Logic Programming*, pages 281–288, 1984.

KK90.   T. Kawamura and T. Kanamori. Preservation of Stronger Equivalence in Unfold/Fold Logic Programming Transformation. *Theoretical Computer Science*, 75(1&2):139–156, 1990.

Llo87.   J. W. Lloyd. *Foundations of Logic Programming*. Symbolic Computation – Artificial Intelligence. Springer-Verlag, Berlin, 1987. Second edition.

LS91.   J. W. Lloyd and J. C. Shepherdson. Partial Evaluation in Logic Programming. *Journal of Logic Programming*, 11:217–242, 1991.

PP91.   M. Proietti and A. Pettorossi. Semantics preserving transformation rules for prolog. In *ACM SIGPLAN Symposium on Partial Evaluation and Semantics-Based Program Manipulation (PEPM '91)*. ACM press, 1991.

Sek91.   H. Seki. Unfold/fold transformation of stratified programs. *Theoretical Computer Science*, 86(1):107–139, 1991.

Sek93.   H. Seki. Unfold/fold transformation of general logic programs for the Well-Founded semantics. *Journal of Logic Programming*, 16(1&2):5–23, 1993.

TS84.   H. Tamaki and T. Sato. Unfold/Fold Transformations of Logic Programs. In Sten-Åke Tärnlund, editor, *Proc. Second Int'l Conf. on Logic Programming*, pages 127–139, 1984.

Transformation Rules for Logic Programs with Goals as Arguments

Alberto Pettorossi[1] and Maurizio Proietti[2]

[1] DISP, Università di Roma Tor Vergata,
Via di Tor Vergata, I-00133 Roma, Italy.
[2] IASI-CNR, Viale Manzoni 30, I-00185, Roma, Italy
{adp,proietti}@iasi.rm.cnr.it,
http://www.iasi.rm.cnr.it/~ {adp,proietti}

Abstract. We introduce a logic language where predicate symbols may have both terms and goals as arguments. We define its operational semantics by extending SLD-resolution with the leftmost selection rule, and we propose a set of transformation rules for manipulating programs written in that language. These transformation rules are shown to be correct in the sense that they preserve the chosen operational semantics. This logic language has higher order capabilities which turn out to be very powerful for the derivation of efficient logic programs. In particular, in our language we can avoid the problem of goal rearrangement which is often encountered during program transformation. Moreover, goals as arguments allow us to perform on logic programs transformation steps similar to the ones performed on functional programs when using higher order generalizations and continuation arguments.

1   Introduction

In the practice of logic programming the idea of having goals as arguments of predicate symbols is not novel (see, for instance, [16,19]). Goals may occur as arguments when writing meta-interpreters, such as:

$solve(true) \leftarrow$
$solve((A, G)) \leftarrow A, solve(G)$

or when expressing the meaning of logical connectives, such as:

$or(P, Q) \leftarrow P$
$or(P, Q) \leftarrow Q$

or when making use of continuations, as indicated by the following program:

$p([\,], Cont) \leftarrow Cont$
$p([X|Xs], Cont) \leftarrow p(Xs, q(X, Cont))$
$q(0, Cont) \leftarrow Cont$

where the goal $p(l, true)$ succeeds iff the list l consists of 0's only.

In this paper we consider an extended logic language which allows variables to range over goals and allows goals to occur as arguments of predicate symbols.

A. Bossi (Ed.): LOPSTR'99, LNCS 1817, pp. 176–195, 2000.

The possibility of storing and manipulating goals as arguments provides 'higher order' capabilities so that in our logic language we can manipulate not only terms (that is, data) but also goals (that is, procedure calls). These capabilities turn out to be useful for performing program manipulations which are often required during program transformation [5,10,17]. Indeed, as we will see, by using goals as arguments we will be able to overcome the goal rearrangement problem, which occurs when for performing a folding step, we are required to modify the positions of the atoms in the body of a clause. This problem is due to the fact that the atoms in the body of a clause cannot always be rearranged without affecting the termination properties of the programs [4].

In our logic language we do not have full higher order capabilities, because in particular, quantification over function or predicate variables is not allowed.

The semantics of our higher order logic programs is a simple extension of the familiar operational semantics of definite logic programs. The operational semantics we consider, is based on SLD-resolution with the leftmost selection rule, also called LD-resolution [1], and we extend unification by allowing goal variables to be bound to goals. We then consider an enhancement of the usual unfold/fold transformation rules so that they may be used also in the case when goals occur as arguments. For instance, we will allow the unfolding of a clause w.r.t. an argument which is an atom. The definition of the semantics of our language guarantees that the transformation rules are correct (see Section 5), and in particular, when defining our semantics, we will take into account the fact that the unfolding of a goal argument may not preserve the set of successes, as indicated by the following example. Let us consider the program:

1. $h \leftarrow p(q)$
2. $p(q) \leftarrow$
3. $q \leftarrow s$

If we unfold the goal argument q in clause 1 using clause 3, we get the clause:

1'. $h \leftarrow p(s)$

and by using LD-resolution in the usual way, the goal h succeeds in the original program, while it fails in the derived program, consisting of clauses 1', 2, and 3. Thus, the set of successes is not preserved by unfolding a goal argument. Similar incorrectness may also arise with other transformation rules, such as folding and goal replacement.

In order to define the operational semantics of our logic language for which suitable enhancements of the unfolding, folding, and goal replacement rules are correct, we will proceed as follows. We first define the syntax of our logic language so that each clause head occurring in our programs has distinct variables, and unifications are realized by means of the equality predicate. Thus, for instance, clause 2 is rewritten as:

2'. $p(G) \leftarrow G = q$

Then the semantics is defined in such a way that, given two goals g_1 and g_2, it gives a value to the equality $g_1 = g_2$ only when g_1 is a goal variable not occurring in the goal g_2 (in particular, our operational semantics is *undefined* for the equality $g = g$, where g is a goal). In other words, we will modify LD-resolution so that a derivation *gets stuck* when it encounters a goal of the form $g_1 = g_2$, where g_1 is either a non-variable goal or a goal variable occurring in g_2. Thus, the derivation starting from the goal h and using the original program (that is, clauses 1, 2′, and 3) gets stuck because the goal $q = q$ is selected, and also the derivation starting from the goal h and using the transformed program (that is, clauses 1′, 2′, and 3) gets stuck because the goal $s = q$ is selected.

Essentially, in our higher order logic language we may introduce new goals, pass them as arguments, and evaluate them, but we cannot inspect their inner structure, because the unification between goals can only be performed via the equality predicate $=$, and as already mentioned, the semantics of the equality $g_1 = g_2$ between goals is defined only when g_1 is a variable not occurring in g_2.

The paper is organized as follows. In the next sections we will introduce the definitions of the syntax (Section 2), the operational semantics (Section 3), and the transformation rules (Section 4) for our logic programs with goals as arguments. The use of the transformation rules according to suitable conditions ensures that the transformation rules are correct in the sense that they preserve the set of successes and the set of finite failures (Section 5). Actually, we will consider two forms of correctness: a *weak* and a *strong* form. The strong form of correctness ensures that a goal succeeds or fails in the original program iff it succeeds or fails, respectively, in the transformed program. The weak form of correctness consists in the 'only-if' part of the strong form, that is, if a goal succeeds or fails in the original program then it succeeds or fails, respectively, in the transformed program. Thus, when the weak form of correctness holds, the transformed program may be *more defined* than the original program in the sense that there may be some goal which has no semantic value (that is, either its evaluation does not terminate or it gets stuck) in the original program, whereas it has a value (that is, it terminates) in the transformed program.

Finally, we show through an example (Section 6) how our extended logic language and our transformation rules can be used for avoiding the problem of rearranging goals while transforming programs for eliminating multiple traversals of data structures.

2   A Logic Language with Goals as Arguments

Let us now introduce the logic language we use. It is constructed starting from the following pairwise disjoint sets:
(i) *individual variables*: $X, X_1, X_2, \ldots$,
(ii) *goal variables*: $G, G_1, G_2, \ldots$,
(iii) *function symbols* (with arity): $f, f_1, f_2, \ldots$, and
(iv) *predicate symbols* (with arity): *true*, *false*, $=, p, p_1, p_2, \ldots$
Individual and goal variables are collectively called *variables*, and they are ranged over by $V, V_1, V_2, \ldots$

Terms: $t, t_1, t_2, \ldots$, *goals*: $g, g_1, g_2, \ldots$, and *arguments*: $u, u_1, u_2, \ldots$, have the following syntax:

$$t ::= X \mid f(t_1, \ldots, t_n)$$
$$g ::= G \mid true \mid false \mid t_1 = t_2 \mid G = g \mid p(u_1, \ldots, u_m) \mid g_1, g_2 \mid g_1; g_2$$
$$u ::= t \mid g$$

The binary operators ',' and ';' denote, respectively, *conjunction* and *disjunction* of goals. They are assumed to be associative with neutral elements *true* and *false*, respectively. Thus, a goal g is the same as $(true, g)$ and $(g, true)$. Similarly, g is the same as $(false; g)$ and $(g; false)$. Goals of the form $p(u_1, \ldots, u_m)$ are also called *atoms*.

Clauses $c, c_1, c_2, \ldots$ have the following syntax:

$$c ::= p(V_1, \ldots, V_m) \leftarrow g$$

where $V_1, \ldots, V_m$ are distinct variables. The atom $p(V_1, \ldots, V_m)$ is called the *head* of clause c and the goal g is called the *body* of c. A clause of the form: $p(V_1, \ldots, V_m) \leftarrow true$ will also be written as: $p(V_1, \ldots, V_m) \leftarrow$.

Programs $P, P_1, P_2, \ldots$ are sets of clauses of the form:

$$p_1(V_1, \ldots, V_{m1}) \leftarrow g_1$$
$$\vdots$$
$$p_k(V_1, \ldots, V_{mk}) \leftarrow g_k$$

where $p_1, \ldots, p_k$ are distinct predicate symbols, and every predicate symbol occurring in g_1 or ... or g_k, is among $p_1, \ldots, p_k$.

Notes on syntax: (1) The assumption that clause heads have only variables as arguments is not restrictive, because one may use equalities in the bodies for binding those variables to terms or goals, as required. (2) The assumption that in every program there exists at most one clause per predicate symbol is not restrictive, because one may use disjunction in the body. In particular, every definite logic program written using the familiar syntax [8], can be rewritten into an equivalent program of our language by suitable introductions of equalities and ';' operators in the bodies of clauses. (3) equality between goals is not symmetric because on the left hand side there must be a goal variable.

For any given syntactic construct r, we use $vars(r)$ to denote the set of variables occurring in r.

3 Operational Semantics

In this section we define a 'big step' operational semantics for our logic language (for an elementary presentation of this technique the reader may refer to [20]). Given a program P, we define the semantics of P as a (possibly empty) ternary relation $P \vdash g \rightarrow b$, where g is a goal and b is either *true* or *false*, denoting that for P and g all the LD-derivations are finite, and either one of them is successful, in which case b is *true*, or all of them are failed, in which case b is *false*.

Given a set of deduction rules, a *deduction tree* τ for $P \vdash g \rightarrow b$ is a tree such that: (i) the root of τ is $P \vdash g \rightarrow b$, and (ii) for every node n of τ with sons $n_1, \ldots, n_k$ (with $k \geq 0$), there exists an instance of a deduction rule whose conclusion is n and whose premises are $n_1, \ldots, n_k$. A *proof* of $P \vdash g \to b$ is a finite deduction tree for $P \vdash g \to b$ where every leaf is a deduction rule which has no premises.

We stipulate that $P \vdash g \to b$ holds iff there exists a proof of $P \vdash g \to b$ when we consider the following set of deduction rules.

(tt) $$\frac{}{P \vdash \mathit{true} \, \to \, \mathit{true}}$$ (ff) $$\frac{}{P \vdash (\mathit{false}, \, g) \, \to \, \mathit{false}}$$

$(te1)$ $$\frac{}{P \vdash (t_1 = t_2, \, g) \, \to \, \mathit{false}}$$ if t_1 and t_2 are not unifiable

$(te2)$ $$\frac{P \vdash g\vartheta \, \to \, b}{P \vdash (t_1 = t_2, \, g) \, \to \, b}$$ if t_1 and t_2 are unifiable and $\vartheta = mgu(t_1, t_2)$

(ge) $$\frac{P \vdash g_2\{G/g_1\} \, \to \, b}{P \vdash ((G = g_1), \, g_2) \, \to \, b}$$ if $G \notin vars(g_1)$

(at) $$\frac{P \vdash (body\{V_1/u_1, \ldots, V_m/u_m\}, \, g) \, \to \, b}{P \vdash (p(u_1, \ldots, u_m), \, g) \, \to \, b}$$ where $p(V_1, \ldots, V_m) \leftarrow body$ is

a renamed apart clause of P

(or) $$\frac{P \vdash (g_1, g) \, \to \, b_1 \qquad P \vdash (g_2, g) \, \to \, b_2}{P \vdash ((g_1; g_2), \, g) \, \to \, b_1 \vee b_2}$$

If $P \vdash g \to \mathit{true}$ we say that g *succeeds* in P. If $P \vdash g \to \mathit{false}$ we say that g *fails* in P. If g neither succeeds nor fails in P we say that g is *undefined* in P.

Notes on semantics: (1) the rules $\dfrac{}{P \vdash \mathit{false} \, \to \, \mathit{false}}$ and $\dfrac{P \vdash g \, \to \, b}{P \vdash (\mathit{true}, g) \, \to \, b}$ which the reader may expect by symmetry, are redundant, because they are derivable as instances of $\dfrac{}{P \vdash (\mathit{false}, g) \, \to \, \mathit{false}}$ and $\dfrac{P \vdash g \, \to \, b}{P \vdash g \, \to \, b}$, respectively, by using the fact that true is the neutral element of a conjunction of goals. (2) $mgu(t_1, t_2)$ denotes a most general unifier of the terms t_1 and t_2. (3) $g\{V_1/u_1, \ldots, V_m/u_m\}$ denotes the substitution of $u_1, \ldots, u_m$ for $V_1, \ldots, V_m$ in g. (4) $\vee$ denotes the boolean or. (5) Our deduction rules for the operational semantics are mutually exclusive, and thus, there exists at most one proof for each $P \vdash g \to b$.

Our deduction rules extend the SLD-resolution for definite logic programs and a conjunction of goals is evaluated with the leftmost selection rule. The evaluation of a disjunction of goals requires the evaluation of each disjunct, and the existence of a proof for $P \vdash g \to b$ implies the *universal termination* of the goal g in the sense of [3]. (Recall that a goal g universally terminates in a program P iff all LD-derivations starting from g and using P, are finite.) It may be the case that for a given program P and goal g, no b exists such that

$P \vdash g \to b$ holds, because every deduction tree with root $P \vdash g \to b$ *either* is infinite *or* has a leaf which is not an instance of any rule conclusion. The latter case may occur when the leaf is of the form: $P \vdash g_0 \to b_0$ and *either* g_0 is a goal variable *or* g_0 is of the form: $g_1 = g_2$ where the goal g_1 is not a goal variable or g_1 occurs in $vars(g_2)$. Thus, for instance, for any $b \in \{true, false\}$, there is no proof for $P \vdash G \to b$ and there is no proof for $P \vdash (G = p, \; G = q) \to b$.

Notice also that the computed answers semantics is *not* captured by our ternary relation $P \vdash g \to b$ and our semantic rules. This choice has been motivated by the fact that we want the unfolding rule to preserve semantics. Indeed, given the following two programs P_1 and P_2:

$$P_1\text{:} \; h(G) \leftarrow G = p, \; G \qquad\qquad P_2\text{:} \; h(G) \leftarrow G = q, \; G$$
$$p \leftarrow q \qquad\qquad\qquad\qquad\qquad p \leftarrow q$$
$$q \leftarrow \qquad\qquad\qquad\qquad\qquad\quad q \leftarrow$$

where P_2 is obtained from P_1 by unfolding p, they are equivalent w.r.t. our operational semantics. However, P_1 and P_2 are not equivalent w.r.t. the computed answer semantics, because for the goal $h(G)$ program P_1 computes the answer $\{G/p\}$, whereas program P_2 computes the answer $\{G/q\}$.

4 The Transformation Rules

In this section we present the transformation rules for our language with goals as arguments. We assume that starting from an initial program P_0 we have constructed the *transformation sequence* $P_0, \ldots, P_i$ [10]. By an application of a transformation rule we get a new program P_{i+1}.

We use $g[u]$ to denote a goal g where we singled out an occurrence of its subconstruct u, where u may be either a term or a goal. By $g[\_]$ we denote the goal $g[u]$ without the occurrence of its subconstruct u. We say that $g[\_]$ is a *goal context*.

Rule R1 (Definition Introduction). It consists in deriving the new program P_{i+1} by adding to the current program P_i a new clause, called *definition clause*, of the form:

$newp(V_1, \ldots, V_m) \leftarrow g$

where: (i) $newp$ is a new predicate symbol not occurring in any program of the sequence $P_0, \ldots, P_i$, (ii) the predicate symbols occurring in g occur in P_0, and (iii) $V_1, \ldots, V_m$ are distinct variables (possibly not all variables) which occur in g.

The set of all definition clauses introduced while constructing the transformation sequence $P_0, \ldots, P_i$, is denoted by Def_i.

Rule R2 (Unfolding). Let c: $h \leftarrow body[p(u_1, \ldots, u_m)]$ be a clause of program P_i. Let c_1: $p(V_1, \ldots, V_m) \leftarrow g$ be the unique, renamed apart clause of $P_0 \cup Def_i$ whose head predicate is p. By *unfolding* c *w.r.t.* $p(u_1, \ldots, u_m)$ *using* c_1 we get the new clause: $h \leftarrow body[g\{V_1/u_1, \ldots, V_m/u_m\}]$. We also get the new program P_{i+1} by replacing in program P_i the clause c by that new clause.

This definition of the unfolding rule is an extension of the usual unfolding rule for definite logic programs and, indeed, for definite logic programs our unfolding rule corresponds to the application of a resolution step to clause c with the selection of the atom $p(u_1, \ldots, u_m)$ and the input clause c_1.

Rule R3 (Folding). Let c: $h \leftarrow body[g\vartheta]$ be a clause of program P_i and c_1: $newp(V_1, \ldots, V_m) \leftarrow g$ be the unique, renamed apart clause in Def_i with head predicate $newp$. Suppose that for every variable V in the set $vars(g) - \{V_1, \ldots, V_m\}$, we have:

- $V\vartheta$ is a variable which does not occur in c outside $g\vartheta$ and
- the variable $V\vartheta$ does not occur in $W\vartheta$, for any variable W occurring in g and different from V.

Then, by *folding c using c_1* we get the new program P_{i+1} by replacing in program P_i the clause c by the clause: $h \leftarrow body[p(V_1, \ldots, V_m)\vartheta]$.

In order to introduce the goal replacement rule (see rule R4 below) we have to introduce the so called *replacement laws*. The replacement of goal g_1 by goal g_2 in the body of a clause of the form: $h \leftarrow body[g_1]$, is allowed when a replacement law holds between g_1 and g_2. We will consider weak and strong replacement laws.

Given a program P, and goals g_1 and g_2, a *strong replacement law* $P \vdash g_1 \Longleftrightarrow g_2$ holds iff
- g_1 and g_2 are equivalent in P w.r.t. the operational semantics defined in Section 3, that is, for every goal context $g[\_]$ and for every $b \in \{true, false\}$, $P \vdash g[g_1] \rightarrow b$ has a proof iff $P \vdash g[g_2] \rightarrow b$ has a proof, and
- the depth of the proof of $P \vdash g[g_2] \rightarrow b$ is not greater than the depth of the proof of $P \vdash g[g_1] \rightarrow b$ (see below for a rigorous definition of *proof depth*).

The latter condition makes $\Longleftrightarrow$ to be an *improvement* relation in the sense of [15]. We will show in the Correctness Theorem of the next section, that the goal replacement rule based on strong replacement laws preserves our operational semantics. Indeed, if we derive program P_2 from program P_1 by an application of the goal replacement rule based on a strong replacement law, then P_1 and P_2 are equivalent in the sense that for every goal g and for every $b \in \{true, false\}$, we have that $P_1 \vdash g \rightarrow b$ iff $P_2 \vdash g \rightarrow b$.

For this result, we do use the assumption that the $\Longleftrightarrow$ relation is an improvement relation. To see this, let us consider the following example:

$$P_1: \; p \leftarrow q \qquad\qquad P_2: \; p \leftarrow p$$
$$q \leftarrow \qquad\qquad\qquad q \leftarrow$$

where P_2 is obtained by replacing q by p in the first clause of P_1. We have that p and q are equivalent in P_1, that is, for every goal context $g[\_]$ and for every

$b \in \{true, false\}$, $P_1 \vdash g[p] \to b$ iff $P_1 \vdash g[q] \to b$, but for the empty goal context
$[\_]$, the proof of $P_1 \vdash p \to true$ has greater depth than the proof of $P_1 \vdash q \to true$.
In fact P_1 and P_2 are not operationally equivalent, because p succeeds in P_1,
while p does not terminate in P_2.

We will also consider the notion of a *weak replacement law*, denoted $P \vdash$
$g_1 \Longrightarrow g_2$, for which we only require that, for every goal context $g[\_]$ and for
every $b \in \{true, false\}$, if $P \vdash g[g_1] \to b$ has a proof then $P \vdash g[g_2] \to b$ has a
proof which has not a greater depth.

For this rule we will prove a weaker correctness result, that is, if we derive program P_2 from program P_1 by an application of the goal replacement rule based
on a weak replacement law, then for every goal g and for every $b \in \{true, false\}$,
if $P_1 \vdash g \to b$ then $P_2 \vdash g \to b$. Thus, program P_2 may be *more defined* than
program P_1, that is, there may be some goal g and some $b \in \{true, false\}$ such
that $P_2 \vdash g \to b$ holds, while $P_1 \vdash g \to b$ has no proof. This notion is justified
by the fact that we often want to apply transformations that may increase the
termination of the program at hand, like for instance, the replacement of the
goal $(g, false)$ by *false*, or the replacement of the goal $(g; true)$ by *true*.

In Definition 2 below, we refine the above notions of weak and strong replacement laws. This refinement is motivated by the fact that the correctness of the
replacement of goal g_1 by goal g_2 in the clause $c: h \leftarrow body[g_1]$, does not depend
on the *local variables* of g_1 and g_2 in c, where the local variables of goal g_i in
c, for $i = 1, 2$, are defined to be those in the set $vars(g_i) - vars(h \leftarrow body[\_])$.
For this reason we find convenient to introduce the notion of a goal g with local
variables V, denoted $g \backslash V$.

Definition 1 (Proof Depth). Let π be the proof for $P \vdash g \to b$ and let m be
the maximal number of instances of the deduction rule (at) in the root-to-leaf
paths of π. Then we say that $P \vdash g \to b$ has a proof depth m, and we write
$P \vdash g \to^m b$.

Definition 2 (Replacement Laws). Given a program P, let g_1 and g_2 be two
goals, and let V_1 and V_2 be two sets of variables.
(i) $P \vdash g_1 \backslash V_1 \Longrightarrow g_2 \backslash V_2$ holds iff for every goal context $g[\_]$ such that $vars(g[\_]) \cap$
$(V_1 \cup V_2) = \emptyset$, and for every $b \in \{true, false\}$, we have that:

$\quad$ if $P \vdash g[g_1] \to b$ then $P \vdash g[g_2] \to b$.

(ii) The relation $P \vdash g_1 \backslash V_1 \Longrightarrow g_2 \backslash V_2$, called a *weak replacement law*, holds
iff for every goal context $g[\_]$ such that $vars(g[\_]) \cap (V_1 \cup V_2) = \emptyset$, and for every
$b \in \{true, false\}$, we have that:

$\quad$ if $P \vdash g[g_1] \to^m b$ then $P \vdash g[g_2] \to^n b$ with $m \geq n$.

(iii) The relation $P \vdash g_1 \backslash V_1 \Longleftrightarrow g_2 \backslash V_2$, called a *strong replacement law*, holds
iff $P \vdash g_1 \backslash V_1 \Longrightarrow g_2 \backslash V_2$ and $P \vdash g_2 \backslash V_2 \Longrightarrow g_1 \backslash V_1$.

(iv) We write $P \vdash g_1 \backslash V_1 \Longleftrightarrow g_2 \backslash V_2$ to mean that $P \vdash g_1 \backslash V_1 \Longrightarrow g_2 \backslash V_2$
and $P \vdash g_2 \backslash V_2 \Longrightarrow g_1 \backslash V_1$ (which is equivalent to $P \vdash g_1 \backslash V_1 \Longleftrightarrow g_2 \backslash V_2$ and
$P \vdash g_2 \backslash V_2 \Longleftrightarrow g_1 \backslash V_1$). Thus, if $P \vdash g_1 \backslash V_1 \Longleftrightarrow g_2 \backslash V_2$ then the proofs for
$P \vdash g_1 \to b$ and for $P \vdash g_2 \to b$ have equal depth.

(v) If $V = \emptyset$ the goal $g\backslash V$ is also written as g. If V is the singleton $\{Z\}$, the goal $g\backslash V$ is also written as $g\backslash Z$.

For any program P we have that the following hold:

1. *Tautologies*:

$$P \vdash true;\, g \implies true \qquad P \vdash g_1;\, g_2 \iff g_2;\, g_1$$
$$P \vdash false,\, g \iff false \quad P \vdash (g_1,\, g_2);\, (g_1,\, g_3) \iff g_1,\, (g_2;\, g_3)$$
$$P \vdash g,\, false \implies false \qquad P \vdash (g_1,\, g_2);\, (g_3,\, g_2) \iff (g_1;\, g_3),\, g_2$$
$$P \vdash g,\, g \iff g \qquad\quad P \vdash (g_1;\, g_2),\, (g_1;\, g_3) \implies g_1;\, (g_2,\, g_3)$$
$$P \vdash g;\, g \iff g$$

In the following replacement laws 2.a, 2.b, and 2.c, as usual for our conventions, V stands for either a goal variable or an individual variable, and u stands for either a term or a goal.

2.a *Generalization + equality introduction*:

$$P \vdash g[u] \iff ((V{=}u),\, g[V])\backslash V \quad \text{if } V \text{ is a variable not occurring in } g[u]$$

2.b *Simplification of equalities*:

$$P \vdash ((V{=}u),\, g[V])\backslash V \iff g[u] \quad \text{if } V \text{ is a variable not occurring in } g[u]$$

2.c *Rearrangement of equalities*:

$$P \vdash (g[(V{=}u),\, g_1])\backslash V \iff ((V{=}u),\, g[g_1])\backslash V \quad \text{if } V \text{ is a variable not occurring in } (g[\_],\, u)$$

When referring to goal variables, the laws 2.a, 2.b, and 2.c will also be called 'goal generalization + equality introduction', 'simplification of goal equalities', and 'rearrangement of goal equalities', respectively.

3. *Rearrangement of term equalities*:

$$P \vdash g,\, (t_1{=}t_2) \implies (t_1{=}t_2),\, g$$

4. *Clark Equality Theory* (CET, see [8]):

$$P \vdash eq_1\backslash Y \iff eq_2\backslash Z \qquad \text{if CET} \vdash \forall X\, (\exists Y\, eq_1 \leftrightarrow \exists Z\, eq_2)$$

where: (i) eq_1 and eq_2 are goals constructed using *true*, *false*, term equalities, conjunctions, and disjunctions, and (ii) $X = vars(eq_1, eq_2) - (Y \cup Z)$.

Notice that, for some program P and for some goals $g, g_1, g_2,$ and g_3, the following do *not* hold:

$$P \vdash true \implies true;\, g$$
$$P \vdash false \implies g,\, false$$
$$P \vdash (t_1{=}t_2),\, g \implies g,\, (t_1{=}t_2)$$
$$P \vdash g_1;\, (g_2,\, g_3) \implies (g_1;\, g_2),\, (g_1;\, g_3)$$
$$P \vdash g_2[g_1] \implies g_2[G],\, (G{=}g_1)$$
$$P \vdash g[(G{=}g_1),\, g_2] \implies (G{=}g_1),\, g[g_2]$$

Rule R4 (Goal Replacement). We get program P_{i+1} from program P_i by replacing clause: $h \leftarrow body[g_1]$ by clause: $h \leftarrow body[g_2]$, if all predicate symbols of (g_1, g_2) occur in P_0, and either (i) $P_0 \vdash g_1\backslash V_1 \implies g_2\backslash V_2$, or (ii) $P_0 \vdash$

$g_1 \backslash V_1 \Longleftrightarrow g_2 \backslash V_2$, where $V_1 = vars(g_1) - vars(h, body[\_])$, and $V_2 = vars(g_2) - vars(h, body[\_])$.

In case (i) we say that the goal replacement is *based on a weak replacement law*. In case (ii) we say that the goal replacement is *based on a strong replacement law*.

Lemma 1 (Replacement). Let g_1, g_2 be goals and V_1, V_2, W be sets of variables. Let $g[\_]$ be a goal context such that $vars(g[\_]) \cap (V_1 \cup V_2) = \emptyset$.

(i) If $P \vdash g_1 \backslash V_1 \Longrightarrow g_2 \backslash V_2$ then $P \vdash g[g_1] \backslash (V_1 \cup W) \Longrightarrow g[g_2] \backslash (V_2 \cup W)$.

(ii) If $P \vdash g_1 \backslash V_1 \Longrightarrow g_2 \backslash V_2$ then $P \vdash g[g_1] \backslash (V_1 \cup W) \Longrightarrow g[g_2] \backslash (V_2 \cup W)$.

5 Correctness of the Transformation Rules

This section is devoted to the proof of the correctness of our transformation rules. We first introduce the notion of *parallel leftmost unfolding* of a clause c.

Let c be a clause in a program P. If c is of the form:

$$p(V_1, \dots, V_m) \leftarrow (a_1, g_1); \dots; (a_k, g_k) \qquad (*)$$

where $k > 0$ and $a_1, \dots, a_k$ are atoms, then the *parallel leftmost unfolding* of clause c in program P is the program Q obtained from P by k applications of the unfolding rule w.r.t. $a_1, \dots, a_k$, respectively.

If the clause c is not of the form (*), then the parallel leftmost unfolding of c is not defined.

Theorem 1 (Correctness). Let us consider a transformation sequence $P_0, \dots, P_k$ constructed by using the rules R1, R2, R3, and R4. Let us suppose that for every h, with $0 \le h < k$, if P_{h+1} has been obtained from P_h by folding clause c using clause c_1, then there exist i, j, with $0 \le i < j \le h$, such that P_j is obtained from P_i by parallel leftmost unfolding of c_1.

Then for every goal g and for every $b \in \{true, false\}$, we have that:

(1) *Improvement*: if $P_0 \cup Def_k \vdash g \to^m b$ then $P_k \vdash g \to^n b$ with $m \ge n$, and

(2) *Soundness*: if all applications of the goal replacement rule are based on strong replacement laws, then: if $P_k \vdash g \to b$ then $P_0 \cup Def_k \vdash g \to b$.

Notice that according to our Correctness Theorem, if some applications of the goal replacement rule are not based on strong replacement laws, then the transformed program P_k may be *more defined* than program $P_0 \cup Def_k$, that is, there may be some goal g and some $b \in \{true, false\}$ such that $P_k \vdash g \to b$ holds, while $P_0 \cup Def_k \vdash g \to b$ has no proof. This fact may derive from applications of the goal replacement rule based on weak replacement laws, such as $P_i \vdash g, false \Longrightarrow false$, for which the $\Longleftrightarrow$ relation does not hold.

Part (1) of the Correctness Theorem follows from Lemmata 2 and 3 below.

Lemma 2 (Improvement). Let P and $NewP$ be programs of the form:

$$P : hd_1 \leftarrow bd_1 \qquad NewP : hd_1 \leftarrow newbd_1$$

$$\vdots \qquad\qquad \vdots$$

$$hd_k \leftarrow bd_k \qquad\qquad hd_k \leftarrow newbd_k$$

For $r = 1, \ldots, k$, let $Y = vars(bd_r) - vars(hd_r)$ and $Z = vars(newbd_r) - vars(hd_r)$ and suppose that: $P \vdash bd_r\backslash Y \Longrightarrow newbd_r\backslash Z$.

Then for all goals g, we have:

if $P \vdash g \rightarrow^m b$ then $NewP \vdash g \rightarrow^n b$ with $m \geq n$.

Proof. We define the size of a proof to be the number of its nodes. We then define a measure μ from the set of proofs to the set $N \times N$ of pairs of natural numbers ordered lexicographically (that is, $\langle m1, m2 \rangle < \langle n1, n2 \rangle$ iff *either* $m1 < n1$ *or* $(m1 = n1$ and $m2 < n2))$. We stipulate that $\mu(\pi) = \langle m, s \rangle$, where m is the depth of π and s is the size of π. We prove this lemma by induction w.r.t. the measure of the proof of $P \vdash g \rightarrow^m b$ (which, by definition, has depth m).

We assume that, for all $\langle m1, s1 \rangle < \langle m, s \rangle$, for all goals g, and for all $b \in \{true, false\}$, if $P \vdash g \rightarrow b$ has a proof of depth $m1$ and size $s1$, then $NewP \vdash g \rightarrow b$ has a proof of depth $n1$, with $m1 \geq n1$. We have to show that $NewP \vdash g \rightarrow b$ has a proof of depth n, with $m \geq n$. We then proceed by cases on the structure of g. We consider the following two cases. The other cases are similar and we omit them.

- Case 1: g is $((G = g_1), g_2)$. Assume that $P \vdash ((G = g_1), g_2) \rightarrow b$ has a proof of depth m and size s. Then, $G \notin vars(g_1)$, $P \vdash ((G = g_1), g_2) \rightarrow b$ has been proved by using rule (ge) as the last step, and $P \vdash g_2\{G/g_1\} \rightarrow b$ has a proof of depth m and size $s-1$. Since $\langle m, s-1 \rangle < \langle m, s \rangle$, by the induction hypothesis $NewP \vdash g_2\{G/g_1\} \rightarrow b$ has a proof of depth n with $m \geq n$ and, by rule (ge), we have that $NewP \vdash ((G = g_1), g_2) \rightarrow b$ has a proof of depth n with $m \geq n$.

- Case 2: g is $(p(u_1, \ldots, u_m), g_1)$. Assume that $P \vdash (p(u_1, \ldots, u_m), g_1) \rightarrow b$ has a proof of depth m and size s. Then, the last step of the proof of $P \vdash (p(u_1, \ldots, u_m), g_1) \rightarrow b$ has been performed by using rule (at), and $P \vdash (bd_r\{V_1/u_1, \ldots, V_m/u_m\}, g_1) \rightarrow b$ has a proof of depth $m-1$ and size $s-1$, where $p(V_1, \ldots, V_m) \leftarrow bd_r$ is a renamed apart clause of P and $p(V_1, \ldots, V_m)$ is hd_r. Now, by (i) the hypothesis that $P \vdash bd_r\backslash Y \Longrightarrow newbd_r\backslash Z$ and (ii) the fact that the substitution $\{V_1/u_1, \ldots, V_m/u_m\}$ does not affect the variables in $Y \cup Z$, we have that $P \vdash (newbd_r\{V_1/u_1, \ldots, V_m/u_m\}, g_1) \rightarrow b$ has a proof of depth $n1$ and size $s1$, with $m-1 \geq n1$. Since $\langle n1, s1 \rangle < \langle m, s \rangle$, by the induction hypothesis there exists a proof of $NewP \vdash (newbd_r\{V_1/u_1, \ldots, V_m/u_m\}, g_1) \rightarrow b$ of depth $n2$ with $n1 \geq n2$. Thus, by using rule (at), we can build a proof of $NewP \vdash (p(u_1, \ldots, u_m), g_1) \rightarrow b$ of depth $n = n2+1$, and thus, $m \geq n$. $\square$

In order to simplify the proof of our next Lemma 3, we notice that we may rearrange any transformation sequence $P_0, \ldots, P_k$ constructed according to the hypothesis of the Correctness Theorem, into a new sequence $P_0, \ldots, P_0 \cup Def_k, \ldots, P_j, \ldots, P_k$ such that: (1) $P_0, \ldots, P_0 \cup Def_k$ is constructed by applications of the definition rule only, and (2) $P_0 \cup Def_k, \ldots, P_j$ is constructed by parallel leftmost unfolding of every clause d in Def_k which is used for an application of the folding rule in the original sequence $P_0, \dots, P_k$.

Lemma 3. Let us consider a transformation sequence $P_0, \dots, P_i, \dots, P_j, \dots, P_k$ such that: (1) $P_0, \dots, P_i$ is constructed by applications of the definition rule only, (2) $P_i = P_0 \cup Def_k$, and (3) $P_i, \dots, P_j$ is constructed by parallel leftmost unfolding of every $d \in Def_k$ which is used for an application of the folding rule in $P_j, \dots, P_k$. For $h = i, \dots, k-1$, let $hd \leftarrow newbd^h$ be a clause in program P_{h+1} derived from the clause $hd \leftarrow bd^h$ in P_h, by an application of the unfolding or folding or goal replacement rule, and let Y be $vars(bd^h) - vars(hd)$ and Z be $vars(newbd^h) - vars(hd)$.

Then, (i) for $h = i, \dots, j-1$, $P_0 \cup Def_k \vdash bd^h \backslash Y \Longrightarrow newbd^h \backslash Z$, and
(ii) for $h = j, \dots, k-1$, $P_j \vdash bd^h \backslash Y \Longrightarrow newbd^h \backslash Z$.

Proof. (i) For every clause $p(V_1, \dots, V_m) \leftarrow g$ in $P_0 \cup Def_k$, we have that:
$P_0 \cup Def_k \vdash p(V_1, \dots, V_m) \Longrightarrow g \backslash Z$, where $Z = vars(g) - \{V_1, \dots, V_m\}$. Thus, Point (i) of the thesis follows from Point (ii) of the Replacement Lemma and the fact that for $h = i, \dots, j-1$, each clause in P_{h+1} is derived from a clause in P_h by the unfolding rule.

(ii) For every definition clause d: $newp(V_1, \dots, V_m) \leftarrow g$ in Def_k which is used for folding in the sequence $P_j, \dots, P_k$, we have that:
(†) $P_j \vdash newp(V_1, \dots, V_m) \Longleftrightarrow g \backslash Z$, where $Z = vars(g) - \{V_1, \dots, V_m\}$. Property (†) is a consequence of the fact that P_j is derived from $P_0 \cup Def_k$ by parallel leftmost unfolding of a set of definition clauses among which is d.

Moreover, for every clause c: $p(V_1, \dots, V_m) \leftarrow g$ in P_0, we have that:
(‡) $P_j \vdash p(V_1, \dots, V_m) \Longrightarrow g \backslash Z$, where $Z = vars(g) - \{V_1, \dots, V_m\}$, because $c \in P_j$.

For $h = j, \dots, k-1$, (1) if P_{h+1} is derived from P_h by the unfolding rule using a clause $newp(V_1, \dots, V_m) \leftarrow g$ which is among those also used for folding (in previous transformation steps), then the thesis follows from Point (ii) of the Replacement Lemma and (†).

(2) If P_{h+1} is derived from P_h by the unfolding rule using a clause c of the form $p(V_1, \dots, V_m) \leftarrow g$ which is *not* among those used for folding, then c belongs to P_0. Thus, the thesis follows from (‡) and Point (ii) of the Replacement Lemma.

(3) If P_{h+1} is derived from P_h by the folding rule using a clause of the form $newp(V_1, \dots, V_m) \leftarrow g$, then the thesis follows from (†) and Point (ii) of the Replacement Lemma.

Finally, (4) if P_{h+1} is derived from P_h by the goal replacement rule based on a replacement law of the form $P_0 \vdash g_1 \backslash Y \Longrightarrow g_2 \backslash Z$, then Point (ii) of the thesis follows from Point (ii) of the Replacement Lemma and the fact that $P_j \vdash g_1 \backslash Y \Longrightarrow g_2 \backslash Z$ also holds, because the predicates of g_1 and g_2 occur in P_0 and the definitions of the predicates in P_0 are not modified during the transformation sequence $P_0, \dots, P_j$. $\square$

In order to get the proof of Part (1) of the Correctness Theorem, it is sufficient to notice that: (A) by Lemma 2 and Point (i) of Lemma 3, we have that: for all goals g, if $P_0 \cup Def_k \vdash g \to^m b$ then $P_j \vdash g \to^r b$ with $m \geq r$, where P_j is the program constructed as indicated in Lemma 3, and (B) by Lemma 2 and Point (ii) of Lemma 3, we have that: for all goals g, if $P_j \vdash g \to^r b$ then $P_k \vdash g \to^n b$ with $r \geq n$.

The proof of Part (2) of the Correctness Theorem is based on the following Lemmata 4 and 5.

Lemma 4 (Soundness). Let P and $NewP$ be programs of the form:

$$P : hd_1 \leftarrow bd_1 \qquad\qquad NewP : hd_1 \leftarrow newbd_1$$
$$\vdots \qquad\qquad\qquad\qquad \vdots$$
$$hd_k \leftarrow bd_k \qquad\qquad\qquad hd_k \leftarrow newbd_k$$

For $r = 1, \ldots, k$, let $Y = vars(bd_r) - vars(hd_r)$ and $Z = vars(newbd_r) - vars(hd_r)$, and suppose that: $P \vdash newbd_r \backslash Z \Longrightarrow bd_r \backslash Y$.

Then for all goals g, we have: if $NewP \vdash g \to b$ then $P \vdash g \to b$.

Proof. We proceed by induction on the size of the proof of $NewP \vdash g \to b$. Assume that, for all $m < n$ and for all goals g, if $NewP \vdash g \to b$ has a proof of size m then $P \vdash g \to b$ has a proof.

We now proceed by cases on the structure of g. We consider the following two cases. The other cases are similar and we omit them.

- Case 1: g is $((G = g_1), g_2)$. Assume that $NewP \vdash ((G = g_1), g_2) \to b$ has a proof of size n. Then, $G \notin vars(g_1)$, $NewP \vdash ((G = g_1), g_2) \to b$ has been proved by using rule (ge) as the last step, and there exists a proof of size $n-1$ of $NewP \vdash g_2\{G/g_1\} \to b$. By the induction hypothesis there exists a proof of $P \vdash g_2\{G/g_1\} \to b$ and, by rule (ge), we have that $P \vdash ((G=g_1), g_2) \to b$ has a proof.

- Case 2: g is $(p(u_1, \ldots, u_m), g_1)$. Assume that $NewP \vdash (p(u_1, \ldots, u_m), g_1) \to b$ has a proof of size n. Then, $NewP \vdash (p(u_1, \ldots, u_m), g_1) \to b$ has been proved by using rule (at) as the last step, and there exists a proof of size $n - 1$ of $NewP \vdash (newbd_r\{V_1/u_1, \ldots, V_m/u_m\}, g_1) \to b$ where $p(V_1, \ldots, V_m) \leftarrow newbd_r$ is a renamed apart clause of $NewP$ and $p(V_1, \ldots, V_m)$ is hd_r. By the induction hypothesis there exists a proof of $P \vdash (newbd_r\{V_1/u_1, \ldots, V_m/u_m\}, g_1) \to b$. Now, by the hypothesis that $P \vdash newbd_r \backslash Z \Longrightarrow bd_r \backslash Y$ and the fact that the substitution $\{V_1/u_1, \ldots, V_m/u_m\}$ does not affect the variables in $Y \cup Z$, we have that $P \vdash (bd_r\{V_1/u_1, \ldots, V_m/u_m\}, g_1) \to b$ has a proof. Thus, by rule (at), $P \vdash (p(u_1, \ldots, u_m), g_1) \to b$ has a proof. □

Lemma 5. Let us consider a transformation sequence $P_0, \ldots, P_k$. For $i = 0, \ldots, k-1$, let $hd \leftarrow newbd$ be a clause in program P_{i+1} derived from the clause $hd \leftarrow bd$ in P_i, by an application of the unfolding rule, or folding rule, or goal replacement rule based on a strong replacement law. Then $P_0 \cup Def_k \vdash newbd \backslash Z \Longrightarrow bd \backslash Y$, where $Y = vars(bd) - vars(hd)$ and $Z = vars(newbd) - vars(hd)$.

Proof. If P_{i+1} is derived from P_i by the unfolding rule using a clause c: $p(V_1, \ldots, V_m) \leftarrow g$ in $P_0 \cup Def_k$, then the thesis follows from Point (i) of the

Replacement Lemma and the fact that $P_0 \cup Def_k \vdash g \backslash Z \implies p(V_1, \dots, V_m)$, where $Z = vars(g) - \{V_1, \dots, V_m\}$. Similarly, if P_{i+1} is derived from P_i by the folding rule using clause d: $newp(V_1, \dots, V_m) \leftarrow g$ in Def_k, then the thesis follows from Point (i) of the Replacement Lemma and the fact that $P_0 \cup Def_k \vdash newp(V_1, \dots, V_m) \implies g \backslash Z$, where $Z = vars(g) - \{V_1, \dots, V_m\}$. Finally, if P_{i+1} is derived from P_i by the goal replacement rule, then the thesis follows from the fact it is based on a strong replacement law and from Point (i) of the Replacement Lemma. $\square$

6   Goals as Arguments for Avoiding Incorrect Goal Rearrangements

In this section we illustrate through an example borrowed from [7], the use of our logic language and our transformation rules. This example indicates how by allowing goals as arguments we can solve the goal rearrangement problem, in the sense that when transforming programs for eliminating multiple traversals of data structures, we can avoid the need of rearranging atoms in the body of clauses.

Let us consider the initial program P_0:

1. $flipcheck(X, Y) \leftarrow flip(X, Y), \ check(Y)$
2. $flip(X, Y) \leftarrow (X = l(N), \ Y = l(N)) \ ;$
   $\qquad\qquad (X = t(L, N, R), \ Y = t(FR, N, FL), \ flip(L, FL), \ flip(R, FR))$
3. $check(X) \leftarrow (X = l(N), \ nat(N)) \ ;$
   $\qquad\qquad (X = t(L, N, R), \ nat(N), \ check(L), \ check(R))$
4. $nat(X) \leftarrow (X = 0) \ ;$
   $\qquad\qquad (X = s(N), \ nat(N))$

where: (i) the term $l(N)$ denotes a leaf with label N and the term $t(L, N, R)$ denotes a tree with label N and the two subtrees L and R, (ii) $nat(X)$ holds iff X is a natural number, (iii) $check(X)$ holds iff all labels in the tree X are natural numbers, and (iv) $flip(X, Y)$ holds iff the tree Y can be obtained by flipping all subtrees of the tree X.

We would like to transform this program and avoid multiple traversals of trees (see the double occurrence of Y in the body of clause 1). We may do so by following two approaches. The first approach is to apply the folding/unfolding rules and the strategy for the *elimination of unnecessary variables* described in [13] or, equivalently, the *conjunctive partial deduction* technique [7] (with the obvious adaptations due to the fact that in our initial program we avoid multiple clauses and use the operator ';' instead). The second approach is to apply the transformation rules we have proposed in Section 4 and to use programs with goals as arguments.

Below we will present the corresponding two derivations. In both derivations we get a program which makes one traversal only of the input trees. However, the first derivation which does *not* use goals as arguments, produces a program, say P_f, which is *not* correct, while the second derivation which uses goals as arguments produces a program, say P_h, which is correct. We have that P_f is *not* correct because during the transformation from P_0 to P_f, we do not preserve universal termination [3]. Indeed, there exists a goal g such that LD-resolution terminates for goal g and program P_0, while it does not terminate for goal g and program P_f (obviously, in order to apply LD-resolution we have to view programs P_0 and P_f as definite logic programs by eliminating ';' in favour of multiple clauses with the same head predicate).

Here is the first derivation from program P_0 to program P_f. In this first derivation we silently assume that clause 1 has been derived from the initial clauses 2, 3, and 4 by applying the definition introduction rule. This allows us to use clause 1 for performing folding steps, and also it allows us to state our correctness results using P_0, instead of $P_0 \cup Def_k$.

We first unfold twice clause 1 and we apply the goal replacement rule whereby deriving the clause:

5. $flipcheck(X,Y) \leftarrow (X=l(N), Y=l(N), nat(N))$;
   $(X=t(L,N,R), Y=t(FR,N,FL),$
   $flip(L,FL), flip(R,FR), nat(N), check(FR), check(FL))$

Then we perform goal rearrangements, which unfortunately do not preserve our operational semantics, and we get:

6. $flipcheck(X,Y) \leftarrow (X=l(N), Y=l(N), nat(N))$;
   $(X=t(L,N,R), Y=t(FR,N,FL),$
   $nat(N), flip(L,FL), check(FL), flip(R,FR), check(FR))$

Now we can fold twice clause 6 using clause 1 and we get the final program P_f consisting of clause 4 together with the following clause:

7. $flipcheck(X,Y) \leftarrow (X=l(N), Y=l(N), nat(N))$;
   $(X=t(L,N,R), Y=t(FR,N,FL),$
   $nat(N), flipcheck(L,FL), flipcheck(R,FR))$

Program P_f performs one traversal only of any input tree given as first argument of *flipcheck*. However, as already mentioned, we have not preserved universal termination. Indeed, the goal $flipcheck(t(l(N),0,l(a)),Y)$ fails in P_0 (that is, $P_0 \vdash flipcheck(t(l(N),0,l(a)),Y) \to false$ holds), while it is undefined in P_f (that is, $P_f \vdash flipcheck(t(l(N),0,l(a)),Y) \to b$ does not hold for any $b \in \{true, false\}$).

Now we present a second derivation starting from the same initial program P_0 and producing a final program P_h which traverses the input tree only once. This derivation is correct in the sense of Point (1) of Theorem 1. In particular, for every goal g of the form: $flipcheck(t_1, t_2)$ where t_1 and t_2 are any two terms, and for every $b \in \{true, false\}$, we have that: if $P_0 \vdash g \to b$ holds, then $P_h \vdash g \to b$ holds. During this second derivation we introduce goal arguments and we make use of the transformation rules introduced in Section 4. The initial step of this derivation is the introduction of the following new definition:

8. $newp(X,Y,G) \leftarrow flip(X,Y), G=check(Y)$

Before continuing our second derivation, let us motivate the introduction of this clause 8 (although this issue is not related to the correctness of our derivation). The incorrect goal rearrangement steps which have led from clause 5 to clause 6, can be avoided by applying, instead, (i) goal generalization + equality introduction and (ii) rearrangement of goal equalities, which are instances of the goal replacement rule, and thus, preserve correctness. Indeed, from clause 5 we can derive by goal generalization + equality introduction the following clause where we have introduced the goal variables GL and GR:

9. $flipcheck(X, Y) \leftarrow (X = l(N), Y = l(N), nat(N))$;
$\qquad\qquad\qquad (X = t(L, N, R), Y = t(FR, N, FL),$
$\qquad\qquad\qquad flip(L, FL), flip(R, FR),$
$\qquad\qquad\qquad nat(N), GR = check(FR), GL = check(FL), GR, GL)$

and then we get the following clause by rearranging the goal equalities:

10. $flipcheck(X, Y) \leftarrow (X = l(N), Y = l(N), nat(N))$;
$\qquad\qquad\qquad (X = t(L, N, R), Y = t(FR, N, FL),$
$\qquad\qquad\qquad flip(L, FL), GL = check(FL),$
$\qquad\qquad\qquad flip(R, FR), GR = check(FR),$
$\qquad\qquad\qquad nat(N), GR, GL)$

Now, this clause 10 explains why we have introduced clause 8. Indeed, by using clause 8 we can avoid the intermediate variables FL and FR which occur in clause 10 by folding each $flip$ atom with the adjacent $check$ atom.

Let us then continue our second derivation starting from clause 8 together with clauses 1, 2, 3, and 4. From clause 8 we perform the transformation steps analogous to those performed in the derivation leading from clause 1 to clause 10. We first unfold clause 8 w.r.t. $flip(X, Y)$ and we get:

11. $newp(X, Y, G) \leftarrow ((X = l(N), Y = l(N))$;
$\qquad\qquad\qquad (X = t(L, N, R), Y = t(FR, N, FL),$
$\qquad\qquad\qquad flip(L, FL), flip(R, FR)))$,
$\qquad\qquad\qquad G = check(Y)$

We then unfold the goal argument $check(Y)$, and after some applications of the goal replacement rule based on weak replacement laws, we get:

12. $newp(X, Y, G) \leftarrow (X = l(N), Y = l(N), G = nat(N))$;
$\qquad\qquad\qquad (X = t(L, N, R), Y = t(FR, N, FL),$
$\qquad\qquad\qquad flip(L, FL), flip(R, FR),$
$\qquad\qquad\qquad G = (nat(N), check(FR), check(FL)))$

We apply the goal generalization + equality introduction rule and the rearrangement of goal equalities rule, and we get:

13. $newp(X, Y, G) \leftarrow (X = l(N), Y = l(N), G = nat(N))$;
$\qquad\qquad\qquad (X = t(L, N, R), Y = t(FR, N, FL),$
$\qquad\qquad\qquad flip(L, FL), V = check(FL), flip(R, FR), U = check(FR),$
$\qquad\qquad\qquad G = (nat(N), U, V))$

Now we can fold clause 13 using clause 8 and we get:

13.f $newp(X, Y, G) \leftarrow (X = l(N),\ Y = l(N),\ G = nat(N))\ ;$
$\qquad (X = t(L, N, R),\ Y = t(FR, N, FL),$
$\qquad newp(L, FL, V),\ newp(R, FR, U),\ G = (nat(N), U, V))$

In order to express *flipcheck* in terms of *newp* we apply the goal generalization + equality introduction rule to clause 1 and we derive:

14. $flipcheck(X, Y) \leftarrow flip(X, Y),\ G = check(Y),\ G$

Then we fold clause 14 using clause 8 and we get:

14.f $flipcheck(X, Y) \leftarrow newp(X, Y, G),\ G$

Thus, the final program P_h consists of the following three clauses:

14.f $flipcheck(X, Y) \leftarrow newp(X, Y, G),\ G$
13.f $newp(X, Y, G) \leftarrow (X = l(N),\ Y = l(N),\ G = nat(N))\ ;$
$\qquad (X = t(L, N, R),\ Y = t(FR, N, FL),$
$\qquad newp(L, FL, V),\ newp(R, FR, U),\ G = (nat(N), U, V))$
4. $nat(X) \leftarrow (X = 0)\ ;$
$\qquad (X = s(N), nat(N))$

Program P_h traverses the input tree only once, because of the structure of the recursive calls of the predicate *newp*. Moreover, the Correctness Theorem ensures that if a goal in the initial program P_0 either succeeds or fails, then also in the final program P_h it either succeeds or fails, respectively. However, a goal which in program P_0 is undefined, may either succeed or fail in program P_h, because as already mentioned, in the derivation we have used replacement laws which are not strong (see the derivation of clause 12 from clause 11).

7   Final Remarks and Related Work

We have proposed a logic language where goals may appear as arguments of predicate symbols. The idea is not novel and, in particular, in a previous paper of ours [11] we have already used goal generalization and we have allowed the use of variables which are bound to goals. Here we have formally introduced the syntax and the operational semantics of a language with goals as arguments and goal variables. The operational semantics we have introduced, extends the familiar operational semantics for definite logic programs with the leftmost selection rule. We have also presented a set of transformation rules for our logic language and we have shown their correctness w.r.t. the given operational semantics. We have shown that variables which range over goals are useful in the context of program transformation for the derivation of efficient logic programs and the use of these variables may avoid the need for atom rearrangement during program transformation, in particular before folding steps. Our extension of definite logic programs makes it possible to perform in the case of logic programs, the kind of transformations which are done in the case of functional programming through the use of higher order generalizations (or lambda abstractions) [12] and *continuations* [18]. For instance, with reference to the example of Section 6, we have that in clause 14.f the third argument G of the predicate *newp* plays the role of a continuation, and indeed, the evaluation of *flipcheck*(X, Y) consists of the evaluation of the goal *newp*(X, Y, G) followed by the evaluation of the continuation which is the goal bound to G.

There are several other proposals in the literature for higher order logic languages (see [6,9] for recent surveys). Our main contribution in this paper is a transformational approach to the development of higher order logic programs, which we believe, has received very little attention so far. Notice that, as already mentioned, our language has only limited higher order capabilities, because quantified function or predicate variables are not allowed.

The Correctness Theorem we have proved about our transformation rules ensures that the if a goal succeeds or fails in the given program then also in the derived program it succeeds or fails, respectively. Since the operational semantics defined in Section 3 models universal termination (that is, the operational semantics of a goal is defined iff all LD-derivations starting from that goal are finite), in this respect our Correctness Theorem extends the results for definite logic programs presented in [3]. (In fact, the transformations presented in [3] also preserve computed answers while ours do not.) Also we would like to notice that our transformation rules extend those considered in [3] because: (i) our language is an extension of definite logic programs, and (ii) our folding rule is more powerful. Indeed, even restricting ourselves to programs that do not contain goal variables and goal arguments, we allow folding steps which use clauses whose bodies contain disjunctions, and this is not possible in [3], where for folding one may use exactly one definition clause whose body is a conjunction of atoms.

The approach we have proposed in the present paper to avoid incorrect goal rearrangements, is complementary to the approach described in [4], where the authors give sufficient conditions for the goal rearrangements to preserve *left termination*. (Recall that a program P left terminates iff all *ground* goals universally terminate in P.) Thus, when these conditions are not met or we are not able to prove their validity, we may apply our technique which avoids incorrect goal rearrangements by using, instead, goal generalization + equality introduction and rearrangement of goal equalities. We have proved in this paper that these transformation rules preserve universal termination, and thus, they also preserve left termination.

Notice, however, that sometimes goal rearrangements may be desirable because they improve program performance by anticipating tests and reducing the time complexity of the execution of logic programs.

Finally, our idea of introducing replacement laws which are based on a notion of improvement has been already considered by various authors in various contexts such as higher order functional languages [15], concurrent constraint logic languages [2], and inductive definitions [14].

We leave for future work the development of suitable strategies for directing the use of the transformation rules we have proposed in this paper.

Acknowledgements. We would like to thank Michael Leuschel for pointing out an error in the preliminary version of this paper and also for helpful comments. Thanks also to the anonymous referees of the LoPSTr 99 Workshop for their suggestions. This work has been partially supported by MURST Progetto Cofinanziato 'Tecniche Formali per la Specifica, l'Analisi, la Verifica, la Sintesi e la Trasformazione di Sistemi Software' (Italy), and Progetto Coordinato CNR 'Verifica, Analisi e Trasformazione dei Programmi Logici' (Italy).

References

1. K. R. Apt and D. Pedreschi. Reasoning about termination of pure logic programs. *Information and Computation*, 106:109–157, 1993.
2. M. Bertolino, S. Etalle, and C. Palamidessi. The replacement operation for CCP programs. In A. Bossi, editor, *Proceedings of LoPSTr '99, Venice, Italy*, Lecture Notes in Computer Science. Springer, 2000. (this volume).
3. A. Bossi and N. Cocco. Preserving universal termination through unfold/fold. In *Proceedings ALP '94*, Lecture Notes in Computer Science 850, pages 269–286. Springer-Verlag, 1994.
4. A. Bossi, N. Cocco, and S. Etalle. Transforming left-terminating programs: The reordering problem. In M. Proietti, editor, *Logic Program Synthesis and Transformation, Proceedings LoPSTr '95, Utrecht, The Netherlands*, Lecture Notes in Computer Science 1048, pages 33–45. Springer, 1996.
5. R. M. Burstall and J. Darlington. A transformation system for developing recursive programs. *Journal of the ACM*, 24(1):44–67, January 1977.
6. P. M. Hill and J. Gallagher. Meta-programming in logic programming. In D. M. Gabbay, C. J. Hogger, and J. A. Robinson, editors, *Handbook of Logic in Artificial Intelligence and Logic Programming*, volume 5, pages 421–497. Oxford University Press, 1998.
7. J. Jørgensen, M. Leuschel, and B. Martens. Conjunctive partial deduction in practice. In J. Gallagher, editor, *Logic Program Synthesis and Transformation, Proceedings of LoPSTr '96, Stockholm, Sweden*, Lecture Notes in Computer Science 1207, pages 59–82. Springer-Verlag, 1997.
8. J. W. Lloyd. *Foundations of Logic Programming*. Springer-Verlag, Berlin, 1987. Second Edition.
9. G. Nadathur and D. A. Miller. Higher-order logic programming. In D. M. Gabbay, C. J. Hogger, and J. A. Robinson, editors, *Handbook of Logic in Artificial Intelligence and Logic Programming*, volume 5, pages 499–590. Oxford University Press, 1998.
10. A. Pettorossi and M. Proietti. Transformation of logic programs: Foundations and techniques. *Journal of Logic Programming*, 19,20:261–320, 1994.
11. A. Pettorossi and M. Proietti. Flexible continuations in logic programs via unfold/fold transformations and goal generalization. In O. Danvy, editor, *Proceedings of the 2nd ACM SIGPLAN Workshop on Continuations, January 14, 1997, ENS, Paris (France) 1997*, pages 9.1–9.22. BRICS Notes Series, N6-93-13, Aahrus, Denmark, 1997.
12. A. Pettorossi and A. Skowron. Higher order generalization in program derivation. In *International Joint Conference on Theory and Practice of Software Development, TAPSOFT '87*, Lecture Notes in Computer Science 250, pages 182–196. Springer-Verlag, 1987.

13. M. Proietti and A. Pettorossi. Unfolding-definition-folding, in this order, for avoiding unnecessary variables in logic programs. *Theoretical Computer Science*, 142(1):89–124, 1995.

14. M. Proietti and A. Pettorossi. Transforming inductive definitions. In D. De Schreye, editor, *Proceedings of the 1999 International Conference on Logic Programming*, pages 486–499. MIT Press, 1999.

15. D. Sands. Total correctness by local improvement in the transformation of functional programs. *ACM Toplas*, 18(2):175–234, 1996.

16. L. S. Sterling and E. Shapiro. *The Art of Prolog*. The MIT Press, 1986.

17. H. Tamaki and T. Sato. Unfold/fold transformation of logic programs. In S.-Å. Tärnlund, editor, *Proceedings of the Second International Conference on Logic Programming, Uppsala, Sweden*, pages 127–138. Uppsala University, 1984.

18. M. Wand. Continuation-based program transformation strategies. *Journal of the ACM*, 27(1):164–180, 1980.

19. D. H. D. Warren. Higher-order extensions to Prolog: are they needed? In Y-H Pao J.E. Hayes, D. Michie, editor, *Machine Intelligence*, volume 10, pages 441–454, Chichester, 1982. Ellis Horwood Ltd.

20. G. Winskel. *The Formal Semantics of Programming Languages: An Introduction*. The MIT Press, 1993.

Algebraic Specification and Program Development by Stepwise Refinement[*]

Extended Abstract

Donald Sannella

Laboratory for Foundations of Computer Science
University of Edinburgh, UK
dts@dcs.ed.ac.uk, www.dcs.ed.ac.uk/~dts/

Abstract. Various formalizations of the concept of "refinement step" as used in the formal development of programs from algebraic specifications are presented and compared.

1 Introduction

Algebraic specification aims to provide a formal basis to support the systematic development of correct programs from specifications by means of verified refinement steps. Obviously, a central piece of the puzzle is how best to formalize concepts like "specification", "program" and "refinement step". Answers are required that are simple, elegant and general and which enjoy useful properties, while at the same time taking proper account of the needs of practice. Here I will concentrate on the last of these concepts, but first I need to deal with the other two.

For "program", I take the usual approach of algebraic specification whereby programs are modelled as *many-sorted algebras* consisting of a collection of sets of data values together with functions over those sets. This level of abstraction is commensurate with the view that the correctness of the input/output behaviour of a program takes precedence over all its other properties. With each algebra is associated a *signature* Σ which names its components (sorts and operations) and thus provides a basic vocabulary for making assertions about its properties. There are various definitions of signature and algebra but the details will not be important here. The class of Σ-algebras is denoted $Alg(\Sigma)$.

For "specification", it will be enough to know that any specification SP determines a signature $Sig(SP)$ and a class $[\![SP]\!]$ of $Sig(SP)$-algebras. These algebras (the *models* of SP) correspond to all the programs that we regard as correct realizations of SP. Algebraic specification is often referred to as a "property-oriented" approach since specifications contain *axioms*, usually in some flavour of first-order logic with equality, describing the properties that models are required to satisfy. But again, the details of what specifications look like will not

---

[*] This research was supported by EPSRC grant GR/K63795 and the ESPRIT-funded CoFI Working Group.

concern us here. Sometimes SP will tightly constrain the behaviour of allowable realizations and $[\![SP]\!]$ will be relatively small, possibly an isomorphism class or even a singleton set; other times it will impose a few requirements but leave the rest unconstrained, and then $[\![SP]\!]$ will be larger. We allow both possibilities; in contrast to approaches to algebraic specification such as [EM85], the "initial model" of SP (if there is one) plays no special rôle.

The rest of this paper will be devoted to various related formalizations of the concept of "refinement step". I use the terms "refinement" and "implementation" interchangeably to refer to a relation between specifications, while "realization" is a relation between an algebra or program and a specification. An idea-oriented presentation of almost all of this material, with examples, can be found in [ST97] and this presentation is based on that. See [ST88], [SST92], [BST99] and the references in [ST97] for a more technical presentation. Someday [ST??] will contain a unified presentation of the whole picture and at that point everybody reading this must immediately go out and buy it. Until then, other starting points for learning about algebraic specification are [Wir90], [LEW96] and [AKK99].

2   Simple Refinement

Given a specification SP, the programming task it defines is to construct an algebra (i.e. program) A such that $A \in [\![SP]\!]$. Rather than attempting to achieve this in a single step, we proceed systematically in a stepwise fashion, incorporating more and more design and implementation decisions with each step. These include choosing between the options of behaviour left open by the specification, between the algorithms that realize this behaviour, between data representation schemes, etc. Each such decision is recorded as a separate step, typically consisting of a local modification to the specification. Developing a program from a specification then involves a sequence of such steps:

$$SP_0 \rightsquigarrow SP_1 \rightsquigarrow \cdots \rightsquigarrow SP_n$$

Here, SP_0 is the original specification of requirements and $SP_{i-1} \rightsquigarrow SP_i$ for any $i = 1, \ldots, n$ is an individual *refinement step*. The aim is to reach a specification (here, SP_n) that is an exact description of an algebra.

A formal definition of $SP \rightsquigarrow SP'$ must incorporate the requirement that any realization of SP' is a correct realization of SP. This gives [SW83,ST88]:

$$SP \rightsquigarrow SP' \quad \text{iff} \quad [\![SP']\!] \subseteq [\![SP]\!]$$

which presupposes that $Sig(SP) = Sig(SP')$. This is the *simple refinement* relation.

Stepwise refinement is sound precisely because the correctness of the final outcome can be inferred from the correctness of the individual refinement steps:

$$\frac{SP_0 \rightsquigarrow SP_1 \rightsquigarrow \cdots \rightsquigarrow SP_n \qquad A \in [\![SP_n]\!]}{A \in [\![SP_0]\!]}$$

In fact, the simple refinement relation is transitive:

$$\frac{SP \rightsquigarrow SP' \qquad SP' \rightsquigarrow SP''}{SP \rightsquigarrow SP''}$$

Typically, the specification formalism will contain operations for building complex specifications from simpler ones. If these operations are monotonic w.r.t. inclusion of model classes (this is a natural requirement that is satisfied by almost all specification-building operations that have ever been proposed) then they preserve simple refinement:

$$\frac{SP_1 \rightsquigarrow SP'_1 \qquad \cdots \qquad SP_n \rightsquigarrow SP'_n}{op(SP_1, \ldots, SP_n) \rightsquigarrow op(SP'_1, \ldots, SP'_n)}$$

This provides one way of decomposing the task of realizing a structured specification into a number of separate subtasks, but it unrealistically requires the structure of the final realization to match the structure of the specification. See Sect. 4 below for a better way.

3 Constructor Implementation

In the context of a sufficiently rich specification language, simple refinement is powerful enough to handle all concrete examples of interest. However, it is not very convenient to use in practice. During stepwise refinement, the successive specifications accumulate more and more details arising from successive design decisions. Some parts become fully determined, and remain unchanged as a part of the specification until the final program is obtained.

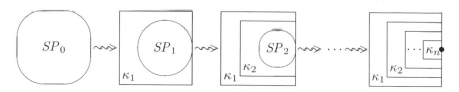

It is more convenient to separate the finished parts from the specification, proceeding with the development of the unresolved parts only.

$$SP_0 \xrightarrow[\kappa_1]{\rightsquigarrow} SP_1 \xrightarrow[\kappa_2]{\rightsquigarrow} SP_2 \xrightarrow[\kappa_3]{\rightsquigarrow} \cdots \xrightarrow[\kappa_n]{\rightsquigarrow} \bullet \ SP_n = EMPTY$$

It is important for the finished parts κ_1, ..., κ_n to be independent of the particular choice of realization for what is left: they should act as constructions extending any realization of the unresolved part to a realization of what is being refined.

Each κ_i amounts to a so-called *parameterised program* [Gog84] with input interface SP_i and output interface SP_{i-1}, or equivalently a *functor* in Standard ML. I call it a *constructor*, not to be confused with value constructors in functional languages. Semantically, it is a function on algebras $\kappa_i : Alg(Sig(SP_i)) \to Alg(Sig(SP_{i-1}))$. Intuitively, κ_i provides a definition of the components of a $Sig(SP_{i-1})$-algebra, given the components of a $Sig(SP_i)$-algebra.

Constructor implementation [ST88] is defined as follows. Suppose that SP and SP' are specifications and κ is a constructor such that $\kappa : Alg(Sig(SP')) \to Alg(Sig(SP))$. Then:

$$SP \underset{\kappa}{\rightsquigarrow} SP' \quad \textbf{iff} \quad \kappa(\llbracket SP' \rrbracket) \subseteq \llbracket SP \rrbracket$$

(Here, $\kappa(\llbracket SP' \rrbracket)$ is the image of $\llbracket SP' \rrbracket$ under κ.) We read $SP \underset{\kappa}{\rightsquigarrow} SP$ as "SP' implements SP via κ".

The correctness of the final outcome of stepwise development may be inferred from the correctness of the individual constructor implementation steps:

$$\frac{SP_0 \underset{\kappa_1}{\rightsquigarrow} SP_1 \underset{\kappa_2}{\rightsquigarrow} \cdots \underset{\kappa_n}{\rightsquigarrow} SP_n = EMPTY}{\kappa_1(\kappa_2(\ldots \kappa_n(empty)\ldots)) \in \llbracket SP_0 \rrbracket}$$

where $EMPTY$ is the empty specification over the empty signature and $empty$ is its (empty) realization. Again, the constructor implementation relation is in fact transitive:

$$\frac{SP \underset{\kappa}{\rightsquigarrow} SP' \qquad SP' \underset{\kappa'}{\rightsquigarrow} SP''}{SP \underset{\kappa \circ \kappa'}{\rightsquigarrow} SP''}$$

4   Problem Decomposition

Decomposition of a programming task into separate subtasks is modelled using a constructor implementation with a multi-argument constructor [SST92]:

$$SP \underset{\kappa}{\rightsquigarrow} \langle SP_1, \ldots, SP_n \rangle \quad \textbf{iff} \quad \kappa(\llbracket SP_1 \rrbracket \times \cdots \times \llbracket SP_n \rrbracket) \subseteq \llbracket SP \rrbracket$$

where $\kappa : Alg(Sig(SP_1)) \times \cdots \times Alg(Sig(SP_n)) \to Alg(Sig(SP))$ is an n-argument constructor. Now the development takes on a tree-like shape. It is complete once a tree is obtained that has empty sequences (of specifications) as its leaves:

$$SP \underset{\kappa}{\rightsquigarrow} \begin{cases} SP_1 \underset{\kappa_1}{\rightsquigarrow} \langle \rangle \\ \quad \vdots \\ SP_n \underset{\kappa_n}{\rightsquigarrow} \begin{cases} SP_{n1} \underset{\kappa_{n1}}{\rightsquigarrow} \left\{ SP_{n11} \underset{\kappa_{n11}}{\rightsquigarrow} \langle \rangle \right. \\ \cdots \\ SP_{nm} \underset{\kappa_{nm}}{\rightsquigarrow} \langle \rangle \end{cases} \end{cases}$$

Then an appropriate instantiation of the constructors in the tree yields a realization of the original requirements specification. The above development tree yields the algebra

$$\kappa(\kappa_1(), \ldots, \kappa_n(\kappa_{n1}(\kappa_{n11}())), \ldots, \kappa_{nm}())) \in [\![SP]\!].$$

The structure of the final realization is determined by the shape of the development tree, which is in turn determined by the decomposition steps. This is in contrast to the naive form of problem decomposition mentioned earlier, where the structure of the final realization is required to match the structure of the specification.

5 Behavioural Implementation

A specification should not include unnecessary constraints, even if they happen to be satisfied by a possible future realization, since this may prevent the developer from choosing a different implementation strategy. This suggests that specifications of programming tasks should not distinguish between programs (modelled as algebras) exhibiting the same *behaviour*.

The intuitive idea of behaviour of an algebra has received considerable attention, see e.g. [BHW95]. In most approaches one distinguishes a certain set *OBS* of sorts as *observable*. Intuitively, these are the sorts of data directly visible to the user (integers, booleans, characters, etc.) in contrast to sorts of "internal" data structures, which are observable only via the functions provided. The behaviour of an algebra is characterised by the set of *observable computations* taking arguments of sorts in *OBS* and producing a result of a sort in *OBS*, i.e. terms of sorts in *OBS* with variables (representing the inputs) of sorts in *OBS* only. Two Σ-algebras A and B are *behaviourally equivalent* (w.r.t. *OBS*), written $A \equiv B$, if all observable computations yield the same results in A and in B.

It turns out to be difficult to write specifications having model classes that are closed under behavioural equivalence, largely because of the use of equality in axioms. One solution is to define $[\![\cdot]\!]$ such that $[\![SP]\!]$ always has this property, but this leads to difficulties in reasoning about specifications. Another is to take account of behavioural equivalence in the notion of implementation.

Behavioural implementation [ST88] is defined as follows. Suppose that SP and SP' are specifications and κ is a constructor such that $\kappa : Alg(Sig(SP')) \to Alg(Sig(SP))$. Then:

$$SP \underset{\kappa}{\overset{\equiv}{\rightsquigarrow}} SP' \quad \text{iff} \quad \forall A \in [\![SP']\!].\exists B \in [\![SP]\!].\kappa(A) \equiv B$$

This is just like constructor implementation except that κ applied to a model of SP' is only required to be a model of SP modulo behavioural equivalence.

A problem with this definition is that stepwise refinement is unsound. The following property does *not* hold:

$$\frac{SP_0 \underset{\kappa_1}{\overset{\equiv}{\rightsquigarrow}} SP_1 \underset{\kappa_2}{\overset{\equiv}{\rightsquigarrow}} \cdots \underset{\kappa_n}{\overset{\equiv}{\rightsquigarrow}} SP_n = EMPTY}{\exists A \in [\![SP_0]\!].\kappa_1(\kappa_2(\ldots \kappa_n(empty)\ldots)) \equiv A}$$

The problem is that $SP_0 \underset{\kappa_1}{\overset{\equiv}{\leadsto}} SP_1$ ensures only that algebras in $[\![SP_1]\!]$ give rise to correct realizations of SP_0. It says nothing about the algebras that are only models of SP_1 up to behavioural equivalence. But such algebras may arise as well because $SP_1 \underset{\kappa_2}{\overset{\equiv}{\leadsto}} SP_2$.

The problem disappears if we modify the definition of behavioural implementation $SP \underset{\kappa}{\overset{\equiv}{\leadsto}} SP'$ to require

$$\forall A \in Alg(Sig(SP')).(\exists A' \in [\![SP']\!].A \equiv A') \Rightarrow (\exists B \in [\![SP]\!].\kappa(A) \equiv B)$$

but then it is very difficult to prove the correctness of behavioural implementations. There is a better way out, originally suggested in [Sch87]. Soundness of stepwise refinement using our original definition of behavioural implementation is recovered, as well as transitivity of the behavioural implementation relation, if we assume that all constructors used are *stable*, that is, that any constructor $\kappa : Alg(Sig(SP')) \to Alg(Sig(SP))$ preserves behavioural equivalence:

Stability assumption: if $A \equiv B$ then $\kappa(A) \equiv \kappa(B)$

We could repeat here the tree-like development picture of Sect. 4 — developments involving decomposition steps based on behavioural implementations with multi-argument (stable) constructors yield correct realizations of the original requirements specification.

There are two reasons why stability is a reasonable assumption. First, recall that constructors correspond to parameterised programs which means that they must be written in some given programming language. The stability of *expressible* constructors can be established in advance for this programming language, and this frees the programmer from the need to prove it during the program development process. Second, there is a close connection between the requirement of stability and the security of encapsulation mechanisms in programming languages supporting abstract data types. A programming language ensures stability if the only way to access an encapsulated data type is via the operations explicitly provided in its output interface. This suggests that stability of constructors is an appropriate thing to expect; following [Sch87] we view the stability requirement as a methodologically justified design criterion for the modularisation facilities of programming languages.

6 Refinement Steps in Extended ML and CASL

The presentation above may be too abstract to see how the ideas apply to the development of concrete programs. It may help to see them in the context of a particular specification and/or programming language.

Extended ML [San91,KST97] is a framework for the formal development of Standard ML programs from specifications. Extended ML specifications look just like Standard ML programs except that axioms are allowed in "signatures" (module interface specifications) and in place of code in module bodies. As noted above, constructors correspond to Standard ML functors. Extended ML functors, with specifications in place of mere signatures as their input and output interfaces, correspond to constructor implementation steps: the well-formedness of functor F(X:SP):SP' = body in Extended ML corresponds to the correctness of $SP' \underset{F}{\leadsto} SP$. There is a close connection with the notion of *steadfast program* in [LOT99]. Extended ML functors are meant to correspond to behavioural implementation steps and the necessary underlying theory for this is in [ST89], but the requisite changes to the semantics of Extended ML are complicated and have not yet been satisfactorily completed. The Extended ML formal development methodology accommodates stepwise refinement with decomposition steps as above, generalized to accommodate development of functors as well as structures (algebras).

CASL, the new *Common Algebraic Specification Language* [CoFI98], has been developed under the auspices of the Common Framework Initiative [Mos97] in an attempt to consolidate past work on the design of algebraic specification languages and provide a focal point for future joint work. *Architectural specifications* in CASL [BST99] relate closely to constructor implementations in the following sense. Consider $SP \underset{\kappa}{\leadsto} \langle SP_1, \ldots, SP_n \rangle$ where κ is a multi-argument constructor. The architectural specification

$$\texttt{arch spec ASP = units } U_1 : SP_1; \ \ldots \ ; \ U_n : SP_n \texttt{ result } T$$

(where T is a so-called *unit term* which builds an algebra from the algebras $U_1, \ldots, U_n$) includes $SP_1, \ldots, SP_n$ and $\kappa = \lambda U_1, \ldots, U_n.T$ but not SP. Its semantics is (glossing over many details) the class $\kappa(\llbracket SP_1 \rrbracket \times \cdots \times \llbracket SP_n \rrbracket)$. Thus $SP \underset{\kappa}{\leadsto} \langle SP_1, \ldots, SP_n \rangle$ corresponds to the simple refinement $SP \leadsto \texttt{ASP}$. CASL accommodates generic units so it also allows development of parameterised programs.

7   Higher Order Extensions

Algebraic specification is normally restricted to first-order. There are three orthogonal dimensions along which the picture above can be extended to higher-order.

First, we can generalize constructor implementations by allowing constructors to be higher-order parameterised programs. If we extend the specification language to permit the specification of such programs (see [SST92,Asp97]) then we can develop them stepwise using the definitions of Sect. 3, with decomposition as in Sect. 4. Both Extended ML and CASL support the development of first-order parameterised programs. In both cases the extension to higher-order parameterised programs has been considered but not yet fully elaborated. Higher-order functors are available in some implementations of Standard ML, cf. [Rus98]. To apply behavioural implementation, one would require an appropriate notion of behavioural equivalence between higher-order parameterised programs.

Second, we can use higher-order logic in axioms. Nothing above depends on the choice of the language of axioms, but the details of the treatment of behavioural equivalence is sensitive to this choice. The treatment in [BHW95] extends smoothly to this case, see [HS96].

Finally, we can allow higher-typed functions in signatures and algebras. Again, the only thing that depends on this is the details of the treatment of behavioural equivalence. Behavioural equivalence of such algebras is characterized by existence of a so-called *pre-logical relation* between them [HS99]. If constructors are defined using lambda calculus then stability is a consequence of the Basic Lemma of pre-logical relations [HLST00].

Acknowledgements. Hardly any of the above is new, and all of it is the product of collaboration. Thanks to Martin Wirsing for starting me off in this direction in [SW83], to Andrzej Tarlecki (especially) for close collaboration on most of the remainder, to Martin Hofmann for collaboration on [HS96], to Furio Honsell for collaboration on [HS99], and to Andrzej, Furio and John Longley for collaboration on [HLST00]. Finally, thanks to the LOPSTR'99 organizers for the excuse to visit Venice.

References

Asp97.   D. Aspinall. Type Systems for Modular Programs and Specifications. Ph.D. thesis, Dept. of Computer Science, Univ. of Edinburgh (1997).

AKK99.   E. Astesiano, H.-J. Kreowski and B. Krieg-Brückner (eds.). *Algebraic Foundations of Systems Specification.* Springer (1999).

BHW95.   M. Bidoit, R. Hennicker and M. Wirsing. Behavioural and abstractor specifications. *Science of Computer Programming* 25:149–186 (1995).

BST99.   M. Bidoit, D. Sannella and A. Tarlecki. Architectural specifications in CASL. *Proc. 7th Intl. Conference on Algebraic Methodology and Software Technology (AMAST'98)*, Manaus. Springer LNCS 1548, 341–357 (1999).

CoFI98.   CoFI Task Group on Language Design. CASL – The CoFI algebraic specification language – Summary (version 1.0). http://www.brics.dk/Projects/CoFI/Documents/CASL/Summary/ (1998).

EM85.   H. Ehrig and B. Mahr. *Fundamentals of Algebraic Specification I: Equations and Initial Semantics.* Springer (1985).

Gog84.   J. Goguen. Parameterized programming. *IEEE Trans. on Software Engineering* SE-10(5):528–543 (1984).

HS96.   M. Hofmann and D. Sannella. On behavioural abstraction and behavioural satisfaction in higher-order logic. *Theoretical Computer Science* 167:3–45 (1996).

HLST00.   F. Honsell, J. Longley, D. Sannella and A. Tarlecki. Constructive data refinement in typed lambda calculus *Proc. 3rd Intl. Conf. on Foundations of Software Science and Computation Structures.* European Joint Conferences on Theory and Practice of Software (ETAPS 2000), Berlin. Springer LNCS 1784, 149–164 (2000).

HS99.   F. Honsell and D. Sannella. Pre-logical relations. *Proc. Computer Science Logic, CSL'99*, Madrid. Springer LNCS 1683, 546–561 (1999).

KST97.   S. Kahrs, D. Sannella and A. Tarlecki. The definition of Extended ML: a gentle introduction. *Theoretical Computer Science* 173:445–484 (1997).

LOT99.   K.-K. Lau, M. Ornaghi and S.-Å. Tärnlund. Steadfast logic programs. *Journal of Logic Programming* 38:259–294 (1999).

LEW96.   J. Loeckx, H.-D. Ehrich and M. Wolf. *Specification of Abstract Data Types.* Wiley (1996).

Mos97.   P. Mosses. CoFI: The Common Framework Initiative for algebraic specification and development. *Proc. 7th Intl. Joint Conf. on Theory and Practice of Software Development,* Lille. Springer LNCS 1214, 115–137 (1997).

Rus98.   C. Russo. Types for Modules. Ph.D. thesis, report ECS-LFCS-98-389, Dept. of Computer Science, Univ. of Edinburgh (1998).

San91.   D. Sannella. Formal program development in Extended ML for the working programmer. *Proc. 3rd BCS/FACS Workshop on Refinement,* Hursley Park. Springer Workshops in Computing, 99–130 (1991).

SST92.   D. Sannella, S. Sokołowski and A. Tarlecki. Toward formal development of programs from algebraic specifications: parameterisation revisited. *Acta Informatica* 29:689–736 (1992).

ST88.   D. Sannella and A. Tarlecki. Toward formal development of programs from algebraic specifications: implementations revisited. *Acta Informatica* 25:233–281 (1988).

ST89.   D. Sannella and A. Tarlecki. Toward formal development of ML programs: foundations and methodology. *Proc. 3rd Joint Conf. on Theory and Practice of Software Development,* Barcelona. Springer LNCS 352, 375–389 (1989).

ST97.   D. Sannella and A. Tarlecki. Essential concepts of algebraic specification and program development. *Formal Aspects of Computing* 9:229–269 (1997).

ST??.   D. Sannella and A. Tarlecki. *Foundations of Algebraic Specifications and Formal Program Development.* Cambridge Univ. Press, to appear.

SW83.   D. Sannella and M. Wirsing. A kernel language for algebraic specification and implementation. *Proc. 1983 Intl. Conf. on Foundations of Computation Theory,* Borgholm. Springer LNCS 158, 413–427 (1983).

Sch87.   O. Schoett. Data Abstraction and the Correctness of Modular Programming. Ph.D. thesis, report CST-42-87, Dept. of Computer Science, Univ. of Edinburgh (1987).

Wir90.   M. Wirsing. Algebraic specification. *Handbook of Theoretical Computer Science* (J. van Leeuwen, ed.). North-Holland (1990).

Making Mercury Programs Tail Recursive

Peter Ross, David Overton, and Zoltan Somogyi

{petdr,dmo,zs}@cs.mu.oz.au
Department of Computer Science and Software Engineering,
University of Melbourne, Victoria 3010, Australia

Abstract. We present two optimizations for making Mercury programs tail recursive. Both operate by taking computations that occur after a recursive call and moving them before the recursive call, modifying them as necessary. The first optimization moves calls to associative predicates; it is a pure source to source transformation. The second optimization moves construction unifications; it required extensions to the mode system (to record aliases) and to the parameter passing convention (to allow arguments to be returned in memory). The two optimizations are designed to work together, and can make a large class of programs tail recursive.

1 Introduction

Recursive calls are often very close to being the last action in a clause. Frequently, however, the recursive call computes a value which must be put into a memory cell or used in a simple computation. Since the Mercury execution algorithm [13] requires both of these kinds of actions to be performed after the call, such clauses are not tail recursive. The code generated for them will therefore execute stack frame setup and teardown code in every iteration, and will require stack space proportional to the depth of recursion. This paper presents two optimizations that in many common cases can transform such code into a tail recursive form by moving code from after the recursive call to before the recursive call. These optimizations have been implemented in the Melbourne Mercury compiler [16].

The first optimization is a pure source to source transformation. It looks for recursive calls followed by associative computations which depend on the outputs of the recursive call. The optimization then creates a specialized version of the predicate in which the associative computation is done before the recursive call. This specialized predicate will have extra arguments that act as *accumulators*: they hold the cumulative results of the associative computations so far.

The second optimization looks for recursive calls followed by construction unifications that put some of the results of that call into memory cells, and moves those construction unifications before the call. This required extending the Mercury mode system to allow a restricted form of partially instantiated data structures and to record aliases, since in the transformed program the cell is not ground when it is created, but will become ground when the recursive call returns. To allow this to happen, we also had to extend the parameter passing conventions of the Mercury abstract machine to allow predicates to return selected output arguments in memory rather than in registers.

A. Bossi (Ed.): LOPSTR'99, LNCS 1817, pp. 196–215, 2000.

Some predicates contain both associative computations and construction unifications after the recursive call. To allow us to make such predicates tail recursive, the accumulator introduction optimization will perform its transformation even when the recursive call is followed by construction unifications as well as associative computations, knowing that the other optimization will move the construction unifications before the call.

The rest of this paper is organized as follows. The rest of this section presents some background. Section 2 describes the accumulator introduction transformation. Section 3 describes the changes needed to allow output arguments to be returned in memory. Section 4 presents benchmarking results. Section 5 discusses how our two optimizations are related to previous work. Section 6 concludes the paper.

1.1 Background

The Mercury language is described in full in the reference manual [11], and the main aspects of the implementation in [13]. Here we concentrate on what is relevant for this paper.

Mercury is a strongly typed language, so the compiler knows the type of every variable. It is also strongly moded. A predicate may have more than one mode, but the compiler treats each mode separately; we call each mode of a predicate (or function) a *procedure*. The compiler reorders conjunctions in the bodies of procedures to ensure that all the consumers of a variable come after its producer; the compiler knows the state of instantiation of every variable at every point in the program.

The Mercury compiler's internal representation of the source program is called the high level data structure, or HLDS for short. The HLDS stores programs in what we call *superhomogeneous form*. In this form,

- the definition of every procedure must be a single clause, whose body may contain arbitrarily nested if-then-elses, negations, conjunctions, disjunctions and *switches* (a switch is a disjunction in which every disjunct unifies the same input variable against distinct function symbols), and
- the atoms (including the clause head) must have one of the forms p(X1,..., Xn), Y = X, or Y = f(X1,...,Xn).

The HLDS annotates every goal with mode information. For unifications, we show this mode information by writing <= for construction unifications, => for deconstruction unifications, == for equality tests, and := for assignments.

2 Accumulator Introduction

This section introduces the source to source transformation that looks for self recursive predicates where the recursive call is followed by an associative computation. This associative computation can then be moved in front of the recursive call. This problem has previously been studied as a transformation based on unfold/fold rules [3, 8, 9] or as a schemata matching transformation [5, 6, 7]. Our transformation is loosely based on Debray's [8] transformation.

2.1 Transformation

Consider a procedure whose body consists of a switch with two arms, where one arm of the switch contains the recursive call. We would like to determine whether or not the computation after the recursive call is associative. In the Mercury implementation, the transformation does this by looking for a *promise* declaration of the form

```
:- promise all [I,A,B,C,ABC]
    (
        (some [AB] p(I, A, B, AB), p(I, AB, C, ABC))
    <=>
        (some [BC] p(I, B, C, BC), p(I, A, BC, ABC))
    ).
```

Promise declarations in general are formulae that the programmer asserts to be true and on whose truth the language implementation is therefore allowed to rely; the implementation is allowed but not required to verify the promise.

This particular promise declaration follows the pattern of an associative computation. An associative predicate is one whose arguments can be divided into a (possibly empty) set of invariant inputs and three nonempty sets, two of inputs and one of outputs. The promise declaration simply states that processing A, B and C from right to left produces the same value for ABC as processing them from left to right.

We illustrate the motivation for our accumulator introduction algorithm by tracing the transformation of the predicate, mirror, in the mode (in, out). The call to mirror([1,2,3], M) would bind M to the list [1,2,3,3,2,1]. Note that append is associative.

The superhomogeneous form [13] of the code, as generated by the Mercury compiler except with meaningful variable names, is as follows, with the code a human programmer would write on the right.

```
mirror(L, M) :-                      mirror([], []).
    ( % switch on L                  mirror([H|T], [H|M1]) :-
        L => [],                         mirror(T, M0),
        M <= []                          append(M0, [H], M1).

    ;

        L => [H|T],
        mirror(T, M0),
        Empty <= [],
        ListH <= [H | Empty],
        append(M0, ListH, M1),
        M <= [H | M1]
    ).
```

Construction unifications are not associative, so a simple associativity analysis might determine that the tail computation is non-associative. However, all of the construction unifications except the last one can safely be moved before the recursive call without breaking the mode constraints of the procedure. This rearrangement of goals is trivial in the Mercury compiler, as at each point in a procedure it knows the state of instantiation of every variable, and two goals can have their order swapped provided that neither goal modifies the instantiation state of any variable referred to by the other goal. (Some other conditions must also be imposed to avoid the introduction of nontermination or unwanted exceptions, but these conditions are not an issue in our examples and we will not discuss them further in this paper.)

The recursive case now ends in `mirror(T, M0)`, `append(M0, ListH, M1)`, `M <= [H | M1]`. Since we will be rearranging the execution order inside this computation, we will introduce a new predicate, `mirror_acc`, with this body, whose arguments are the variables which occur both in this code fragment and in the rest of the code of `mirror`:

```
mirror_acc(T, M, ListH, H) :-
    mirror(T, M0),
    append(M0, ListH, M1),
    M <= [H | M1].
```

We will fold the end of the recursive case of `mirror` with this new predicate. The compiler will be able to use last call optimisation on this call and, as we shall see, we can make `mirror_acc` tail recursive as well. This requires first unfolding the call to `mirror` in `mirror_acc` with the original definition of `mirror`. This of course requires a renaming apart step; we have put an `A_` prefix on the variables that came from `mirror_acc`.

```
mirror_acc(A_T, A_M, A_ListH, A_H) :-
    ( % switch on A_T
        A_T => [],
        A_M0 <= [],
        append(A_M0, A_ListH, A_M1),
        A_M <= [A_H | A_M1]
    ;
        A_T => [H|T],
        Empty <= [],
        ListH <= [H | Empty],
        mirror(T, M0),
        append(M0, ListH, M1),
        A_M0 <= [H | M1],
        append(A_M0, A_ListH, A_M1),
        A_M <= [A_H | A_M1]
    ).
```

The second call to `append` depends on the preceding construction unification, so their order cannot be swapped. However we can inform the compiler that a call to append can be equivalent to a construction unification:

```
:- promise all [L,H,T] ( L = [H|T] <=> append([H],T,L) ).
```

Using this construction equivalence law, we can replace `A_M0 <= [H | M1]`, `append(A_M0, A_ListH, A_M1)` with `append([H], M1, A_M0)`, `append(A_M0, A_ListH, A_M1)`. Applying the associativity law, we transform again to append

(M1, A_ListH, New), append([H], New, A_M1) where New is a new variable of the same type as M1, A_ListH and A_M1. (The associative law requires the types of those three variables to be the same.) Another application of the construction equivalence law, this time in the other direction, leaves us with append(M1, A_ListH, New), A_M1 <= [H | New]).

Now the two calls to append are next to each other, so the associative law allows the two calls to append to be rearranged to become append(ListH, A_ListH, Tmp), append(M0, Tmp, New), where Tmp is a new variable of the same type as ListH, A_ListH, M0 and New. The first call to append no longer depends on the recursive call, so it can be moved before the recursive call. This results in the following code:

```
mirror_acc(A_T, A_M, A_ListH) :-
    ( % switch on A_T
        A_T => [],
        A_M0 <= [],
        append(A_M0, A_ListH, A_M1),
        A_M <= [A_H | A_M1]
    ;
        A_T => [H|T],
        Empty <= [],
        ListH <= [H | Empty],
        append(ListH, A_ListH, Tmp),
        mirror(T, M0),
        append(M0, Tmp, New),
        A_M1 <=  [H | New]
        A_M <= [A_H | A_M1]
    ).
```

We now use the original definition of mirror_acc to do folding in both mirror and the previous version of mirror_acc to obtain the following completely transformed code:

```
mirror(L, M) :-
    ( % switch on L
        L => [],
        M <= []
    ;
        L => [H|T],
        Empty <= [],
        ListH <= [H | Empty],
        mirror_acc(T, M, ListH, H)
    ).

mirror_acc(A_T, A_M, A_ListH, A_H) :-
    ( % switch on A_T
        A_T => [],
        A_M0 <= [],
        append(A_M0, A_ListH, A_M1),
```

```
        A_M <= [A_H | A_M1]
    ;
        A_T => [H|T],
        Empty <= [],
        ListH <= [H | Empty],
        append(ListH, A_ListH, Tmp),
        mirror_acc(T, A_M1, Tmp, H),
        A_M <= [A_H | A_M1]
    ).
```

The call to **append** in the base case is redundant. However, it is only redundant because, for this particular predicate, the base case initializes the answer to be the identity element for **append**. Partial deduction [12] can replace this call with A_M1 = A_ListH.

In the recursive case, application of the associativity law has rearranged the order of the arguments to **append**. The variable, ListH, is now placed at the start of the list, rather than the end. Thus the complexity of the call to **append** now becomes $O(1)$ rather than $O(N)$, improving the big-O complexity of the algorithm as a whole. Unfortunately the complexity can also change in the reverse direction. To prevent this from happening we introduce a heuristic. The heuristic is based on the idea that the accumulator data structure is usually 'bigger' than the individual data items being accumulated. This heuristic requires knowing, for each associative predicate, which argument position(s) control the runtime of calls to that predicate; for **append** this is the first argument. (This information may be available in programmer declarations, built into the compiler, or derived by the compiler via a program analysis such as the termination analysis algorithm of [14].) The heuristic says that after the rearrangement of the code, the accumulator variable should not be located in any of these argument positions.

This optimisation is sufficient to introduce tail recursion in predicates in which the recursive call is followed by one or more independent associative computations. The algorithm can also transform predicates where the recursive call is followed by one or more chains of independent associative calls, which have the additional property of commutativity. A commutative call is one which obeys the following law:

```
:- promise all [A,B,AB] ( p(A, B, AB) <=> p(B, A, AB) ).
```

The properties of commutativity and associativity allow us to transform a chain of calls into an equivalent chain of calls of which only one is required by the mode constraints of the procedure to be after the recursive call. For example the following two definitions of sum are equivalent and the one on the right is in a form suitable for our algorithm.

```
sum([], 0).                      sum([], 0).
sum([H|T], S) :-                 sum([H|T], S) :-
    sum(T, S0),                      plus(H, H, TwoH),
    plus(H, S0, S1),                 sum(T, S0),
    plus(H, S1, S).                  plus(TwoH, S0, S).
```

For predicates such as `mirror` in which the code after the recursive call includes construction unification as well, achieving tail recursion also requires the optimisation described in section 3.

2.2   Algorithm

The following definitions are needed to allow the presentation of the algorithm to be as concise as possible. The operator, $\triangleright$, has the following meaning: $C_b \triangleright C_a$ is true iff the goal C_b depends on the goal C_a, which means that C_a changes the state of instantiation of some variable that occurs in C_b. This means that C_a and C_b must appear in the program in their original order; they cannot have their order swapped. The operator, $\triangleright^+$, is the transitive closure of $\triangleright$. The function $nonlocals(G)$ returns the set of variables of the goal, G, that are also used elsewhere in the predicate.

The initial stage of the algorithm, shown in Figure 1, partitions the goals following the final recursive call in the recursive case into five sets: the set of goals which can be safely moved before the recursive call (*before*), and four sets of goals which cannot. The first of these sets (*assoc*) contains only calls to associative predicates; the second and third (*construct* and *construct_assoc*) contain only construction unifications, with *construct_assoc* containing the constructions that depend on members of the *assoc* set and *construct* containing the constructions that do not; and the fourth set (*reject*) contains everything else. The algorithm goes on to the second stage only if the *reject* set is empty.

The second stage of the algorithm, shown in Figure 2, is responsible for ensuring that the transformation does not worsen the big-O computational complexity of the predicate. It checks the complexity doesn't worsen using the heuristic from section 2.1, if the heuristic reports it does worsen then the algorithm terminates. It also swaps the order of the arguments to all the associative calls and determines the substitutions that will be used to mimic the unfold/fold process that was used as the justification of the algorithm.

Finally, the third stage, shown in Figure 3, creates the accumulator version of the predicate by applying the substitutions determined from stage 2. It also redefines the original predicate to call the accumulator version.

2.3   Example

As an aid to understanding the algorithm, we will walk through the algorithm for the `mirror` predicate from section 2.1. First, we present the original code of the predicate annotated to show how the algorithm refers to its various parts:

```
mirror(L, M) :-    % Inv={} In={L} Out={M}
    ( % switch on L
        L => [H | T],                  % C 1,1
        mirror(T, MO),                 % C 1,2      In'={T} Out'={MO}
        Empty <= [],                   % C 1,3
        ListH <= [H | Empty],          % C 1,4
        append(MO, ListH, M1),         % C 1,5
        M <= [H | M1]                  % C 1,6
```

$Let\ p(Inv,\ In,\ Out)$:-
   $switch($
      $\langle C_{1,1} \ldots C_{1,k-1}, p(Inv, In', Out'), C_{1,k+1} \ldots C_{1,m} \rangle,$
      $\langle C_{2,1} \ldots C_{2,n} \rangle$
   $).$
   $where\ 1 \le k < m \wedge \neg(\exists l, l > k \wedge C_{1,l} = p(\_))$

$reject = construct\_assoc = construct = assoc = before = \emptyset$
$for\ i = k + 1\ to\ m:$
   $if\ (C_{1,i} \triangleright C_{1,j} \Rightarrow (1,j) \in (\{(1,1) \ldots (1,k-1)\} \cup before))$
      $before = before \cup (1,i)$
   $else\ if\ (C_{1,i}$ is an associative call such that
         (its invariant input arguments depend only on Inv
         $\wedge$ exactly one of its two associative input arguments occurs in $Out')$
         $\wedge C_{1,i} \triangleright C_{1,j} \Rightarrow (1,j) \in (\{(1,1) \ldots (1,k)\} \cup before))$
      $assoc = assoc \cup (1,i)$
   $else\ if\ (C_{1,i}$ is a construction unification
         $\wedge C_{1,i} \triangleright C_{1,j} \Rightarrow (1,j) \in (\{(1,1) \ldots (1,k)\} \cup before \cup construct))$
      $construct = construct \cup (1,i)$
   $else\ if\ (C_{1,i}$ is a construction unification
         $\wedge C_{1,i} \triangleright C_{1,j} \Rightarrow (1,j) \in (\{(1,1) \ldots (1,k)\} \cup before \cup assoc \cup construct\_assoc)$
         $\wedge C_{1,i} \triangleright^{+} C_{1,j} \Rightarrow (1,j) \in (\{(1,1) \ldots (1,k)\} \cup before \cup \{C_{1,l}\} \cup construct\_assoc$
         where $(C_{1,l} \in assoc \wedge$
         $C_{1,i}$ can be expressed as a call to the same predicate as $C_{1,l}))$
      $construct\_assoc = construct\_assoc \cup (1,i)$
   $else$
      $reject = reject \cup (1,i)$
$if\ (reject \ne \emptyset)$
   transformation is not applicable, exit

Fig. 1. The first stage

```
    ;
        L => [],              % C 2,1
        M <= []               % C 2,2
    ).
```

Note that the order of the arms of a switch does not matter, since exactly one of the arms will be taken. Note also that although in this example, all the conjuncts are calls or unifications, we do not require this in general; our algorithm would work just fine if e.g. $C_{1,6}$ were replaced with a compound goal (e.g. a disjunction).

We now present the values of the variables computed by our algorithm at the end of each stage of the transformation:

Stage 1:

$before$	$= \{(1,3),(1,4)\}$	$assoc$ $= \{(1,5)\}$
$construct$	$= \{\}$	$construct\_assoc = \{(1,6)\}$
$reject$	$= \{\}$	

Stage 2:

$before = \{(1,1),(1,3),(1,4)\}$ $after = \{(1,5),(1,6)\}$

$init\_accs = \{ListH, H\}$

$acc\_var\_subst = \{ListH \to A\_ListH, H \to A\_H\}$

$during\_assoc\_input = M0$ $inv\_input = \{\}$

$before\_assoc\_input = ListH$ $assoc\_output = M1$

$acc\_var = A\_ListH$ $new\_acc = New$

$CS_{1,5} = append(ListH, M0, M1)$

$assoc\_call\_subst = \{M0 \to A\_ListH, M1 \to NewListH\}$

$rec\_call\_subst = \{M0 \to M1, ListH \to NewListH\}$

$before = before \cup \{(1,1)\ldots(1,k-1)\}$

$after = assoc \cup construct \cup construct\_assoc$

$init\_accs = \bigcup_{i \in before} nonlocals(C_i) \cap \bigcup_{i \in after} nonlocals(C_i)$

$acc\_var\_subst = \emptyset$

for each $var \in init\_accs$
   create a new variable, A_var
   $acc\_var\_subst = \{(var \to A\_var)\} \cup acc\_var\_subst$

$increase\_complexity = false$

$rec\_call\_subst = \emptyset$

$assoc\_call\_subst = \emptyset$

for each $a \in assoc$
   let inv_input
     be the set of invariant input arguments in C_a
   let $during\_assoc\_input$
     be the associative input argument in C_a that is in Out'
   let $before\_assoc\_input$
     be the associative input argument in C_a that is not in Out'
   let $assoc\_output$
     be the associative output argument in C_a

   let acc_var be the unique variable such that
     $(before\_assoc\_input \to acc\_var) \in acc\_var\_subst$

   let CS_a be C_a with $during\_assoc\_input$ and $before\_assoc\_input$
   having their positions swapped
   if ($during\_assoc\_input$ is in an inefficient position in CS_a)
     $increase\_complexity = true$

   create a new variable, new_acc
   $assoc\_call\_subst = \{during\_assoc\_input \to acc\_var,$
     $assoc\_output \to new\_acc\} \cup assoc\_call\_subst$
   $rec\_call\_subst = \{during\_assoc\_input \to assoc\_output,$
     $before\_assoc\_input \to new\_acc\} \cup rec\_call\_subst$

if ($increase\_complexity$)
   transformation would increase big-O complexity, exit

Fig. 2. The second stage

Stage 3:

$call\_to\_head = \{M0 \rightarrow M\}$ $head\_to\_call = \{M \rightarrow M0\}$

$p\_acc \qquad = mirror\_acc$

$call \qquad = mirror\_acc(T, M0, ListH, H)$

$base\_call \quad = mirror\_acc(T, M, ListH, H)$

$rec\_call \quad = mirror\_acc(T, M1, NewListH, H)$

$R_{1,5} \qquad = append(ListH, A\_ListH, NewListH)$

$R_{1,6} \qquad = M <= [A\_H|M1]$

$B_{2,1} \qquad = L => [] \qquad\qquad B_{2,2} \qquad = M0 <= []$

$B_{1,5} \qquad = append(M0, A\_ListH, M1)$

$B_{1,6} \qquad = M <= [A\_H|M1] \quad Acc \qquad = \{A\_ListH, A\_H\}$

```
call_to_head = ∅
head_to_call = ∅
for each CV ∈ Out'
    let HV be the variable from Out corresponding to CV in Out'
    call_to_head = {CV → HV} ∪ call_to_head
    head_to_call = {HV → CV} ∪ head_to_call

create new predicate, p_acc
call = p_acc(Inv, In', Out', init_accs)
base_call = rename_goal(call, call_to_head)
rec_call = rename_goal(call, rec_call_subst)
let C_before be the sequence C_{1,j} where (1,j) ∈ before

redefine p as p(Inv, In, Out) :-
    switch(
        ⟨C_before, base_call⟩,
        ⟨C_{2,1} ... C_{2,n}⟩
    ).

for each (1,j) ∈ assoc
    R_{1,j} = rename(CS_{1,j}, assoc_call_subst)
for each (1,j) ∈ construct ∪ construct_assoc
    R_{1,j} = rename(C_{1,j}, acc_var_subst)
for i = 1 to n
    B_{2,i} = rename_goal(C_{2,i}, head_to_call)
for each (1,j) ∈ assoc ∪ construct ∪ construct_assoc
    B_{1,j} = rename_goal(C_{1,j}, acc_var_subst)

Acc = rename_vars(init_accs, acc_var_subst)
let R_assoc be the sequence R_{1,j} where (1,j) ∈ assoc
let R_construct be the sequence R_{1,j} where (1,j) ∈ construct ∪ construct_assoc
let B_after be the sequence B_{1,j} where
    (1,j) ∈ assoc ∪ construct ∪ construct_assoc

define p_acc as
    p_acc(Inv, In, Out, Acc) :-
        switch(
            ⟨C_before, R_assoc, rec_call, R_construct⟩,
            ⟨B_{2,1} ... B_{2,n}, B_after⟩
        ).
```

Fig. 3. The third stage

The final result of the algorithm is these two definitions:

```
mirror(L, M) :-
    ( % switch on L
        L => [H | T],
        Empty <= [],
        ListH <= [H | Empty],
        mirror_acc(T, M, ListH, H)
    ;
        L => [],
        M <= []
    ).

mirror_acc(L, M, A_ListH, A_H) :-
    ( % switch on L
        L => [H | T],
        Empty <= [],
        ListH <= [H | Empty],
        append(ListH, A_ListH, NewListH),
        mirror_acc(T, M1, NewListH, H),
        M <= [A_H | M1]
    ;
        L => [],
        M0 <= [],
        append(M0, A_ListH, M1),
        M <= [A_H | M1]
    ).
```

3   Last Call Modulo Constructors Optimization

If a predicate that would be tail recursive in Prolog is not tail recursive in Mercury, the reason is usually that the current Mercury implementation returns all output arguments of a call in registers. If an output argument needs to be placed somewhere in memory, this must be done after returning from the call.

For example, consider the recursive clause of append(in, in, out):

```
append(A, B, C) :-
    A = [H | T],
    C = [H | NT],
    append(T, B, NT).
```

In Prolog, *last call optimization* [1] would ensure that this clause is tail-recursive. In Mercury, however, the recursive call to append would return NT in a register which then needs to be copied into the correct memory location (i.e. the second argument of the cons cell). Actually, with the current release of Mercury, the situation is even worse. The mode checker does not allow constructions of partially-instantiated data structures. This means that the mode checker will actually delay the entire construction unification C = [H | NT] until after the recursive call.

Somogyi, Henderson and Conway [13] briefly outline a solution to these problems: reorder the code so that the construction unifications come before the call, then create a new version of the called predicate which returns the relevant arguments in memory and pass it the addresses in which to place the results.

We have taken this outline and used it as the basis for a new optimization pass in the Mercury compiler which we call the *last call modulo constructors* optimization (LCMC).[1] Before describing the optimization itself we describe changes that were required to the mode system, code generator and abstract machine to support it.

3.1   Mode System, Abstract Machine, and Code Generation

We start with a brief overview of the mode system as implemented in the Melbourne Mercury Compiler, release 0.9 [16]. The instantiation state (*inst*) of a variable is one of the following:

free
: A variable having instantiation state free is an unbound variable with no aliases (i.e. the variable is not constrained to be part of another data structure).

ground(uniqueness)
: A variable having instantiation state ground(uniqueness) is bound to a ground term whose structure is unknown. The uniqueness field describes the number of references to the variable.

bound(uniqueness, functors)
: A variable having instantiation state bound(uniqueness, functors) is bound to a term whose top-level functor is in the set functors. The functors field contains, for each possible functor that the variable may be bound to, the name of the functor and the instantiation states of its arguments.

any(uniqueness)
: A variable having instantiation state any(uniqueness) is a constrained variable.

not_reached
: A variable having instantiation state not_reached is an output from a goal that cannot succeed.

defined_inst(inst_name)
: A variable having instantiation state defined_inst(inst_name) has a named instantiation state which may be looked up in the *inst table* for the procedure. This is used for describing recursive insts.

The *mode* of a predicate argument is a mapping from its initial inst to its final inst. The two most common argument modes, ground -> ground and free -> ground, are abbreviated in and out, respectively.

The *instmap* data structure maps variables to insts. Mode analysis uses abstract interpretation to determine the instmap at each point in a goal and stores the changes to the instmap across a goal in an *instmap delta*. Mode analysis

---

[1] This term comes from a similar idea described by Wadler [17] which he calls *tail recursion modulo cons*.

also schedules the goals within a conjunction, re-ordering them if necessary, and selects which mode to use for each predicate call.

Mercury's mode system requires that precise information about the insts of all variables be known at all points in the execution of a goal. Use of partially instantiated data structures, which is required for LCMC, creates aliasing between variables which we need to keep track of if we are to determine how further instantiation of one variable affects the variables to which it is aliased.

Andrew Bromage has recently extended the mode system to allow the tracking of definite aliases. He introduces a new kind of inst, `alias(inst_key)`, where two variables are definitely aliased iff their insts are both `alias` specifying the same `inst_key`. The actual inst of the variables is determined by looking up the current instantiation of the `inst_key` in an *inst key table*.

At the abstract machine level, a variable whose instantiation after expansion of aliases is `ground` or `bound` is represented by a word containing its value, while a variable whose inst is `free` is represented by an uninitialized word. This is not sufficient for our needs. We have therefore added a new basic inst, `free_alias`, which is similar to `free` except that a variable whose inst is `free_alias` is represented by a word that contains the address where its value will be placed when the variable is instantiated.

During mode analysis, uninstantiated parts of a partially instantiated data structure have the inst `free_alias` rather than `free`. In most places during mode analysis, `free` and `free_alias` insts are treated the same. The exception to this is in the unification of two free variables. While it is still a mode error to attempt to unify two `free` variables, as in previous versions of Mercury, two variables whose insts are `free` and `free_alias` may now be unified; after the unification, both will have the inst `free_alias`. We do not allow the unification of two variables whose insts are both `free_alias`. This is because this would require a `free_alias` variable to record the address of more than one memory location to be filled in when the variable is instantiated. While this could be implemented, using either terminated pointer chains as in the WAM [1], or circular pointer chains as in PARMA [15], the overhead required is very likely to outweigh the benefits gained by LCMC. (Note that the PARMA scheme has actually been implemented for Mercury by the HAL project [10].)

An argument of a procedure whose mode is `free_alias -> ground` will be passed by reference. The code generator will reserve an input register for this argument, and it will place the address of the memory location to be filled in in this register before calling the procedure. When a variable whose inst is `free_alias` is bound, the code generator emits code to place its value in the memory location that the representation of the `free_alias` variable points to.

3.2 The LCMC Transformation

The LCMC optimization itself is a very simple transformation. The LCMC pass occurs after other passes that may increase the chances of being able to apply LCMC. These include simplification, inlining and accumulator introduction. At this stage, mode analysis has selected an initial scheduling order for each procedure which avoids construction of partially instantiated terms.

LCMC traverses the goal for each procedure in turn. A procedure is determined to be a candidate for LCMC if any path through the goal contains a final conjunction where the last call in the conjunction is followed only by construction unifications. The algorithm used is described more formally in Figure 4.

Procedure: LCMC()
Input: G_{in}, the goal of the procedure to be transformed
Output: G_{out}, the transformed goal

if
    G_{in} is a disjunction of sub-goals, $disj(G_1, \ldots, G_n)$
then
    $G_{out} = disj(\text{LCMC}(G_1), \ldots, \text{LCMC}(G_n))$
else if
    G_{in} is a switch of sub-goals, $switch(G_1, \ldots, G_n)$
then
    $G_{out} = switch(\text{LCMC}(G_1), \ldots, \text{LCMC}(G_n))$
else if
    G_{in} is an if-then-else, $ite(G_C, G_T, G_E)$, with condition G_C,
    then goal G_T, and else goal G_E
then
    $G_{out} = ite(G_C, \text{LCMC}(G_T), \text{LCMC}(G_E))$
else if
    G_{in} is a conjunction of sub-goals, $conj(G_1, \ldots, G_n)$
then
    if
        $\exists k.\ 1 < k < n \wedge G_k$ is a call
        $\wedge\ \forall i.\ k < i \leq n \Rightarrow G_i$ is a construction unification
    then
        let $G_{PBR} = \text{PBR}(G_k, \langle G_{k+1}, \ldots, G_n \rangle)$
        $G_{out} = conj(G_1, \ldots, G_{k-1}, G_{k+1}, \ldots, G_n, G_{PBR})$
    else
        $G_{out} = conj(G_1, \ldots, G_{n-1}, \text{LCMC}(G_n))$
else
    $G_{out} = G_{in}$

Fig. 4. The LCMC transformation

For all conjunctions where LCMC can be applied, the conjunction is re-ordered so that the constructions appear before the call. Now the required mode for the called predicate will be different from the previously-determined mode. The PBR() procedure in Figure 5 determines which output arguments of the call become pass-by-reference. These arguments will have an initial instantiation of free_alias rather than free. LCMC tries to find an existing procedure of the called predicate that matches the mode required. If found, the call is replaced by a call to this procedure. If it is not found, it will need to be created. This is done by taking a copy of the existing procedure and changing the modes of its arguments. The new procedure then has LCMC run on it. If the called predicate is the same as the calling predicate, this will result in a tail-recursive procedure.

After running LCMC on a procedure, it is mode checked to update the inst-map deltas and to ensure that it is mode correct. This includes checking that there are no unifications involving two free_alias insts.

Procedure: PBR()

Input: G_{in}, a call goal, $call(P, V, M)$
              where P is the predicate being called,
              $V = \langle V_1, \ldots, V_k \rangle$ the argument variables of the call,
              $M = \langle M_1, \ldots, M_k \rangle$ the modes of the arguments,
              and k the arity of P.
          $\langle G_1, \ldots, G_n \rangle$, a sequence of construction unification goals

Output: G_{out}, a goal which calls a new pass-by-reference procedure

for $i = 1$ to k
do
    if
        $\exists I. \ M_i = \mathtt{free} \ \verb|->| \ I$
        $\wedge \ (I = \mathtt{ground} \vee I = \mathtt{bound(\_, \_)})$
        $\wedge \ V_i$ appears on the right hand side of one of the
            construction unifications $G_1, \ldots, G_n$
    then
        $M_i' = \mathtt{free\_alias} \ \verb|->| \ I$
    else
        $M_i' = M_i$
done
$M' = \langle M_1', \ldots, M_k' \rangle$
$G_{out} = call(P, V, M')$

Fig. 5. The PBR procedure

Let us look at how the transformation is applied to the procedure `append(in, in, out)` which we will refer to as mode 0 of the predicate `append/3`. The HLDS representation for this procedure, before LCMC, is shown below. The comments show the change in instantiation state of the variables after each sub-goal (the uniqueness field is left out since it is not relevant to LCMC).

```
% mode 0 of append/3
:- mode append(in, in, out).

append(Xs, Ys, Zs) :-
    % Initial insts: Xs -> ground, Ys -> ground, Zs -> free
    (
        Xs => [],
        Zs := Ys                % Zs -> ground
    ;
        Xs => [X | Xs1],        % X -> ground, Xs1 -> ground
        append(Xs1, Ys, Zs0),   % call mode 0 of append/3
                                % Zs0 -> ground
        Zs <= [X | Zs0]         % Zs -> bound([ground | ground])
    ).                          % Zs -> ground
```

LCMC discovers that in the second arm of the switch, construction of Zs can be moved before the recursive call. Zs0 now has an inst of `free_alias` before the call so LCMC tries to find a mode of `append/3` that matches this inst. The required mode is not found so it is created (mode 1) by copying mode 0 and changing the initial inst of Zs. At this stage, the HLDS for mode 0 is:

```
% mode 0 of append/3
:- mode append(in, in, out).

append(Xs, Ys, Zs) :-
    % Initial insts: Xs -> ground, Ys -> ground, Zs -> free
    (
        Xs => [],
        Zs := Ys                 % Zs -> ground
    ;
        Xs => [X | Xs1]          % X -> ground,  Xs1 -> ground
        Zs <= [X | Zs0]          % Zs -> bound([ground | alias(IK0)])
                                 % Zs0 -> alias(IK0)
                                 % IK0 -> free_alias
        append(Xs1, Ys, Zs0)     % call mode 1 of append/3
                                 % Zs -> bound([ground | alias(IK1)])
                                 % Zs0 -> alias(IK1)
                                 % IK1 -> ground
    ).                           % Zs -> ground
```

LCMC is now run on the new procedure, mode 1. When it re-orders the call and construction it finds that an appropriate mode of append/3 already exists (i.e. mode 1). The HLDS for mode 1 looks the same as mode 0 except that the mode of the third argument is free_alias -> ground rather than out (free -> ground).

Finally, we show the C code generated by the compiler for the tail recursive mode 1 of append. (We have made the code more readable by e.g. shortening label names and removing type casts.) The arguments Xs, Ys and Zs are passed in registers r1, r2 and r3, respectively.

```
/* code for predicate 'append'/3 in mode 1 */
Define_static(append_3_1);
    if (r1 == mkword(mktag(0), mkbody(0)))
        GOTO_LABEL(append_3_1_i2);
Define_label(append_3_1_i4);
    tag_incr_hp(r4, mktag(1), 2);
    field(mktag(1), r4, 0) = field(mktag(1), r1, 0);
    *r3 = r4;
    r3 = &field(mktag(1), r4, 1);
    r1 = field(mktag(1), r1, 1);
    if (r1 != mkword(mktag(0), mkbody(0)))
        GOTO_LABEL(append_3_1_i4);
Define_label(append_3_1_i2);
    *r3 = r2;
    proceed();
```

The code first checks whether Xs (in r1) is the empty list, and branches to label append_3_1_i2 if it is. If it is not, it falls through to the code for the recursive

212 P. Ross, D. Overton, and Z. Somogyi

case. This allocates a new two-word cell on the heap, and places a pointer to this cell tagged with the tag value for cons (1), which represents the value of Zs, in r4. It places the value of the Zs where the caller expects it, which is the memory location whose address the caller passed in r3. It fills in the first word of the new cell with X, and puts the address of the second into r3, to tell the recursive call where to put the value of Zs0. Extracting Xs1 from the second field of the cons cell of Xs and putting it into r1 completes the setup for the recursive call, since Ys is already in r2. The recursive call is an unconditional jump to the start of the procedure, which low-level optimizations in the Mercury compiler turn into the conditional jump to the start of the recursive case, as shown above. The code of the base case implements the assignment Zs := Ys by copying Ys to where the caller expects Zs.

The LCMC optimization does not guarantee a tail call in every procedure it transforms. The transformed call will be a tail call if and only if it returns exactly the same sequence of outputs in exactly the same locations as its containing procedure. If it does not, the call must be followed by code that places the output arguments of the containing procedure in their proper places. In such cases, the optimization may still be useful as it may allow a tail call somewhere in the new pass-by-reference procedure by reducing the number of output registers of the procedure. This is seen in the append example where the call from mode 0 to mode 1 is not a tail call because mode 0 needs to save the value of Zs on the stack across the call and then place it in a register before it returns. However, the recursive call from mode 1 to itself is tail recursive because it can place Zs in the required location in memory as soon as it is constructed, so there is nothing that needs to be done after the recursive call.

Since the compiler runs LCMC recursively on each new procedure at the point where it is created, we can check whether the optimization is actually going to give us a tail call somewhere in the new procedure and, if not, abandon the optimization for this procedure.

The overall effect is that although our optimization does not depend on the last call being a recursive call, the last call will be a recursive call in most of the situations in which our optimization can be usefully applied.

The mirror_acc/4 predicate that was created by the transformation in section 2 can also be transformed into tail recursive form by the LCMC transformation. Thus, the original mirror/2 predicate, which could not be made tail recursive by either optimization by itself, can be made tail recursive by combining the two optimizations.

4   Results

To measure the effectiveness of our optimizations, we benchmarked a set of small programs on a PC with 450 MHz Intel PIII CPU, 512 KB of L2 cache, 256 MB of memory, running Linux 2.2.12. The benchmark programs all process lists, and they were tested with their input being a list of 30 integers. Their executions were repeated several thousand times to eliminate the uncertainties involved in measuring small time intervals. The results are presented in the following table in the form of normalized runtimes; the raw data is available from our web site.

The table shows two sets of results: without and with garbage collection. Within each set, the columns show performance without either of the optimizations we presented in this paper, with just LCMC, with just accumulator introduction, and with both. In all four cases, all the other optimizations of the Mercury compiler were turned on with the exception of unused argument elimination, because unused argument elimination makes relating a call back to a promise using that call difficult. (We intend to move unused argument elimination after the tail recursion optimizations, but this requires first modifying its implementation to accept the modes produced by LCMC.)

Table 1. Normalised Benchmark Results

	without gc				with gc			
	None	LCMC	Acc	Both	None	LCMC	Acc	Both
append	100.0	90.4	100.0	90.7	100.0	97.6	99.4	97.7
sumlist	100.0	99.9	80.3	80.2	100.0	99.9	79.2	79.2
nrev	100.0	74.1	13.1	13.9	100.0	96.2	12.5	12.5
sumdbl	100.0	99.9	99.9	90.0	100.0	99.2	99.2	98.6
mirror	100.0	72.9	100.0	10.3	100.0	95.7	99.2	9.5

As is to be expected, `append` and `sumlist` only achieve a speed increase when the correct optimization is enabled. Naive reverse (`nrev`) benefits from both optimizations. LCMC makes the call to `append` tail recursive, which improves the performance of its caller `nrev`. Accumulator introduction allows a speed increase by reducing the big-O complexity of the algorithm (effectively turning it into non-naive reverse) and by making the `nrev` predicate tail recursive. However turning on LCMC after turning on accumulator introduction on slows the code down slightly because in the accumulator version of nrev, the first argument of append is always a list of length one, and the fixed overhead of the LCMC transformation thus cannot be compensated for by LCMC making `append` tail recursive. The predicate `sumdbl`, which in one traversal both sums a list of integers and returns another list which has each element doubled is a case where you don't get any significant speedups unless both optimizations are turned on. (Such predicates can be expected to be produced by deforestation.) The predicate `mirror` from section 2.1 also requires both optimizations to turned on for it to become tail recursive. However, mirror can also benefit from LCMC alone because of its use of `append`.

At the moment, Mercury uses the Boehm conservative garbage collector for C [4]. Using this collector requires a function call on every memory allocation, whereas in the no-gc case, Mercury allocates memory by simply incrementing the heap pointer. (The Boehm collector also lacks provision for efficiently recovering memory without garbage collection, e.g. between different repetitions of the same test.) Since memory allocation accounts for a bigger fraction of the runtime of the program with gc than without gc, we get smaller relative speedups with gc than with without gc for optimizations that do not eliminate memory allocations themselves. LCMC cannot eliminate memory allocations. Accumulator introduction can eliminate memory allocations, and will do so whenever it reduces the big-O complexity of a predicate that allocates memory every iteration. The nrev and mirror predicates both benefit from this effect.

5 Related Work

As stated earlier the accumulator introduction transformation was based on Debray's work [8]. However Debray only showed how the transformation works with predicates which have the additional property of commutativity. Thus there is no need for the associative call to have its arguments rearranged, nor the introduction of the heuristic to ensure the big O complexity never increases. Brough and Hogger [5] allude to transformation not necessarily improving the efficiency, but only state that applicability of the transform should be related to the knowledge of the calling modes of each predicate.

The other significant facet of the accumulator introduction transformation is the possibility of leaving a predicate in a state which doesn't make the predicate tail recursive but allows the LCMC optimization to be applied.

Optimizations similar to LCMC have often been suggested in the literature of both functional [17] and logic [13] programming. Most of these suggestions have not been implemented. The major exceptions are Prolog systems in which the issues involved in implementing LCMC are completely different.

One paper we know of which addresses the issue in the context of a moded logic programming language is Bigot and Debray [2]. They describe an algorithm for deciding when to return output values in registers and when to return them in memory. However, their technique requires profiling information (the number of times each procedure is called from each one of its call sites) which the Mercury profiler cannot yet supply, and in any case, their algorithm would require significant extensions to handle separate compilation. Our implementation of LCMC probably captures most of the benefit with much less implementation complexity.

6 Conclusion

We have presented two optimizations that can improve the operational efficiency of a program. The optimizations are applicable when only independent associative goals and/or construction unifications occur after the recursive call. Both optimizations can be automatically applied and have been implemented in the Melbourne Mercury compiler. We have also shown that both optimizations can be combined to optimize a program which neither optimization would optimize by itself.

The accumulator introduction optimization is included with the current stable release, Mercury 0.9. The LCMC optimization is implemented on a separate branch of the compiler source tree which contains the alias tracking analysis which is still in an experimental stage. The source code is available upon request.

We thank the anonymous referees for their valuable comments, the attendees at the LOPSTR conference for their stimulating discussions, and the Australian Research Council for their support.

References

[1] Hassan Aït-Kaci *Warren's Abstract Machine: A Tutorial Reconstruction.* MIT Press, 1991.

[2] Peter A. Bigot and Saumya Debray. Return value placement and tail call optimization in high level languages. *Journal of Logic Programming*, 38(1):1–29, January 1999.

[3] Charlene Bloch. Source-to-source transformation of logic programs. Master's thesis, Weizmann Institue of Science, November 1984.

[4] Hans-Juergen Boehm. Dynamic memory allocation and garbage collection. *Computers in Physics*, 9(3):297–303, May/June 1995.

[5] D. R. Brough and C. J. Hogger. Compiling associativity into logic programs. *Journal of Logic Programming*, 4(4):345–359, December 1987.

[6] D. R. Brough and C. J. Hogger. Grammar-related transformations of logic programs. *New Generation Computing*, 9:115–134, 1991.

[7] Halime Büyükyildiz and Pierre Flener. Generalised logic program transformation schemas. In N.E. Fuchs, editor, *Proceedings of the Seventh International Workshop on Logic Program Synthesis and Transformation*, pages 45–65, 1997.

[8] Saumya K. Debray. Optimizing almost-tail-recursive Prolog programs. In *Proceedings of the International Symposium on Functional Programming Languages and Computer Architecture*, pages 204–219, 1985.

[9] Saumya K. Debray. Unfold/fold transformations and loop optimization of logic programs. In *Proceedings of the ACM SIGPLAN Conference on Programming Language Design and Implementation*, pages 297–307, 1988.

[10] Bart Demoen, Maria Garcia de la Banda, Warwick Harvey, Kim Marriott, and Peter J. Stuckey. Herbrand constraint solving in HAL. In *Proceedings of the Sixteenth International Conference on Logic Programming*, pages 260–274, 1999.

[11] Fergus Henderson, Thomas Conway, Zoltan Somogyi, and David Jeffery. The Mercury language reference manual. Technical Report 96/10, Department of Computer Science, University of Melbourne, Australia, 1996.

[12] A. Pettorossi and M. Proietti. Transformation of logic programs: Foundations and techniques. *Journal of Logic Programming*, 19,20:261–320, 1994.

[13] Zoltan Somogyi, Fergus Henderson, and Thomas Conway. The execution algorithm of Mercury: an efficient purely declarative logic programming language. *Journal of Logic Programming*, 29(1–3):17–64, 1996.

[14] Chris Speirs, Zoltan Somogyi, and Harald Søndergaard. Termination analysis for Mercury. In *Proceedings of the Fourth International Static Analysis Symposium*, pages 157–171, 1997.

[15] Andrew Taylor. *High Performance Prolog Implementation.* PhD thesis, University of Sydney, 1991.

[16] Mercury Team. Mercury 0.9. Available from http://www.cs.mu.oz.au/mercury/, December 1999.

[17] P. Wadler. Listlessness is better than laziness: Lazy evaluation and garbage collection at compile-time. In *Proceedings of ACM Symposium on Lisp and Functional Programming*, pages 45–52, 1984.

The Replacement Operation for CCP Programs

Marco Bertolino[1], Sandro Etalle[2], and Catuscia Palamidessi[3]

[1] S.I.A.C. bertolino@siac.it
[2] Universiteit Maastricht ealle@cs.unimaas.nl
[3] Penn State University catuscia@cse.psu.edu

Abstract. The *replacement* is a very powerful transformation operation which – both within the functional paradigm as well as within the logic programming one – can mimic the most common transformation operations such as unfold, fold, switching, distribution. Because of this flexibility, it can be incorrect if used without specific applicability conditions.

In this paper we present applicability conditions which ensure the correctness of the replacement operation in the context of Concurrent Constraint Programs. Furthermore we show that, under these conditions, the replacement generalizes both the unfolding operation as well as a restricted form of folding operation.

1 Introduction

Concurrent constraint programming ([26]) (ccp, for short) is a concurrent programming paradigm which derives from replacing the *store-as-valuation* concept of von Neumann computing by the *store-as-constraint* model. The computational model of ccp is based on a global *store*, represented by a constraint, which expresses some partial information on the values of the variables involved in the computation. The concurrent execution of different processes, which interact through the common store, refines the partial information of the values of the variables by adding (*telling*) constraints to the store. Communication and synchronization are achieved by allowing processes to test (*ask*) if the store entails a constraint before proceeding in the computation.

Central to the development of large and efficient applications is the study of optimization techniques. To this end, while there exists a history and a wide literature on transformations for sequential languages, ranging from theoretical studies to implemented tools, there are only few and relatively recent attempts to apply these techniques to concurrent languages. To the best of our knowledge, the only papers addressing this issue are [10,11,29,23,14,17,13,9]. In our opinion, this situation can be ascribed to the non-determinism and the synchronization mechanisms present in concurrent languages, which substantially complicate their semantics. In this context, transformation techniques have to employ more sophisticated analysis tools.

The area closest to ccp with a large literature on transformation operations is the area of Constraint Logic Programs (CLP). For this paradigm, the literature

A. Bossi (Ed.): LOPSTR'99, LNCS 1817, pp. 216–233, 2000.

on transformations can be divided into two main branches. On one hand we find methods which focus exclusively on the manipulation of the constraint for compile-time [18,19] and for low-level local optimization [15]. On the other hand there are techniques such as the unfold/fold transformation systems, which were developed initially for Logic Programs [28] and then applied to CLP [16,1,8] and to ccp in [9]. These ones focus primarily on the declarative side of the program.

The *Replacement* is a program transformation technique flexible enough to encompass both the above kinds of optimization: it can be profitably used to manipulate both the constraint and the "declarative" side of a program. In fact the replacement operation, which was introduced in the field of Logic Programming by Tamaki and Sato [28] and later further developed and applied to CLP in [16,1,7], syntactically consists in replacing an agent in the body of a program definition by another one. It is therefore a very general operation and it is able to mimic many other transformations, such as thinning, fattening [3] and folding. In the logic programming area, a lot of research [4,5,1,6,7,12,16,22,28,27] has been devoted to the definition of *applicability conditions* sufficient to guarantee the correctness of replacement w.r.t. several different semantics. See [21] for a survey on transformation techniques for logic languages.

The goal of this paper is to provide some natural and relatively simple applicability conditions which ensure the correctness of the replacement for ccp, i.e. that the transformed program is equivalent to the original one. Of course, the notion of equivalence depends on the semantics one refers to. In the case of ccp programs the notion of semantics usually considered is the set of final stores, i.e. the stores that can be obtained at the end of a computation (we say that a computation ends when it cannot proceed anymore). These are often called "observables". Sometimes also the stores obtained as limit of the intermediate stores in an infinite computation are considered part of the observables, but in this paper we will not take them into account. In this paper we will actually consider a stronger semantics, namely *simulation equivalence*, or *reciprocal simulation*. The reason for this choice is that observables-equivalence, in a concurrent context, is too weak for ensuring the correctness of transformation techniques such as the replacement. Basically this is due to lack of compositionality. When replacing an agent A with A' we will require that the two agents be *simulation-equivalent*. Ultimately, what we aim at is a set of conditions which guarantee that the program resulting from the replacement operation is simulation-equivalent to the original one, in which case we say that the operation is *correct*. Since simulation-equivalence implies observables-equivalence, correctness implies that the two programs are also observables-equivalent.

It turns out that the simulation-equivalence of the replacing and the replaced agents alone is not sufficient to guarantee the correctness of the operation. In fact, we will show that it guarantees only *partial* correctness i.e. that the resulting program is simulated by the original one, but not vice-versa. In order to guarantee total correctness we have to ensure that *the replacement must not introduce unwanted loops*. Now, consider for example the contrived program:

$$p(x) \;\text{:-}\; q(x)$$
$$q(x) \;\text{:-}\; (\; ask(x = [\,]) \to \textbf{stop}$$
$$+\; ask(\exists_{y,ys}\; x = [y|ys]) \to \exists_{y,ys}\; tell(x = [y|ys]) \parallel p(ys))$$

Here, $q(x)$ is clearly equivalent to $p(x)$; but if we replace $q(x)$ with $p(x)$ in the body of the first definition we obtain the definition $p(x)$:- $p(x)$, which is certainly not equivalent to the original one.

To avoid unwanted loops, in this paper we follow the inspiration of [4,7,25] (which focus on logic programs, CLP and functional programs, respectively), and we individuate two situations in which the operation certainly does not introduce any unwanted loop: The simplest one is (a): *when the replacing agent is independent from the definition that is going to be transformed*. This is the case in which the definition of the replacing agent does not depend on the definition being transformed.

Clearly, this condition is sufficient to guarantee that no extra loops are introduced by the transformation. For instance, it rules out the situation described above, in which we replaced $q(x)$ with $p(x)$. Moreover, it is immediate to check. The disadvantage is that it clearly does not allow to introduce recursion inside a definition: For instance in the above example we might want to replace $p(ys)$ with $q(ys)$. Notice that this replacement *does* introduce a loop in the form of a direct recursion inside the definition of p. Such a step would be clearly forbidden by the condition (a) above. In order to be able to perform also this second replacement we need an applicability condition alternative to (a). Here we provide such an alternative condition, namely, (b): *when the replacing agent is at least as efficient as the replaced one*. Referring to the simulation semantics this is the case when the following holds: if the replaced agent can compute an "answer" constraint c with a transition sequence which uses n procedure expansions, then the replacing agent can also compute the answer c for the replacing one in m procedure expansions with $m \leq n$. This is undoubtedly a desirable situation which fits well in the natural context in which the transformation is performed in order to increase program's execution speed. Moreover, in the above example we have that $q(ys)$ is equivalent to $p(ys)$ and more efficient than $p(ys)$, because it requires one procedure expansion less to "reach" the same answer. Thus condition (b) is flexible enough to allow the above replacement and therefore to introduce recursion, which can be seen as an example of *wanted* loop.

2   Preliminaries

In this section we briefly recall the definition of ccp. We refer to [26] for more details. The language ccp is parametric w.r.t. a cylindric constraint system $\mathbf{C} = \langle \mathcal{C}, \leq, \wedge, true, false, Var, \exists, \delta \rangle$. Roughly speaking, such system represents a set of logical formulas $\mathcal{C}$ (constraints) closed under conjunction ($\wedge$) and existential quantifier ($\exists$). The relation $\leq \subseteq \mathcal{C} \times \mathcal{C}$ is an ordering relation whose inverse represents the notion of *logical entailment*. *Var*, with typical elements $x, y, \ldots$, is the set of variables which can appear in the constraints. δ is a function from $Var \times Var$ into constraints, which gives *true* on all the pairs of identical variables (diagonal elements). Intuitively, δ_{xy} represents the equality constraint between x and y. In the following, the notation $\tilde{\chi}$ indicates a sequence of the form $\chi_1, \ldots, \chi_n$. The processes are described by the following grammar

$$Processes \ P ::= [D, A]$$
$$Declarations \ D ::= \epsilon \mid p(\tilde{x}) :\text{-} A \mid D, D$$
$$Agents \ A ::= \mathbf{stop} \mid \mathbf{tell}(c) \mid \sum_{i=1}^{n} \mathbf{ask}(c_i) \rightarrow A_i \mid A \parallel A \mid \exists_x A \mid p(\tilde{x})$$

The agent **stop** represents successful termination. The basic actions are given by $\mathbf{ask}(c)$ and $\mathbf{tell}(c)$ constructs, where c is a *finite constraint*, i.e. an algebraic element of C. These actions work on a common *store* which ranges over C. $\mathbf{ask}(c)$ is a test on the current store and its execution does not modify the store. We say that $\mathbf{ask}(c)$ is a *guard* and that is *enabled* in d iff $c \le d$. If d is the current store, then the execution of $\mathbf{tell}(c)$ sets the store to $c \wedge d$. The *guarded choice* agent $\sum_{i=1}^{n} g_i \rightarrow A_i$ selects nondeterministically one g_i which is enabled, and then behaves like A_i. If no guards are enabled, then it *suspends*, waiting for other (parallel) agents to add information to the store. Parallel composition is represented by $\parallel$. The situation in which all components of a system of parallel agents suspend is called *global suspension* or *deadlock*. The agent $\exists_x A$ behaves like A, with x considered *local* to A. Finally, the agent $p(\tilde{x})$ is a procedure call, where p is the name of the procedure and $\tilde{x}$ is the list of the actual parameters. The meaning of $p(\tilde{x})$ is given by a procedure declaration of the form $p(\tilde{y}) :\text{-} A$, where $\tilde{y}$ is the list of the formal parameters. A set of declarations constitutes a *program*.

The operational model of ccp, informally introduced above, is described by a transition system $T = (Conf, \longrightarrow)$, where the set of configurations is defined as $Conf = Processes \times C$. Sometimes we will need to indicate the the number (0 or 1) of procedure expansions taking place during a transition. In that case we will use the notation $\longrightarrow_n$, where n is the number of procedure expansions. Table 1 describes the rules of T.

The guarded choice operator models global non-determinism (**R2**), in the sense that it depends on the current store whether or not a guard is enabled, and the current store is subject to modifications by the external environment (**R1**). **R3** and **R4** describe parallelism as interleaving. To describe locality (**R5**) the syntax has been extended by an agent $\exists_x^d A$ in which x is local to A and d is the store that has been produced locally on x. Initially the local store is empty, i.e. $\exists_x A = \exists_x^{true} A$. The procedure expansion is modeled by **R6**. $\Delta_{\tilde{y}}^{\tilde{x}}$ stands for $\exists_{\tilde{\alpha}}^{\delta_{\tilde{x}\tilde{\alpha}}} \exists_{\tilde{y}}^{\delta_{\tilde{\alpha}\tilde{y}}}$ and it is used to establish the link between the formal parameters $\tilde{y}$ and the actual parameters $\tilde{x}$. The notation $\delta_{x_1,\ldots,x_n \alpha_1,\ldots,\alpha_n}$ represents the conjunction of the constraints $\delta_{x_1\alpha_1}, \ldots, \delta_{x_n\alpha_n}$. The variables $\tilde{\alpha}$ are introduced in order to avoid problems related to name clashes between $\tilde{x}$ and $\tilde{y}$; they are assumed to occur neither in the procedure declaration nor in the procedure call.

Note that in a transition, only the agent part of the process is modified. Namely, if $\langle [D, A], c \rangle \longrightarrow \langle [D', A'], c' \rangle$, then $D' = D$. However, in order to define the notion of simulation, we find it convenient to have the program explicit in the configuration.

Table 1. The transition system T.

R1 $\langle [D, \textbf{tell}(c)], d \rangle \longrightarrow_0 \langle [D, \textbf{stop}], c \wedge d \rangle$

R2 $\langle [D, \sum_{i=1}^n g_i \rightarrow A_i], d \rangle \longrightarrow_0 \langle [D, A_j], d \rangle$ $j \in [1, n]$ and $g_j = \textbf{ask}(c)$ and $c \leq d$

R3 $\dfrac{\langle [D, A], c \rangle \longrightarrow_n \langle [D, A'], c' \rangle}{\langle [D, B \parallel A], c \rangle \longrightarrow_n \langle [D, B \parallel A'], c' \rangle}$

R4 $\dfrac{\langle [D, A], c \rangle \longrightarrow_n \langle [D, A'], c' \rangle}{\langle [D, A \parallel B], c \rangle \longrightarrow_n \langle [D, A' \parallel B], c' \rangle}$

R5 $\dfrac{\langle [D, A], d \wedge \exists_x c \rangle \longrightarrow_n \langle [D, B], d' \rangle}{\langle [D, \exists_x^d A], c \rangle \longrightarrow_n \langle [D, \exists_x^{d'} B], c \wedge \exists_x d' \rangle}$

R6 $\langle [D, p(\tilde{x})], c \rangle \longrightarrow_1 \langle [D, \Delta_{\tilde{y}}^{\tilde{x}} A], c \rangle$ $p(\tilde{y}) :- A \in D$

We describe now what we intend to *observe* about a process. Intuitively, for every possible initial store (input) we want to collect the results (outputs) of all possible finite computations.

Definition 1 (Observables). *Given a process P, we define its* observables *as follows:*

$$\mathcal{O}(P) = \{ \langle c, c' \rangle \mid \text{ there exists } P' \text{ s.t. } \langle P, c \rangle \longrightarrow^* \langle P, c' \rangle \not\longrightarrow \}$$

where $\not\longrightarrow$ denotes the absence of outgoing transitions and $\longrightarrow^*$ denotes the reflexive and transitive closure of $\longrightarrow$. □

In some cases we will need to refer to the number of procedure expansions taking place during a sequence of transitions. We will then use the notation $\longrightarrow_n^*$, where $n \geq 0$ represents such number. Formally:

$$\langle P, c \rangle \longrightarrow_0^* \langle P, c \rangle$$
$$\langle P, c \rangle \longrightarrow_{n+m}^* \langle P', c' \rangle \text{ if } \langle P, c \rangle \longrightarrow_n \langle P'', c'' \rangle \text{ and } \langle P'', c'' \rangle \longrightarrow_m^* \langle P', c' \rangle$$

3   Simulation

In this section we introduce the notion of simulation for ccp programs and agents. This will be the key semantic concept throughout the paper, and will allow us to characterize – among other things – whether a transformation is correct or not.

The main reason why we introduce the notion of simulation is that it has strong properties (like compositionality) that are crucial for proving the correctness of the replacement. Moreover, simulation semantics is correct with respect to the observables.

Our notion of simulation is inspired by the homonymous notion in theory of concurrency, see for instance [30]. In process algebras like CCS simulation equivalence is considered too weak, because it is not correct w.r.t. maximal trace semantics, which is the standard notion of observables. Researchers in concurrency theory usually consider, instead, the stricter notion of *bisimulation* [20]. In the case of ccp, however, the standard notion of observable (final stores) is more abstract, and the asynchronous nature of communication allows us to maintain a more abstract equivalence also when considering the issue of compositionality, in the sense that less information is needed to achieve the closure under contexts. Furthermore, being a weaker relation, simulation has the advantage of allowing us to use transformation rules which are applicable in more cases.

In our definition of simulation for ccp, the main differences w.r.t. the classical notion is that we consider the simulation at the level of the stores rather than of the actions. This is because of the asynchronous nature of ccp communication: the relevant changes during a computations are those made in the store; actions are relevant only for their effect on the store. This is reflected by the definition of the transition system: the transition relation is unlabeled and the configurations contain the store. In CCS, on the contrary, transitions are labeled by actions and there is no concept of store. Another difference is that we impose a condition on terminal configurations: when a process terminates we require that the simulating process eventually terminates as well and produces the same store. We introduce this condition, which has no analogous in the classical notion of simulation, in order to achieve correctness w.r.t. the observables. Finally, we require a simulation to be joint-closed (see below). Again, this condition has no counterpart in CCS, and it is needed here to ensure compositionality.

Definition 2. *A relation* $\mathcal{R} \subseteq \mathrm{Conf} \times \mathrm{Conf}$ *is* joint-closed *iff for every* $d \in \mathcal{C}$ *and every pair* $(\langle Proc, c \rangle, \langle Proc', c' \rangle) \in \mathcal{R}$ *we have that* $(\langle Proc, c \wedge d \rangle, \langle Proc', c' \wedge d \rangle) \in \mathcal{R}$. $\square$

Recall that a *program* is a set of declarations. In the sequel we indicate programs by D, D' etc., and processes by P, P' etc.

Definition 3 (Simulation on agents). *A relation* $\mathcal{S} \subseteq \mathrm{Conf} \times \mathrm{Conf}$ *is a simulation iff it is joint-closed, and for every pair* $(\langle [D_1, A_1], c_1 \rangle, \langle [D_2, A_2], c_2 \rangle)$ *in* $\mathcal{S}$ *the following two conditions hold:*

(i) *If* $\langle [D_1, A_1], c_1 \rangle \longrightarrow \langle [D_1, A'_1], c'_1 \rangle$, *then for some* $A'_2, c'_2, \langle [D_2, A_2], c_2 \rangle \longrightarrow^*$ $\langle [D_2, A'_2], c'_2 \rangle$, $c'_2 \geq c'_1$, *and* $(\langle [D_1, A'_1], c'_1 \rangle, \langle [D_2, A'_2], c'_2 \rangle) \in \mathcal{S}$.
(ii) *If* $\langle [D_1, A_1], c_1 \rangle \not\longrightarrow$, *then for some* $A'_2, \langle [D_2, A_2], c_2 \rangle \longrightarrow^* \langle [D_2, A'_2], c_1 \rangle \not\longrightarrow$. $\square$

As a notational convention, if $(\langle P, c \rangle, \langle P', c' \rangle) \in \mathcal{S}$ for some simulation $\mathcal{S}$, we say that $\langle P', c' \rangle$ *simulates* $\langle P, c \rangle$ and we write $\langle P, c \rangle \trianglelefteq \langle P', c' \rangle$. Furthermore, we say that the process P' *simulates* P, notation $P \trianglelefteq P'$, iff $\langle P, true \rangle \trianglelefteq \langle P', true \rangle$. Note that, by joint-closedness, $P \trianglelefteq P'$ implies that $\langle P, c \rangle \trianglelefteq \langle P', c \rangle$ for every $c \in \mathcal{C}$.

The following proposition states the correctness of simulation w.r.t. the observables:

Proposition 4. *If $P \trianglelefteq P'$, then $\mathcal{O}(P) \subseteq \mathcal{O}(P')$.*

Proof (Sketch) Let $\langle c, d \rangle \in \mathcal{O}(P)$. Then there exist $P_0, P_1, \ldots P_n$ and $c_0, c_1, \ldots c_n$, with $n \geq 0$, such that

$$\langle P, c \rangle = \langle P_0, c_0 \rangle \longrightarrow \langle P_1, c_1 \rangle \longrightarrow \ldots \longrightarrow \langle P_n, c_n \rangle = \langle P_n, d \rangle \not\longrightarrow$$

Since $P \trianglelefteq P'$, one can show by induction on n that there exist $P'_0, P'_1, \ldots P'_n, P'_{n+1}$ and $c'_0, c'_1, \ldots c'_n$ such that $\forall i \in \{1, \ldots, n\}$, $\langle P_i, c_i \rangle \trianglelefteq \langle P'_i, c'_i \rangle$, $c_i \leq c'_i$, and

$$\langle P', c \rangle = \langle P'_0, c'_0 \rangle \longrightarrow^* \langle P'_1, c'_1 \rangle \longrightarrow^* \ldots \longrightarrow^* \langle P'_n, c'_n \rangle \longrightarrow^* \langle P'_{n+1}, d \rangle \not\longrightarrow$$

Hence we have $\langle c, d \rangle \in \mathcal{O}(P')$. $\qquad\qquad\qquad\qquad\qquad\qquad\qquad\qquad\qquad$ □

We extend now the definition of simulation to agents and to programs. The first notion will provide the basis for the correctness of the replacement operation. The second notion will allow expressing a sufficient condition for correctness: when a transformed program is reciprocally similar to the original one, then we can be sure that the transformation is correct.

Definition 5 (Simulation and equivalence on agents and programs).
Let D, D' be two programs, and A, A' be two agents. We say that

- *A' simulates A in D, written $A \trianglelefteq_D A'$, iff $[D, A] \trianglelefteq [D, A']$.*
- *A' is equivalent to A in D iff $A \trianglelefteq_D A'$ and $A' \trianglelefteq_D A$.*
- *D' simulates D, written $D \trianglelefteq D'$, iff for every agent A, $[D, A] \trianglelefteq [D', A]$.*
- *D is equivalent to D' iff $D \trianglelefteq D'$ and $D' \trianglelefteq D$.* □

Example 6. Consider the following programs

$$D : \{\ p(x) :\!\!-\ q(x) \qquad\qquad D' : \{\ p(x) :\!\!-\ tell(x = a) \qquad D'' : \{\ p(x) :\!\!-\ p(x).$$
$$\qquad q(x) :\!\!-\ tell(x = a)\ \} \qquad\quad q(x) :\!\!-\ tell(x = a)\ \} \qquad\quad q(x) :\!\!-\ tell(x = a)\ \}$$

It is straightforward to check that $[D, p(x)]$, $[D, q(x)]$, $[D', p(x)]$, $[D', q(x)]$, $[D''$, $q(x)]$ all simulate each other; moreover, they all also simulate $[D'', p(x)]$, while $[D'', p(x)]$ does not simulate any of them. Consequently, $p(x)$ simulates $q(x)$ in D and in D', but not in D'', while $q(x)$ simulates $p(x)$ in all three programs. Finally, D and D' are equivalent to each other and they both simulate D'', while D'' does not simulate D nor D'. □

Simulation satisfies the following properties.

Proposition 7.

1. *The relations $\trianglelefteq$ (on configurations, processes and programs) and $\trianglelefteq_D$ are reflexive and transitive.*
2. *The simulation between agents is preserved by contexts, that is, if $A \trianglelefteq_D A'$, then $C[A] \trianglelefteq_D C[A']$ for any context $C[\ ]$ (compositionality).* □

Proof

1. Immediate, by reflexivity and transitivity of the entailment relation of the constraint system

2. By case analysis on the various operators. We illustrate here the case of the parallel operator, which is usually the one which causes problems. For the full proof we refer to [2]. Assume that $[D, A] \trianglelefteq [D, A']$. We want to show that for any agent B, $[D, A \parallel B] \trianglelefteq [D, A' \parallel B]$. To this purpose, define

$$\mathcal{S} = \{(\langle [D, B_1 \parallel B], c_1 \rangle, \langle [D, B_2 \parallel B], c_2 \rangle) \mid \langle [D, B_1], c_1 \rangle \trianglelefteq \langle [D, B_2], c_2 \rangle,$$
$$c_1 \leq c_2 \text{ and } B \in Agents\}$$

By definition, $(\langle [D, A \parallel B], true \rangle, \langle [D, A' \parallel B], true \rangle) \in \mathcal{S}$. We show now that $\mathcal{S}$ is a simulation. It is easy to see that $\mathcal{S}$ is joint-closed. Further, let $(\langle [D, B_1 \parallel B], c_1 \rangle, \langle [D, B_2 \parallel B], c_2 \rangle) \in \mathcal{S}$. We need to show that the properties (i) and (ii) of Definition 3 are verified.

(i) Whenever we have a transition from $\langle [D, B_1 \parallel B], c_1 \rangle$, it is either a transition of the form

   a) $\langle [D, B_1 \parallel B], c_1 \rangle \longrightarrow \langle [D, B_1' \parallel B], c_1' \rangle$ (i.e. B_1 makes a step and B is idle), or

   b) $\langle [D, B_1 \parallel B], c_1 \rangle \longrightarrow \langle [D, B_1 \parallel B'], c_1' \rangle$ (i.e. B makes a step and B_1 is idle).

   We consider the two cases separately.

   a) If it is B_1 which makes the step, then we have also $\langle [D, B_1], c_1 \rangle \longrightarrow \langle [D, B_1'], c_1' \rangle$ and, by definition of $\mathcal{S}$, we can derive $\langle [D, B_2], c_2 \rangle \longrightarrow^* \langle [D, B_2'], c_2' \rangle$, with $c_1' \leq c_2'$ and $\langle [D, B_1'], c_1' \rangle \trianglelefteq \langle [D, B_2'], c_2' \rangle$. Consequently we have $\langle [D, B_2 \parallel B], c_2 \rangle \longrightarrow^* \langle [D, B_2' \parallel B], c_2' \rangle$ with $(\langle [D, B_1' \parallel B], c_1' \rangle, \langle [D, B_2' \parallel B], c_2' \rangle) \in \mathcal{S}$ and $c_1' \leq c_2'$.

   b) If it is B which makes the step, then let $c_1' = c_1 \wedge c'$ for some suitable c'. Since $c_1 \leq c_2$, we will also have $\langle [D, B_2 \parallel B], c_2 \rangle \longrightarrow \langle [D, B_2 \parallel B'], c_2' \rangle$ with $c_2' = c_2 \wedge c'$. By the condition of joint-closedness, $\langle [D, B_1'], c_1' \rangle \trianglelefteq \langle [D, B_2'], c_2' \rangle$ holds. Furthermore $c_1' = c_1 \wedge c' \leq c_2 \wedge c' = c_2'$. Hence $(\langle [D, B_1 \parallel B'], c_1' \rangle, \langle [D, B_2 \parallel B'], c_2' \rangle) \in \mathcal{S}$ and $c_1' \leq c_2'$.

(ii) If $\langle [D, B_1 \parallel B], c_1 \rangle \not\longrightarrow$, then $\langle [D, B_1], c_1 \rangle \not\longrightarrow$ and $\langle [D, B], c_1 \rangle \not\longrightarrow$. By definition of $\mathcal{S}$ we have that $\langle [D, B_2], c_2 \rangle \longrightarrow^* \langle [D, B_2'], c_1 \rangle \not\longrightarrow$, from which we derive $\langle [D, B_2 \parallel B], c_2 \rangle \longrightarrow^* \langle [D, B_2' \parallel B], c_1 \rangle \not\longrightarrow$.

4   The Replacement Operation and Its Partial Correctness

Given a program D, the replacement operation consists in replacing a number of agents $\{A_1, \ldots, A_n\}$ with new agents $\{A_1', \ldots, A_n'\}$ in the bodies of some of the definitions of D. Here, what we are looking for are conditions sufficient to ensure that the resulting program is equivalent to D. In this section we make the first step in this direction by showing that if each A_i simulates A_i' (in D) then D simulates the program D' resulting from the transformation. In other words, the transformation is *partially correct*.

As mentioned in Proposition 7, the property of "being simulated by" is carried over through context, therefore when we replace A by A' in the body of the definition $p(x)$:- $C[A]$, we can – without loss of generality – look at it as if we were actually replacing its whole body, i.e. $C[A]$ by $C[A']$. This simplifies the notation of the following result, which is the main point of this section and relates the notion of simulation between agents to the notion of simulation between programs.

Theorem 8 (Partial Correctness). *Consider the following ccp programs*

$$D = \{\, p_i(\tilde{x}_i) \text{ :- } A_i \}_{i \in \{1,\ldots,n\}} \,\cup\, E$$
$$D' = \{\, p_i(\tilde{x}_i) \text{ :- } A'_i \}_{i \in \{1,\ldots,n\}} \,\cup\, E$$

If, for each $i \in \{1,\ldots,n\}$, $A'_i \trianglelefteq_D A_i$ holds, then $D' \trianglelefteq D$ holds.

Proof Let $\mathcal{S}$ be the relation

$$\mathcal{S} = \{(\langle [D',F],c\rangle, \langle [D,H],d\rangle) \mid \langle [D,F],c\rangle \trianglelefteq \langle [D,H],d\rangle\}.$$

In order to prove the thesis it is sufficient to show that $\mathcal{S}$ is a simulation. It is easy to see that $\mathcal{S}$ is joint-closed. We prove now that it satisfies the properties (i) and (ii) of Definition 3.

Let $(\langle [D',F],c\rangle, \langle [D,H],d\rangle)$ be a generic pair in $\mathcal{S}$.

(i) Assume that

$$\langle [D',F],c\rangle \longrightarrow \langle [D',F'],c'\rangle \tag{1}$$

We must prove that there exist H' and d' such that $\langle [D,H],d\rangle \longrightarrow^* \langle [D,H'],d'\rangle$ with $c' \le d'$ and $(\langle [D',F'],c'\rangle, \langle [D,H'],d'\rangle) \in \mathcal{S}$. We consider two cases, depending on whether the transition (1) contains or not a procedure expansion in the part of D' which is different from D.

1. Assume that (1) contains no procedure expansions, or else they are confined to the E part of D'. In this case the same transition can take place also in D, i.e. we have $\langle [D,F],c\rangle \longrightarrow \langle [D,F'],c'\rangle$. By definition of $\mathcal{S}$ we know that $\langle [D,F],c\rangle \trianglelefteq \langle [D,H],d\rangle$. Hence there exist H', d' such that $\langle [P,H],d\rangle \longrightarrow^* \langle [D,H'],d'\rangle$ with $c' \le d'$ and $\langle [D,F'],c'\rangle \trianglelefteq \langle [D,H'],d'\rangle$. By definition of $\mathcal{S}$, we have $(\langle [D',F'],c'\rangle, \langle [D,H'],d'\rangle) \in \mathcal{S}$.

2. Assume now that (1) contains a procedure expansion in the subset $\{\, p_i(\tilde{x}_i) \text{ :- } A'_i \}_{i \in \{1,\ldots,n\}}$ of D'. Then F must have the form $C[\, p_i(\tilde{y})\,]$ where $C[\,]$ is some context and $i \in \{1,\ldots,n\}$. Hence $F' = C[\Delta_{\tilde{x}}^{\tilde{y}} A'_i]$ and $c' = c$. If we consider the corresponding procedure expansion in D, we have $\langle [D,F],c\rangle \longrightarrow \langle [D,G],c\rangle$, where Let $G = C[\Delta_{\tilde{x}}^{\tilde{y}} A_i]$. Since $A'_i \trianglelefteq_D A_i$, by Proposition 7 we have that $\langle [D,F'],c\rangle \trianglelefteq \langle [D,G],c\rangle$. Finally, by definition of $\mathcal{S}$, we have $\langle [D,F],c\rangle \trianglelefteq \langle [D,H],d\rangle$. Hence there exists H' and d' such that $\langle [D,H],d\rangle \longrightarrow^* \langle [D,H'],d'\rangle$ with $c \le d'$ and $\langle [D,G],c\rangle \trianglelefteq \langle [D,H'],d'\rangle$. By transitivity of $\trianglelefteq$, we deduce that $\langle [D,F'],c\rangle \trianglelefteq \langle [D,H'],d'\rangle$, which implies $(\langle [D',F'],c\rangle, \langle [D,H'],d'\rangle) \in \mathcal{S}$.

(ii) Assume that $\langle [D', F], c \rangle \not\longmapsto$. Then $\langle [D, F], c \rangle \not\longmapsto$ as well. By definition of $\mathcal{S}$ we have $\langle [D, F], c \rangle \trianglelefteq \langle [D, H], d \rangle$. Hence there exists H' such that $\langle [D, H], d \rangle \longrightarrow^* \langle [D, H'], c \rangle \not\longmapsto$.   □

Theorem 8 ensures that if the replacing agents are simulated by the replaced ones then the resulting program is simulated by the original one, i.e. the transformation is *partially* correct. In order to achieve *total correctness* we also have to find conditions which ensure that the resulting program simulates the original one. For this purpose, it would be nice if the converse of the above result would hold, namely, if $A_i \trianglelefteq_D A_i'$ would imply $D \trianglelefteq D'$. Unfortunately this is not the case: Consider again the programs in Example 6, recall that $p(x)$ simulates and is simulated by $q(x)$ in D. Now notice that D'' is the result of replacing $q(x)$ by $p(x)$ in the body of the first definition of D. The fact that D'' is simulated by D, but does not simulate D, shows that the converse of the above theorem does not hold. Hence, in order to obtain applicability conditions for the total correctness of the replacement operation we have to devise new additional tools.

5   Total Correctness by Independence

Example 6 shows a case of program transformation (from D to D'') in which total correctness is not achieved. If we look at the details of the transformation, we note that the replacement of $q(x)$ by $p(x)$ introduces a loop in the program. As we mentioned in the introduction, ensuring that no unwanted loops are brought into the program is the crucial point of ensuring total correctness. In fact, the easiest way to ensure total correctness for the transformation is to require that the definition of the replacing agents does not *depend on* the definitions that are about to be transformed. To formalize this concept, we introduce the following definition.

Definition 9 (Dependency). *Let D be a program, and p and q be predicate symbols. We say that* p *refers to* q *in D if there is a a definition in D with p in the head and q in the body. We say that* p *depends on* q *in D if (p, q) is in the reflexive and transitive closure of the relation* refers to. *Finally, we say that an agent A depends on p if in A occurs a predicate which depends on p.*   □

We can now state our first result on total correctness. Because of space reasons, for its proof we refer to [2].

Theorem 10 (Total Correctness 1). *Consider the following ccp programs*

$$D = \{\, p_i(\tilde{x}_i) :\!- A_i \}_{i \in \{1,\dots,n\}} \cup E$$
$$D' = \{\, p_i(\tilde{x}_i) :\!- A_i' \}_{i \in \{1,\dots,n\}} \cup E$$

If, for each $i \in \{1 \dots n\}$, the following two conditions hold:

(1) A_i is equivalent to A_i' in D,
(2) for every $j \in \{1, \dots, n\}$, A_i' does not depend on p_j.

then D is equivalent to D'.   □

In other words, if condition (2) is satisfied, then the converse of Theorem 8 holds. Condition (2) corresponds to the condition (a) mentioned in the introduction, and it ensures, syntactically, that no loops are introduced by the transformation. This confirms our claim that, as long as the replacing agents are equivalent to the replaced ones, if the transformation is not correct then it is only because of the introduction of some unwanted loop.

6 Total Correctness by Improvements

In this section we propose a second method for guaranteeing that no unwanted loops are introduced. While the one seen in Theorem 10 is syntactic (based on Condition (2)), the one we propose here is based on the semantics, and formalizes the requirement (b) mentioned in the introduction. The resulting approach is more complex than the one based on Theorem 10 but it is often more useful for program optimization. The crucial concept here is the one of *improving simulation*, which is a notion of simulation between agents that takes into account the number of procedure expansions in the transitions.

Definition 11 (Improving simulation on configurations). *A relation $S \subseteq$ Conf $\times$ Conf is an improving simulation iff it joint-closed and for every pair $(\langle [D_1, A_1], c_1 \rangle, \langle [D_2, A_2], c_2 \rangle) \in S$ the following two conditions hold:*

(i) *If $\langle [D_1, A_1], c_1 \rangle \longrightarrow_{n_1} \langle [D_1, A_1'], c_1' \rangle$ then for some $A_2', c_2', n_2, \langle [D_2, A_2], c_2 \rangle \longrightarrow_{n_2}^{*}$*
    $\langle [D_2, A_2'], c_2' \rangle$, $n_1 \geq n_2$, $c_1' \leq c_2'$, and $(\langle [D_1, A_1'], c_1' \rangle, \langle [D_2, A_2'], c_2' \rangle) \in S$.
(ii) *If $\langle [D_1, A_1], c_1 \rangle \not\longrightarrow$, then for some $A_2', \langle [D_2, A_2], c_2 \rangle \longrightarrow_0^{*} \langle [D_2, A_2'], c_1 \rangle \not\longrightarrow$.*
$\hfill\square$

As a notational convention, if $(\langle P, c \rangle, \langle P', c' \rangle) \in S$ for some improving simulation S, then we say that $\langle P', c' \rangle$ *improves on* $\langle P, c \rangle$ and we write $\langle P, c \rangle \preceq \langle P', c' \rangle$. Again, we further say that the process P' *improves on* the process P ($P \preceq P'$) iff $\langle P, true \rangle \preceq \langle P', true \rangle$.

Now, in order to present the other results concerning the total correctness of the replacement operation, we need to extend the concept of improving simulation to agents and programs.

Definition 12 (Improvement relation on agents and programs). *Let D, D' be two programs, and let A, A' be two agents. We say that:*

- *A' improves on A in D, written $A \preceq_D A'$, iff $[D, A] \preceq [D, A']$.*
- *D' improves on D iff, for every agent A, $[D, A] \preceq [D', A]$.*
$\hfill\square$

The relation of improvement is strictly more restrictive than the one of simulation: if an agent (resp. process, program) *improves on* another one then it certainly simulates it as well. Of course, the converse is not true. Consider again the programs in Example 6. It is straightforward to check that:

- In D, $q(x)$ improves on $p(x)$, but not vice-versa;
- In D', $q(x)$ improves on $p(x)$, and vice-versa;
- In D'', $q(x)$ improves on $p(x)$ but not vice-versa ($p(x)$ does not even simulate $q(x)$ in D'').

Furthermore, we also have that D' improves on D, while D simulates D' but it is not an improvement on it. In fact in D' the agent $p(x)$ after a single procedure expansion performs the action *tell*, while in D the same agent must perform two procedure expansions before performing the *tell* action.

Proposition 7 applies to the improvement relation as well: all improvement relations are reflexive and transitive. Moreover, the improvement relation between agents is invariant under contexts.

We are now ready to state our main result.

Theorem 13 (Total Correctness 2). *Consider the following ccp programs*

$$D = \{ p_i(\tilde{x}_i) :\!\!- A_i \}_{i \in \{1,\dots,n\}} \cup E$$
$$D' = \{ p_i(\tilde{x}_i) :\!\!- A'_i \}_{i \in \{1,\dots,n\}} \cup E$$

1. *If, for each $i \in \{1,\dots,n\}$, $A_i \preceq_D A'_i$ holds, then D' improves on D.*
2. *If, in addition, for each $i \in \{1,\dots,n\}$, $A'_i \trianglelefteq_D A_i$, then D' is equivalent to D.*

Proof We prove only Part (1). Part (2) is a consequence of the combination of Part (1) and Theorem 8.

Let $\mathcal{S}$ be the relation

$$\mathcal{S} = \{((\langle [D, F], c\rangle, \langle [D', H], d\rangle)) \mid \langle [D, F], c\rangle \preceq \langle [D, H], d\rangle\}.$$

In order to prove the thesis it is sufficient to show that $\mathcal{S}$ is an improving simulation. It is easy to see that $\mathcal{S}$ is joint-closed. We prove now that it satisfies the properties (i) and (ii) of Definition 11.

Let $((\langle [D, F], c\rangle, \langle [D', H], d\rangle))$ be a generic pair in $\mathcal{S}$.

(i) Assume that $\langle [D, F], c\rangle \longrightarrow_n \langle [D, F'], c'\rangle$, where $n = 0$ or $n = 1$. We must prove that there exist H' and d' such that $\langle [D', H], d\rangle \longrightarrow_m^* \langle [D', H'], d'\rangle$ with $m \leq n$, $c' \leq d'$, and $((\langle [D, F'], c'\rangle, \langle [D', H'], d'\rangle)) \in \mathcal{S}$.

By definition of $\mathcal{S}$ we have $\langle [D, F], c\rangle \preceq \langle [D, H], d\rangle$, hence there exist H', m and d' such that

$$\langle [D, H], d\rangle \longrightarrow_k^* \langle [D, H'], d'\rangle \tag{2}$$

with $m \leq n$, $c' \leq d'$, and $\langle [D, F'], c'\rangle \preceq \langle [D, H'], d'\rangle$.

We consider two cases, depending on whether the transition sequence (2) contains or not a procedure expansion in the part of D' which is different from D.

   1. Assume that (2) contains no procedure expansions, or else they are confined to the E part of D'. In this case the same transitions can take place also in D', i.e. we have $\langle [D', H], d\rangle \longrightarrow_k^* \langle [D', H'], d'\rangle$. Furthermore, by definition of $\mathcal{S}$, we have $((\langle [D, F'], c'\rangle, \langle [D', H'], d'\rangle)) \in \mathcal{S}$.

2. Assume now that (2) contains a procedure expansion in the subset $\{ p_i(\tilde{x}_i) :\!\!- A'_i \}_{i \in \{1,\ldots,n\}}$ of D'. Since m can only be 1, then (2) must be of the form

$$\langle [D,H], d \rangle \longrightarrow_0^* \langle [D,G], e \rangle \longrightarrow_1 \langle [D,L], e \rangle \longrightarrow_0^* \langle [D,H'], d' \rangle$$

where $G = C[p_i(\tilde{y}_i)]$ and $L = C[\Delta_{\tilde{x}_i}^{\tilde{y}_i} A_i]$. If we replace D by D' we obtain

$$\langle [D',H], d \rangle \longrightarrow_0^* \langle [D',G], e \rangle \longrightarrow_1 \langle [D',L'], e \rangle$$

where $L' = C[\Delta_{\tilde{x}_i}^{\tilde{y}_i} A'_i]$. Furthermore, since $A_i \preceq_D A'_i$, by Proposition 7 we have that $\langle [D,L], e \rangle \preceq \langle [D,L'], e \rangle$. Hence

$$\langle [D,L'], e \rangle \longrightarrow_0^* \langle [D,H''], d'' \rangle$$

with $d' \leq d''$ and $\langle [D,H'], d' \rangle \preceq \langle [D,H''], d'' \rangle$. Since there are no procedure expansions, the same sequence of transitions can be obtained in D':

$$\langle [D',L'], e \rangle \longrightarrow_0^* \langle [D',H''], d'' \rangle$$

Finally, observe that, by transitivity of $\preceq$ we have $\langle [D,F'], c' \rangle \preceq \langle [D,H''], d'' \rangle$. Hence, by definition of $\mathcal{S}$, we obtain $(\langle [D,F'], c' \rangle, \langle [D',H''], d'' \rangle) \in \mathcal{S}$.

(ii) Assume that $\langle [D,F], c \rangle \not\longrightarrow$. By definition of $\mathcal{S}$, $(\langle [D,F], c \rangle, \langle [D,H], d \rangle) \in \mathcal{S}$, hence there exists H' such that $\langle [D,H], d \rangle \longrightarrow_0^* \langle [D,H'], c \rangle \not\longrightarrow$. Since there are no procedure expansions, the same sequence of transitions can be obtained in D': $\langle [D',H], d \rangle \longrightarrow_0^* \langle [D',H'], c \rangle \not\longrightarrow$.   □

Two remarks are in order: First, when we apply the replacement operation in order to improve the efficiency of a program it is natural to require that the replacing agent be equivalent to and more efficient than the replaced one. The above theorem shows the pleasing properties that under those circumstances the replacement is always correct and that it yields a program which is an improvement on the initial one. Secondly, from Proposition 4 it follows that, when the above theorem applies, then also the semantics of the observables is preserved, i.e. for any agent A, $\mathcal{O}([D',A]) = \mathcal{O}([D,A])$ holds.

7   An Extended Example: Minimum and Maximum Element of a List

In order to illustrate some of the possible uses of the applicability conditions formulated above, we use here a typical example of an unfold-fold transformation system. Let D be the following ccp program

```
min(list,m) :- (    ask (∃x,w,xs list = [x,w|xs]) → ∃z,x,xs (tell(list = [x|xs]) || min(xs,z)
                || smaller(x,z,m)                    )
              + ask (∃x list = [x]) → ∃x (tell(list = [x]) || tell(m = x)))

max(list,m) :- (    ask (∃x,w,xs list = [x,w,|xs]) → ∃z,x,xs (tell(list = [x|xs]) || max(xs,z)
                || greater(x,z,m)                    )
              +    ask (∃x list = [x]) → ∃x (tell(list = [x]) || tell(m = x)))

minmax(l,min,max) :- min(l,min) || max(l,max)
```

Where smaller and greater are defined in the obvious way. Here min(list,m) returns in m the minimum value of the non-empty list list: in the first branch of the ask choice, min checks if list contains more than one element, in which case is call itself recursively. On the other hand, if list contains only one element x, then the second branch is followed and m is set equal to x. max works in the same way, and minmax reports both the minimum and the maximum of the values in the list. Notice that the definition of minmax traverses the input list twice. This is a source of inefficiency, which can be fixed via an unfold/fold transformation. The first operation we encounter is the *unfolding*, which consists of replacing an atom with the body of its definition. Consider the program

$$D = \{ \, d_1 : \;\; q(\tilde{y}) :\!\!- C[p(\tilde{v})]$$
$$\phantom{D = \{ \,} d_2 : \;\; p(\tilde{x}) :\!\!- A \} \cup E$$

then *unfolding* $p(\tilde{v})$ in d_1 means replacing d_1 with $d_1' : \;\; q(\tilde{y}) :\!\!- C[\Delta_{\tilde{x}}^{\tilde{v}} A]$. This operation can be regarded as an instance of replacement. In fact, its correctness follows in a straightforward manner from Theorem 13: it is easy to show that in the above program $\Delta_{\tilde{x}}^{\tilde{v}} A$ is *equivalent to*, and *improves on* $p(\tilde{v})$. By applying twice the unfolding operation to the definition of minmax, we obtain the following definition.

minmax(l,min,max) :-
  (ask $(\exists_{x,w,xs}$ l $= $ [x,w|xs]) $\rightarrow \exists_{z,x,xs}$ (tell(l $=$ [x|xs]) ‖ min(xs,z) ‖ smaller(x,z,min))
  +ask $(\exists_x$ l $=$ [x]) $\rightarrow \exists_x$ (tell(l $=$ [x]) ‖ tell(min $=$ x)))
‖
  (ask $(\exists_{x',w',xs'}$ l $= $ [x',w'|xs']) $\rightarrow$
               $\exists_{z',x',xs'}$ (tell(l $=$ [x'|xs']) ‖ max(xz',z') ‖ greater(x',z',max))
  +ask $(\exists_{x'}$ l $=$ [x']) $\rightarrow \exists_{x'}$ (tell(l $=$ [x']) ‖ tell(max $=$ x')))

Now, it is straightforward to prove that if $a \wedge b = false$, then $(((ask(a) \rightarrow A) + (ask(b) \rightarrow B)) \, \| \, ((ask(a) \rightarrow C) + (ask(b) \rightarrow D)))$ improves on $(ask(a) \rightarrow (A \, \| \, C)) + (ask(b) \rightarrow (B \, \| \, D))$ and vice-versa. Thus, by Theorem 13, we can safely apply a replacement operation which yields

minmax(l,min,max) :-
    ask $(\exists_{x,w,xs}$ l $=$ [x,w|xs]) $\rightarrow$
        ($\exists_{z,x,xs}$ (tell(l $=$ [x|xs]) ‖ min(xs,z) ‖ smaller(x,z,min))
        ‖ $\exists_{z',x',xs'}$ (tell(l $=$ [x'|xs']) ‖ max(xs',z') ‖ greater(x',z',max)))
  + ask $(\exists_x$ l $=$ [x]) $\rightarrow$ ($\exists_x$ (tell(l $=$ [x]) ‖ tell(min $=$ x)))
                  ‖ $\exists_{x'}$ (tell(l $=$ [x']) ‖ tell(max $=$ x'))

Now, with other (intuitively immediate) replacement operations whose correctness is guaranteed by Theorem 13, we obtain the following definition.

minmax(l,min,max) :-
    ask$(\exists_{x,w,xs}$ l $=$ [x,w|xs]) $\rightarrow \exists_{z,z',x,xs}$ (tell(l $=$ [x|xs]) ‖ smaller(x,z,min) ‖ min(xs,z)
                                      ‖ max(xs,z') ‖ greater(x,z',max))
 + ask$(\exists_x$ l $=$ [x]) $\rightarrow \exists_x$ (tell(min $=$ x) ‖ tell(max $=$ x) ‖ tell(l $=$ [x]))

We are now ready for the last operation, which corresponds to a folding one: we replace min(xs, z) ‖ max(xs, z') with minmax(xs, z, z').

minmax(I,min,max) :-
    ask($\exists_{x,w,xs}$ I = [x,w|xs]) → $\exists_{z,z',x,xs}$ (tell(I = [x|xs]) || minmax(xs,z,z')
                              || smaller(x,z,min) || greater(x,z',max))
  + ask($\exists_x$ I = [x]) → $\exists_x$ (tell(I = [x]) || tell(min = x) || tell(max = x))

Notice that this operation has made *recursive* the definition of minmax. As we mentioned in the introduction, this is an example of a *wanted loop*. Clearly, for this last operation we could have not applied Theorem 10

As the mimmax example shows, the applicability conditions we propose for the replacement operation are flexible enough to let this operation mimic both unfolding, folding and usual (yet not trivial) "cleaning-up" operations. (See Appendix A for a list of agents which can be interchanged). Actually, it is possible to devise a fold-unfold transformation system whose proof of correctness is based on Theorem 13. This has been done in [2]. Such a system is not quite as powerful as a tailored folding operation such as the one presented in [9] (which, on the other hand, ensure only a weaker form of correctness of the transformation), but this accounts for the flexibility of the conditions we presented.

8   Concluding Remarks

For experts in transformations, the applicability conditions outlined in Theorem 13 are not fully surprising: similar concepts were first employed in Logic Programming (for instance in [28,4,5,7]) and then applied to functional programs in [24,25]. However, this is the first time that they are applied to a concurrent context. To the best of our knowledge, this is the first paper which treats the notion of replacement in a concurrent language.

Acknowledgements. We would like to thank the anonymous referees of LOP-STR and of APPIA-GULP-PRODE for the useful suggestions.

References

1. N. Bensaou and I. Guessarian. Transforming constraint logic programs. *Theoretical Computer Science*, 206(1–2):81–125, 1998.
2. M. Bertolino. Transformazione dei programmi concorrenti Tesi di Laurea, Dip. Informatica e Scienze dell' Informazione, Università di Genova, Genova, Italy, 1997.
3. A. Bossi and N. Cocco. Basic Transformation Operations which preserve Computed Answer Substitutions of Logic Programs. *Journal of Logic Programming*, 16(1&2):47–87, 1993.
4. A. Bossi, N. Cocco, and S. Etalle. On Safe Folding. In M. Bruynooghe and M. Wirsing, editors, *Programming Language Implementation and Logic Programming - Proceedings PLILP'92*, volume 631 of *Lecture Notes in Computer Science*, pages 172–186. Springer-Verlag, 1992.
5. A. Bossi, N. Cocco, and S. Etalle. Simultaneous replacement in normal programs. *Journal of Logic and Computation*, 6(1):79–120, February 1996.

6. J. Cook and J.P. Gallagher. A transformation system for definite programs based on termination analysis. In F. Turini, editor, *Proc. Fourth Workshop on Logic Program Synthesis and Transformation*. Springer-Verlag, 1994.

7. S. Etalle and M. Gabbrielli. On the correctness of the replacement operation for clp modules. *Journal of Functional and Logic Programming*, February 1996. available at http://www.cs.tu-berlin.de/journal/jflp.

8. S. Etalle and M. Gabbrielli. Transformations of CLP modules. *Theoretical Computer Science*, 166(1):101–146, 1996.

9. S. Etalle, M. Gabbrielli, and M. C. Meo. Unfold/Fold Transformations of CCP Programs. In D. Sangiorgi and R. de Simone, editors, *CONCUR98 – 1998 International Conference on Concurrency Theory*, LNCS 1466, pages 348–363. Springer-Verlag, 1998.

10. N. De Francesco and A. Santone. Unfold/fold transformation of concurrent processes. In H. Kuchen and S.Doaitse Swierstra, editors, *Proc. 8th Int'l Symp. on Programming Languages: Implementations, Logics and Programs*, volume 1140, pages 167–181. Springer-Verlag, 1996.

11. H. Fujita, A. Okumura, and K. Furukawa. Partial evaluation of GHC programs based on the UR-set with constraints. In R.A. Kowalski and K.A. Bowen, editors, *Logic Programming: Fifth International Conference and Symposium, volume 2*, pages 924–941. Cambridge, MA: MIT Press, 1988.

12. P.A. Gardner and J.C. Shepherdson. Unfold/fold transformations of logic programs. In J-L Lassez and G. Plotkin, editors, *Computational Logic: Essays in Honor of Alan Robinson*. MIT Press, 1991.

13. M. Gengler and M. Martel. Self-applicable partial evaluation for the pi-calculus. In *ACM SIGPLAN Symposium on Partial Evaluation and Semantics-Based Program Manipulation (PEPM '97)*, pages 36–46. ACM, 1997.

14. H. Hosoya, N. Kobayashi, and A. Yonezawa. Partial evaluation scheme for concurrent languages and its correctness. In L. Bougé et al., editors, *Euro-Par'96 - Parallel Processing, Lyon, France. (Lecture Notes in Computer Science, vol. 1123)*, pages 625–632. Berlin: Springer-Verlag, 1996.

15. Niels Jørgensen, Kim Marriott, and Spiro Michaylov. Some global compile-time optimizations for CLP($\mathcal{R}$). In Vijay Saraswat and Kazunori Ueda, editors, *International Logic Programming Symposium*, pages 420–434, San Diego, 1991. MIT Press.

16. M.J. Maher. A transformation system for deductive databases with perfect model semantics. *Theoretical Computer Science*, 110(2):377–403, March 1993.

17. M. Marinescu and B. Goldberg. Partial-evaluation techniques for concurrent programs. In *ACM SIGPLAN Symposium on Partial Evaluation and Semantics-Based Program Manipulation (PEPM '97)*, pages 47–62. ACM, 1997.

18. Kim Marriott and Harald Søndergaard. Analysis of constraint logic programs. In Saumya Debray and Manuel Hermenegildo, editors, *Proceedings North American Conference on Logic Programming*. MIT Press, 1990.

19. Kim Marriott and Peter J. Stuckey. The 3 r's of optimizing constraint logic programs: Refinement, removal and reordering. In *POPL'93: Proceedings ACM SIGPLAN Symposium on Principles of Programming Languages*, Charleston, January 1993.

20. D.M.R. Park. Concurrency and automata on infinite sequences. In P. Deussen, editor, *Proc. of the 5th GI conference*, Lecture Notes in Computer Science, pages 167–183. Springer-Verlag, 1981.

21. A. Pettorossi and M. Proietti. Transformation of logic programs: Foundations and techniques. *Journal of Logic Programming*, 19,20:261–320, 1994.

22. M. Proietti and A. Pettorossi. Synthesis and transformation of logic programs using unfold/fold proofs. *Journal of Logic Programming*, 41(2-3):197–230, 1999.
23. D. Sahlin. Partial Evaluation of AKL. In *Proceedings of the First International Conference on Concurrent Constraint Programming*, 1995.
24. D. Sands. Total correctness by local improvement in program transformation. In *Proceedings of the 22nd Annual ACM SIGPLAN-SIGACT Symposium on Principles of Programming Languages (POPL)*. ACM Press, 1995.
25. D. Sands. Total correctness by local improvement in the transformation of functional programs. *ACM Transactions on Programming Languages and Systems*, 18(2):175–234, 1996.
26. V.A. Saraswat, M. Rinard, and P. Panangaden. Semantics foundations of concurrent constraint programming. In *Proc. Eighteenth Annual ACM Symp. on Principles of Programming Languages*. ACM Press, 1991.
27. T. Sato. Equivalence-preserving first-order unfold/fold transformation system. *Theoretical Computer Science*, 105(1):57–84, 1992.
28. H. Tamaki and T. Sato. Unfold/Fold Transformations of Logic Programs. In Sten-Åke Tärnlund, editor, *Proc. Second Int'l Conf. on Logic Programming*, pages 127–139, 1984.
29. K. Ueda and K. Furukawa. Transformation rules for GHC Programs. In *Proc. Int'l Conf. on Fifth Generation Computer Systems*, pages 582–591. Institute for New Generation Computer Technology, Tokyo, 1988.
30. R.J. van Glabbeek. The linear time - branching time spectrum. In J.C.M. Baeten and J.W. Klop, editors, *Proc. of CONCUR 90*, volume 458 of *Lecture Notes in Computer Science*, pages 278–297, Amsterdam, 1990. Springer-Verlag.

A   Appendix: Mutually Replaceable Agents

In this appendix we present a list of mutually replaceable agents, that is, agents which, under the reported applicability conditions, are equivalent to each others (in all programs) and which improve on each other (in all programs). In virtue of Theorem 13 these agents can (under the given conditions) be freely interchanged. Hence the name "mutually replaceable". The technical proofs are presented in [2, Appendix 2].

Here, for the sake of simplicity, we write $A \equiv B$ as a shorthand for "A is mutually replaceable with B".

Properties of the Parallel Operator

- $A \parallel stop \equiv A$
- $A \parallel B \equiv B \parallel A$
- $A \parallel (B \parallel C) \equiv (A \parallel B) \parallel C$

Properties of the Tell Operator

- $tell(true) \equiv stop$
- $tell(c) \parallel tell(d) \equiv tell(c \wedge d)$

Properties of the Ask Operator

- $ask(true) \to A \equiv A$
- $ask(c) \to (ask(d) \to A) \equiv ask(c \wedge d) \to A$

Properties of the Hiding Operator

- $\exists_x A \equiv A$ provided that $x \notin FV(A)$
- $\exists_{\tilde{x}} A \parallel \exists_{\tilde{x}} B \equiv \exists_{\tilde{x}} (A \parallel \exists_{\tilde{x}} B)$
- $\exists_{\tilde{x}} \exists_{\tilde{y}} A \equiv \exists_{\tilde{y}} \exists_{\tilde{x}} A$
- $\exists_{\tilde{x}}^d \exists_{\tilde{y}}^e A \equiv \exists_{\tilde{y}}^e \exists_{\tilde{x}}^d A$ provided that $\exists_{\tilde{y}} d = d$, $\exists_{\tilde{x}} e = e$
- $\exists_{\tilde{x}}^d \exists_{\tilde{y}}^e A \equiv \exists_{\tilde{x}\tilde{y}}^{d \wedge e} A$ provided that $\exists_{\tilde{y}} d = d$
- $\exists_{\tilde{x}}^{c \wedge e} \exists_{\tilde{y}}^d A \equiv \exists_{\tilde{x}}^c \exists_{\tilde{y}}^{e \wedge d} A$ provided that $\exists_{\tilde{y}} e = e$

Mixed Properties

- $\exists_{\tilde{x}} tell(c) \equiv tell(\exists_{\tilde{x}} c)$
- $\exists_{\tilde{x}} (tell(c) \parallel A) \equiv tell(\exists_{\tilde{x}} c) \parallel \exists_{\tilde{x}}^c A$
- $\exists_{\tilde{x}} \sum_{i=1}^n ask(c_i) \to A_i \equiv \sum_{i=1}^n ask(c_i) \to \exists_{\tilde{x}} A_i$ provided that $\exists_{\tilde{x}} c_i = c_i$ for every $i \in \{1, \ldots, n\}$
- $((ask(a) \to A + ask(b) \to B) \parallel (ask(a) \to C + ask(b) \to D)) \equiv ((ask(a) \to (A \parallel C)) + (ask(b) \to (B \parallel D)))$ provided that $a \wedge b = false$
- $tell(d) \parallel \sum_{i=1}^n ask(c_i) \to A_i \equiv tell(d) \parallel A_j$ provided that $c_j \leq d$ and for every $k \in \{1, \ldots, n\}, k \neq j \Rightarrow d \wedge c_k = false$

Annotations for Prolog – A Concept and Runtime Handling

Marija Kulaš

FernUniversität Hagen, FB Informatik, D-58084 Hagen, Germany
marija.kulas@fernuni-hagen.de

Abstract. A concept of annotations for rendering procedural aspects of Prolog is introduced, built around well-known procedural concepts of Standard Prolog. Annotations describe properties of predicates. Such properties can be pre or post conditions, which must hold true when a predicate is called or exited, respectively. We introduce two more kinds of annotations, fail and redo annotations, hence incorporating a whole *model* of Prolog execution into our language. This enables natural rendering of many procedural properties of Prolog which cannot be expressed with only pre/post conditions, like non-failure. Every annotation can be narrowed down to a subset of calls, via *calling premiss*. With the novel idea of *context* we supersede program-point assertions. The annotations are defined simply as Prolog goals, making them fully *parametric* and therefore comfortable for debugging. All examples presented are actual runs of our system Nope.

1 Introduction

This work was motivated by the need for more accurate and more verifiable documentation for Prolog programs. Even in pure logic programs, there is no easy equation "specification = implementation", as pointed out in [11]. All the more so in Prolog, due to the non-logical predicates like cut, var, assert. Unambiguous, terse and still readable comments are hard to write. Perhaps even more difficult is the question, how trustworthy the comment is, i.e. how closely does it match its target? There has been much important research in rendering and verifying aspects of Prolog execution, starting with the introduction of mode declarations. Sec. 7 presents a short survey of related research, biased towards declarative efforts. We indicate along the way what we feel to be missing in the existing approaches. In Sec. 3 a remedy is proposed in the form of call annotations. Sec. 4 is the central part of the paper: it generalizes the concept of call annotations and provides a transformational semantics. Sec. 5 outlines some enhancements of the annotation language. Sec. 6 allows a close look into the merits of the approach, by means of several illustrations. Sec. 8 points out some possible continuations of this work.

A. Bossi (Ed.): LOPSTR'99, LNCS 1817, pp. 234–254, 2000.

2   Modes

While in principle every argument of a predicate may be arbitrarily instantiated, i. e. it can be anything from a variable over terms with variables down to a ground term, in practice there are always restrictions.

To set up the terminology, let us name the degree of instantiation of an invocation of a predicate a *calling pattern*, or call substitution. Similarly, on exit we obtain a corresponding *exit pattern*, or answer substitution. We shall regard a calling pattern and a corresponding exit pattern of a predicate as a *mode* of the predicate, like in the approach of [18]. We say that T is *instantiated* if nonvar(T) holds, and *uninstantiated* if var(T) holds. We say that a term T gets *more instantiated* (gets *changed*) if some variable in T gets instantiated.

The classic mode declarations, introduced by [20] and first provided in DEC-10 Prolog to underpin compiled code optimization, specify the usage of each argument of a predicate by choosing one of the three mode symbols: mode '+' specifies that the corresponding argument in any call of the predicate will always be instantiated (input argument), mode '-' specifies that the argument will always be uninstantiated (output argument), and mode '?' specifies that there is no restriction on the form of the argument.

3   From Modes to Call Annotations

The classic mode language is very simple and useful, but often not expressive enough, the var/nonvar discrimination being too coarse grained for many practical purposes. For example, sometimes we need to specify that an argument has to be ground at the time of call, as in the case of Prolog negation. Namely, if a non-ground negation is called, Prolog might compute an unsound answer ('safe' versus 'floundering' negation).

What would help, in our opinion, is the possibility of expressing the intended calling patterns like this

$$\text{call} \backslash + \ X \Rightarrow \text{ground}(X)$$

to be read as "negated goals shall be ground at the time of call". Let us name such a declaration a *call annotation*. We propose the following syntactic variants.

$$\text{call Goal} \Rightarrow \text{MustHold}$$
$$\text{call Goal with Template} \Rightarrow \text{MustHold}$$
$$\text{call Goal \{ with Template \} within Context} \Rightarrow \text{MustHold}$$

We've just seen an example for the first variant, namely the safe negation annotation. There will be diverse examples in this paper, each tested with Nope. Nope is an (almost standard) Prolog module that recognizes our annotations and checks them at run-time.

The second variant is an enhancement of the goal specification in Prolog, namely a template allows us to specify the calling pattern more precisely than with head unifications alone. In fact, arbitrarily precise, since a template can be any Prolog goal. The default template is true.

The third variant introduces the idea of *context*, a way of specifying sets of program points. The contexts are partially ordered (*context subsumption*). The default context is _, which subsumes any other context, so an annotation without a context part applies in any context.

Definition 1 (call annotation). *Let P be a predicate of arity n. A call annotation for P/n is a Prolog goal*

$$\text{call } \textsf{Premiss} \Rightarrow \textsf{Constraint}$$

where Premiss ::= Goal { with Template } { within Context }. *Here* Goal *is a Prolog goal for P/n, i. e. a Prolog term of the form* P(S_1, .., S_n). Context *is a context (see Sec. 3.3).* Template, Constraint *are arbitrary Prolog goals.*

Technical Note: Declarations or Goals. We show our annotations mostly in the traditional, declaration form :- Annotation. to make them stick out, but please note that they are simply *goals* and can be called like any other Prolog goals, amounting to *parametric* annotations. (In case you wonder which predicate is here being called, it's the arrow.)

Technical Note: What May be Annotated. The annotation language is implemented by means of goal replacement, see page 242. Therefore, in principle there is nothing to prevent us from annotating *arbitrary* goals and not just *atomary* ones (as opposed to composite predications like negation, conjunction, disjunction, or if-then-else). For example, it is just a question of slowing down the parser a notch to allow arbitrary negated goals, making it possible to express safe negation in its most general form (as above). The default parser of our implementation will recognize annotated negation, but conjunction, disjunction and if-then-else will be transparent, i. e. any annotations for these built-in 'predicates' of Standard Prolog will be ignored, as opposed to all other built-ins (and of course all user-defined predicates).

Technical Note: Broken Annotations in Nope. This note shall explain the illustrations. If an annotation does not hold (with respect to the given program and a goal), our runtime checker Nope will issue a warning. The default warning in Nope shows the violated annotation, with its arrow broken. For the safe negation example it would look like

/* NOPE call \+member(A,[1,2]) $\not\Rightarrow$ ground(member(A,[1,2])) */

This can be overridden via an explicit use of the else/2 utility (defined on page 242):

call \+ X $\Rightarrow$ ground(X) else write(floundering)

customizing the warning into /* NOPE floundering */. Also, the warning handler of Nope has different severity levels. For example, the utility bark/0 appearing in Sec. 6.3 tunes the warning handler to interrupt Prolog for each warning.

3.1   Soft Success

Owing to the defaults for Template and Context, we may assume every call annotation in the form call Goal with Template within Context $\Rightarrow$ Constraint. There is also a normal form, employed in the implementation of Nope (see page 242).

Definition 2 (normal form). *We say that* call Goal with Template within Context $\Rightarrow$ Constraint, *where* Goal $\equiv P(S_1, .., S_n)$, *has the normal form* call GoalSkeleton with FullTemplate within Context $\Rightarrow$ Constraint, *where* GoalSkeleton *is the full generalization of* Goal: GoalSkeleton $\equiv P(X_1, .., X_n)$ *with* $X_1, .., X_n$ *distinct new variables, and all the specializations are made explicit via* FullTemplate $\equiv (X_1 = S_1, .., X_n = S_n,$ Template).

An observant reader might object that unifying a goal Q with Goal and computing Template is not the same as unifying Q with GoalSkeleton and computing FullTemplate, see var(3) versus var(X), X=3. But the annotations shall not be applied via unification, since we consider matching (subsumption) to be the more natural choice for our purpose. Recall the traditional concept of Pattern *subsuming* Object if Object is an instance of Pattern, i.e. if Object can be unified with Pattern without further instantiating any variables in Object. We generalize this so as to accommodate not only equality but arbitrary goals in Template: everything goes but there is an invariant, the user's goal, which may not be changed.

Definition 3 (succeeds soft). *Let* Goal *and* Invariant *be arbitrary Prolog goals. We say that* Goal *succeeds soft on* Invariant *if* Goal *succeeds without changing* Invariant.

More formally: If Goal succeeds with an answer substitution σ, then σ may only rename Invariant, written as σ(Invariant) $\cong$ Invariant.

Soft succeeding goals are not only of the kind \+ \+ G. Nope provides a predicate call_soft(G, J) that succeeds only softly on J for any G and any J. The advantage over \+ \+ G is that soft success allows for *local variables*, because the variables of G not occurring in J may get instantiated.

In Def. 8 we define applicability of annotations via soft success. Owing to this we may have arbitrary premises, like p(X,Y) with X=Y.

3.2   Simple Context

It is useful to be able to access the immediate ancestor (parent) of a goal Q, i.e. the goal which called Q. To this effect, we introduce contexts.

Definition 4 (parent of a goal). *The head of a clause is the parent of each body goal. If a goal is issued at the top-level of a Prolog interpreter, we will say that its parent is the goal* false.

A *context* specifies the parent of the annotated goal. In the simplest case, it can be any atomary Prolog goal. So the meaning of an annotation for Q within

Context shall be to check on Q occurring anywhere in the clause bodies of Context. Alternatively, one can view contexts as specifying *sets of program points*, namely those points where the annotated goal is allowed to appear (in this first simple case: all points in the bodies of Context).

Furthermore, sometimes it is useful to exclude contexts. For example, if we only want to check the non-recursive calls of a predicate P, we need to express "check P within any context but P". For such purposes we allow *negative contexts*, represented as dash-prefixed atomary Prolog goals. The meaning of -Context is the complement of the set of program points represented by Context, i. e. this can be any point in the program (plus top-level, 'defining' false/0) outside of the definition of Context.

In the following we shall further refine the idea of a context. But first we have some questions for our contexts so far. One key question about contexts is their inheritance, i. e. when is an annotation for Q within X pertinent to Q within Y? Also, when is an annotation bound to a context CA pertinent to a goal within a context CQ? To settle these questions, we define a partial ordering for contexts.

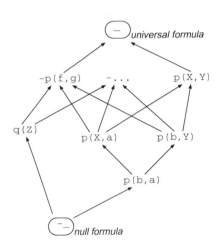

Fig. 1. Poset of simple contexts

We start from the natural lattice of first-order atomary formulas (augmented by a 'universal' and a 'null' formulas) modulo renaming, as introduced by [17]. The partial ordering $\preceq$ being "is instance of", the greatest lower bound of two atoms being their most general unifier (or the special bottom element *null formula*) and the least upper bound being their most specific generalizer (or the special top element *universal formula*).

Next we enhance the language. Our language is the following set $\mathcal{C}$ of atomary and non-atomary formulas (plus the universal and the null formula): the first order language – modulo renaming – made of standard Prolog variables, function and predicate symbols, and a unary operator -. Atoms Q of this language we call *positive contexts*, and non-atoms -Q we call *negative (negated) contexts*. The universal formula is represented here by _, and the null formula is represented by -_.

It remains to enhance the partial ordering.

Definition 5 (partial ordering of contexts). *For positive contexts X and Y we define:* $-X \preceq \_$, $X \preceq Y$ *if X is an instance of Y,* $X \prec -Y$ *if X is not unifiable with Y,* $-X \preceq -Y$ *if* $Y \preceq X$.

If we assign to every atom Q from $\mathcal{C}$ the set of its ground instances, and to -Q all the other ground atoms in the Herbrand base $\mathsf{B}_\mathcal{C}$ for $\mathcal{C}$, we obtain an isomorphism between $(C, \preceq)$ and a sub-poset of $(\mathcal{P}(B_C), \subseteq)$. Due to this isomorphism, $(C, \preceq)$ is a poset and the seeming asymmetry of the definition actually is a perfect duality:

$$X \prec\text{-}Y \quad \text{iff} \quad Y \prec\text{-}X \quad \text{iff} \quad X, Y \text{ are not unifiable.}$$

Definition 6 (context subsumes). *If $CQ \preceq CA$, then we say: the context CA subsumes the context CQ.*

We chose the names CA and CQ to suggest *annotation context* as opposed to *query context*. The interesting case is namely when an annotation context subsumes the actual query context, meaning the annotation may fire.

Definition 7 (context inheritance). *If $X \prec Y$, then an annotation for Q within Y shall be inherited to X, i.e. it is also an annotation for Q within X.*

A self-contained example of context inheritance follows.

```
:- dynamic a/0, b/0, c/0, d/0.
:- call a =¿ b.
:- call a within parent =¿ c.
:- call a within - parent =¿ d.

parent :- a.
```

— ?- a.
/* NOPE call a ⇏ b */
/* NOPE call a within - parent ⇏ d */

no

— ?- parent.
/* NOPE call a ⇏ b */
/* NOPE call a within parent ⇏ c */

no

3.3   (Generalized) Context

Assertions can be divided into predicate assertions, stating properties of a predicate, and program-point assertions, stating properties that shall hold when the code at a given point in the program is about to be executed. Traditionally, the two classes have different syntax, predicate assertions being written as declarations, and program-point assertions being scattered all over the program code (like in [7]). Our annotations are predicate assertions. However, due to contexts, as defined so far, we can capture some sets of program points. For illustrations see Sec. 6.3 and Sec. 6.7.

There is only a small step necessary to be able to capture also individual program points. For example, say we have a program-point annotation $\mathcal{A}$ placed as follows:

$$H \text{ :- } B_1, .., B_i, \mathcal{A}, B_{i+1}, .., B_n. \qquad \% \text{ k-th clause for the predicate of } H$$

then we can simulate it in Nope as

$$\text{call } B_{i+1} \text{ within } H^*pp(k,i) \Rightarrow \mathcal{A}$$

In other words, we enhance the context specification by an optional part, program-point, linked to the simple context by an asterisk. A non-asterisk term Context is regarded as an abbreviation of Context * _ meaning "any program point within the simple context Context". The program-point is a Datalog term representing the intended program point(s) like pp(K,J), where K is the serial number of the clause in the definition of the parent goal, and J is the serial number of the body subgoal (counting each conjunct/disjunct/implication-part). The partial ordering $\preceq$ of simple contexts shall be lifted in the obvious way to generalized contexts.

3.4   Calling Premiss

For the premiss of an annotation we will also use the more evocative name *calling premiss*.

Definition 8 (calling premiss subsumes goal). *We say that a calling premiss Goal with Template within Context subsumes the call port of Q (for short: subsumes Q), if at that port Q=Goal, Template succeeds soft on Q, and also Context subsumes the parent of Q.*

More formally: Let Parent be the parent goal of Q. The following three conditions must hold. If σ is the answer substitution for Q=Goal, then $\sigma(Q) \cong Q$. If θ is an answer for σ(Template), then $\theta(Q) \cong Q$. Lastly, $\sigma(\text{Parent}) \preceq \sigma(\text{Context})$.

A logical reading of this definition (leaving out the contexts) shall be:
$$\forall\, \mathcal{V}(Q): \exists\, \mathcal{V}(\text{Template}) \backslash \mathcal{V}(Q): \quad X_1 = Q_1, .., X_n = Q_n \vdash X_1 = G_1, .., X_n = G_n, \text{Template}.$$
Here $\mathcal{V}$(Term) is the set of variables in Term, and $X_1, .., X_n$ are new variables. $Q_1, .., Q_n$ are respectively the first, .., nth arguments of Q, i. e. the actual calling substitution, and similarly $G_1, .., G_n$ are the arguments of Goal, i. e. the calling substitution monitored by the annotation. The monitored substitution together with Template constitutes the *full*, or *normalized* monitored template. So the actual calling substitution shall imply the monitored template.

Observe that this allows local variables, namely variables that don't occur in Goal can be used to create and propagate values from the calling premiss through to the constraint.

Now we can define what does it mean to apply a call annotation.

Definition 9 (applicable). *An annotation is applicable on a goal Q if its calling premiss subsumes Q.*

Definition 10 (call annotation satisfied/violated). *An applicable call annotation is satisfied/violated for a goal Q, if its constraint succeeds/fails at the call port of Q.*

Definition 11 (correctness wrt annotations and queries). *An annotated program is said to be correct if, during the computation of arbitrary queries (from the given set of allowed queries), all the applicable annotations are satisfied.*

4   Following the Execution Model

In the previous section we suggested annotating the call port of a goal, in order to grasp more precisely the intended calling patterns. So what about the other three ports? Here we refer to the classic model of Prolog execution [2], abstracting a goal to a black box with four ports, known from the debugging sessions.

Following this model, we propose a language of annotations as a step towards capturing procedural aspects of Prolog. This language has the advantage of there being a workable consent among Prolog users on what the box trace model of Prolog execution means.

Definition 12 (port annotation). *Let P be a predicate of arity n. A* Port *annotation for P/n is a Prolog goal of the form*

$$\textsf{Event} \Rightarrow \textsf{Constraint}$$

where

```
Event    ::= Port Premiss
Port     ::= call — exit — fail — redo
Premiss ::= Goal { with Template } { within Context }
```

Here Goal is a Prolog goal for P/n, i. e. a Prolog term of the form $P(S_1, .., S_n)$. *Context is a context. Template, Constraint are arbitrary Prolog goals.*

As in [5], we deal only with *partial correctness*, because we do not claim whether goals actually succeed, fail or redo. Or even get called. Also, as the transformational semantics below reveals, our annotation language provides for accessing the values of variables on call and on exit from a query, similar to [5]. Thus, our language is also a language of *binary assertions*. The actual calling pattern is accessible on the left of $\Rightarrow$, and, in case of exit and redo annotations, the exit pattern is on the right. This circumvents the need for language primitives to access the call/exit values.

$P(T_1, .., T_n) \overset{\text{CALL}}{\rightsquigarrow}$
    call_soft(FullTemplate, $P(T_1, .., T_n)$) $\rightarrow$
        (Constraint else Warning), $P(T_1, .., T_n)$
    ; $P(T_1, .., T_n)$

$P(T_1, .., T_n) \overset{\text{EXIT}}{\rightsquigarrow}$
    call_soft(FullTemplate, $P(T_1, .., T_n)$) $\rightarrow$
        $P(T_1, .., T_n)$, (Constraint else Warning)
    ; $P(T_1, .., T_n)$

$P(T_1, .., T_n) \overset{\text{FAIL}}{\rightsquigarrow}$
    call_soft(FullTemplate, $P(T_1, .., T_n)$) $\rightarrow$
        ($P(T_1, .., T_n)$; (Constraint else Warning), fail)
    ; $P(T_1, .., T_n)$

$P(T_1, .., T_n) \overset{\text{REDO}}{\rightsquigarrow}$
    call_soft(FullTemplate, $P(T_1, .., T_n)$) $\rightarrow$
        $P(T_1, .., T_n)$, (true; (Constraint else Warning), fail)
    ; $P(T_1, .., T_n)$

Fig. 2. The program transformation of Nope

Applicability of a port annotation is defined as in Def. 9. To define the meaning of port annotations, we can adopt Def. 10. But observe that a premiss shall always match the *call* port of the goal (therefore we dubbed it 'calling premiss'). In this paper we do not define the concept of a port.

But still, we do give a precise semantics of our annotations, via a program transformation. Namely, we show the essentials of our implementation of the run-time checking of annotations. The implementation bases upon the following program transformation. Every annotation for a predicate P imposes a virtual transformation, a *goal replacement*, on the user's program: *Any user's goal* $P(T_1, .., T_n)$, *at the program points specified by the annotation, be they top-level or in some clause bodies, will be computed as if replaced according to the Fig. 2. The labels on the arrows indicate the respective* Port *of the annotation.*

Note that a call annotation hence corresponds to a (global) precondition, and an exit annotation to a (global) postcondition. The usual coupling is achieved via an own (local) precondition, as illustrated in Sec. 6.1.

Lemma 1 (non-interference of port annotations). *Port annotations in Nope are not interfering with the success set: A query about the user's program Π computes the same answers and in the same sequence when posed to $\Pi + \Delta$, where Δ denotes arbitrary port annotations with terminating and pure templates and constraints.*

Annotations with a non-terminating template or constraint are clearly a bad idea. But otherwise, this lemma imposes the too strong restriction of purity upon templates and constraints. In practice, users profit from annotations with side-effects. Like [7], we guarantee that no amount of annotation tweaking will change any variables of a user's query. As for the rest of dangers, we simply count on users to be sensible in their choice of side-effects. Lemma 1 follows from the program transformation of Nope (Fig. 2), where call_soft/2 and else/2 have the following definitions:

```
call`soft(Test, Invariant) :-
    copy`term(Invariant, InvariantCopy),
    once(Test),  % Test succeeds, but does it change Invariant?
    variant(Invariant, InvariantCopy).  % Other variables may be instantiated.

else(Constraint, Warning) :-  % Constraint else Warning
    \+ Constraint -¿ (\+ Warning -¿ true; true); true.
```

Here variant/2 checks whether its arguments are renamings of each other.

Lemma 2 (compositionality of port annotations). *Port annotations in Nope are compositional: If Premiss₀ of a given annotation $\mathcal{A}_0$ subsumes the call port of Q, then Constraint₀ is going to be computed at the Port₀ of Q, no matter how many annotations, for what ports and in what order, were given until the call.*

This lemma follows from the program transformation of Nope.

5   Enhancing the Language

A special case of constraint is false: it can never succeed, but it can nevertheless be useful, as shown in [5]: If we prove that the program, containing a false postcondition for a predicate, is correct, then we know that the matching queries can never succeed (they must fail or loop). So *non-success* can be expressed as

exit Premiss ⇒ false

and can be exploited for integrity constraints like negative examples. To also have positive examples, we need *non-failure*, which is not expressible using pre/post-conditions alone. But, as shall be shown in Sec. 6.6, in Nope this can be expressed as

ff Premiss ⇒ false

where ff is the new *'port' of finite failure*, which can be either *derived* from the basic four ports (see Sec. 6.6), or built in.

So the subset assertions of [7] look in Nope like

ff qsort([2,1],[1,2]) ⇒ false

Similarly to finite failure, we can derive the event of building a resolvent, the *unify port* ('bootstrapping' the annotation language).

6   Illustrations

Here we give several short examples in support of our claim that the port annotations are a versatile and an intuitively appealing means to specify general mode information, to express and support the verification of hypothetical invariants, to write customized tracers, to alert to unwanted events, and generally enhance the prototyping and self-reflective capacities of Prolog.

6.1   Mergesort and Its Partial Specification

Our introductory example shows how annotations can help in debugging. Fig. 3 gives an implementation of the predicate merge/3. The predicate is specified to expect as inputs two sorted lists of integers, and to merge them into a sorted output list. This specification is captured in the form of two annotations.

The implementation of merge/3 is buggy. Usually the user discovers this by asking some queries and analyzing the answers of Prolog. However, due to the annotations, 'watching over' the specification, the analysis part can be delegated

:- ensure loaded(library(nope)). *% how to activate NOPE*

% Precondition: the inputs should make sense
:- call merge(X, Y, Z) =¿ sorted(X), sorted(Y)
         else format('inputs ~w and ~w must be sorted', [X,Y]).

% Postcondition
:- exit merge(X, Y, Z) with sorted(X), sorted(Y) =¿ sorted(Z).

merge([X—Xs], [Y—Ys], [X—Zs]) :- X¿Y, merge(Xs, [Y—Ys], Zs).
merge([X—Xs], [Y—Ys], [X,X—Zs]) :- X =:= Y, merge(Xs, Ys, Zs).
merge([X—Xs], [Y—Ys], [Y—Zs]) :- X¡Y, merge([X—Xs], Ys, Zs).
merge([], [X—Xs], [X—Xs]).
merge(Xs, [], Xs).

sorted([]). sorted([']). sorted([X,Y—L]) :- X =¡ Y, sorted([Y—L]).

Fig. 3. Program with annotations

to Nope. As soon as a goal is computed which violates one of the annotations, Nope alerts us to this fact.

For example, after loading the program, we can have the following interaction.

— ?- merge([3,1], [], ').
/* NOPE inputs [3,1] and [] must be sorted */

yes
— ?- merge([1], [2], M).
/* NOPE exit merge([1],[2],[2,1])with sorted([1]),sorted([2]) $\not\Rightarrow$ sorted([2,1]) */

M = [2,1] ?

The second message of Nope is warning us that the postcondition is violated, namely the merging algorithm produces unsorted lists (the first and the third clause for merge/3 have swapped comparisons).

An avid reader might object that we do not need the template sorted(X), sorted(Y) in the postcondition, since this is already being taken care of by the precondition. This is not quite true. Note that there can be arbitrarily many annotations for a predicate, even for the same port of it, and they will be composed via conjunction. But still, each annotation is regarded as an independent entity, in the sense of not having to take into account any other annotations. So our exit annotations actually do not assume that any call annotations have to be satisfied. For example, if we omit the template above and prove the following two annotations to hold

call merge(X,Y,Z) $\Rightarrow$ sorted(X), sorted(Y)
exit merge(X,Y,Z) $\Rightarrow$ sorted(Z)

with respect to the program and a closed set of top-level queries, then we know that merge/3 is only going to be called with sorted inputs, and that the output is also going to be sorted. But if the call annotation fails for a certain goal, the exit annotation is still going to be checked in Nope, requiring too much of the predicate (namely, that merge/3 is always going to deliver a sorted output, regardless of inputs).

   This example was about error *monitoring* by means of annotations. At almost no extra cost we can have error *diagnosis*, by means of two generic annotations [9].

6.2 Some Modes

To express that \+ does not alter its argument, we use the following mode declaration

   exit \+ X with copy'term(X,X0) $\Rightarrow$ variant(X,X0)

This example showed how to access the call/exit values of variables.

   For our next few examples we need to discriminate between a Prolog term which already is a list (i.e., all its instances are lists), and a Prolog term that can be instantiated to a list (i.e., some of its instances are lists). Let us name the former a *complete list*, and the latter an *incomplete list*. A complete list is a Prolog list structure ·(Head,Tail) with the ultimate tail [], and an incomplete list can be either a variable or a so-called *partial list*, namely a Prolog list structure whose ultimate tail is a variable. The type predicates for complete list vs. partial list shall bear traditional names is_list/1 vs. is_partiallist/1 and shall be defined as follows.

   is'list(X) :-
      var(X) -¿ fail; X=[]; X=['—Y], is'list(Y).

   is'partiallist(X) :-
      var(X) -¿ fail; X=['—Y], var(Y); X=['—Y], is'partiallist(Y).

Now we are able to pin down the mode of the classic predicate list/1:

   :- exit list(X) with copy'term(X,X0) =¿ var(X0); is'list(X0); is'partiallist(X0).
   :- exit list(X) =¿ is'list(X).

   list([]).
   list(['—T]) :- list(T).

claiming that a successful list/1 query has been called with a complete or an incomplete list, and will succeed with a complete list.

   The constraint that the first argument of append/2 from [15] be a complete list can be expressed (and documented) through the following two annotations.

```
:- call append(X,Y) with var(X), \+ Y=[] =¿ false else write(divergence).
:- call append(X,Y) with var(X), \+ \+ Y=[] =¿ false else write(trivial answers).
```

```
% append(-, `) :- !, fail. % reject incomplete lists  %% now catched by the ann's
append([], []).
append([L—Ls], List0) :- append(L, List1, List0), append(Ls, List1).
```

Note that, by using the default context, we do not need to actually check the list completeness, but only the var property, since each recursive call of append/2 will be checked. Note also how the constraint false serves to alert, at runtime, to unwanted events like ill-defined modes.

6.3   Use of Contexts and Parametricity

Due to parametricity and contexts, our annotations can be seen as macro definitions for program-point annotations. For example,

```
lr alert(Q) :-
    functor(Q,F,N), functor(Q0,F,N),
    (call Q within Q0 =¿ \+ subsumes noc(Q,Q0) else bark, write(lr:Q)).
```

```
subsumes noc(X,Y) :- groundcopy(Y,Yg), X=Yg.
```

```
:- lr alert(append(`,`)).
```

monitors leftmost (assuming left-to-right execution) recursive calls of append/2, like

```
— ?- append(X,[Y]).
/* NOPE lr:append(`347,[`94]) */
Prolog interruption (h for help)? c
/* NOPE lr:append(`758,[`94]) */
Prolog interruption (h for help)? a
Execution aborted
```

6.4   Uniform Conditioning

As a hint on the merits of conditioning even the call annotations (in order to express dependencies between the input arguments), see

```
call functor(T,F,N) with var(T) ⇒ nonvar(F), nonvar(N)
```

Observe that here we can get rid of the template, via a less readable but equivalent

```
call functor(T,F,N) ⇒ var(T) -¿ nonvar(F), nonvar(N); true
```

However, this does not hold in general. Namely, the *call* values of variables are normally not identical with their exit values. Thus, templates are not redundant, even in case of pure logic programs.[1] For programs with side-effects just more so, because (in case of exit, fail and redo) on the left of the arrow we have the state *before*, and on the right of the arrow: the state *after* the computation of Q.

Perhaps more convincing will be a less trivial example. The mode specification for the 'univ' operator for term creation and decomposition comprises seven error-cases in Standard Prolog (8.5.3.3.a-g in the source [8], or Sec. 98 in the reference book [4]). These can be expressed in Nope quite readably, especially since the 'natural' preconditions var(T) or Y\==[] can be separated from the constraints.

:- call T=..[] with var(T) ⇒ false else domain`error(non`empty`list). *% case f*

:- call T=..[X—Y] with var(T) ⇒ length(Y,N), Max`arity=255, N=¡Max`arity else representation`error(max`arity). *% case g*

:- call T=..List with var(T) ⇒ \+ var(List), \+ is`partiallist(List) else instantiation`error. *% case a modified, see examples below*

:- call T=..[X—Y] with var(T) ⇒ nonvar(X) else instantiation`error. *% case c*

:- call T=..List ⇒ var(List); is`list(List); is`partiallist(List) else type`error(list). *% case b corrected as in [4]*

:- call T=..[X—Y] with Y\==[] ⇒ var(X);atom(X) else type`error(atom). *% case d*

:- call T=..[X] ⇒ \+ compound(X) else type`error(atomic). *% case e*

The differences between this specification and the specifications of [8] and [4] can be summarized in the following table.

— ?- f(a) =.. L. *% [8] finds type_error(list), [4] and Nope find no error.*
— ?- T =.. a.   *% All find type_error(list), [4] additionally finds instantiation_error.*
— ?- T =.. L.   *% [8] finds type_error(list), [4] and Nope find instantiation_error.*

6.5   Tracing

The Byrd tracer (see Sec. 6.7) is a special case of annotation composition. We do not have to bear with all four ports of a general goal pattern if we only want a specific port of a specific goal pattern traced.

```
fail`alert(X) :- fail X =¿ write('Fail: '), write(X), nl.
:- fail`alert(p(X)).

p(1) :- p(2), p(3).
p(2) :- p(4).
p(4).
```

---

[1] Another reason is the subsumption on the left vs. unification on the right of the arrow, but that is not a vital design decision of the language, the way the call/exit values are.

```
    — ?- p(K).
Fail: p(3)
Fail: p(4)
Fail: p(2)

K = 2 ?
```

6.6   Finite Failure

The fail-port is capturing 'no (more)' rather than 'no'. Often we are interested only in genuine 'no', the finite failure. We can derive the *whole* of this new event from the basic four events, for example by emulating the Prolog stack:

```
ff(( Q with T within Ctx =¿ C )) :-
    (call Q with T within Ctx =¿ asserta(lemma(Q:call))),
    (redo Q with T within Ctx =¿ asserta(lemma(Q:redo))),
    (exit Q with T within Ctx =¿ once(retract(lemma(`:`)))),
    (fail Q with T within Ctx =¿ once(retract(lemma(Q:What)))), What=call -¿ C; true).
```

Alternatively, we can provide finite failure as a regular annotation, say ff, on a par with call/exit/fail/redo. This is a matter of only adding a new entry in the transformation table of Nope, and allows for superior code. Either way, we may now write

```
ff`alert(X) :- ff X =¿ write(finitely`fails:X), nl.
:- ff`alert(p(`)).
```

and obtain the desired behaviour:

```
    — ?- p(K).
finitely`fails: p(3)

K = 2 ?
```

Non-failure, which is not expressible using pre/post-conditions alone, can now be expressed as ff Premiss ⇒ false.

   In a similar way, we can derive the event of building a resolvent, the *unify port*, from the four basic events.

6.7   Byrd Invariant

Correctness of the original Byrd's trace algorithm [2] depends essentially on the claim that only one flipflop/0 predicate, defined as alternatively succeeding and failing, suffices to handle arbitrarily many predicates. Of the annotation languages known to us, only [7] can express such a claim, by resorting to program-point assertions. Contexts make this expressible in a predicate assertion.

```
:- dynamic tracing/0, notracing/0.
flipflop :- retract(tracing), assert(notracing).
flipflop :- retract(notracing), assert(tracing), fail.
tracing.
```

% Byrd's trace invariant
```
:- call call(Goal) within break(Goal) =¿ notracing. % for any Goal
```

```
break(Goal) :-
    trace(call, Goal), (call(Goal); trace(fail, Goal), fail),
    (trace(exit, Goal); trace(redo, Goal), fail).
```

```
trace(Port, Goal) :- tab(1), write(Port:Goal).
```

% Example. For every traced predicate a new first clause will be asserta'ed.
```
p(X) :- flipflop, !, break(p(X)).
p(1) :- p(2), p(3).
p(2) :- p(4).
p(4).
```

6.8   Safe Negation

Here we show a special case of the safe negation problem. A non-directed graph is given as a set of edges, written as a symmetric relation edge/2. We would like to know if the following program for transitive closure is 'safe', i.e. whether it would compute only sound answers.

% path(U, V, P) :-
%   P represents a cycle-free path between the nodes U and V as a list [U,..,V].
%   Cycle-free means here: No node occurs in P twice.

```
path(U, V, P) :- % safe to use in all modes
    path1(U, [V], P).
```

% path1(U, [V—Visited], [Un, .., U1, V — Visited]) :-
%   [Un, .., U1, V] is a path from U to V. No Ui occurs in [V—Visited]. No Ui occurs twice.
% Visited must be 'ground', i.e. may contain no variables.

```
path1(U, [V—Visited], [U, V—Visited]) :-
    edge(U, V), \+ member(U, [V—Visited]).
```

```
path1(U, [V—Visited], Path) :-
    edge(W, V), \+ member(W, [V—Visited]), path1(U, [W, V—Visited], Path).
```

Lemma 3 (path:nonfloundering). *The previous program does not flounder (wrt an arbitrary path/3 query), since the following annotation holds of it:*

```
call \+ member(X, L) ⇒ ground(X), ground(L)
```

This annotation is a consequence of the following two easier-to-prove ones:

exit edge(X, Y) $\Rightarrow$ ground(X), ground(Y)
call path1(U, [V—Visited], W) $\Rightarrow$ ground(Visited)

A straightforward inductive proof of the correctness of the program wrt the last two annotations and arbitrary path/3 queries follows from the verification condition of [5], being that we only have here a pre and a post condition. For the general case of port annotations, an extension to this verification condition can be proved.

7   Related Work

Due to lack of space, we discuss in this paper only approaches with, in our view, 'strong declarative emphasis', and left out the 'more procedural' ones, which are covered to some extent in [9].

Mode Languages.   The DEC-10 modes are de facto standard, which is reflected in the Standard Prolog sources [8]. The big asset of these modes is their simplicity, a very important criterion for a mode language, given the reluctance of users to put down any declarations at all. In [16] more precise (and complex) specification was possible. The trend of inventing new, finely tuned mode symbols was perpetuated in some other dialects of Prolog, with the result that mode declarations became rather arbitrary and complicated to use.

Somogyi [18] brought a vital simplification: the two implicit components of using a predicate, namely the calling pattern and the exit pattern, should be separated. Here, a mode is a *mapping* from an initial to a final state of instantiation of the arguments of the predicate, such that nothing gets less instantiated. This is a refinement of the classic concept of modes, making them simple and flexible. His concept of modes is scheduled for implementation within the Mercury project [6].

Modes and Beyond.   Naish [11] initiated the research into new, general kinds of declarations. His idea was to associate with some predicates of a program Π so-called type-predicates. Intended is the following relationship: the specification Σ corresponding to Π is the same as Π except that each clause $p(T_1, .., T_n)$:− B is replaced by $p(T_1, .., T_n)$:− B, p_type($T_1, .., T_n$). He designed and implemented a concrete declarative mode language [12]. The mode language generalizes upon directional types by putting constraints on type variables.

A further major step towards the goal of more declarative rendering of Prolog code is the LPTP framework of Stärk [19], proposing a first-order language capable of stating that a general goal succeeds, fails or (universally) terminates, together with a powerful calculus (formalizing a suitable execution model) for interactively proving these properties. The inherent limitation here is purity: only a logical subset of Prolog (no cut, var or assert/retract allowed) can be treated.

A different approach was put forward by Drabent and Małuszyński [5]: they introduced a general Prolog-like language to formulate pre/post conditions for predicates of a Prolog program. Each predicate must have one pair of pre/post conditions (*assertion*), which may be arbitrarily complex. For example, a predicate p/1 not changing its argument could have the assertion consisting of the trivial precondition true, and the postcondition .$p_1 = p_1$., meaning that upon exiting the predicate p, the corresponding calling pattern (designated by the left-dot) of the only argument of the predicate (designated by p_1) has to be identical to the exit pattern (designated by the right-dot). Here the dot syntax serves to differentiate between the two argument values, call and exit values. The authors coined the term *binary assertions* for assertions that have the means of accessing these two sets of argument values. The most popular language in the spirit of this general scheme is from the generic framework CIAO of Hermenegildo et al. [7]. Their language of assertions is a subset of Prolog. This has the distinct advantage of avoiding the introduction of an entirely new language, which would have to be learned (and liked) first. Here are some examples of their annotations.

```
:- calls qsort(A,B) : list(A).
:- success qsort(A,B) : list(A) =¿ list(B).
:- comp qsort(A,B) : (list(A), var(B)) + does˙not˙fail.
```

The first annotation is a (global) precondition, the second one a postcondition corresponding to the concept of assertion in [5], since it accommodates an own precondition, given before the arrow. The third annotation serves to express some properties of the computation like non-failure. Behind the somewhat patchworky syntax is a more serious issue of expressive power: pre/post conditions alone do not suffice to express every property of execution, e. g. non-failure. As stated in [7], *"no property which refers to (a sequence of) intermediate states in the computation (...) can be easily expressed using* calls *and* success *assertions only"*. This shortcoming of the pre/post conditions is here being compensated for by handing the more tricky properties over to Prolog.

Arguably a more natural way is to start from an explicit execution model of Prolog. The model should ideally be simple and complete. One such model happens to be generally known. The 4-port model [2], which is the basis of the standard Prolog debugger, is a *complete* execution model of Prolog, in the sense of entailing every aspect of Prolog execution necessary for verification, and therefore all the information one might need. This model maps a query Q to its standard trace $\mathcal{T}(Q)$, which is a sequence of *events* of the form Port F($T_1, .., T_N$), where Port may be one of {call, exit, fail, redo}, F/N are predicates, T_i are terms, representing the 'atomary' steps of the Prolog interpreter during the execution of Q (as defined in [2]).

This idea originates in probably the first proposal of Prolog annotations ever made, O'Keefe's public domain program Advice [14]. The annotations of Advice are of the form advise(Goal, Port, Action), which supersedes pre/post conditions.

Comparison to Nope. The generalized declarations of [11] would correspond to an exit annotation in Nope. A concept like complete list (see Sec. 6.2) cannot be expressed in [12], types being closed under instantiation. Regarding [19], our annotation language cannot state e. g. that a goal succeeds, only that, *if* the goal succeeds, then a constraint must hold. On the other hand, [19] is confined to pure logic programming so cannot represent degrees of instantiation.

Now we round off the comparisons to the three most closely related languages to our own, [5], [7] and [14]. Our approach accommodates pre/post conditions in the form of binary assertions as pioneered in [5], and also uses Prolog as the annotation language like [7]. But in contrast to these, our approach is taking into account that our object language is not an arbitrary one but Prolog, with its specific procedural semantics, so we stretched the general idea of pre/post conditions to accommodate specific events from a well-known *model* of Prolog execution. Therefore we can more naturally express procedural properties of Prolog. As an additional bonus, our annotations are written in terms of procedural concepts known by everybody who ever tried the Prolog debugger. One novelty of our approach is that each one of the annotations can be restricted to a subset of calls by means of templates and contexts (*calling premiss*). All annotations are uniform and *parametric*, since they are defined as Prolog goals, which makes them particularly suitable for dynamic checking. The novel idea of *context* allows expressing program-point assertions. The annotations are applied via a general kind of matching instead of unification.

On the other hand, [7] allows the user to choose between two checking regimes for pre and post conditions, one using their variant of subsumption akin to our soft success (but without local variables), and the other using unification (doubly negated to prevent interference). Default is the subsumption. In our approach, templates are checked using subsumption ('for all') and constraints using unification ('exists').

Advice [14] differs from Nope mainly in that it has unary assertions (i. e. the calling pattern is not available), uses unification instead of matching, has no contexts, and negated occurences of a predicate cannot be checked on their own (as no built-ins can be checked). The second item is of course an advantage of Advice over Nope, since matching can be emulated by unification but not vice versa.

8   Outlook

Similar to [3] and [7], we advocate dividing the burden of analysis between static and dynamic phases. The outline of our scenario: 1) Static analysis of some acceptable classes of annotations, with respect to the cost of analysis and the realistic gain for the user. The shining example of a widely accepted static check in logic programming is the singleton variable warning [13]: a variable occuring only once in a clause indicates a probable programming error. Quick and useful, this test[2] became classic. 2) Having a stock of basic static tests, which are being taken care of by fast algorithms, the next objective is to provide some kind of

---

[2] amusingly enough, even this could be represented via port annotations, monitoring the predicates for loading code, e. g. call assertz(C) $\Rightarrow$ \+ thereis_singleton_in(C).

calculus, enabling us to prove more complex annotations from the basic ones. 3) The rest of annotations are checked at runtime.

We envisage much further work on annotation languages for describing procedural properties of Prolog, especially in view of practical relevance. A competitive instance of Prolog has to accommodate foreign languages and programming paradigms like modules, constraints or agents, getting ever more complex on the way.

Acknowledgments. Many thanks for valuable comments upon previous drafts of this paper and other bits are due to C. Beierle, G. Meyer, R. Stärk, I. Đurđanović, M. Hermenegildo, U. Neumerkel, M. Carlsson, Vuk and the anonymous referees. This research was supported by the Deutsche Forschungsgemeinschaft (DFG), grant Be 1700/3-1.

References

1. Edinburgh University A. I. Applications Institute. Edinburgh Prolog tools. ftp://sunsite.doc.ic.ac.uk/packages/prolog-pd-software/tools.tar.Z, 1988.
2. Lawrence Byrd. Understanding the control flow of Prolog programs. In S. A. Tärnlund, editor, *Proc. of the Logic Programming Workshop*, pages 127–138, Debrecen, Hungary, 1980. Also as D. A. I. Research Paper No. 151.
3. P. W. Dart and J. Zobel. Efficient run-time type checking of typed logic programs. *J. of Logic Programming*, pages 31–69, 1992.
4. P. Deransart, A. Ed-Dbali, and L. Cervoni. *Prolog: The Standard (reference manual)*. Springer-Verlag, 1996.
5. W. Drabent and J. Małuszyński. Inductive assertion method for logic programs. *Theoretical Computer Science*, 59:133–155, 1988.
6. F. Henderson, T. Conway, Z. Somogyi, D. Jeffery, P. Schachte, S. Taylor, and C. Speirs. *The Mercury Language Reference Manual*. http://www.cs.mu.oz.au/research/mercury, 1998. Release 0.8.
7. M. Hermenegildo, G. Puebla, and F. Bueno. Using global analysis, partial specifications, and an extensible assertion language for program validation and debugging. In K. R. Apt, V. W. Marek, M. Truszczynski, and D. S. Warren, editors, *The Logic Programming Paradigm: A 25-Year Perspective*. Springer-Verlag, 1999.
8. ISO Prolog Standard drafts. http://www.logic-programming.org/prolog_std.html. Part I.
9. M. Kulaš. Debugging Prolog using annotations. In *WLPE'99: 10th Workshop on Logic Programming Environments*, Las Cruces, NM, 1999. Also in ENTCS, http://www.elsevier.nl/locate/entcs.
10. Gregor Meyer. Type checking and type inferencing for logic programs with subtypes and parametric polymorphism. Informatik Berichte 200, FernUniversität Hagen, 1996. See also tutorial notes of ICLP'97. Source distribution http://www.fernuni-hagen.de/pi8/typical.
11. L. Naish. Types and intended meaning. In F. Pfenning, editor, *Types in Logic Programming*, pages 189–215. MIT Press, 1992.
12. L. Naish. Mode checking using constrained regular trees. Technical Report 98/3, Department of Computer Science, University of Melbourne, 1998. Also as http://www.cs.mu.oz.au/~lee/papers/modealg/.

13. Richard A. O'Keefe. *vcheck.pl.* In DEC-10 Prolog Library [1]. Check for misspelled variables, 1982.
14. Richard A. O'Keefe. *advice.pl.* In DEC-10 Prolog Library [1]. Interlisp-like advice package, 1984.
15. Quintus Corp., Palo Alto, CA. *Quintus Prolog Language and Library*, 1991. Release 3.1.
16. Quintus Corp., Palo Alto, CA. *Quintus Prolog Reference Pages*, 1991. Release 3.1.
17. J. C. Reynolds. Transformational systems and the algebraic structure of atomic formulas. In B. Meltzer and D. Michie, editors, *Machine Intelligence 5*. Edinburgh University Press, 1970.
18. Z. Somogyi. A system of precise modes for logic programs. In *Proc. of the ICLP*, 1987.
19. Robert F. Stärk. The theoretical foundations of LPTP (a logic program theorem prover). *J. of Logic Programming*, 36(3):241–269, 1998. Source distribution http://www.inf.ethz.ch/personal/staerk/lptp.html. Release 1.05.
20. D. H. D. Warren. Implementing Prolog – Compiling predicate logic programs. Research Reports 39 and 40, University of Edinburgh, Dept. of Artificial Intelligence, 1977.

Verification by Testing for Recursive Program Schemes

Daniel Le Métayer, Valérie-Anne Nicolas, and Olivier Ridoux

IRISA/INRIA, Campus de Beaulieu, F-35042 Rennes Cedex, France
{lemetayer|vnicolas|ridoux}@irisa.fr

Abstract. In this paper, we explore the testing-verification relationship with the objective of mechanizing the generation of test data. We consider program classes defined as recursive program schemes and we show that complete and finite test data sets can be associated with such classes, that is to say that these test data sets allow us to distinguish every two different functions in these schemes. This technique is applied to the verification of simple properties of programs.

1 Introduction

The only way to improve confidence that a program really achieves its intended purpose is to confront it with other means of expressing this purpose. Typically, such means can be properties that the program is supposed to satisfy or test data sets with oracles characterizing the expected behavior of the program. However, despite the fact that they both contribute to the same final objective, verification and testing remain two independent research areas and we haven't seen much cross-fertilization between them so far (except in specific domains like protocol design). We believe that testing can be formalized in a fruitful way in order to cooperate harmoniously with verification. Our goal in this paper is to support this claim by putting forward a technique for the automatic verification of (simple) properties of programs that relies both on program analysis and program testing.

Since the systematic construction of complete test data sets is out of reach in general, we propose to tackle this problem by restricting it to classes of programs and properties. The key idea underlying this work is a transposition to recursive programs of the well-known property that $n+1$ values are sufficient to identify a polynomial of degree n. We introduce a hierarchy of common recursive program (or property) schemes which define infinite classes of functions. The main result of the paper shows that each scheme can be associated with a finite complete test data set. The test data sets are complete in the sense that they are sufficient to distinguish any two distinct functions in the class.

This result essentially provides a way to reduce program equivalence to program testing (with respect to a given hierarchy of program schemes). In this paper, we show how this technique can also be used in conjunction with abstract interpretation to prove simple properties of programs. One must have in

A. Bossi (Ed.): LOPSTR'99, LNCS 1817, pp. 255–272, 2000.

mind that we do not want to prove the complete correctness of a program via testing. Instead, partial correctness properties will be proved via testing. More than on a list of scheme hierarchies, we want to dwell on a new method for proving program properties, relying on the association of test data sets to schemes, independently of the syntactic shape of these schemes.

In the following section we introduce a simple hierarchy of unary recursive schemes to illustrate our ideas, and we proceed with the technical contribution of the paper, which makes it possible to associate schemes with complete test data sets. Section 3 extends this result to some more complex unary and binary scheme hierarchies our method can deal with. Section 4 describes the use of these results to prove properties of programs, and Section 5 shows the relevance of our method on some application examples. Section 6 sketches the more general context of this work.

2   A Simple Hierarchy of Recursive Schemes

The process that we describe in Section 4 relies on our ability to associate complete test data sets with schemes. In this section, we provide a sketch of the proof of this result for a simple hierarchy of recursive schemes introduced in Definition 2. The interested reader can find in [NIC98] the definition of the whole framework.

A test data set is complete with respect to a scheme if it allows to decide the equality of any two functions of the scheme. This is stated in Definition 1.

Definition 1
D is a complete test data set for a class C of functions if and only if

$$\forall f \in C, \ \forall g \in C, \ (f \neq g \Rightarrow \exists x \in D \ s.t. \ (f(x) \neq g(x)))$$

In other words, D is a complete test data set for a class C of functions if and only if $\forall f \in C, \ \forall g \in C, \ ((\forall x \in D \ , \ f(x) = g(x)) \Rightarrow (f = g))$.

Definition 2

$$S^1_1 = \{\lambda x. \ Succ^k(x) \mid k \in I\!N\} \ \bigcup \ \{\lambda x. \ k \mid k \in I\!N\}$$
$$S^1_{i+1} = \{f \mid f(0) = k$$
$$f(n+1) = g(f(n)) \ , \ k \in I\!N \ , \ g \in S^1_i\}$$

The scheme of lower level in the hierarchy S^1 (S^1_1) is made of all the successor and all the constant unary functions on $I\!N$. Functions in scheme S^1_i follow a recursive pattern where the result is a constant in the basic case, and a composition of a recursive call with a function belonging to a scheme of lower level in the hierarchy in the recursive case. The schemes S^1_i are inspired by previous work on inductive data types and the associated inductive program schemes [PDM89]. These schemes are called unary schemes because they allow the definition of some unary functions (in Section 3, we consider some binary schemes to express functions on pairs of natural numbers). The first observation to be made about functions of the S_i^1 schemes is that they can be split into two different classes of functions: the first class contains increasing functions,[1] in fact even only *separable* functions in a sense made precise below. Functions of the second class, that we call *periodic* have a finite codomain. For example, in S_1^1, the class of separable functions is the set of successor functions, and the class of periodic functions is the set of constant functions.

Definition 3

Two functions f and g from $\mathbb{N}$ to $\mathbb{N}$ are said α-separable if and only if there exists α open intervals $I_1, \ldots, I_\alpha$ with $I_i =]A_i, A_{i+1}[$, $A_1 = -1$, $A_{\alpha+1} = \infty$, $i > j \Rightarrow A_i > A_j$ and

$$\forall i \in [1, \alpha], (even(i) \Rightarrow (\forall x \in I_i, (f(x) < g(x)) \quad and \quad f(A_{i+1}) \geq g(A_{i+1})))$$

$$\forall i \in [1, \alpha], (odd(i) \Rightarrow (\forall x \in I_i, (f(x) > g(x)) \quad and \quad f(A_{i+1}) \leq g(A_{i+1})))$$

Two functions f and g are α-separable if it is possible to decompose $\mathbb{N}$ into α intervals $I_1, \ldots, I_\alpha$ such that one of the two functions is strictly greater than the other on each interval. In the definition, α is the least value satisfying this property. The relevance of α-separability for testing stems from Property 1, which follows directly from Definition 3 ($card(D)$ denotes the cardinality of the set D):

Property 1

If f and g are α-separable and D is a subset of $\mathbb{N}$ such that $\forall x \in D, f(x) = g(x)$ then $card(D) < \alpha$.

Property 1 means that two α-separable functions can at most be equal on $\alpha - 1$ values. It is thus necessary and sufficient to test them on α values to distinguish them. For example, $\{0, \ldots, \alpha - 1\}$ is a complete test data set for any pair of α-separable functions, and so for any set of α-separable functions.

We now turn our attention to periodic functions. A periodic function begins returning some distinct values, afterwards it has a cyclic behavior.

Definition 4

A function f from $\mathbb{N}$ to $\mathbb{N}$ is said δ-periodic if and only if $\exists \lambda \geq 0$, $\exists \pi > 0$, s.t. $(\lambda + \pi \leq \delta)$ and

$$\forall x \geq \lambda . \forall y \geq \lambda . (x \bmod \pi = y \bmod \pi \Rightarrow f(x) = f(y))$$
$$\wedge \forall x < \lambda + \pi . \forall y < \lambda + \pi . (f(x) = f(y) \Rightarrow x = y)$$

where mod is the modulo function.

Notice that the whole behavior of a δ-periodic function can be determined by just knowing its behavior on the first $(\lambda + \pi + 1)$ natural numbers (the λ first values give the initial non-cyclic behavior, the following π values give the cyclic behavior and the last one the value of the period).

The relevance of periodicity for testing is expressed by the following property, which is a direct consequence of Definition 4:

---

[1] A unary function f is increasing if $\forall x.f(x) \geq x$.

Property 2
If C is a set of δ-periodic functions then $\{0,\ldots,\delta\}$ is a complete test data set for C.

The notions of separability and periodicity can be generalized to sets of functions and the above results can be gathered as follows:

Property 3
If a class C of functions is the union of a class C_1 of δ-periodic functions and of a class C_2 of increasing α-separable functions then $\{0,\ldots,\mu\}$ is a complete test data set for C with $\mu = max(\delta, \alpha - 1)$.

This result can be proven using Property 1 and Property 2 and showing that the test values necessary to distinguish two functions from C_1 or C_2 respectively are sufficient to distinguish a function from C_1 and a function from C_2. It relies mainly on the fact that functions of C_2 are injective whereas functions of C_1 are not (the test of a function of C_1 on the value δ will yield a value already obtained by its test on the previous test data).

The observation made at the beginning of this section can now be stated formally:

Property 4
$\forall i,\ S_i^1 = C_i^1 \bigcup C_i^2$ *with C_i^1 i-periodic and C_i^2 increasing i-separable.*

This property is proven by induction on i, relying on lemmas which establish the propagation of separability and periodicity through the hierarchy of schemes [NIC98].

Property 4 and Property 3 joined together allow us to derive Property 5, which is the fundamental property on which all the other results presented in this paper rely.

Property 5
$\forall i,\ \{0,\ldots,i\}$ *is a complete test data set for S_i^1.*

We have considered only one simple hierarchy of schemes so far. It has mainly allowed us to introduce the key ideas of our method. In the next section, we show how the result presented above can be used to derive complete test data sets for other unary and binary schemes.

3   Extension to Some Other Scheme Hierarchies

In this section, we first present a larger hierarchy of program schemes where the recursive call is not direct (the recursive call to the function does not need to be applied to the argument n directly) and then consider some binary functions in Section 3.2. We can benefit from the result presented in the previous section to associate test data sets to these more complex scheme hierarchies.

3.1 A More Complex Unary Scheme Hierarchy

In this section, we consider a slight generalization of the unary scheme hierarchy S^1 presented in Section 2. The difference is that our new $\{S_n^2, \ n \in \mathbb{N}\}$ hierarchy allows recursive calls which do not need to apply directly to the argument n:

Definition 5

$$S_i^2 = \{f \mid f(0) = k$$
$$f(n+1) = g(f(h(n))) \ , \ k \in \mathbb{N}, \ g \in S_i^1, \ h \in S_i^1\}$$

One first difference with respect to S_n^1 schemes is that S_n^2 do not contain only total functions. Depending on the value of the function h, the recursive call to f can apply to an argument greater than the initial one. Consequently, we begin with characterizing a definition domain for the functions of S_n^2.

Property 6
Consider the following definition of f

$$f(0) \quad = k$$
$$f(n+1) = g(f(h(n)))$$

with $g \in S_i^1$ and $h \in S_i^1$.
Function f is total if and only if f is defined on each value of the set $\{1, \ldots, i\}$.

For a function h which is i-periodic, the resulting function f, when it terminates, is neither periodic (as defined in Definition 4) nor increasing α-separable. However, it has a cyclic behavior (just like periodic functions) but it may repeat certain values where periodic functions ensure distinct values. Nevertheless, the following property allows us to distinguish this new kind of function from the periodic and increasing α-separable ones.

Property 7
Consider the following definition of f

$$f(0) \quad = k$$
$$f(n+1) = g(f(h(n)))$$

with $h \in S_i^1$ i-periodic and $g \in S_i^1$.
If f is total then the set $\{0, \ldots, 2i\}$ is sufficient to determine f (i.e. to determine the value of its period and its behavior on a period).

Gathering the above results, we can prove that: $\forall n \ . \ S_{n+1}^1 \subset S_n^2$. We are now able to derive a complete test data set for the total functions of the S_n^2 scheme.

Property 8
$\forall n \ . \ \{0, \ldots, 2n\}$ is a complete test data set for the total functions of the S_n^2 scheme.

3.2   Some Binary Scheme Hierarchies

All the functions considered so far are unary. We now turn our attention to binary functions (n-ary functions can be treated in a similar way). The following schemes capture some common recursive definition patterns:

Definition 6

$$B^1(X_1, X_2) = \{f \mid f(0,m) = h(m)$$
$$f(n+1,m) = g(f(n,m)) \ , \ g \in X_1, \ h \in X_2\}$$

$$B^2(X_1, X_2) = \{f \mid f(0,m) = h(m)$$
$$f(n+1,m) = f(n, g(m)) \ , \ h \in X_1, \ g \in X_2\}$$

$$B^3(X) \quad = \{f \mid f(0,m) = k$$
$$f(n+1,m) = g(m, f(n,m)) \ , \ k \in \mathbb{N}, \ g \in X\}$$

Binary schemes B^1 and B^2 are parameterized by the unary schemes associated with the functions occurring in their definitions, and binary scheme B^3 is parameterized by one of the binary schemes of the definition. Property 4 shows that each unary scheme S_i^1 is made of two classes of functions corresponding to δ-periodic functions and increasing α-separable functions. In order to establish the required results for binary schemes, we need to consider these two subclasses separately. We call them P_i and I_i (for Periodic and Increasing respectively).

Definition 7

$$P_1 \quad = \{\lambda x. \ k \mid k \in \mathbb{N}\}$$
$$P_{i+1} = \{f \mid f(0) = k$$
$$f(n+1) = g(f(n)) \ , \ k \in \mathbb{N}, \ g \in P_i\}$$

$$I_1 \quad = \{\lambda x. \ (x+k) \mid k \in \mathbb{N}\}$$
$$I_{i+1} = \{f \mid f(0) = k$$
$$f(n+1) = g(f(n)) \ , \ k \geq i-1, \ g \in I_i'\}$$

$$I_1' \quad = \{\lambda x. \ (x+k) \mid k > 0\}$$
$$I_{i+1}' = \{f \mid f(0) = k$$
$$f(n+1) = g(f(n)) \ , \ k \neq 0, \ g \in I_i'\}$$
$$\bigcup \{f \mid f(0) = 0$$
$$f(n+1) = g(f(n)) \ , \ g \in I_i''\}$$

$$I_1'' \quad = \{\lambda x. \ (x+k) \mid k > 1\}$$
$$I_{i+1}'' = \{f \mid f(0) = k$$
$$f(n+1) = g(f(n)) \ , \ k > 1, \ g \in I_i'\}$$
$$\bigcup \{f \mid f(0) = 0$$
$$f(n+1) = g(f(n)) \ , \ g \in I_i''\}$$
$$\bigcup \{f \mid f(0) = 1$$
$$f(n+1) = g(f(n)) \ , \ g \in I_i''\}$$

The sub-class of functions I_i' is used to exclude the possibility that $g = id$ in the definition of I_{i+1}. The intermediate scheme I_i'' allows us to remove syntactically the different possible definitions of the identity function and the successor function.

We can now state the main results concerning binary schemes.

The following properties allow us to associate a complete test data set to most of the parameterized schemes of Definition 6. The first property concerns the scheme $B^1(X_1, X_2)$.

Property 9

$(\{0\} \times \{0, \ldots, j-1\}) \cup (\{1\} \times \{0, \ldots, i-1\})$ is a complete test data set for $B^1(I_i, I_j)$.

$\{0, \ldots, i\} \times \{0, \ldots, j\}$ is a complete test data set for $B^1(I_i, P_j)$.

$\{0, \ldots, i+1\} \times \{0, \ldots, j\}$ is a complete test data set for $B^1(P_i, P_j)$.

The next properties establish the same kind of results as Property 9 for the schemes $B^2(X_1, X_2)$ and $B^3(X)$ respectively.

Property 10

$(\{0\} \times \{0, \ldots, i-1\}) \cup (\{1\} \times \{0, \ldots, j-1\})$ is a complete test data set for $B^2(I_i, I_j)$.

$(\{0\} \times \{0, \ldots, i-1\}) \cup (\{1\} \times \{0, \ldots, j\})$ is a complete test data set for $B^2(I_i, P_j)$.

Property 11

$\{(0, 0)\} \cup (\{1\} \times \{1, \ldots, i\}) \cup (\{1, \ldots, j\} \times \{1\})$ is a complete test data set for $B^3(B^1(I_i, I_j))$.

The whole proof of these properties is detailed in [NIC98].

Note that we have proposed some complete test data sets for the more common instantiations of the binary schemes. The ones which have not been treated correspond to unusual combinations in real programs. For example, the scheme $B^1(P_i, I_j)$ is defined by:

$$B^1(P_i, I_j) = \{f \mid f(0, m) = h(m) \\ f(n+1, m) = g(f(n, m)) , \ g \in P_i, \ h \in I_j\}$$

Actually, it is the recursive application of a periodic function, ending with a call to an increasing function.

Furthermore, it is interesting to notice that these unusual combinations lead to not easily testable program schemes. For the scheme $B^1(P_i, I_j)$ for example, the difficulty comes from the fact that there is no way to ensure that a finite number of arguments of the increasing function h produces a set of results covering the domain of g (modulo its periodicity).

In Section 4 we illustrate the use of the results presented in Sections 2 and 3 to derive complete test data sets to prove properties of programs.

4 Verification of Properties Using Complete Test Data Sets

Let us consider a simple program for reversing lists, written in a first-order functional language. Function Rev reverses a list, and function App adds an element (the second argument) at the end of a list (the first argument):

$$\begin{aligned} Rev(nil) &= nil \\ Rev(n:l) &= App(Rev(l), n) \end{aligned}$$

$$\begin{aligned} App(nil, m) &= m:nil \\ App(n:l, m) &= n:App(l, m) \end{aligned}$$

One property that a *reverse* program must satisfy is the fact that the length of its result must be equal to the length of its argument. In order to check this property, we have to express it as a function computing the expected length of the result of Rev from the length of its argument. Obviously, this function is the identity Id here.

The next stage consists in deriving an abstract version of Rev computing the length of the result of Rev from the length of its argument. Though the choice of an actual abstraction is dependent on the property to be proved and is not automatic, its application to the program can be achieved automatically, applying the abstract interpretation technique [CC77]. We choose the natural numbers $\mathbb{N}$ as the abstract domain and the abstraction function associates each list with its length. Non-list values are abstracted in a one point domain because they are not relevant to the analysis considered here. Rather than keeping these dummy arguments, we abstract a function with some non-list arguments into a function with fewer arguments. The primitives of interest here are basically the list constructor (denoted by ":" in our programming language) and the empty list nil. Not surprisingly, their abstractions are, respectively, the successor function $Succ = \lambda x.(x+1)$ and the constant $\lambda x.0$. Thus, we get the following abstract interpretation $Lrev$ for the Rev function.[2]

$$\begin{aligned} Lrev(0) &= 0 \\ Lrev(n+1) &= Lapp(Lrev(n)) \end{aligned}$$

$$\begin{aligned} Lapp(0) &= 1 \\ Lapp(n+1) &= Succ(Lapp(n)) \end{aligned}$$

Now we are left with comparing $Lrev$ with the identity function. Of course, in this simple case we could rely on symbolic manipulations and inductive proof techniques to show that $Lapp$ is equivalent to the function $Succ$ and then replace it in the body of $Lrev$. But it is well known that mechanizing these techniques is difficult in general. What we do instead is to analyze the definitions of $Lrev$ and

---

[2] Note that the second argument of App is not of type list, which explains why $Lapp$ has a single argument

Id to derive a complete test data set to decide their equivalence (or provide a counter-example if they turn out to be different). The goal of this simple syntactic analysis (called *scheme inference*) is to identify the scheme (or skeleton) of each function and find its position in the hierarchy of schemes.

We do not dwell on the scheme inference algorithm here. It is achieved by pattern matching on the structure of the definition of the functions and relies on a set of inference rules akin to a type inference system. Details about its implementation can be found in [NIC98]. For example, the definition of $Lrev$ matches the generic pattern of the schemes S_i^1 defined in Section 2 :

$$
\begin{aligned}
f(0) \quad &= k \\
f(n+1) &= g(f(n))
\end{aligned}
$$

with $k = 0$ and $g = Lapp$. The definition of $Lapp$ matches the generic pattern with $k = 1$ and $g = Succ$, which belongs to scheme S_1^1. So $Lapp$ is associated with scheme S_2^1 and $Lrev$ is associated[3] with scheme S_3^1.

It is not difficult to show that the schemes S_i^1 define a hierarchy which is strictly increasing with respect to set inclusion (in other words $i < i' \Rightarrow S_i^1 \subset S_{i'}^1$). Id belongs to the scheme S_1^1, so we have to take the least upper bound of S_1^1 and S_3^1, which is S_3^1. This shows that it is enough to test Id and $Lrev$ on the values 0, 1, 2, and 3 to decide their equality. In order to express these values in terms of the original program, we just have to use the correspondence relation between the abstract and the concrete domains. Here, this means that it is enough to test the program Rev on four randomly chosen lists of lengths 0, 1, 2, and 3 to decide if Rev always returns lists of the same length as its argument. In practice, one can prefer to choose lists made of distinct elements, which have a greater power of discrimination and can allow the detection of bugs apart from the property of interest.

To summarize, the four main stages of the test data derivation process are the following:

Abstraction of the program: Program $\rightarrow$ Abstract program

$\downarrow$

Scheme inference: Abstract program $\rightarrow$ $Scheme_1$
Property $\rightarrow$ $Scheme_2$

$\downarrow$

Abstract test data inference: $Lub(Scheme_1, Scheme_2) \rightarrow$ Abstract test data

$\downarrow$

Concrete test data generation: Abstract test data $\rightarrow$ Concrete test data

---

[3] Since both Id and $Lrev$ are semantically equal to the identity function, we could have expected that they are just associated with S_1^1, but we have to keep in mind that this knowledge is not available at this stage (in fact, it is exactly what we are trying to prove).

5   The Method at Work

In the previous section, we have used the *Reverse* program and the *Id* property to explain the different stages of the method introduced in Section 2. In this section, we present further examples illustrating it. We are still considering list functions, and our aim is to prove properties about the lengths of their arguments and results. So, we are using the same abstraction as the one used in the previous section. We start with a replacement program, which is supposed to return a list whose length is the product of the lengths of its arguments ; we continue with two sort programs returning a list of the same length as their argument.

5.1   A Replacement Program

Let us consider a program *Rep* replacing each element of its first list argument by its second argument. This program can be written:

$$Rep(nil, l_2) \quad = nil$$
$$Rep(n : l_1, l_2) \quad = Apnd(l_2, Rep(l_1, l_2))$$

$$Apnd(nil, l_2) \quad = l_2$$
$$Apnd(n : l_1, l_2) = n : Apnd(l_1, l_2)$$

We would like to check that the length of the result of *Rep* is the product of the lengths of its argument. The product function can be written as follows:

$$Mult(0, m) \quad = 0$$
$$Mult(n + 1, m) = Add(m, Mult(n, m))$$

$$Add(0, m) \quad = m$$
$$Add(n + 1, m) \quad = Succ(Add(n, m))$$

The abstract interpretation outlined in Section 4 returns the following abstract function for *Rep*:

$$Lrep(0, n_2) \quad = 0$$
$$Lrep(n_1 + 1, n_2) \quad = Lapnd(n_2, Lrep(n_1, n_2))$$

$$Lapnd(0, n_2) \quad = n_2$$
$$Lapnd(n_1 + 1, n_2) = Succ(Lapnd(n_1, n_2))$$

The scheme inference algorithm associates the scheme $B^3(B^1(I_1, I_1))$ with both *Lrep* and *Mult* (the scheme returned for *Lapnd* and *Add* is $B^1(I_1, I_1)$ since $\lambda x.x$ and *Succ* both belong to I_1). So $D = \{(0, 1), (1, 0), (1, 1)\}$ is a complete test data set for *Lrep* and it is sufficient to test *Rep* on lists of the lengths indicated by D to decide if the length of its result is indeed the product of the lengths of its arguments.

5.2   A Selection Sort Program

A selection sort program $Selsort$ can be defined as follows in our functional programming language:

$$
\begin{aligned}
Selsort(nil) \;&= nil \\
Selsort(n:l) \;&= \textbf{let } (n_1, l_1) = Maxl(l, n) \\
&\quad\; \textbf{in } n_1 : Selsort(l_1)
\end{aligned}
$$

$$
\begin{aligned}
Maxl(nil, m) \;&= (m, nil) \\
Maxl(n:l, m) \;&= \textbf{let } (n_1, l_1) = Maxl(l, n) \\
&\quad\; \textbf{in } (Max(m, n_1), Min(m, n_1) : l_1)
\end{aligned}
$$

The abstract interpretation returns the following abstract function for this program:

$$
\begin{aligned}
Lselsort(0) \;&= 0 \\
Lselsort(n+1) \;&= Succ(Lselsort(Lmaxl(n)))
\end{aligned}
$$

$$
\begin{aligned}
Lmaxl(0) \;&= 0 \\
Lmaxl(n+1) \;&= Succ(Lmaxl(n))
\end{aligned}
$$

Note that $Lmaxl$ is of arity 1 since $Maxl$ has only one list argument, which allowed us to simplify the function by removing the let expression. The scheme inference returns the scheme S_2^2 for $Lselsort$ ($Lmaxl$ being associated with the scheme S_2^1). Since the identity function belongs to S_1^2, $\{0, 1, 2, 3\}$ is a complete test data set to decide if $Lselsort = Id$; it is thus sufficient to test the program $Selsort$ on four randomly chosen lists of length 0, 1, 2, and 3 to decide if it possesses the required property.

Note that a standard proof of this property (that program $Selsort$ respects the length) would have used an induction on the length of the argument. So, it would have required a non-trivial proof technique, while our method boils down to the comparison of test outputs.

However, it should be clear that only errors which have an impact on the length of the result are guaranteed to be detected using this test data set (since it is the very purpose of this test). Let us imagine for example that we have forgotten the introduction of the value $Min(m, n_1)$ in the result of $Maxl$:

$$
\begin{aligned}
Maxl(nil, m) \;&= (m, nil) \\
Maxl(n:l, m) \;&= \textbf{let } (n_1, l_1) = Maxl(l, n) \\
&\quad\; \textbf{in } (Max(m, n_1), l_1)
\end{aligned}
$$

The mistake would be revealed through the application of $Selsort$ to a list of length 2. But if we had inadvertently replaced Max by Min, the bug would not necessarily be captured by a test data set including random list of lengths 0, 1, 2, and 3. In this case however, if we consider the extra condition that the lists of the test data set contain different elements, then the bug is detected.

5.3   An Insertion Sort Program

Insertion sort can be defined as follows:

$$Insort(nil) \quad = nil$$
$$Insort(n:l) \quad = Insert(Insort(l), n)$$

$$Insert(nil, m) \; = m : nil$$
$$Insert(n:l, m) = Max(n, m) : (Insert(l, Min(n, m)))$$

The abstract interpretation of this program returns the following abstract function:

$$Linsort(0) \quad\;\; = 0$$
$$Linsort(n+1) = Linsert(Linsort(n))$$

$$Linsert(0) \quad\;\; = 1$$
$$Linsert(n+1) = Succ(Linsert(n))$$

The scheme inferred for $Linsort$ is S_3^1, so $Insort$ has the same complete test data set as $Selsort$. As an illustration of the accurateness of this test data set, let us consider a wrong definition of $Insert$:

$$Insort'(nil) \quad\;\; = nil$$
$$Insort'(n:l) \quad\;\; = Insert'(Insort'(l), n)$$

$$Insert'(nil, m) \; = m : nil$$
$$Insert'(n:l, m) = Max(n, m) : (Min(n, m) : nil)$$

The abstract interpretation of $Insort'$ is the function

$$Linsort'(0) \quad\;\; = 0$$
$$Linsort'(n+1) = Linsert'(Linsort'(n))$$

$$Linsert'(0) \quad\;\; = 1$$
$$Linsert'(n+1) = 2$$

$Linsert'$ can be cast into the S_i^1 schemes as:

$$Linsert'(0) \quad\;\; = 1$$
$$Linsert'(n+1) = \bar{2}(Linsert'(n))$$

where $\bar{2}$ denotes $\lambda x.\ 2$, the constant function which returns 2.

So $Linsert'$ also belongs to S_2^1; as a consequence $Linsort'$ and $Linsort$ belong to the same scheme S_3^1.

It turns out that the erroneous definition $Insort'$ returns correct results for lists of length less than or equal to 2. Thus, it is indeed necessary to include a list of length 3 into the test data set to capture this bug.

6   Related Work

6.1   Program Testing and Program Verification

The work presented here stands at the crossroad of three main trends of activities: program testing, program analysis and program verification. It presents similarities but also differences with each of them.

The main departure with respect to "traditional" verification techniques and formal development methods like Z [SPI92], VDM [JON90], LARCH [GH93], B [ABR96] is that we trade generality for mechanization. Our goal is not to provide complete correctness proofs of a program but rather to "formally test" it against specific properties. This strategy is shared by the program analysis community, but the verifications that are made possible by our method are out of reach of static analysis techniques. These techniques rely on iterative algorithms to compute fixed points of recursive equations [CC77]. Restrictions have to be introduced in order to ensure the termination of these iterations. One typical restriction is to impose that the abstract domains are finite (or, more generally, that no infinitely increasing chain of values can be constructed by the algorithm). The kind of restriction introduced in this paper is of a different nature: it is a restriction on the structure of the definition of the program. One advantage of this kind of restriction (which is due to its syntactic nature) is that it can also be used in a top-down process, to favor the construction of more easily testable programs. Another advantage is that it can be checked mechanically (in contrast with classical test hypotheses). Further work is needed to decide if traditional program analysis techniques can be extended to take advantage of such restrictions.

Most of the properties we have proven using testing in this paper also could have been proven using inductive proof techniques. Our method can be seen as a factorization of the proving effort in the association between a test data set and a scheme. Moreover, in the context of a syntactically restricted formalism, determining the scheme of a function is easier than directing a proof by induction.

The research activities in software testing can be classified into two very distinct categories:

1. General theories of testing have been proposed including notions like test data adequacy [BA82, WEY83, DO91], testability [FRE91, GAU95], robustness [GG75], reliability [DO91], ideal test data sets [GG75], valid and unbiased test data sets [GAU95], test hypotheses [GAU95], etc. But test criteria with the desired qualities usually lead to infinite test data sets or test hypotheses which do not necessarily hold.

2. On the practical side, a number of test coverage criteria have been put forward [BEI90, NTA88, RW85]. Some of them are supported by test coverage measure tools [OW91]. These tools are automatic but they only provide *a posteriori* information about the test coverage of a given test data set. In any case, these criteria are not exactly formal in the sense that there is no link between the satisfaction of a test coverage criterion (at least for the effective ones) and the correctness of the program.

A distinctive feature of our work with respect to testing (which makes it closer to verification) is that it is not limited to the detection of bugs in a program: we know that a program which passes a complete test data set satisfies the tested property. Also, since our test data generation process takes both the program and a property into account, it can be seen as an hybrid of structural and functional testing. Such an integration has already been advocated in a more general framework in the past [RC85], but without any mechanical procedure. A similar approach has been successfully investigated for protocol testing [FJJV96, BP94], but these contributions focus on the control aspects of programs (rather than on data). They are thus complementary to our work.

6.2   Program Testing and Program Learning

By another way, one can compare our testing technique, and more generally the test generation process, with techniques from the program learning community. These techniques are about synthesizing programs from examples [BIE78] (as opposed to generating test data sets from programs). This trend of research is concerned with both the learning procedures and the classes of functions that can be learned. The framework that is common to all these methods is called *inductive inference.*

The programs that are learned belong in fact to restricted fragments of a programming language. This is because inductive learning uses a notion of *learning bias* to narrow the search space. The role of the learning bias is to make the learning process feasible and as efficient as possible. A learning bias restricts the language in which the concept to be learned is expressed. Such a bias makes the learning process incomplete because the intended concept may be better expressed outside the learning bias, or even may not be expressible in the learning bias. However, a learning bias establishes a formal relation between the examples and the concept that is learned.

Tools and methods exist for program testing and program learning. However, a deeper examination of these two activities shows that they are based on very different hypotheses.

In the learning activity, a finite suite of examples or traces is used to generate a program that is guaranteed to satisfy the examples. In other words, if one considers the suite of examples as a test data set, it is certain that the generated program will pass it. Note also that the input document is assumed to be correct. A learning bias is used to narrow the search space and to infer only regular programs. This restriction is in the same spirit as testing hypotheses, which also assume regularity in the tested programs.

In the context of structural testing, test data sets are generated from a program according to a test criterium (e.g., all-instructions, all-def-use). But finite test data sets are generally not robust (which means that they can accept incorrect programs). Finally, the input document (the program) cannot be assumed to be correct. This shows that the situation is less favorable than in the context of program learning. The basic reason is that classical approaches to the generation of test data sets deal with general programs (i.e., written in Turing-complete languages), whereas program learning deals with biased programs.

A solution to make the situation of test data sets generation more favorable is to borrow from program learning some of its hypotheses. We will call *testing bias* a syntactic restriction that corresponds in program testing to a learning bias in program learning. Our method goes in this direction, taking inspiration from automated program learning to do test generation via a testing bias. Here, testing biases are defined as recursive function schemes and our method deals with hierarchies of testing biases.

The relation between program learning and program testing has been recognized in the past by several authors [WEY83, BG96]. In fact, Bergadano *et al.* actually use program learning as a means for generating test data sets. In their case, a program learning process generates incrementally a family of programs that are "close" to the program to be tested. Each time a new program is produced, a new test case is added to the set of examples. The new test case must be such that it distinguishes the new program from the program to be tested. Our technique does not actually perform program learning. We mainly use it as a fruitful metaphor to establish a tight relation between a finite set of input/output data, a program and a property. The key idea is that the program must belong to a "learnable" family. On the contrary, usual testing theories either involve infinite sets of data, or lack a well defined relation between test data sets and programs.

7   Conclusion

The approach put forward in this paper is based on a tight integration of static analysis and testing techniques for program verification. These techniques are traditionally studied by different communities without much cross-fertilization. Furthermore, considering the three types of documents used in programming, i.e., properties (e.g., specifications), programs, and data (e.g., test data and examples), one can observe that all point-to-point relations between these documents have been explored in both directions (e.g., the program-data relation corresponds to testing and program learning). However, it is seldom the case that the relation between the three types of documents is considered globally. We think that great benefits can be gained from a better understanding of the connections between them [LMNR98].

Our method is both formal and automatic. Once the abstraction is chosen (that is to say, the abstract domain and the abstraction function), all the different stages of the method are fully automated. There is no way to find automatically the abstraction, it is the only point in our method for which the user has to be a bit intuitive. From a practical point of view, it is possible to construct libraries of abstractions by associating some different generic abstractions to several inductive types. This could be an help for the user. Our method has been implemented in a prototype system which, as a consequence, does not require any specific knowledge from the user. This system is powerful enough to deal with all the examples used in this paper. It is our belief that there is plenty of room for software engineering tools between the following two extremes: unrestricted, but only semi-automated, techniques requiring significant efforts from highly qualified users, and fully automated processes with restricted power [LM97].

Of course, the price to pay for complete mechanization is to limit one's ambitions: we have introduced restrictions on both programs and properties to be verified. Note however that the restriction on programs is weaker than the restriction on properties since it is only their abstraction that must belong to one scheme of the hierarchy. Because of the restriction on properties, our method should be seen as an extended type checker rather than a program verification technique. For instance, a typical type checker can verify that a program returns a result of type list, when our technique can also provide information about the length of this list. Further works are needed to assess the impact of the current limitations of the method and to suggest ways to enhance it to increase its practical significance. We just sketch now some extensions which are currently under investigation.

So far, we have studied only the *length* abstraction presented in this paper. We are now considering other properties on integers (like size, or depth) and other structured types (like trees, or general inductive types). One important constraint on the schemes (which plays a crucial role in the proofs of our results) is their uniformity with respect to the structured data type (natural numbers here). This choice is inspired by previous work on inductive data types and the associated inductive program schemes [PDM89]. Uniformity means that conditions in programs are based only on the structure of the arguments. It can be seen as a programming discipline, favoring the construction of programs which can be tested or verified more easily. It is also possible to alleviate this limitation on the source programs since it is only their abstraction that must belong to a scheme. One possible solution is to derive two approximate abstract versions of the program representing a lower bound and an upper bound of the property of the result. Consider for example a modification of the replacement program *Rep* of Section 5.1 to include a conditional statement on the elements of its first argument, replacing only the values different from zero. We can then derive two abstract functions corresponding to the two extreme cases: the first one returns its first argument (when no element is replaced) and the second one is the product (when all the elements are replaced). Further work is needed to assess the significance of this extension.

More generally, different works on protocol testing and verification of properties by model-checking have already shown that restricted formalisms could be of great use in the search for automation. We believe that domain specific languages could also gain benefits from our method and be the ideal target to exercise it.

References

[ABR96]   J.-R. ABRIAL. *The B-Book: Assigning Programs to Meanings.* Cambridge University Press, 1996.

[BA82]   T.A. BUDD and D. ANGLUIN. Two Notions of Correctness and Their Relation to Testing. *Acta Informatica,* 18, 1982.

[BEI90]   B. BEIZER. *Software Testing Techniques, 2nd Edition.* Van Nostrand Reinhold, 1990.

[BG96]   F. BERGADANO and D. GUNETTI. Testing by means of inductive program learning. *ACM transactions on Software Engineering and Methodology,* 5(2), 1996.

[BIE78]   A. BIERMANN. The inference of regular LISP programs from examples. *IEEE transactions on Systems, Man, and Cybernetics,* 8(8), 1978.

[BP94]   G.V. BOCHMANN and A. PETRENKO. Protocol Testing: Review of Methods and Relevance for Software Testing. *Proceedings of ISSTA,* August 1994.

[CC77]   P. COUSOT and R. COUSOT. Abstract interpretation: a unified lattice model for static analysis of programs by construction or approximation of fixpoints. *Proceedings of the 4th POPL,* 1977.

[DO91]   R.A. DEMILLO and A.J. OFFUTT. Constraint-Based Automatic Test Data Generation. *IEEE Transactions on Software Engineering,* 17(9), September 1991.

[FJJV96]   J.-C. FERNANDEZ, C. JARD, T. JÉRON, and C.G. VIHO. Using on-the-fly verification techniques for the generation of test suites. *Proceedings of the Conference on Computer-Aided Verification,* July 1996.

[FRE91]   R.S. FREEDMAN. Testability of Software Components. *IEEE Transactions on Software Engineering,* 17(6), June 1991.

[GAU95]   M-C. GAUDEL. Testing can be formal, too. *Proceedings of TAPSOFT,* 1995.

[GG75]   J.B. GOODENOUGH and S.L. GERHART. Toward a Theory of Test Data Selection. *IEEE Transactions on Software Engineering,* 1(2), June 1975.

[GH93]   J.V. GUTTAG and J.J. HORNING. Larch: languages and tools for formal specification. *Texts and Monographs in Computer Science,* 1993.

[JON90]   C.B. JONES. *Systematic software development using VDM.* Prentice Hall International, second edition, 1990.

[LM97]   D. LE MÉTAYER. Program analysis for software engineering: new applications, new requirements, new tools. *ACM Sigplan Notices,* (1), Janvier 1997.

[LMNR98]   D. LE MÉTAYER, V.-A. NICOLAS, and O. RIDOUX. Exploring the Software Development Trilogy. *IEEE Software,* November 1998.

[NIC98]   V.-A. NICOLAS. *Preuves de Propriétés de Classes de Programmes par Dérivation Systématique de Jeux de Test.* PhD thesis, Université de Rennes 1, December 1998.

[NTA88]   S.C. NTAFOS. A Comparison of Some Structural Testing Strategies. *IEEE Transactions on Software Engineering,* 14(6), June 1988.

[OW91]   T.J. OSTRAND and E.J. WEYUKER. Data Flow-Based Test Adequacy Analysis for Languages with Pointers. *Proceedings of POPL,* January 1991.

[PDM89]   B. PIERCE, S. DIETZEN, and S. MICHAYLOV. Programming in Higher-Order Typed Lambda-Calculi. *Research report CMU-CS-89-111,* March 1989.

[RC85]   D.J. RICHARDSON and L.A. CLARKE. Partition Analysis: A Method Combining Testing and Verification. *IEEE Transactions on Software Engineering*, 11(12), December 1985.

[RW85]   S. RAPPS and E.J. WEYUKER. Selecting Software Test Data Using Dataflow Information. *IEEE Transactions on Software Engineering*, 11(4), April 1985.

[SPI92]   M. SPIVEY. *The Z notation - A reference manual*. International Series in Computer Science. Prentice Hall International, second edition, 1992.

[WEY83]   E.J. WEYUKER. Assessing test data adequacy through program inference. *ACM Transactions on Programming Languages and Systems*, 5(4), October 1983.

Combined Static and Dynamic Assertion-Based Debugging of Constraint Logic Programs*

Germán Puebla, Francisco Bueno, and Manuel Hermenegildo

Department of Computer Science,
Technical University of Madrid (UPM)
{german,bueno,herme}@fi.upm.es

Abstract. We propose a general framework for assertion-based debugging of constraint logic programs. Assertions are linguistic constructions for expressing properties of programs. We define several assertion schemas for writing (partial) specifications for constraint logic programs using quite general properties, including user-defined programs. The framework is aimed at detecting deviations of the program behavior (symptoms) with respect to the given assertions, either at compile-time (i.e., statically) or run-time (i.e., dynamically). We provide techniques for using information from global analysis both to detect at compile-time assertions which do not hold in at least one of the possible executions (i.e., static symptoms) and assertions which hold for all possible executions (i.e., statically proved assertions). We also provide program transformations which introduce tests in the program for checking at run-time those assertions whose status cannot be determined at compile-time. Both the static and the dynamic checking are provably safe in the sense that all errors flagged are definite violations of the specifications. Finally, we report briefly on the currently implemented instances of the generic framework.

1 Introduction

As (constraint) logic programming (CLP) systems [23] mature and larger applications are built, an increased need arises for advanced development and debugging environments. Such environments will likely comprise a variety of tools ranging from declarative diagnosers to execution visualizers (see, for example, [12] for a more comprehensive discussion of tools and possible debugging scenarios). In this paper we concentrate our attention on the particular issue of program validation and debugging via direct static and/or dynamic checking of user-provided assertions.

We assume that a (partial) specification is available with the program and written in terms of assertions [5,3,13,14,24,27]. Classical examples of assertions are the type declarations used in languages such as Gödel [22] or Mercury [29] (and in functional languages). However, herein we are interested in supporting a more general setting in which, on one hand assertions can be of a more general

---

* This work has been supported in part by projects ESPRIT LTR #22532 DiSCiPl and CICYT TIC99-1151 EDIPIA. The authors would also like to thank Jan Małuszyński, Włodek Drabent and Pierre Deransart for many interesting discussions on assertions.

A. Bossi (Ed.): LOPSTR'99, LNCS 1817, pp. 273–292, 2000.

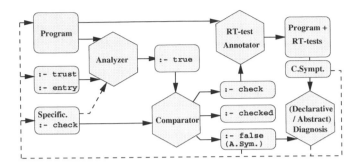

Fig. 1. A Combined Framework for Program Development and Debugging

nature, including properties which are *undecidable*, and, on the other hand, only a small number of assertions may be present in the program, i.e., the assertions are *optional*. In particular, we do not wish to limit the programming language or the language of assertions unnecessarily in order to make the assertions decidable.

Consequently, the proposed framework needs to deal throughout with *approximations* [6,10,20,19]. It is imperative that such approximations be performed in a safe manner, in the sense that if an "error" (more formally, a *symptom*) is flagged, then it is indeed a violation of the specification. However, while the system can be complete with respect to decidable properties (e.g., certain type systems), it cannot be complete in general, in the sense that when undecidable properties are used in assertions, there may be errors with respect to such assertions that are not detected at compile-time. This is a tradeoff that we accept in return for the greater flexibility. However, in order to detect as many errors as possible, the framework combines *static* (i.e., compile-time) and *dynamic* (i.e., run-time) checking of assertions. In particular, run-time checks are (optionally) generated for assertions which cannot be statically determined to hold or not.

Our approach is strongly motivated by the availability of powerful and mature static analyzers for (constraint) logic programs (see, e.g., [5,7,16,17,25] and their references), generally based on abstract interpretation [10]. These systems can statically infer a wide range of properties (from types to determinacy or termination) accurately and efficiently, for realistic programs. Thus, we would like to take advantage of standard program analysis tools, rather than developing new abstract procedures, such as concrete [3,13,14] or abstract [8,9] diagnosers and debuggers, or using traditional proof-based methods [1,2,11,15,30].

Figure 1 presents the general architecture of the type of debugging environment that we propose.[1] Hexagons represent the different tools involved and arrows indicate the communication paths among such tools. It is a design decision of the framework implementation that most of such communication be performed in terms of assertions, and that, rather than having different languages for each tool, the same assertion language be used for all of them. This facilitates

---

[1] The implementation includes also other techniques, such as traditional procedural debugging and visualization, which are however beyond the scope of the work presented in this paper.

communication among the different tools, enables easy reuse of information, and makes such communication understandable for the user.

Assertions are also used to write a (partial) specification of the (possibly partially developed) program. Because these assertions are to be checked we will refer to them as *"check"* assertions.[2] All these assertions (and those which will be mentioned later) are written in the same syntax [27], with a prefix denoting their status (*check, trust, ...*). The program analyzer generates an approximation of the actual semantics of the program, expressed using assertions with the flag *true* (in the case of CLP programs standard analysis techniques –e.g., [17,16]– are used for this purpose). The comparator, using the abstract operations of the analyzer, compares the user requirements and the information generated by the analysis. This process produces three different kinds of results, which are in turn represented by three different kinds of assertions:

- Verified requirements (represented by *checked* assertions).
- Requirements identified not to hold (represented by *false* assertions). In this case an *abstract symptom* has been found and diagnosis should start.
- None of the above, i.e., the analyzer/comparator pair cannot prove that a requirement holds nor that it does not hold (and some assertions remain in *check* status). Run-time tests are then introduced to test the requirement (which may produce "concrete" symptoms). Clearly, this may introduce significant overhead and can be turned off after program testing.

Given this overall design, in this work we concentrate on formally defining assertions, some assertion schemas, and the notions of correctness and errors of a program with respect to those assertions. We then present techniques for static and dynamic checking of the assertions. This paper is complementary to other more informal ones in which we present the framework from a more application-oriented perspective. Details on the assertion language at the user-level can be found in [27]. Details on the debugging framework and on the use of assertions within it from a user's perspective can be found in [26] (which also includes a discussion on the practicality of the approach) and in [21] (which also includes a preliminary performance evaluation).

In this paper, after the necessary preliminaries of Section 2, we define formally our notion of assertion and of assertion-based debugging and validation in Section 3, and some particular kinds of assertions in Section 4. We then formalize dynamic and static debugging in sections 5 and 6, respectively. Finally, Section 7 briefly reports on the implemented instances of the proposed framework.

2   Preliminaries and Notation

A *constraint* is essentially a conjunction of expressions built from predefined predicates (such as term equations or inequalities over the reals) whose arguments are constructed using predefined functions (such as real addition). We let $\bar{\exists}_L \theta$ be

---

[2] The user may provide additional information by means of *"entry"* assertions (which describe the external calls to a module) and *"trust"* assertions (which provide information that the analyzer can use even if it cannot prove it) [5,27].

the constraint θ restricted to the variables of the syntactic object L. We denote constraint entailment by $\models$, so that $c_1 \models c_2$ denotes that c_1 entails c_2.

An *atom* has the form $p(t_1, ..., t_n)$ where p is a predicate symbol and the t_i are terms. A *literal* is either an atom or a constraint. A *goal* is a finite sequence of literals. A *rule* is of the form $H\!:\!-B$ where H, the *head*, is an atom and B, the *body*, is a possibly empty finite sequence of literals. A *constraint logic program*, or *program*, is a finite set of rules. The *definition* of an atom A in program P, $defn_P(A)$, is the set of variable renamings of rules in P such that each renaming has A as a head and has distinct new local variables. We assume that all rule heads are normalized, i.e., H is of the form $p(X_1, ..., X_n)$ where $X_1, ..., X_n$ are distinct free variables. This is not restrictive since programs can always be normalized, and it facilitates the presentation. However, in the examples (and in the implementation of our framework) we use non-normalized programs.

The operational semantics of a program is in terms of its "derivations" which are sequences of reductions between "states". A *state* $\langle G \mid \theta \rangle$ consists of a goal G and a constraint store (or *store* for short) θ. A state $\langle L :: G \mid \theta \rangle$ where L is a literal can be *reduced* as follows:

1. If L is a constraint and $\theta \wedge L$ is satisfiable, it is reduced to $\langle G \mid \theta \wedge L \rangle$.
2. If L is an atom, it is reduced to $\langle B :: G \mid \theta \rangle$ for some rule $(L\!:\!-B) \in defn_P(L)$.

where :: denotes concatenation of sequences and we assume for simplicity that the underlying constraint solver is complete. We use $S \leadsto_P S'$ to indicate that in program P a reduction can be applied to state S to obtain state S'. Also, $S \leadsto_P^* S'$ indicates that there is a sequence of reduction steps from state S to state S'. A *derivation* from state S for program P is a sequence of states $S_0 \leadsto_P S_1 \leadsto_P ... \leadsto_P S_n$ where S_0 is S and there is a reduction from each S_i to S_{i+1}. Given a non-empty derivation D, we denote by *curr_state(D)* and *curr_store(D)* the last state in the derivation, and the store in such last state, respectively. E.g., if D is the derivation $S_0 \leadsto_P^* S_n$ with $S_n = \langle G \mid \theta \rangle$ then *curr_state(D)* $= S_n$ and *curr_store(D)* $= \theta$. A *query* is a pair (L, θ) where L is a literal and θ a store for which the CLP system starts a computation from state $\langle L \mid \theta \rangle$. The set of all derivations from Q for P is denoted *derivations(P, Q)*. We will denote sets of queries by $\mathcal{Q}$. We extend *derivations* to operate on sets of queries as follows: *derivations* $(P, \mathcal{Q}) = \bigcup_{Q \in \mathcal{Q}}$ *derivations* (P, Q).

The observational behavior of a program is given by its "answers" to queries. A finite derivation from a query (L, θ) for program P is *finished* if the last state in the derivation cannot be reduced. A finished derivation from a query (L, θ) is *successful* if the last state is of the form $\langle nil \mid \theta' \rangle$, where nil denotes the empty sequence. The constraint $\exists_L \theta'$ is an *answer* to S. We denote by *answers(P, Q)* the set of answers to query Q. A finished derivation is *failed* if the last state is not of the form $\langle nil \mid \theta \rangle$. Note that *derivations* $(P, \mathcal{Q})$ contains not only finished derivations but also all intermediate derivations from a query. A query Q *finitely fails* in P if *derivations(P, Q)* is finite and contains no successful derivation.

3   Assertions and Program Correctness

We now provide a formal definition of assertions and of correctness of a program w.r.t. a set of assertions. Our definition of assertion is very open. In the next section we will provide several more specific schemas for assertions which correspond to the traditional *pre-* and *post*conditions.

Definition 1 (Condition on Derivations). *Let $\mathcal{D}$ be the set of all derivations. A condition on derivations is any boolean function $f : \mathcal{D} \to \{true, false\}$ which is total.*

Definition 2 (Assertion). *An* assertion *A for a program P is a pair (app_A, sat_A) of conditions on derivations.*

Conditions on derivations are boolean functions which are decidable for any derivation. As an intuition, given an assertion A, the role of app_A is to indicate whether A is *applicable* to a derivation D. If it is, then sat_A should take the value *true* on D for the assertion to hold.

Definition 3 (Evaluation of an Assertion on a Derivation). *Given an assertion $A = (app_A, sat_A)$ for program P, the* evaluation of A on a derivation D, denoted $solve(A, D, P)$, is defined as:

$$solve(A, D, P) = app_A(D) \to sat_A(D).$$

Assertions have often been used for performing debugging with respect to partial correctness, i.e., to ensure that the program does not produce unexpected results for *valid* queries, i.e., queries which are "expected". The set of valid queries to the program is represented by $\mathcal{Q}$. We now provide several simple definitions which will be instrumental.

Definition 4 (Error Set). *Given an assertion A, the* error set *of A in a program P for a set of queries $\mathcal{Q}$ is*

$$E(A, P, \mathcal{Q}) = \{D \in derivations(P, \mathcal{Q}) | \neg solve(A, D, P)\}.$$

Definition 5 (False Assertion). *An assertion A is* false *in a program P for a set of queries $\mathcal{Q}$ iff $E(A, P, \mathcal{Q}) \neq \emptyset$.*

Definition 6 (Checked Assertion). *An assertion A is* checked *in a program P for a set of queries $\mathcal{Q}$ iff $E(A, P, \mathcal{Q}) = \emptyset$.*

The definitions of *false* and *checked* assertions are complementary. Thus, it is clear that given a program P and a set of queries $\mathcal{Q}$, any assertion A is either false or checked. The goal of assertion checking is to determine whether each assertion A is false or checked in P for $\mathcal{Q}$. There are two kinds of approaches to doing this. One is based on actually trying all possible execution paths (derivations) for all possible queries. When it is not possible to try all derivations an alternative is to explore a hopefully representative set of them. This approach is explored in Section 5. The second approach is to use global analysis techniques and is based on computing safe approximations of the program behavior statically. This approach is studied in Section 6.

Definition 7 (Partial Correctness). *A program P is* partially correct *w.r.t. a set of assertions $\mathcal{A}$ and a set of queries $\mathcal{Q}$ iff $\forall A \in \mathcal{A}$ A is checked in P for $\mathcal{Q}$.*

If all the assertions are checked, then the program is partially correct. Thus, our framework is of use both for *validation* and for detection of errors. Finally, in addition to checked and false assertions, we will also consider *true* assertions. True assertions differ from checked assertions in that true assertions hold in the program for any set of queries Q.

Definition 8 (True Assertion). *An assertion A is* true *in program P iff* $\forall Q : E(A, P, Q) = \emptyset$.

Clearly, any assertion which is true in P is also checked for any Q, but not vice-versa. Since true assertions hold for any possible query they can be regarded as query-independent properties of the program. Thus, true assertions can be used to express analysis information, as already done, for example, in [5]. This information can then be reused when analyzing the program for different queries.

4   Assertion Schemas

An *assertion schema* is an expression which, given a syntactic object AS, produces an assertion $A = (app_A, sat_A)$ by syntactic manipulation only. In other words, assertion schemas are syntactic sugar for writing certain kinds of assertions which are used very often. Assertions described using the given assertion schemas will be denoted as AS in order to distinguish them from the actual assertion A. In what follows we use r and $r(O)$ to represent a variable renaming and the result of applying it to some syntactic object O, respectively.

Condition Literals: In the assertion schemas pre- and postconditions will be used. For simplicity, in the formalization (but not in the implementation) pre- and postconditions in assertions are assumed to be literals (rather than for example conjunctions and/or disjunctions of literals).[3] We call such literals *condition literals* and assume that they have a particular meaning associated.

Definition 9 (Meaning of a Literal). *The* meaning of a literal L, denoted $|L|$ *is a set of constraints. If L is a constraint, we define $|L| = \{L\}$. If L is an atom we assume that a definition of the form $|L'| = \{\theta_1,\ldots,\theta_n\}$ is given s.t. $L = r(L')$. Then $|L| = r(\{\theta_1,\ldots,\theta_n\})$.*

Intuitively, the meaning of a literal contains the "weakest" constraints which make the literal take the value *true*. A constraint θ is *weaker* than another constraint θ' iff $\theta' \models \theta$. We denote by M a set of meanings of literals.

Example 1. Consider defining $|list(A)|=\{A = [], A = [B|C] \wedge list(C)\}$ and $|sorted(A)|=\{A = [], A = [B], A = [B, C|D] \wedge B \leq C \wedge E = [C|D] \wedge sorted(E)\}$.

Definition 10 (Holds Trivially). *A literal L holds trivially for θ in M, denoted $\theta \models_M L$ iff $\exists \theta' \in |L|$ s.t. $\theta \models \theta'$ and $\exists c : (c \wedge \theta' \not\models false) \wedge (\theta' \wedge c \models \theta)$.*

---

[3] However, it is straightforward to lift up this restriction, and in the implementation of the framework conjunctions and disjunctions are indeed allowed.

Example 2. Assume that $\theta = (A = f)$ and $M = \{|list(A)|, |sorted(B)|\}$. Since $\forall \theta' \in |list(A)| : \theta \not\models \theta'$, as we would expect, $\theta \not\models_M list(A)$. Assume now that $\theta = (A = [\_|Xs])$. Though A is compatible with a list, it is not actually a (nil terminated) list. Again in this case $\forall \theta' \in |list(A)| : \theta \not\models \theta'$ and thus again $\theta \not\models_M list(A)$. The intuition behind this is that we cannot guarantee that A is actually a list given θ since a possible instance of A in θ is $A = [\_|f]$, which is clearly not a list. Finally, assume that $\theta = (A = [B] \wedge B = 1)$. In such case $\exists \theta' = (A = [B|C] \wedge C = [])$ s.t. $\theta \models \theta'$ and $\exists c = (B = 1)$ s.t. $(c \wedge \theta' \not\models false) \wedge (\theta' \wedge c \models \theta)$. Thus, in this last case $\theta \models_M list(A)$.

Calls Assertions: This assertion schema is used to describe preconditions for predicates. Given a program P and an expression $AS = calls(p, Precond)$, where p is a normalized atom and $Precond$ a condition literal which refers to the variables of p, we obtain an assertion A for program P whose app_{AS} and sat_{AS} are defined as:

$$app_{calls(p,Precond)}(D) = \begin{cases} true & \text{if } curr\_state(D) = \langle q :: G \mathbin{|} \theta \rangle \wedge q = r(p) \\ false & \text{otherwise} \end{cases}$$

$$sat_{calls(p,Precond)}(D) = curr\_store(D) \models_M r(Precond).$$

Clearly, there is no way an assertion $calls(p, Precond)$ can be violated unless the next literal q to be reduced is of the same predicate as p.

Example 3. The procedure `partition(A,B,C,D)` expects a list in A to "partition" it into two other lists based on the "pivot" B. Thus, the following assertion states that it should be called with A a list. It appears in the schema oriented syntax that we use herein, as well as in the program oriented syntax of [27].

```
:- calls partition(A,B,C,D) : list(A).
% { calls( partition(A,B,C,D) , list(A) ) }
```

Success Assertions: Success assertions are used in order to express postconditions of predicates. These postconditions may be required to hold on success of the predicate for any call to the predicate, i.e., the precondition is *true*, or only for calls satisfying certain preconditions. Given a program P and an expression $AS = success(p, Pre, Post)$, where p is a normalized atom, and both Pre and $Post$ condition literals which refer to the variables of p, we obtain an assertion A for P whose app_{AS} and sat_{AS} are defined as follows:

$$app_{success(p,Pre,Post)}(D) = \begin{cases} true & \text{if } curr\_state(D) = \langle G \mathbin{|} \theta \rangle \wedge \exists q \exists \theta' \exists r : \\ & \langle q :: G \mathbin{|} \theta' \rangle \in D \wedge q = r(p) \wedge \theta' \models_M r(Pre) \\ false & \text{otherwise} \end{cases}$$

$$sat_{success(p,Pre,Post)}(D) = \forall\, S = \langle q :: G \mathbin{|} \theta' \rangle \in D \text{ s.t. } \exists r\ q = r(p) :$$
$$\theta' \models_M r(Pre) \rightarrow curr\_store(D) \models_M r(Post).$$

Note that, for a given assertion A and derivation D, several states of the form $\langle q :: G \mathbin{|} \theta' \rangle$ s.t. $q = r(p)$ may exist in D in which the precondition, i.e., *r(Pre)* holds. As a result, the postcondition *r(Post)* will have to be checked several times with different renamings r which relate the variables of p, and thus (some of) those in *Post*, with different states in D.

Example 4. The following assertion states that if a procedure `qsort(A,B)` succeeds when called with A a list then B should be sorted on success.

```
:- success qsort(A,B) : list(A) => sorted(B).
% { success( qsort(A,B) , list(A) , sorted(B) ) }
```

5   Run-Time Checking of Assertions

The main idea behind run-time checking of assertions is, given a program P, a set of queries $\mathcal{Q}$, and a set of assertions $\mathcal{A}$, to directly apply Definitions 5 and 6 in order to determine whether the assertions in $\mathcal{A}$ are checked or false, i.e., obtaining (a subset of) the derivations by running the program and determining whether they belong to the error set of the assertions. It is not to be expected that Definition 6 can be used to determine that an assertion is checked, as this would require checking the derivations from all valid queries, which is in general an infinite set and thus checking would not terminate. In this situation, and as mentioned before, an alternative is to perform run-time checking for a hopefully representative set of queries. Though this does not allow fully validating the program in general, it allows detecting many incorrectness problems.

An important observation is that in constraint logic programming it seems natural to define the meaning of condition literals as CLP programs rather than as (recursive) sets. We thus restrict the admissible conditions of assertions to those literals L_p for which a definition of the corresponding predicate p exists s.t. $answers(P, (L_p, true)) = |L_p|$. We argue that this is not too strong a restriction given the high expressive power of CLP languages.[4] Note that the approach also implies that the program P must contain the definitions of all the predicates p for literals L_p used in conditions of assertions. Thus, from now on we assume the program P contains the definition of M as CLP predicates. We believe that this choice of a language for writing conditions is in fact of practical interest because it facilitates the job of programmers, which do not need to learn a specification language in addition to the CLP language they are already familiar with.

Example 5. Consider defining `list(A)` and `sorted(A)` of Example 1 as:

```
list([]).                sorted([]).      sorted([_]).
list([_|L]) :- list(L).  sorted([X,Y|L]) :- X =< Y, sorted([Y|L]).
```

Once we have decided to define condition literals in CLP,[5] the next question is how to determine the value of $\theta \models_M L$ using the underlying CLP system. At first sight, one possibility would be to compute $answers(P, (L, \theta))$. Clearly, if such set is empty, $\theta \not\models_M L$. However, $\theta \models_M L$ is not guaranteed to hold if $answers(P, (L, \theta))$ is not empty. This is why we introduce the definition below.

Definition 11 (Succeeds Trivially). *A literal L succeeds trivially for θ in P, denoted $\theta \Rightarrow_P L$, iff $\exists \theta' \in answers(P, (L, \theta))$ s.t. $\theta \models \theta'$.*

---

[4] Note that the scheme of [27,26] allows approximate definitions of such predicates and sufficient conditions for proving and disproving them.

[5] Note that, given a logic expression built using literals, conjunctions, and disjunctions, it is always possible to write such expression as a predicate definition.

Intuitively, a literal L succeeds trivially if L succeeds for θ in P without adding new "relevant" constraints to θ. Note that, if L is a constraint, this means that L was already entailed by θ. For program predicate atoms, it means that θ was constrained enough to make L succeed without adding relevant constraints to θ. This means that we are considering condition literals as *instantiation* checks [27,21]. They are true iff the variables they check for are at least as constrained as their predicate definition requires. Note that the notion of L succeeding trivially for θ in P corresponds to $\theta \models_M L$.

Lemma 1 (Checking of Condition Literals). *Let L be a condition literal in an assertion for program P. If $answers(P, (L, true)) = |L|$ then for any θ, $\theta \models_M L$ iff $\theta \Rightarrow_P L$.*

Proof. $\theta \models_M L \Rightarrow \theta' \in |L| = answers(P, (L, true)) \wedge \theta \models \theta' \Rightarrow \theta' \in answers(P, (L, \theta')) \wedge \theta \models \theta' \Rightarrow \theta' \in answers(P, (L, \theta)) \wedge \theta \models \theta'$. Conversely, $\theta \Rightarrow_P L \Rightarrow \theta' \in answers(P, (L, \theta)) \wedge \theta \models \theta' \Rightarrow \theta' \models \theta \wedge \theta \models \theta' \Rightarrow \theta \in answers(P, (L, \theta)) \Rightarrow \exists \theta'' \in answers(P, (L, true)) = |L| \exists c : (c \wedge \theta'' \not\models false) \wedge (\theta'' \wedge c \models \theta)$.

The lemma above allows us to use in a sound way the results of $\theta \Rightarrow_P L$ as the value of $\theta \models_M L$. Unfortunately, from a practical point of view, computing $\theta \Rightarrow_P L$ is problematic, since it may require computing $answers(P, (L, \theta))$, which may not terminate. Thus, unless we introduce some restrictions, run-time checking may introduce non-termination into terminating programs.

Existing CLP systems do compute $derivations(P, Q)$ using some fixed strategy, which induces an ordering on the set of derivations. A strategy is determined by a *search rule* which indicates the order in which the program rules that can be used to reduce an atom should be tried, coupled with a strategy to decide which of the unfinished derivations should be further reduced. The typical search strategy is LIFO, which implies a depth-first search. We denote by SR a search rule together with a search strategy, and by $derivations_{SR}(P, Q)$ the sequence of derivations from Q in P under strategy SR.

Definition 12 ($derivations_{SR}^1$). *Let P be a program and Q a query. We denote by $derivations_{SR}^1(P, Q)$ the prefix of $derivations_{SR}(P, Q)$ s.t.*

1. *If $answers(P, Q) = \emptyset$ then $derivations_{SR}^1(P, Q) = derivations_{SR}(P, Q)$.*
2. *Otherwise, let $derivations_{SR}(P, Q)$ be the sequence $D_1 :: \ldots :: D_n :: DS$ s.t. $\forall i \in \{1, \ldots, n-1\} : D_i$ is not successful and D_n is successful. Then, $derivations_{SR}^1(P, Q) = D_1 :: \ldots :: D_n$.*

Definition 13 (Test). *A literal L is a test iff $\forall \theta$:*

1. *$derivations_{SR}^1(P, (L, \theta))$ is finite, and if θ_1 is its answer then*
2. *$\forall \theta' \in answers(P, (L, \theta)) : (\theta_1 \wedge \theta' \models false \vee \theta' \models \theta_1)$.*

Example 6. Literals `sorted(B)` and `list(B)` for the predicates defined in Example 5 are tests, since for every possible initial state the execution of, e.g., `list(B)`, this literal either (1) finitely fails if B is constrained to be incompatible with a list, (2) succeeds once without adding "relevant" constraints if B is constrained to a list, or (3) has a leftmost successful derivation which constrains B to a list in such a way that this constraint is incompatible with the answers of the rest of successful derivations. E.g., for `list(X)` there is an infinite number of answers `X=[]`, `X=[_]`, `X=[_|_]`, ..., but they are pairwise incompatible (they have no common instance).

Theorem 1. *If L is a test then $\forall \theta : \theta \Rightarrow_P L$ iff $\exists D \in derivations^1_{SR}(P, (L, \theta))$ s.t. D is successful with answer θ_1 and $\theta \models \theta_1$.*

Proof. Since $\theta_1 \in answers(P, (L, \theta))$, if $\theta \models \theta_1$ then $\theta \Rightarrow_P L$. The converse also holds. We prove it by contradiction. If $\theta \Rightarrow_P L$ then $\exists \theta' \in answers(P, (L, \theta))$: $\theta \models \theta'$. Assume θ' is not θ_1 and $\theta \not\models \theta_1$. Then L cannot be a test, which is a contradiction. If L was a test then either (1) $\theta' \wedge \theta_1 \models false$ or (2) $\theta' \models \theta_1$. Since $\theta \models \theta'$ then (1) $\theta \wedge \theta_1 \models \theta' \wedge \theta_1 \models false$, which is impossible, since θ_1 is an answer for initial store θ and therefore compatible with it, or (2) $\theta \models \theta_1$, which is a contradiction.

Theorem 1 guarantees that checking of pre- and postconditions, which are required to be tests, is decidable, since it suffices to check only for the first successful derivation in a (sub)set of derivations (search space) which is finite. I.e., either there is a first answer computed in a finite number of reductions, or there is no answer and the checking finitely fails. In our framework we only admit *tests* as conditions in assertions which are going to be checked at run-time. This guarantees that run-time checking will not introduce non-termination.

5.1   An Operational Semantics for CLP Programs with Assertions

We now provide an operational semantics which checks whether assertions hold or not while computing the derivations from a query. A *check literal* is a syntactic object $check(L, A)$ where L is either an atom or a constraint and A (an identifier for) the assertion which generated the check literal. In this semantics, a *literal* is now an atom, a constraint, or a check literal. A CLP program with assertions is a pair $(P, \mathcal{A})$, where P is a program, as defined in Section 2, and $\mathcal{A}$ is a set of assertions.[6]

In the case of programs with assertions finished derivations can be, in addition to successful and failed, also "erroneous". We introduce a class of distinguished states of the form $\langle \epsilon \mathbin{\text{I}} A \rangle$ which cannot be further reduced. A finished derivation D is *erroneous* if $curr\_state(D) = \langle \epsilon \mathbin{\text{I}} A \rangle$, where A is (an identifier for) an assertion. Erroneous derivations indicate that the assertion A has been violated.

Let $\mathcal{A}[L]$ denote a renaming of the set of assertions $\mathcal{A}$ where assertions for the predicate of atom L have been renamed to match the variables of L. A state $\langle L :: G \mathbin{\text{I}} \theta \rangle$, where L is a literal can be *reduced* as follows:

1. If L is a constraint and $\theta \wedge L$ is satisfiable, it is reduced to $\langle G \mathbin{\text{I}} \theta \wedge L \rangle$.
2. If L is an atom,
    - if $\exists A = calls(L, Cond) \in \mathcal{A}[L]$ s.t. $\theta \not\Rightarrow_P Cond$, then it is reduced to $\langle \epsilon \mathbin{\text{I}} A \rangle$.

---

[6] Program point assertions can be introduced by just allowing check literals to appear in the body of rules [27]. However, for simplicity we do not discuss program point assertions in this paper.

- otherwise, let $PostC = \{check(S, A) | \exists A = success(L, C, S) \in \mathcal{A}[L] \wedge \theta \Rightarrow_P C\}$, if $\exists (L\text{:-}B) \in defn_P(L)$ then the state is reduced to $\langle B :: PostC :: G \mid \theta \rangle$.

3. If L is a check literal $check(Prop, A)$,
   - if $\theta \Rightarrow_P Prop$ then it is reduced to $\langle G \mid \theta \rangle$
   - otherwise it is reduced to $\langle \epsilon \mid A \rangle$.

Note that we define $PostC$ above as a set though it should actually be a sequence of $check$ literals. We do so since the order in which the $check$ literals are checked is irrelevant. We will use $\leadsto_{(P,\mathcal{A})}$ to refer to reductions performed using the above operational semantics of programs with assertions. Also, the set of derivations from a set of queries $\mathcal{Q}$ in a program P using the semantics with assertions is denoted $derivations_{\mathcal{A}}(P, \mathcal{Q})$.

Theorem 2 (Run-time Checking). *Given a program P, a set of assertions $\mathcal{A}$, and a set of queries $\mathcal{Q}$,*

$$\mathcal{A} \text{ is false iff } \exists D \in derivations_{\mathcal{A}}(P, \mathcal{Q}) : curr\_state(D) = \langle \epsilon, A \rangle.$$

Proof. $\mathcal{A}$ is false $\Leftrightarrow E(\mathcal{A}, P, \mathcal{Q}) \neq \emptyset \Leftrightarrow \exists D \in derivations(P, \mathcal{Q}) \neg solve(A, D, P)$. Let $D = S \leadsto_P^* S_n$ and let $sat_A(D)$ be false. Let $S_n = \langle G \mid \theta \rangle$. It can be proved that $\neg solve(A, D, P) \Leftrightarrow \exists D' \in derivations_{\mathcal{A}}(P, \mathcal{Q})$ s.t. $D' = S \leadsto_{(P,\mathcal{A})}^* S'_{n-1} \leadsto_{(P,\mathcal{A})} \langle check(Prop, A) :: G \mid \theta \rangle \leadsto_{(P,\mathcal{A})} \langle \epsilon, A \rangle$.

Theorem 2 guarantees that we can use the proposed operational semantics for programs with assertions in order to detect violation of assertions. Moreover, Theorem 3 below guarantees that the behavior of a partially correct program is the same under the operational semantics of Section 2 and under the semantics with assertions. If P is partially correct, it is straightforward to define a one-to-one relation between derivations $S \leadsto_P^* S_n$ and derivations $S \leadsto_{(P,\mathcal{A})}^* S'_n$, so that the two kinds of derivations only differ in the reductions of the distinguished literals of the form $check(L, A)$. We denote the corresponding isomorphism between derivations of the two kinds by $\approx$.

Theorem 3. *Let P be a program, $\mathcal{A}$ a set of assertions, and $\mathcal{Q}$ a set of queries. If P is partially correct w.r.t. $\mathcal{A}$ then $derivations(P, \mathcal{Q}) \approx derivations_{\mathcal{A}}(P, \mathcal{Q})$.*

Therefore, the semantics with assertions can also be used to obtain answers to the original query. Even though this semantics can be used to perform run-time checking, an important disadvantage is that existing CLP systems do not implement such semantics. Modification of a CLP system with that aim is not a trivial task due to the complexity of typical implementations. Thus, it seems desirable to be able to perform run-time checking on top of existing systems without having to modify them. Writing a meta-interpreter which implements this semantics on top of a CLP system is not a difficult task. However, the drawback of this approach is its inefficiency due to the overhead introduced by the meta-interpretation level.[7] A second approach, which is the one used in our implementation, is based on program transformation.

---

[7] An alternative approach is to reduce such overhead by partially evaluating the meta-interpreter w.r.t. the program with assertions prior to performing run-time checking.

5.2   A Program Transformation for Run-Time Checking

We now present a program transformation technique which given a program
P, obtains another program P' which checks the assertions while running on a
standard CLP system. The meta-interpretation level mentioned above is eliminated since the process of assertion checking is compiled into P'. The program
transformation from P into P' given a set of assertions $\mathcal{A}$ is as follows. Let
$new(P,p)$ denote a function which returns an atom of a new predicate symbol
different from all predicates defined in P with same arity and arguments as p.
Let $renaming(\mathcal{A}, p, p')$ denote a function which returns a set of assertions identical to $\mathcal{A}$ except for the assertions referred to p which are now referred to p', and
let $renaming(P, p, p')$ denote a function which returns a set of rules identical to
P except for the rules of predicate p which are now referred to p'. We obtain
$P' = rtchecks(\mathcal{A}, P)$, such that:

$$rtchecks(\mathcal{A}, P) = \begin{cases} rtchecks(\mathcal{A}', P') & \text{if } \mathcal{A} = \{A\} \cup \mathcal{A}'' \\ P & \text{if } \mathcal{A} = \emptyset \end{cases}$$

where

$\mathcal{A}' = renaming(\mathcal{A}'', p, p')$
$P' = renaming(P, p, p') \cup \{CL\}$
$p' = new(P, p)$
$CL = \begin{cases} p\text{:-}check(C, A),\ p'. & \text{if } A = calls(p, C) \\ p\text{:-}(ts(C)\text{->}p', check(S, A); p'). & \text{if } A = success(p, C, S) \end{cases}$

As usual, the construct $(cond$ -> $then$; $else)$ is the Prolog if-then-else.
The program above contains two undefined predicates: $check(C, A)$ and $ts(C)$.
$check(C, A)$ must check whether C holds or not and raise an error if it does
not. $ts(C)$ must return true iff for the current constraint store θ, $\theta \Rightarrow_P C$.
As an example, for the particular case of Prolog, $check(C, A)$ can be defined
as "check(C,A) :- (ts(C) -> true ; error(A))." where error(A) is a
predicate which informs about the false assertion A; $ts(C)$ can be defined as
"ts(C) :- copy_term(C,C1), call(C1), variant(C,C1).".

Note that the above transformation will introduce nested levels of conditionals when there are several assertions for the same predicate. This is prevented
in the implementation using an equivalent transformation, which avoids nesting
conditionals. However, the transformation presented is easier to prove correct.
The following theorem guarantees that the transformed program detects that an
assertion is false iff it is actually false.

Theorem 4 (Program Transformation). *Let P be a program, $\mathcal{A}$ a set of
assertions, and let $P' = rtchecks(\mathcal{A}, P)$. Given a set of queries $\mathcal{Q}$, $\forall A \in \mathcal{A}$:
$E(A, P, \mathcal{Q}) \neq \emptyset$ iff $\exists D \in derivations(P', \mathcal{Q})$ s.t. $\exists S \in D$ with S of the form
$\langle error(A) :: G \mid \theta \rangle$.*

Proof. (Sketch) There is a direct correspondence between $derivations(P', \mathcal{Q})$
and $derivations_{\mathcal{A}}(P, \mathcal{Q})$. The result then follows directly from Theorem 2.

6   Compile-Time Checking of Assertions

In this section we present some techniques for detecting errors at compile-time rather than at run-time, and also proving assertions to hold, i.e., (partially) validating specifications. With this aim, we assume the existence of a global analyzer, typically based on abstract interpretation [10] which is capable of computing at compile-time certain characteristics of the run-time behavior of the program. In particular, we consider the case in which the analysis provides safe approximations of the calling and success patterns for predicates.

Note that it is not to be expected that all assertions are checkable at compile-time, either because the properties in the assertions are not decidable or because the available analyzers are not accurate enough. Those which cannot be checked at compile-time can, in general, (optionally) be checked at run-time.

Abstract Interpretation. Abstract interpretation [10] is a technique for static program analysis in which execution of the program is simulated on an *abstract domain* (D_α) which is simpler than the actual, *concrete domain* (D). An abstract value is a finite representation of a, possibly infinite, set of actual values in the concrete domain (D). The set of all possible abstract semantic values represents an abstract domain D_α which is usually a complete lattice or cpo which is ascending chain finite. However, for this study, abstract interpretation is restricted to complete lattices over sets both for the concrete $\langle 2^D, \subseteq \rangle$ and abstract $\langle D_\alpha, \sqsubseteq \rangle$ domains.

Abstract values and sets of concrete values are related via a pair of monotonic mappings $\langle \alpha, \gamma \rangle$: *abstraction* $\alpha : 2^D \to D_\alpha$, and *concretization* $\gamma : D_\alpha \to 2^D$, such that $\forall x \in 2^D : \gamma(\alpha(x)) \supseteq x$ and $\forall y \in D_\alpha : \alpha(\gamma(y)) = y$. In general $\sqsubseteq$ is induced by $\subseteq$ and α. Similarly, the operations of *least upper bound* ($\sqcup$) and *greatest lower bound* ($\sqcap$) mimic those of 2^D in a precise sense:

$$\forall \lambda, \lambda' \in D_\alpha : \lambda \sqsubseteq \lambda' \leftrightarrow \gamma(\lambda) \subseteq \gamma(\lambda')$$
$$\forall \lambda_1, \lambda_2, \lambda' \in D_\alpha : \lambda_1 \sqcup \lambda_2 = \lambda' \Leftrightarrow \gamma(\lambda_1) \cup \gamma(\lambda_2) = \gamma(\lambda')$$
$$\forall \lambda_1, \lambda_2, \lambda' \in D_\alpha : \lambda_1 \sqcap \lambda_2 = \lambda' \Leftrightarrow \gamma(\lambda_1) \cap \gamma(\lambda_2) = \gamma(\lambda')$$

Goal dependent abstract interpretation takes as input a program P, an abstract domain D_α, and a description Q_α of the possible initial queries to the program given as a set of abstract queries. An *abstract query* is a pair (L, λ), where L is an atom (for one of the exported predicates) and $\lambda \in D_\alpha$ an abstract constraint which describes the initial stores for L. A set of abstract queries Q_α represents a set of queries, denoted $\gamma(Q_\alpha)$, which is defined as $\gamma(Q_\alpha) = \{(L, \theta) \mid (L, \lambda) \in Q_\alpha \wedge \theta \in \gamma(\lambda)\}$. Such an abstract interpretation computes a set of triples $Analysis(P, Q_\alpha, D_\alpha) = \{\langle L_p, \lambda^c, \lambda^s \rangle \mid p \text{ is a predicate of } P\}$. For each predicate p in a program P we denote L_p a representative of the class of all normalized atoms for p, and we assume that the abstract interpretation based analysis computes exactly one tuple $\langle L_p, \lambda^c, \lambda^s \rangle$ for each predicate p.[8] If p is detected to be dead code then $\lambda^c = \lambda^s = \bot$. As usual in abstract interpretation, $\bot$ denotes the abstract constraint such that $\gamma(\bot) = \emptyset$, whereas $\top$

---

[8] This assumption corresponds to a mono-variant analysis. Extension to a multivariant analysis is straightforward, but we prefer to keep the presentation simple.

denotes the most general abstract constraint, i.e., $\gamma(\top) = D$. We now provide a couple of definitions which will be used below for stating correctness of abstract interpretation-based compile-time checking.

Definition 14 (Calling Context). *Consider a program P, a predicate p and a set of queries $\mathcal{Q}$. The* calling context *of p for P and $\mathcal{Q}$ is $C(p, P, \mathcal{Q}) = \{ \bar{\exists}_{L_p} \theta |$ $\exists D \in derivations(P, \mathcal{Q}) : curr\_state(D) = \langle L_p :: G \mid \theta \rangle \}$.*

Definition 15 (Success Context). *Consider a program P, a predicate p, a constraint store θ, and a set of queries $\mathcal{Q}$. The* success context *of p and θ for P and $\mathcal{Q}$ is $S(p, \theta, P, \mathcal{Q}) = \{ \bar{\exists}_{L_p} \theta' | \exists D \in derivations(P, \mathcal{Q}) \exists G : \langle L_p :: G \mid \theta \rangle \in D$ and $curr\_state(D) = \langle G \mid \theta' \rangle \}$.*

We can restrict the constraints in the calling and success contexts to the variables in L_p since this does not affect the evaluation of calls and success assertions. Correctness of abstract interpretation guarantees that for any $\langle L_p, \lambda^c, \lambda^s \rangle$ in $Analysis(P, \mathcal{Q}_\alpha, D_\alpha)$, $\gamma(\lambda^c) \supseteq C(p, P, \gamma(\mathcal{Q}_\alpha))$ and $\gamma(\lambda^s) \supseteq \bigcup_{\theta \in \gamma(\lambda^c)} S(p, \theta, P, \gamma(\mathcal{Q}_\alpha))$. In order to ensure correctness of compile-time checking for a set of queries $\mathcal{Q}$, the analyzer must be provided with a suitable $\mathcal{Q}_\alpha$ such that $\gamma(\mathcal{Q}_\alpha) \supseteq \mathcal{Q}$. In our implementation of the framework, $\mathcal{Q}_\alpha$ is expressed by means of *entry* assertions [27].

Exploiting Information from Abstract Interpretation. Before presenting the actual sufficient conditions that we propose for performing compile-time checking of assertions, we present some definitions and results which will then be instrumental.

Definition 16 (Trivial Success Set). *Given a literal L and a program P we define the* trivial success set *of L in P as $TS(L, P) = \{\bar{\exists}_L \theta \mid \theta \Rightarrow_P L\}$.*

This definition is an adaptation of that presented in [28], where analysis information is used to optimize automatically parallelized programs.

Definition 17 (Abstract Trivial Success Subset). *An abstract constraint $\lambda^-_{TS(L,P)}$ is an* abstract trivial success subset *of L in P iff $\gamma(\lambda^-_{TS(L,P)}) \subseteq TS(L, P)$.*

Lemma 2. *Let λ be an abstract constraint and let $\lambda^-_{TS(L,P)}$ be an abstract trivial success subset of L in P.*

1. *If $\lambda \sqsubseteq \lambda^-_{TS(L,P)}$ then $\forall \theta \in \gamma(\lambda) : \theta \Rightarrow_P L$.*
2. *If $\lambda \sqcap \lambda^-_{TS(L,P)} \neq \bot$ then $\exists \theta \in \gamma(\lambda) : \theta \Rightarrow_P L$.*

Proof. Let TS denote $TS(L, P)$.

1. $\lambda \sqsubseteq \lambda^-_{TS} \Rightarrow \gamma(\lambda) \subseteq \gamma(\lambda^-_{TS}) \subseteq TS \Rightarrow \forall \theta \in \gamma(\lambda) : \theta \in TS$.
2. $\lambda \sqcap \lambda^-_{TS} \neq \bot \Rightarrow \gamma(\lambda) \cap \gamma(\lambda^-_{TS}) \neq \emptyset \Rightarrow \exists \theta \in \gamma(\lambda) : \theta \in \gamma(\lambda^-_{TS}) \subseteq TS$.

Definition 18 (Abstract Trivial Success Superset). *An abstract constraint* $\lambda^{+}_{TS(L,P)}$ *is an* abstract trivial success superset *of* L *in* P *iff* $\gamma(\lambda^{+}_{TS(L,P)}) \supseteq TS(L,P)$.

Lemma 3. *Let* λ *be an abstract constraint and let* $\lambda^{+}_{TS(L,P)}$ *be an abstract trivial success superset of* L *in* P.

1. *If* $\lambda^{+}_{TS(L,P)} \sqsubseteq \lambda$ *then* $\forall\, \theta : if\, \theta \Rightarrow_P L$ *then* $\theta \in \gamma(\lambda)$.
2. *If* $\lambda \sqcap \lambda^{+}_{TS(L,P)} = \perp$ *then* $\forall\, \theta \in \gamma(\lambda) : \theta \not\Rightarrow_P L$.

Proof. Let TS denote $TS(L,P)$.

1. $\lambda^{+}_{TS} \sqsubseteq \lambda \Rightarrow TS \subseteq \gamma(\lambda^{+}_{TS}) \subseteq \gamma(\lambda) \Rightarrow \forall\, \theta \in TS : \theta \in \gamma(\lambda)$.
2. $\lambda \sqcap \lambda^{+}_{TS} = \perp \Rightarrow \gamma(\lambda) \cap \gamma(\lambda^{+}_{TS}) = \emptyset \Rightarrow \gamma(\lambda) \cap TS = \emptyset$.

In order to apply Lemma 2 and Lemma 3 effectively, accurate $\lambda^{+}_{TS(L,P)}$ and $\lambda^{-}_{TS(L,P)}$ are required. It is possible to find a correct $\lambda^{+}_{TS(L,P)}$, which may also hopefully be accurate, by simply analyzing the program with the set of abstract queries $\mathcal{Q}_\alpha = \{(L, \top)\}$. Since our analysis is goal-dependent, the initial abstract constraint $\top$ is used in order to guarantee that the information which will be obtained is valid for any call to L. The result of analysis will contain a tuple of the form $\langle L, \top, \lambda^s \rangle$ and thus we can take $\lambda^{+}_{TS(L,P)} = \lambda^s$, as correctness of the analysis guarantees that λ^s is a superset approximation of $TS(L,P)$.

Unfortunately, obtaining a (non-trivial) correct $\lambda^{-}_{TS(L,P)}$ in an automatic way is not so easy, assuming that analysis provides superset approximations. In [28], correct $\lambda^{-}_{TS(L,P)}$ for built-in predicates were computed by hand and provided to the system as a table of "builtin abstract behaviors". This is possible because the semantics of built-ins is known in advance and does not depend on P (also, computing by hand is well justified in this case because, in general, code for built-ins is not available since for efficiency they are often written in a lower-level language –e.g., C– and analyzing their definition is thus not straightforward).

In the case of user defined predicates, precomputing $\lambda^{-}_{TS(L,P)}$ is not possible since their semantics is not known in advance. However, the user can provide *trust* assertions [27] which provide this information. Also, since in this case the code of the predicate is present, analysis of the definition of the predicate p of L can also be applied and will be effective if analysis is *precise* for L, i.e., $\gamma(\lambda^s) = \bigcup_{\theta \in \gamma(\lambda^c)} S(p, \theta, P, \mathcal{Q})$ rather than $\gamma(\lambda^s) \supseteq \bigcup_{\theta \in \gamma(\lambda^c)} S(p, \theta, P, \mathcal{Q})$. In this situation we can use λ^s as (the best possible) $\lambda^{-}_{TS(L,P)}$. Requiring that the analysis be precise for any arbitrary literal L is not realistic. However, if the success set of L corresponds exactly to some abstract constraint λ_L, i.e., $TS(L,P) = \gamma(\lambda_L)$, then analysis can often be precise enough to compute $\langle L, \lambda^c, \lambda^s \rangle$ with $\lambda^s = \lambda_L$. This implies that not all the tests that the user could write can be proved to hold at compile-time, but only those of them which coincide with some abstract constraint. This means that if we only want to perform compile-time validation, then it is best to use tests which are perfectly captured by the abstract domain. An interesting situation in which this occurs is the use of regular programs as type definitions (as with the property (type) list defined in Example 5). There is a direct mapping from type definitions (i.e., the abstract values in the domain) to regular programs and vice-versa which allows accurately relating any abstract value to any program defining a type (i.e., to any regular program).

Checked Assertions. We now provide sufficient conditions for proving at compile-time that an assertion is never violated. Detecting checked assertions at compile-time is quite useful. First, if all assertions are found to be checked, then the program has been validated. Second, even if only some assertions are found to be checked, performing run-time checking for those assertions can be avoided, thus improving efficiency of the program with run-time checks. Finally, knowing that some assertions have been checked also allows the user to focus debugging on the remaining assertions.

Theorem 5 (Checked Calls Assertion). *Let* P *be a program,* $A = calls(p, Precond)$ *an assertion,* Q *a set of queries, and let* Q_α *be s.t.* $\gamma(Q_\alpha) \supseteq Q$. *Assume that* $\langle p, \lambda^c, \lambda^s \rangle \in Analysis(P, Q_\alpha, D_\alpha)$. *A is checked in* P *for* Q *if* $\lambda^c \sqsubseteq \lambda^-_{TS(Precond,P)}$.

Proof of theorem 5 is trivial since λ^c is a safe approximation of the calling context of the predicate of p. Thus, it provides a sufficient condition for a calls assertion to be checked.

Theorem 6 (Checked Success Assertion). *Let* P *be a program,* $A = success(p, Pre, Post)$ *an assertion,* Q *a set of queries, and let* Q_α *be s.t.* $\gamma(Q_\alpha) \supseteq Q$. *Assume that* $\langle p, \lambda^c, \lambda^s \rangle \in Analysis(P, Q_\alpha, D_\alpha)$. *A is checked in* P *for* Q *if (1)* $\lambda^c \sqcap \lambda^+_{TS(Pre,P)} = \bot$ *or (2)* $\lambda^s \sqsubseteq \lambda^-_{TS(Post,P)}$.

Theorem 6 states that there are two situations in which a success assertion is checked. Case 1 indicates that the precondition is never satisfied, and thus the assertion holds and the postcondition does not need to be tested. Case 2 indicates that the postcondition holds for all stores in the success contexts, which is a safe approximation of the current stores of derivations in which the assertion is applicable.

False Assertions. Our aim now is to establish sufficient conditions which ensure statically that there is an erroneous derivation $D \in derivations(P, Q)$, i.e., without having to actually compute $derivations(P, Q)$. Unfortunately, this is a bit trickier than it may seem at first sight if analysis over-approximates computation states, as is the usual case.

Theorem 7 (False Calls Assertion). *Assuming the premises of Theorem 5, then A is false in* P *for* Q *if* $C(p, P, Q) \neq \emptyset$ *and* $\lambda^c \sqcap \lambda^+_{TS(Precond,P)} = \bot$.

In order to prove that a calls assertion is false it is not enough to prove that $\lambda^+_{TS(Precond,P)} \sqsubseteq \lambda^c$ as the contexts which violate the assertion may not appear in the real execution but rather may have been introduced due to the loss of accuracy of analysis w.r.t. the actual computation. Furthermore, even if λ^c and $\lambda^+_{TS(Precond,P)}$ are incompatible, it may be the case that there are no calls for predicate P in $derivations(P, Q)$ (and analysis is not capable of detecting so). This is why the condition $C(p, P, Q) \neq \emptyset$ is also required.

Theorem 8 (False Success Assertion). *Assuming the premises of Theorem 6, then A is false in P for Q if $\lambda^c \sqcap \lambda^-_{TS(Pre,P)} \neq \bot$ and $\lambda^s \sqcap \lambda^+_{TS(Post,P)} = \bot$ and $\exists\, \theta \in \gamma(\lambda^c \sqcap \lambda^-_{TS(Pre,P)}) : S(p, \theta, P, Q) \neq \emptyset$.*

Now again, λ^s is an over-approximation, and in particular it can approximate the empty set. This is the rationale behind the final extra condition.

If an assertion A is *false* then the program is not correct w.r.t. A. Detecting the mininal part of the program responsible for the incorrectness, i.e., diagnosis of a *static symptom*, is an interesting problem. However, such static diagnosis is out of the scope of this paper. This is the subject of on-going research.

True Assertions. As with checked assertions, if an assertion is true then it is guaranteed that it will not raise any error. From the point of view of assertion checking, the only difference between them is that checked assertions may raise errors if the program were used with a different set of queries.

Note that an assertion $calls(p, Precond)$ can never be found to be true, as the calling context of p depends on the query. If we pose no restriction on the queries we can always find a calling state which violates the assertion, unless $Precond$ is a tautology.

Theorem 9 (True Success Assertion). *Assuming the premises of Theorem 6, then A is true in P if $\lambda^+_{TS(Pre,P)} \sqsubseteq \lambda^c$ and $\lambda^s \sqsubseteq \lambda^-_{TS(Post,P)}$.*

The first condition guarantees that λ^s describes any store which is a descendent of a calling state of p which satisfied the precondition. The second condition ensures that any store described by λ^s satisfies the postcondition. Thus, any store in the success context which originated from a calling state which satisfied the precondition satisfies the postcondition.

Equivalent Assertions. It may be the case that some assertions are not detected as checked or false at compile-time. One possibility here is to default to run-time checking of the remaining assertions. However, it is possible that part of the assertion(s) can be replaced at compile-time by a simpler one, i.e., one which can be checked more efficiently.

Definition 19 (Equivalent Assertions). *Two assertions A, A' are equivalent in program P for a set of queries Q iff $E(A, P, Q) = E(A', P, Q)$.*

If A and A' are equivalent but A' is simpler then obviously A' should be used instead for run-time checking. Generating equivalent assertions at compile-time by simplification of assertions can be done using techniques such as abstract specialization (see, e.g., [28]). For simplicity, we do not discuss here how to obtain simpler versions of assertions. However, the implementation of the framework discussed below simplifies whenever possible those assertions which cannot be guaranteed to be false nor checked at compile-time.

7   Implementation

We have implemented the schema of Figure 1 as a *generic framework*. This genericity means that different instances of the tools involved in the schema for different CLP dialects can be generated in a straightforward way. To date, we have developed two different debugging environments as instances of the proposed framework: CiaoPP [19], the Ciao system[9] preprocessor and CHIPRE [26], an assertion-based, type inferencing and checking tool (in collaboration with Pawel Pietrzak from the U. of Linköping and Cosytec). The type analysis used is an adaptation to $CLP(\mathcal{FD})$ of the regular approximation approach of [16]. CiaoPP and CHIPRE share a common source (sub-)language (ISO-Prolog + finite domain constraints) and the Ciao assertion language [27],[10] so that source and output programs (annotated with assertions and/or run-time tests) within this (sub-)language can be easily exchanged. CHIPRE has been interfaced by Cosytec with the CHIP system (adding a graphical user interface) and is currently under industrial evaluation. CiaoPP is a more general tool which can perform a number of program development tasks including: (a) Inference of properties of program predicates and literals, including types (using [16]), modes and other variable instantiation properties (using the CLP version of the PLAI abstract interpreter [17]), non-failure, determinacy, bounds on computational cost, bounds on sizes of terms, etc. (b) Static debugging including checking how programs call system libraries and also the assertions present in other modules used by the program. (c) Several kinds of source to source program transformations such as specialization, parallelization, inclusion of run-time tests, etc. Information generated by analysis, assertions in system libraries, and any assertions optionally included in user programs are all written in the assertion language.[11]

The actual evaluation of the practical benefits of these tools is beyond the scope of this paper, but we believe that the significant industrial interest shown is encouraging. Also, it has certainly been observed during use by the system developers and a few early users that these tools can indeed detect some bugs much earlier in the program development process than with any previously available tools. Interestingly, this has been observed even when no specifications are available from the user: in these systems the system developers have included a rich set of assertions inside library modules (such as those defining the system built-ins and standard libraries) for the predicates defined in these modules. As a result, symptoms in user programs are often flagged during compilation simply because the analyzer/comparator pair detects that assertions for the system library predicates are violated by program predicates.

---

[9] Ciao [4] is a next-generation, GNU-licensed Prolog system (available from http://www.clip.dia.fi.upm.es/Software). The language subsumes standard ISO-Prolog and is specifically designed to be very extensible and to support modular program analysis, debugging, and optimization. Ciao is based on the &-Prolog/SICStus concurrent Prolog engine.

[10] As mentioned before, for clarity of the presentation in this work we have only addressed a subset of the assertion language.

[11] The full assertion language is also used by an automatic documentation generator for LP/CLP programs, LPdoc [18], which derives information from program assertions and machine-readable comments, and which generates manuals in many formats including postscript, pdf, info, HTML, etc.

References

1. K. R. Apt and E. Marchiori. Reasoning about Prolog programs: from modes through types to assertions. *Formal Aspects of Computing*, 6(6):743–765, 1994.
2. K. R. Apt and D. Pedreschi. Reasoning about termination of pure PROLOG programs. *Information and Computation*, 1(106):109–157, 1993.
3. J. Boye, W. Drabent, and J. Małuszyński. Declarative diagnosis of constraint programs: an assertion-based approach. In *Proc. of the 3rd. Int'l Workshop on Automated Debugging–AADEBUG'97*, pages 123–141, Linköping, Sweden, May 1997. U. of Linköping Press.
4. F. Bueno, D. Cabeza, M. Carro, M. Hermenegildo, P. López-García, and G. Puebla. The Ciao Prolog System. Reference Manual. The Ciao System Documentation Series–TR CLIP3/97.1, School of Computer Science, Technical University of Madrid (UPM), August 1997.
5. F. Bueno, D. Cabeza, M. Hermenegildo, and G. Puebla. Global Analysis of Standard Prolog Programs. In *European Symposium on Programming*, number 1058 in LNCS, pages 108–124, Sweden, April 1996. Springer-Verlag.
6. F. Bueno, P. Deransart, W. Drabent, G. Ferrand, M. Hermenegildo, J. Maluszynski, and G. Puebla. On the Role of Semantic Approximations in Validation and Diagnosis of Constraint Logic Programs. In *Proc. of the 3rd. Int'l Workshop on Automated Debugging–AADEBUG'97*, pages 155–170, Linköping, Sweden, May 1997. U. of Linköping Press.
7. B. Le Charlier and P. Van Hentenryck. Experimental Evaluation of a Generic Abstract Interpretation Algorithm for Prolog. *ACM Transactions on Programming Languages and Systems*, 16(1):35–101, 1994.
8. M. Comini, G. Levi, M. C. Meo, and G. Vitiello. Proving properties of logic programs by abstract diagnosis. In M. Dams, editor, *Analysis and Verification of Multiple-Agent Languages, 5th LOMAPS Workshop*, number 1192 in Lecture Notes in Computer Science, pages 22–50. Springer-Verlag, 1996.
9. M. Comini, G. Levi, and G. Vitiello. Abstract debugging of logic programs. In L. Fribourg and F. Turini, editors, *Proc. Logic Program Synthesis and Transformation and Metaprogramming in Logic 1994*, volume 883 of *Lecture Notes in Computer Science*, pages 440–450, Berlin, 1994. Springer-Verlag.
10. P. Cousot and R. Cousot. Abstract Interpretation: a Unified Lattice Model for Static Analysis of Programs by Construction or Approximation of Fixpoints. In *Fourth ACM Symposium on Principles of Programming Languages*, pages 238–252, 1977.
11. P. Deransart. Proof methods of declarative properties of definite programs. *Theoretical Computer Science*, 118:99–166, 1993.
12. P. Deransart, M. Hermenegildo, and J. Maluszynski. Debugging of Constraint Programs: The DiSCiPl Approach. In P. Deransart, M. Hermenegildo, and J. Maluszynski, editors, *Analysis and Visualization Tools for Constraint Programming*. Springer-Verlag, 2000. To appear.
13. W. Drabent, S. Nadjm-Tehrani, and J. Małuszyński. The Use of Assertions in Algorithmic Debugging. In *Proceedings of the Intl. Conf. on Fifth Generation Computer Systems*, pages 573–581, 1988.
14. W. Drabent, S. Nadjm-Tehrani, and J. Maluszynski. Algorithmic debugging with assertions. In H. Abramson and M.H.Rogers, editors, *Meta-programming in Logic Programming*, pages 501–522. MIT Press, 1989.
15. G. Ferrand. Error diagnosis in logic programming. *J. Logic Programming*, 4:177–198, 1987.

16. J.P. Gallagher and D.A. de Waal. Fast and precise regular approximations of logic programs. In Pascal Van Hentenryck, editor, *Proc. of the 11th International Conference on Logic Programming*, pages 599–613. MIT Press, 1994.

17. M. García de la Banda, M. Hermenegildo, M. Bruynooghe, V. Dumortier, G. Janssens, and W. Simoens. Global Analysis of Constraint Logic Programs. *ACM Transactions on Programming Languages and Systems*, 18(5):564–615, 1996.

18. M. Hermenegildo. A Documentation Generator for Logic Programming Systems. In *ICLP'99 Workshop on Logic Programming Environments*, pages 80–97. N.M. State University, December 1999.

19. M. Hermenegildo, F. Bueno, G. Puebla, and P. López-García. Program Analysis, Debugging and Optimization Using the Ciao System Preprocessor. In *1999 International Conference on Logic Programming*, pages 52–66, Cambridge, MA, November 1999. MIT Press.

20. M. Hermenegildo and The CLIP Group. Programming with Global Analysis. In *Proceedings of ILPS'97*, pages 49–52, Cambridge, MA, October 1997. MIT Press. (abstract of invited talk).

21. M. Hermenegildo, G. Puebla, and F. Bueno. Using Global Analysis, Partial Specifications, and an Extensible Assertion Language for Program Validation and Debugging. In K. R. Apt, V. Marek, M. Truszczynski, and D. S. Warren, editors, *The Logic Programming Paradigm: a 25-Year Perspective*, pages 161–192. Springer-Verlag, July 1999.

22. P. Hill and J. Lloyd. *The Goedel Programming Language*. MIT Press, Cambridge MA, 1994.

23. J. Jaffar and M.J. Maher. Constraint Logic Programming: A Survey. *Journal of Logic Programming*, 19/20:503–581, 1994.

24. D. Le Métayer. Proving properties of programs defined over recursive data structures. In *ACM Symposium on Partial Evaluation and Semantics-Based Program Manipulation*, pages 88–99, 1995.

25. K. Muthukumar and M. Hermenegildo. Compile-time Derivation of Variable Dependency Using Abstract Interpretation. *Journal of Logic Programming*, 13(2/3):315–347, July 1992.

26. G. Puebla, F. Bueno, and M. Hermenegildo. A Generic Preprocessor for Program Validation and Debugging. In P. Deransart, M. Hermenegildo, and J. Maluszynski, editors, *Analysis and Visualization Tools for Constraint Programming*. Springer-Verlag, 2000. To appear.

27. G. Puebla, F. Bueno, and M. Hermenegildo. An Assertion Language for Debugging of Constraint Logic Programs. In P. Deransart, M. Hermenegildo, and J. Maluszynski, editors, *Analysis and Visualization Tools for Constraint Programming*. Springer-Verlag, 2000. To appear.

28. G. Puebla and M. Hermenegildo. Abstract Multiple Specialization and its Application to Program Parallelization. *J. of Logic Programming. Special Issue on Synthesis, Transformation and Analysis of Logic Programs*, 41(2&3):279–316, November 1999.

29. Z. Somogyi, F. Henderson, and T. Conway. The execution algorithm of Mercury: an efficient purely declarative logic programming language. *JLP*, 29(1–3), October 1996.

30. E. Vetillard. *Utilisation de Declarations en Programmation Logique avec Constraintes*. PhD thesis, U. of Aix-Marseilles II, 1994.

Context-Moving Transformations for Function Verification[*]

Jürgen Giesl

Computer Science Dept., University of New Mexico, Albuquerque, NM 87131, USA,
E-mail: giesl@cs.unm.edu

Abstract. Several induction theorem provers have been developed
which support mechanized verification of functional programs. Unfortunately, a major problem is that they often fail in verifying tail recursive functions (which correspond to imperative programs). However, in
practice imperative programs are used almost exclusively.
We present an automatic transformation to tackle this problem. It transforms functions which are hard to verify into functions whose correctness
can be shown by the existing provers. In contrast to classical program
transformations, the aim of our technique is not to increase efficiency, but
to increase verifiability. Therefore, this paper introduces a novel application area for program transformations and it shows that such techniques
can in fact solve some of the most urgent current challenge problems in
automated verification and induction theorem proving.

1 Introduction

To guarantee the correctness of programs, a formal verification is required. However, mathematical correctness proofs are usually very expensive and time-con-
suming. Therefore, program verification should be *automated* as far as possible.

As *induction*[1] is the essential proof method for verification, several systems
have been developed for automated induction proving. These systems are successfully used for *functional* programs, but a major problem for their practical
application is that they are often not suitable for verifying *imperative* programs.
The reason is that the translation of imperative programs into the functional
input language of these systems always yields *tail recursive* functions which are
particularly hard to verify. Thus, developing techniques for proofs about tail
recursive functions is one of the most important research topics in this area.

In Sect. 2 we present our functional programming language and give a brief
introduction to induction proving. We illustrate that the reason for the difficulties in verifying tail recursive functions is that their accumulator parameter is
usually initialized with a fixed value, but this value is changed in recursive calls.

This paper introduces a new framework for mechanized verification of such
functions by first transforming them into functions which are better suitable for
verification and by afterwards applying the existing induction provers for their

---

[*] This work was supported by the DFG under grant GI 274/4-1.
[1] In this paper, "induction" stands for *mathematical induction*, i.e., it should not be
confused with induction in the sense of machine learning.

A. Bossi (Ed.): LOPSTR'99, LNCS 1817, pp. 293–312, 2000.

verification. To solve the verification problems with tail recursive functions, the *context* around recursive accumulator arguments has to be shifted away, such that the accumulator parameter is no longer changed in recursive calls. For that purpose, we introduce two automatic transformation techniques in Sect. 3 - 5. While of course our transformations are not always applicable, they proved successful on a representative collection of tail recursive functions, cf. [Gie99b]. In this way, correctness of many imperative programs can be proved *automatically* without inventing loop invariants or generalizations.

2   Functional Programs and Their Verification

We consider a first order functional language with eager semantics and (non-parameterized and free) algebraic data types. As an example, regard the data type nat for natural numbers whose objects are built with the *constructors* 0 and s : nat $\rightarrow$ nat (for the successor function). Thus, the constructor ground terms represent the data objects of the respective data type. In the following, we often write "1" instead of "s(0)", etc. For every n-ary constructor c there are n *selector* functions $d_1, \ldots, d_n$ which serve as inverse functions to c (i.e., $d_i(c(x_1, \ldots, x_n)) \equiv x_i$). For example, for the unary constructor s we have the selector function p such that $p(s(m)) \equiv m$ (i.e., p is the predecessor function).

In particular, every program F contains the type bool whose objects are built with the (nullary) constructors true and false. Moreover, there is a built-in equality function = : $\tau \times \tau \rightarrow$ bool for every data type τ. To distinguish the function symbol = from the equality predicate symbol, we denote the latter by "$\equiv$". The *functions* of a *functional program* F have the following form.

$$\textbf{function } f(x_1 : \tau_1, \ldots, x_n : \tau_n) : \tau \Leftarrow$$
$$\textbf{if } b_1 \textbf{ then } r_1$$
$$\vdots$$
$$\textbf{if } b_m \textbf{ then } r_m$$

Here, "**if** b_i **then** r_i" is called the i-th *case* of f with *condition* b_i and *result* r_i. For functions with just one case of the form "**if** true **then** r" we write "**function** $f(x_1 : \tau_1, \ldots, x_n : \tau_n) : \tau \Leftarrow r$". To ease readability, if b_m is true, then we often denote the last case by "**else** r_m". As an example, consider the following function (which calls an auxiliary algorithm + for addition).

$$\textbf{function times}(x, y : \text{nat}) : \text{nat} \Leftarrow$$
$$\textbf{if } x \neq 0 \textbf{ then } y + \text{times}(p(x), y)$$
$$\textbf{else } 0$$

If a function f is called with a tuple of ground terms t^* as arguments, then t^* is evaluated first (to constructor ground terms q^*). Now the condition $b_1[x^*/q^*]$ of the first case is checked. If it evaluates to true, then $r_1[x^*/q^*]$ is evaluated. Otherwise, the condition of the second case is checked, etc. So the conditions of a functional program as above are tested from top to bottom.

Our aim is to verify statements about the algorithms of a functional program.

We only consider universally quantified equations $\forall_{...}\, s \equiv t$ and we often omit the quantifiers to ease readability. Let s, t contain the tuple of variables x^*. Then $s \equiv t$ is *inductively true* for the program F, denoted $F \models_{\text{ind}} s \equiv t$, if for all those data objects q^* where evaluation of $s[x^*/q^*]$ or evaluation of $t[x^*/q^*]$ is defined, evaluation of the other term $t[x^*/q^*]$ resp. $s[x^*/q^*]$ is defined as well, and if both evaluations yield the same result. For example, the conjecture

$$\text{times}(\text{times}(x, y), z) \equiv \text{times}(x, \text{times}(y, z)) \tag{1}$$

is inductively true, since $\text{times}(\text{times}(x, y), z)$ and $\text{times}(x, \text{times}(y, z))$ evaluate to the same result for all instantiations with data objects. Similar notions of inductive truth are widely used in program verification and induction theorem proving. For an extension of inductive truth to more general formulas and for a model theoretic characterization see e.g. [ZKK88,Wal94,BR95,Gie99c].

To prove inductive truth automatically, several *induction theorem provers* have been developed, e.g. [BM79,KM87,ZKK88,BSH$^+$93,Wal94,BR95,BM98]. For instance, these systems can prove conjecture (1) by *structural* induction on the variable x. If we abbreviate (1) by $\varphi(x, y, z)$, then in the induction base case they would prove $\varphi(0, y, z)$ and in the step case (where $x \neq 0$), they would show that the induction hypothesis $\varphi(\mathsf{p}(x), y, z)$ implies the induction conclusion $\varphi(x, y, z)$.

However, one of the main problems for the application of these induction theorem provers in practice is that most of them can only handle functional algorithms with recursion, but they are not designed to verify imperative algorithms containing loops.

The classical techniques for the verification of imperative programs (like the so-called Hoare-calculus [Hoa69]) allow the proof of partial correctness statements of the form $\{\varphi_{\text{pre}}\}\ \mathcal{P}\ \{\varphi_{\text{post}}\}$. The semantics of this expression is that in case of termination, the program $\mathcal{P}$ transforms all program states which satisfy the precondition φ_{pre} into program states satisfying the postcondition φ_{post}. As an example, regard the following imperative program for multiplication.

> **procedure** multiply $(x, y, z : \mathsf{nat}) \Leftarrow$
> $z := 0;$
> **while** $x \neq 0$ **do** $x := \mathsf{p}(x);$
> $z := y + z$ **od**

To verify that this imperative program is equivalent to the functional program times, one has to prove the statement

$\{x \equiv x_0 \wedge y \equiv y_0 \wedge z \equiv 0\}$ **while** $x \neq 0$ **do** $x := \mathsf{p}(x); z := y + z$ **od** $\{z \equiv \text{times}(x_0, y_0)\}.$

Here, x_0 and y_0 are additional variables which represent the initial values of the variables x and y. However, in the Hoare-calculus, for that purpose one needs a *loop invariant* which is a consequence of the precondition and which (together with the exit condition $x = 0$ of the loop) implies the postcondition $z \equiv \text{times}(x_0, y_0)$. In our example, the proof succeeds with the loop invariant

$$z + \text{times}(x, y) \equiv \text{times}(x_0, y_0). \tag{2}$$

The search for loop invariants is the main difficulty when verifying imperative programs. Of course, it would be desirable that programmers develop suitable loop invariants while writing their programs, but in reality this is still often not the case. Thus, for an *automation* of program verification, suitable loop invariants would have to be discovered mechanically. However, while there exist some heuristics and techniques for the choice of loop invariants [SI98], in general this task seems difficult to mechanize [Dij85].

Therefore, in the following we present an alternative approach for automated verification of imperative programs. For that purpose our aim was to use the existing powerful induction theorem provers. As the input language of these systems is restricted to functional programs, one first has to translate imperative programs into functional ones. Such a translation can easily be done automatically, cf. [McC60,Gie99a].

In this translation, every **while**-loop is transformed into a separate function. For the loop of the procedure multiply we obtain the following algorithm mult which takes the input values of x, y, and z as arguments. If the loop-condition is satisfied (i.e., if $x \neq 0$), then mult is called recursively with the new values of x, y, and z. Otherwise, mult returns the value of z. The whole imperative procedure multiply corresponds to the following functional algorithm with the same name which calls the auxiliary function mult with the initial value $z \equiv 0$.

function multiply $(x, y : \text{nat}) : \text{nat} \Leftarrow$ **function** mult $(x, y, z : \text{nat}) : \text{nat} \Leftarrow$
   mult$(x, y, 0)$ **if** $x \neq 0$ **then** mult$(\text{p}(x), y, y + z)$
                                                  else z

Thus, while the above functions may look unnatural on their own, verification of such functions is indeed an important practical problem, since this is required in order to verify (very natural) imperative procedures like multiply.

Now induction provers may be used to prove conjectures about the functions multiply and mult. However, it turns out that the functional algorithms resulting from this translation have a certain characteristic form which makes them unsuitable for verification tasks. In fact, this difficulty corresponds to the problem of finding loop invariants for the original imperative program.

To verify the equivalence of multiply and times using the transformed functions multiply and mult, one now has to prove multiply$(x, y) \equiv$ times(x, y), i.e.,

$$\text{mult}(x, y, 0) \equiv \text{times}(x, y). \tag{3}$$

Using structural induction on x, the base formula mult$(0, y, 0) \equiv$ times$(0, y)$ can easily be proved, but there is a problem with the induction step. In the case $x \neq 0$ we have to show that the induction hypothesis

$$\text{mult}(\text{p}(x), y, 0) \equiv \text{times}(\text{p}(x), y) \tag{IH}$$

implies the induction conclusion mult$(x, y, 0) \equiv$ times(x, y). Using the algorithms of mult and times, the induction conclusion can be transformed into

$$\text{mult}(\text{p}(x), y, y) \equiv y + \text{times}(\text{p}(x), y). \tag{IC}$$

However, the desired proof fails, since the induction hypothesis (IH) cannot be successfully used for the proof of (IC).

The reason for this failure is due to the *tail recursive* form of mult (i.e., there is no context around mult's recursive call). Instead, its result is computed in the *accumulator* parameter z. The accumulator z is initialized with 0, but this value is changed in the recursive calls of mult. For that reason the induction hypothesis (where $z \equiv 0$) does not correspond to the induction conclusion (where $z \equiv y$).

The classical solution for this problem is to *generalize* the conjecture (3) to a stronger conjecture which is easier to prove. For instance, in our example one needs the following generalization which can be proved by a suitable induction.

$$\mathsf{mult}(x, y, z) \equiv z + \mathsf{times}(x, y) \tag{4}$$

Thus, developing generalization techniques is one of the main challenges in induction theorem proving [Aub79,BM79,HBS92,Wal94,IS97,IB99]. Note that the generalization (4) corresponds to the loop invariant (2) that one would need for a direct verification of the imperative program multiply in the Hoare-calculus. So in fact, finding suitable generalizations is closely related to the search for loop invariants.[2]

In this paper we propose a new approach to avoid the need for generalizations or loop invariants. The idea is to transform functions like mult, which are difficult to verify, into algorithms like times which are much better amenable to automated induction proofs. For example, the well-known induction theorem proving system NQTHM [BM79,BM98] fails in proving (3), whereas after a transformation of multiply and mult into times this conjecture becomes trivial. This approach of verifying imperative programs via a translation into functional programs is based on the observation that in functional languages there often exists a formulation of the algorithms which is easy to verify (whereas this formulation cannot be expressed in iterative form). The aim of our technique is to find such a formulation automatically.

Our approach has the advantage that the transformation solves the verification problems resulting from a tail recursive algorithm once and for all. On the other hand, when using generalizations or loop invariants one has to find a new generalization (or a new loop invariant, respectively) for every new conjecture about such an algorithm. Moreover, most techniques for finding generalizations or loop invariants have to be guided by the system user, since they rely on the presence of suitable lemmata. By these lemmata the user often has to provide the main idea for the generalization resp. the loop invariant. In contrast, our transformation works automatically.

---

[2] A difference between verifying functional programs by induction and verifying imperative programs by loop invariants and inductive assertions is that for imperative programs one uses a "forward" induction starting with the initial values of the program variables and for functional programs a "reversed" induction is used which goes back from their final values to the initial ones. However, the required loop invariants resp. the corresponding generalizations are easily interchangeable, cf. [RY76].

In particular, automatic generalization techniques fail for many conjectures which contain *several* occurrences of a tail recursive function. As an example, regard the associativity of multiply or, in other words,

$$\mathsf{mult}(\mathsf{mult}(x, y, 0), z, 0) \equiv \mathsf{mult}(x, \mathsf{mult}(y, z, 0), 0). \tag{5}$$

Similar to (3), a direct proof by structural induction on x does not succeed. So again, the standard solution would be to generalize the conjecture (5) by replacing the fixed value 0 by suitable terms. For example, one may generalize (5) to

$$\mathsf{mult}(\mathsf{mult}(x, y, \underline{v}), z, 0) \equiv \mathsf{mult}(x, \mathsf{mult}(y, z, 0), \underline{\mathsf{mult}(v, z, 0)}).$$

To ease readability, we have underlined those terms where the generalization took place. While the proof of this conjecture is not too hard (using the distributivity of + over multiply), we are not aware of any technique which would find this generalization (or the corresponding loop invariant) automatically, because it is difficult to synthesize the correct replacement of the third argument in the right-hand side (by $\mathsf{mult}(v, z, 0)$). The problem is that the disturbing 0's occurring in (5) cannot just be generalized to new variables, since this would yield a flawed conjecture. Thus, finding generalizations for conjectures with several occurrences of a tail recursive function is often particularly hard, as different occurrences of an instantiated accumulator may have to be generalized to different new terms.[3] On the other hand, our transformation allows us to prove such conjectures without user interaction. Essentially, the reason is that while generalizations and loop invariants depend on both the algorithms and the conjectures to be proved, the transformation only depends on the algorithms.

The area of program transformation is a well examined field which has found many applications in software engineering, program synthesis, and compiler construction. For surveys see e.g. [BW82,Par90,MPS93,PP96,PP98]. However, the transformations developed for these applications had a goal which is fundamentally different from ours. Our aim is to transform programs into new programs which are easier to verify. In contrast to that, the classical transformation methods aim to increase efficiency. Such transformations are unsuitable for our purpose, since a more efficient algorithm is often harder to verify than a less efficient easier algorithm. Moreover, we want to transform tail recursive algorithms into non-tail recursive ones, but in the usual applications of program transformation, non-tail recursive programs are transformed into tail recursive ones ("recursion removal", cf. e.g. [Coo66,DB76,BD77,Wan80,BW82,AK82,HK92]).

As the goals of the existing program transformations are often opposite to ours, a promising approach is to use these classical transformations *in the reverse*

---

[3]   An alternative generalization of (5) is $\mathsf{mult}(\mathsf{mult}(x, y, 0), z, \underline{v}) \equiv \mathsf{mult}(x, \mathsf{mult}(y, z, 0), \underline{v})$. This generalization is easier to find (as we just replaced both third arguments of the left- and right-hand side by the same new variable v). However, it is not easy to verify (its proof is essentially as hard as the proof of the original conjecture (5)).

direction. To our knowledge, such an application of these transformations for the purpose of verification has rarely been investigated before. In this way, we indeed obtained valuable inspirations for the development of our transformation rules in Sect. 3 - 5. However, our rules go far beyond the reversed standard program transformation methods, because these methods had to be modified substantially to be applicable for the programs resulting in our context.

3   Context Moving

The only difference between mult and times is that the context $y + \ldots$ to compute times' result is outside of the recursive call, whereas in mult the context $y + \ldots$ is in the recursive argument for the accumulator z. This change of the accumulator in recursive calls is responsible for the verification problems with mult.

For that reason, we now introduce a transformation rule which allows to *move* the context away from recursive accumulator arguments to a position outside of the recursive call. In this way, the former result $\mathsf{mult}(\mathsf{p}(x), y, y + z)$ can be replaced by $y + \mathsf{mult}(\mathsf{p}(x), y, z)$. So the algorithm mult is transformed into

$$
\begin{aligned}
&\textbf{function } \mathsf{mult}\,(x, y, z : \mathsf{nat}) : \mathsf{nat} \Leftarrow \\
&\quad \textbf{if } x \neq 0 \textbf{ then } y + \mathsf{mult}(\mathsf{p}(x), y, z) \\
&\quad\quad\quad \textbf{else }\ z.
\end{aligned}
$$

To develop a rule for context moving, we have to find sufficient criteria which ensure that such a transformation is equivalence preserving. For our rule, we regard algorithms of the form (6) where the last argument z is used as an accumulator. Our aim is to move the contexts $r_1, \ldots, r_k$ of the recursive accumulator arguments to the top, i.e., to transform the algorithm (6) into (7).

$$
\begin{array}{ll}
\textbf{function }\ f\,(x^* : \tau^*, z : \tau) : \tau \Leftarrow & \textbf{function }\ f\,(x^* : \tau^*, z : \tau) : \tau \Leftarrow \\
\quad \textbf{if } b_1 \quad \textbf{then } f(r_1^*, r_1) & \quad \textbf{if } b_1 \quad \textbf{then } r_1[z/f(r_1^*, z)] \\
\quad\quad \vdots & \quad\quad \vdots \\
\quad \textbf{if } b_k \quad \textbf{then } f(r_k^*, r_k) \quad (6) & \quad \textbf{if } b_k \quad \textbf{then } r_k[z/f(r_k^*, z)] \quad (7) \\
\quad \textbf{if } b_{k+1} \textbf{ then } r_{k+1} & \quad \textbf{if } b_{k+1} \textbf{ then } r_{k+1} \\
\quad\quad \vdots & \quad\quad \vdots \\
\quad \textbf{if } b_m \quad \textbf{then } r_m & \quad \textbf{if } b_m \quad \textbf{then } r_m.
\end{array}
$$

We demand $m > k \geq 1$, but the order of the f-cases is irrelevant and the transformation may also be applied if the accumulator z is not f's *last* parameter. (We just used the above formulation to ease readability.)

First of all, note that the intermediate values of the parameter z are not the same in the two versions of f. Thus, to guarantee that evaluation of both versions of f leads to the same cases in the same order, we must demand that the accumulator z does not occur in the conditions $b_1, \ldots, b_m$ or in $r_1^*, \ldots, r_k^*$.

Let u^*, w be constructor ground terms. Now for both versions of f, evaluation of $f(u^*, w)$ leads to the same f-cases $i_1, \ldots, i_d$ where $i_1, \ldots, i_{d-1} \in \{1, \ldots, k\}$ and $i_d \in \{k+1, \ldots, m\}$ (provided that the evaluation is defined). Let $t[r^*, s]$

abbreviate $t[x^*/r^*, z/s]$ (where for terms t containing at most the variables x^*, we also write $t[r^*]$) and let $a_h^* = r_{i_h}^*[r_{i_{h-1}}^*[\ldots [r_{i_1}^*[u^*]]\ldots]]$, where $a_0^* = u^*$. Then with the old definition of f we obtain the result (8) and with the new definition we obtain (9).

$$r_{i_d}[a_{d-1}^*, r_{i_{d-1}}[a_{d-2}^*, \ldots r_{i_2}[a_1^*, r_{i_1}[a_0^*, w]]\ldots]] \tag{8}$$

$$r_{i_1}[a_0^*, r_{i_2}[a_1^*, \ldots r_{i_{d-1}}[a_{d-2}^*, r_{i_d}[a_{d-1}^*, w]]\ldots]]. \tag{9}$$

For example, the original algorithm mult computes a result of the form

$$y_x + (y_{x-1} + (\ldots (y_2 + (y_1 + z))\ldots))$$

where y_i denotes the number which is added in the i-th execution of the algorithm. On the other hand, the new version of mult computes the result

$$y_1 + (y_2 + (\ldots (y_{x-1} + (y_x + z))\ldots)).$$

Therefore, the crucial condition for the soundness of this transformation is the *left-commutativity* of the contexts $r_1, \ldots, r_k$ moved, cf. [BW82]. In other words, for all $i \in \{1, \ldots, m\}$ and all $i' \in \{1, \ldots, k\}$ we demand

$$r_i[x^*, r_{i'}[y^*, z]] \equiv r_{i'}[y^*, r_i[x^*, z]].$$

Then (8) and (9) are indeed equal as can be proved by subsequently moving the inner $r_{i_j}[a_{j-1}^*, \ldots]$ contexts of (8) to the top. So for mult, we only have to prove $x + (y + z) \equiv y + (x + z)$ and $y + z \equiv y + z$ (which can easily be verified by the existing induction theorem provers).

Note also that since in the schema (6), $r_1, \ldots, r_m$ denote arbitrary *terms*, such a context moving would also be possible if one would exchange the arguments of $+$ in mult's recursive call. Then r_1 would be $z + y$ and the required left-commutativity conditions would read $(z + y) + x \equiv (z + x) + y$ and $z + y \equiv z + y$.

However, context moving may only be done, if all terms $r_1, \ldots, r_m$ contain the accumulator z. Otherwise f's new definition could be total although the original definition was partial. For example, if f has the (first) case

if $x \neq 0$ then $f(x, 0)$

then $f(x, z)$ does not terminate for $x \neq 0$. However, if we would not demand that z occurred in the recursive accumulator argument, then context moving could transform this case into "**if $x \neq 0$ then 0**". The resulting function is clearly not equivalent to the original one, because now the result of $f(x, z)$ is 0 for $x \neq 0$.

Finally, we also have to demand that in $r_1, \ldots, r_m$, the accumulator z may not occur within arguments of functions dependent on f. Here, every function is *dependent* on itself and moreover, if g is dependent on f and g occurs in the algorithm h, then h is also dependent on f. So in particular, this requirement excludes nested recursive calls with the argument z. Otherwise, the transformation would not preserve the semantics. As an example regard the following function, where the algorithm one(z) returns 1 for all arguments z.

$$\textbf{function } f(x, z : \text{nat}) : \text{nat} \Leftarrow$$
$$\textbf{if } x \neq 0 \textbf{ then } f(p(x), f(z, 0))$$
$$\textbf{else } \text{one}(z)$$

By moving the context $f(\ldots, 0)$ to the top, the result of the first case would be transformed into $f(f(p(x), z), 0)$. The original algorithm satisfies all previously developed conditions. However, the original algorithm is total, whereas after the transformation $f(x, z)$ does not terminate any more for $x \neq 0$. Under the above requirements, the transformation of (6) into (7) is sound.

Theorem 1 (Soundness of Context Moving). *Let F be a functional program containing the algorithm (6) and let F' result from F by replacing (6) with (7). Then for all data objects t^*, t, and q, $f(t^*, t)$ evaluates to q in the program F iff it does so in F', provided that the following requirements are fulfilled:*

(A) $z \notin \mathcal{V}(b_1) \cup \ldots \cup \mathcal{V}(b_m)$
(B) $z \notin \mathcal{V}(r_1^*) \cup \ldots \cup \mathcal{V}(r_k^*)$
(C) For all $i \in \{1, \ldots, m\}$, $i' \in \{1, \ldots, k\}$: $F \models_{\text{ind}} r_i[x^*, r_{i'}[y^*, z]] \equiv r_{i'}[y^*, r_i[x^*, z]]$
(D) $z \in \mathcal{V}(r_1) \cap \ldots \cap \mathcal{V}(r_m)$
(E) In $r_1, \ldots, r_m$, z does not occur in arguments of functions dependent on f.

Proof. We first prove the following context moving lemma for all constructor ground terms u^*, v^*, w and all $i' \in \{1, \ldots, k\}$:

$$F \models_{\text{ind}} r_{i'}[v^*, f(u^*, w)] \equiv f(u^*, r_{i'}[v^*, w]). \tag{10}$$

We use an induction on u^* w.r.t. the relation $\succ_f$. Here, $u^* \succ_f q^*$ holds for the constructor ground terms u^* and q^* iff there exists a constructor ground term u such that $f(u^*, u)$ is defined in F and such that F-evaluation of $f(u^*, u)$ leads to a recursive call $f(q^*, q)$ for some constructor ground term q. The well-foundedness of $\succ_f$ is due to the requirements (A), (B), and (E).

If one of the two terms in the equation (10) is defined, then there is an $i \in \{1, \ldots, m\}$ such that $b_i[u^*] \equiv_F$ true and $b_j[u^*] \equiv_F$ false for all $1 \leq j < i$, where $s \equiv_F t$ abbreviates $F \models_{\text{ind}} s \equiv t$. (Here we need condition (D) to infer the definedness of $f(u^*, w)$ from the definedness of $r_{i'}[v^*, f(u^*, w)]$.) If $i \geq k + 1$, then

$$r_{i'}[v^*, f(u^*, w)] \equiv_F r_{i'}[v^*, r_i[u^*, w]]$$
$$\equiv_F r_i[u^*, r_{i'}[v^*, w]], \text{ by (C)}$$
$$\equiv_F f(u^*, r_{i'}[v^*, w]), \text{ since } z \in \mathcal{V}(r_i) \text{ (by (D))}.$$

If $i \leq k$, then we have

$$r_{i'}[v^*, f(u^*, w)] \equiv_F r_{i'}[v^*, f(r_i^*[u^*], r_i[u^*, w])]$$
$$\equiv_F f(r_i^*[u^*], r_{i'}[v^*, r_i[u^*, w]]), \text{ by the induction hypothesis}$$
$$\equiv_F f(r_i^*[u^*], r_i[u^*, r_{i'}[v^*, w]]), \text{ by (C)}$$
$$\equiv_F f(u^*, r_{i'}[v^*, w]), \qquad \text{since } z \in \mathcal{V}(r_i) \text{ (by (D))}.$$

Thus, Lemma (10) is proved and now the "only if"-direction of Thm. 1 can also be shown by induction w.r.t. $\succ_f$. There must be an $i' \in \{1, \ldots, m\}$ such that

$b_{i'}[t^*] \equiv_F$ true and $b_{j'}[t^*] \equiv_F$ false for all $1 \leq j' < i'$. The induction hypothesis implies $b_{i'}[t^*] \equiv_{F'}$ true and $b_{j'}[t^*] \equiv_{F'}$ false as well.

If $i' \geq k+1$, then the conjecture follows from $f(t^*, t) \equiv_F r_{i'}[t^*, t]$, $f(t^*, t) \equiv_{F'} r_{i'}[t^*, t]$, and the induction hypothesis. If $i' \leq k$, then we have $f(t^*, t) \equiv_F f(r_{i'}^*[t^*], r_{i'}[t^*, t]) \equiv_F q$ for some constructor ground term q. By Lemma (10) we obtain $r_{i'}[t^*, f(r_{i'}^*[t^*], t)] \equiv_F q$. Note that for all f-subterms $f(s^*, s)$ in this term, s^* evaluates to constructor ground terms q^* with $t^* \succ_f q^*$. For f-subterms where the root is in $r_{i'}$, this follows from Condition (E). Thus, the induction hypothesis implies $r_{i'}[t^*, f(r_{i'}^*[t^*], t)] \equiv_{F'} q$ and hence, we also have $f(t^*, t) \equiv_{F'} q$.

So the "only if"-direction of Thm. 1 is proved. The proof for the "if"-direction of Thm. 1 is completely analogous (where instead of $\succ_f$ one uses an induction on the length of $f(t^*, t)$'s evaluation in F'). $\qquad\square$

The algorithm obtained from mult by context moving is significantly easier to verify. As mult's (former) accumulator z is no longer changed, it can now be eliminated by replacing all its occurrences by 0. The semantics of the main function multiply remains unchanged by this transformation.

function multiply $(x, y : $ nat$) : $ nat $\Leftarrow$ **function** mult $(x, y : $ nat$) : $ nat $\Leftarrow$
   mult(x, y) **if** $x \neq 0$ **then** $y + $ mult$($p$(x), y)$
                             else 0

Now mult indeed corresponds to the algorithm times and thus, the complicated generalizations or loop invariants of Sect. 2 are no longer required. Thus, the verification problems for this algorithm are solved.

Similarly, context moving can also be applied to transform an algorithm like

function plus $(x, z : $ nat$) : $ nat $\Leftarrow$ **function** plus $(x, z : $ nat$) : $ nat $\Leftarrow$
   if $x \neq 0$ **then** plus$($p$(x),$ s$(z))$ into   **if** $x \neq 0$ **then** s$($plus$($p$(x), z))$
      else z **else** $z,$

which is much better suited for verification tasks. Here, for condition (C) we only have to prove s$($s$(z)) \equiv $ s$($s$(z))$ and s$(z) \equiv $ s(z) (which is trivial).

To apply context moving mechanically, the conditions (A) - (E) for its application have to be checked automatically. While the conditions (A), (B), (D), and (E) are just syntactic, the left-commutativity condition (C) has to be checked by an underlying induction theorem prover. In many cases, this is not a hard task, since for algorithms like plus the terms $r_i[x^*, r_{i'}[y^*, z]]$ and $r_{i'}[y^*, r_i[x^*, z]]$ are already *syntactically* equal and for algorithms like mult, the required left-commutativity follows from the associativity and commutativity of "$+$". To ease the proof of such conjectures about auxiliary algorithms, we follow the strategy to apply our transformations to those algorithms first which depend on few other algorithms. Thus, we would attempt to transform "$+$" before transforming mult. In this way, one can usually avoid the need for generalizations when performing the required left-commutativity proofs. Finally, note that of course, context moving should only be done if at least one of the recursive arguments $r_1, \ldots, r_k$ is different from z (otherwise the algorithm would not change).

Our context moving rule has some similarities to the reversal of a technique known in program transformation (*operand commutation*, cf. e.g. [Coo66,DB76, BW82]). However, our rule generalizes this (reversed) technique substantially.

For example, directly reversing the formulation in [BW82] would result in a rule which would also impose applicability conditions on the functions *that call* the transformed function f (by demanding that f's accumulator would have to be initialized in a certain way). In this way, the applicability of the reversed rule would be unnecessarily restricted (and unnecessarily difficult to check). Therefore, we developed a rule where context moving is separated from the subsequent replacement of the (former) accumulator by initial values like 0. Moreover, in [BW82] the problems concerning the occurrence of the accumulator z and of nested recursive calls are not examined (i.e., the requirements (D) and (E) are missing there). Another important difference is that our rule allows the use of *several different* recursive arguments $r_1, \ldots, r_k$ and the use of *several* non-recursive cases with *arbitrary* results (whereas reversing the formulation in [BW82] would only allow one single recursive case and it would only allow the non-recursive result z instead of the arbitrary terms $r_{k+1}, \ldots, r_m$). Note that for this reason in our rule we have to regard *all* cases of an algorithm at once.

As an example where this flexibility of our transformation rule is needed consider the following algorithm to compute the multiplication of all elements in a list, where however occurring 0's are ignored. We use a data type list for lists of naturals with the constructors nil : list and cons : nat × list → list, where car : list → nat and cdr : list → list are the selectors to cons. Moreover, "*" abbreviates a multiplication algorithm like times or multiply.

procedure prod $(l$: list, z : nat) $\Leftarrow$
    $z := \mathsf{s}(0)$;
    while $l \neq$ nil **do**   **if** car$(l) \neq 0$ **then** $z :=$ car$(l) * z$;
                $l :=$ cdr(l) **od**

This procedure can be translated automatically into the following functions (here, we re-ordered the cases of pr to ease readability).

function prod $(l$: list) : nat $\Leftarrow$ **function** pr $(l$: list, z : nat) : nat $\Leftarrow$
pr$(l, \mathsf{s}(0))$ **if** $l =$ nil   **then** z
                                                            if car$(l) \neq 0$ **then** pr$($cdr$(l),$ car$(l) * z)$
                                                                        else pr$($cdr$(l), z)$

To transform the algorithm pr, we indeed need a technique which can handle algorithms with several recursive cases. Since $*$ is left-commutative, context moving and replacing z with $\mathsf{s}(0)$ results in

function prod $(l$: list) : nat $\Leftarrow$ **function** pr $(l$: list) : nat $\Leftarrow$
pr(l) **if** $l =$ nil   **then** $\mathsf{s}(0)$
                                                            if car$(l) \neq 0$ **then** car$(l) *$ pr$($cdr$(l))$
                                                                        else pr$($cdr$(l))$.

Further algorithms with several recursive and non-recursive cases where context moving is required are presented in [Gie99b].

Context moving is also related to a technique in [Moo75]. However, in contrast to our rule, his transformation is not equivalence-preserving, but it corresponds to a *generalization* of the conjecture. For that reason this approach faces the danger of over-generalization (e.g., the associativity law for multiply is generalized into a flawed conjecture). It turns out that for almost all algorithms considered in [Moo75] our transformation techniques can generate *equivalent* algorithms that are easy to verify. So for such examples, generalizations are no longer needed.

4   Context Splitting

Because of the required left-commutativity, context moving is not always applicable. As an example regard the following imperative procedure for uniting lists. We use a data type llist for lists of list's. Its constructors are empty and add with the selectors hd and tl. So add(z, k) represents the insertion of the list z in front of the list of lists k and hd(add(z, k)) yields z. Moreover, we use an algorithm app for list-concatenation. Then after execution of union(k, z), the value of z is the union of all lists in k.

$$\textbf{procedure } \mathsf{union}(k : \mathsf{llist}, z : \mathsf{list}) \Leftarrow$$
$$z := \mathsf{nil};$$
$$\textbf{while } k \neq \mathsf{empty} \textbf{ do } z := \mathsf{app}(\mathsf{hd}(k), z);$$
$$k := \mathsf{tl}(k) \qquad \textbf{od}$$

Translation of union into functional algorithms yields

$$\textbf{function } \mathsf{union}\,(k : \mathsf{llist}) : \mathsf{list} \Leftarrow \qquad \textbf{function } \mathsf{uni}\,(k : \mathsf{llist}, z : \mathsf{list}) : \mathsf{list} \Leftarrow$$
$$\mathsf{uni}(k, \mathsf{nil}) \qquad\qquad \textbf{if } k \neq \mathsf{empty} \textbf{ then } \mathsf{uni}(\mathsf{tl}(k), \mathsf{app}(\mathsf{hd}(k), z))$$
$$\textbf{else } z.$$

These functions are again unsuited for verification, because the accumulator z of uni is initially called with nil, but this value is changed in the recursive calls. Context moving is not possible, because the context app$(\mathsf{hd}(k), \ldots)$ is not left-commutative. This motivates the development of the following *context splitting* transformation. Given a list of lists $k = [z_1, \ldots, z_n]$, the result of uni(k, nil) is

$$\mathsf{app}(z_n, \mathsf{app}(z_{n-1}, \ldots \mathsf{app}(z_3, \mathsf{app}(z_2, z_1)) \ldots)). \tag{11}$$

In order to move the context of uni's recursive accumulator argument to the top, our aim is to compute this result in a way such that z_1 is moved as far to the "outside" in this term as possible (whereas z_n may be moved to the "inside"). Although app is not commutative, it is at least *associative*. So (11) is equal to

$$\mathsf{app}(\mathsf{app}(\ldots \mathsf{app}(\mathsf{app}(z_n, z_{n-1}), z_{n-2}) \ldots, z_2), z_1). \tag{12}$$

This gives an idea on how the algorithm uni may be transformed into a new (unary) algorithm uni$'$ such that uni$'(k)$ computes uni(k, nil). The result of uni$'([z_1, \ldots, z_n])$ should be app(uni$'([z_2, \ldots, z_n]), z_1)$. Similarly, uni$'([z_2, \ldots, z_n])$ should yield app(uni$'([z_3, \ldots, z_n]), z_2)$, etc. Finally, uni$'([z_n])$ is app(uni$'(\mathsf{empty})$,

z_n). To obtain the result (12), $\mathsf{app}(\mathsf{uni}'(\mathsf{empty}), z_n)$ must be equal to z_n. Hence, $\mathsf{uni}'(\mathsf{empty})$ should yield app's neutral argument nil. Thus, we obtain the following new algorithms, which are well suited for verification tasks.

function union $(k : \mathsf{llist})$: list $\Leftarrow$ **function** uni′ $(k : \mathsf{llist})$: list $\Leftarrow$
    uni′(k) **if** $k \neq$ empty **then** $\mathsf{app}(\mathsf{uni}'(\mathsf{tl}(k)), \mathsf{hd}(k))$
                                                    else nil

So the idea is to *split up* the former context $\mathsf{app}(\mathsf{hd}(k), \ldots)$ into an *outer* part $\mathsf{app}(\ldots, \ldots)$ and an *inner* part $\mathsf{hd}(k)$. If the outer context is associative, then one can transform tail recursive results of the form $f(\ldots, \mathsf{app}(\mathsf{hd}(k), z))$ into results of the form $\mathsf{app}(f'(\ldots), \mathsf{hd}(k))$. In general, our context splitting rule generates a new algorithm (14) from an algorithm of the form (13).

function $f(x^* : \tau^*, z : \tau) : \tau \Leftarrow$ **function** $f'(x^* : \tau^*) : \tau \Leftarrow$
  if b_1 **then** $f(r_1^*, p[r_1, z])$ **if** b_1 **then** $p[f'(r_1^*), r_1]$
           $\vdots$ $\vdots$

  if b_k **then** $f(r_k^*, p[r_k, z])$ (13)   **if** b_k **then** $p[f'(r_k^*), r_k]$ (14)
  if b_{k+1} **then** $p[r_{k+1}, z]$ **if** b_{k+1} **then** r_{k+1}
           $\vdots$ $\vdots$

  if b_m **then** $p[r_m, z]$ **if** b_m **then** r_m.

Here, p is a term of type τ containing exactly the two new variables x_1 and x_2 of type τ and $p[t_1, t_2]$ abbreviates $p[x_1/t_1, x_2/t_2]$. Then our transformation splits the contexts into their common top part p and their specific part r_i and it moves the common part p to the top of recursive results. (This allows an elimination of the accumulator z.) If there are several possible choices for p, then we use the heuristic to choose p as small and r_i as big as possible. Let e be a constructor ground term which is a neutral argument of p, i.e., $F \models_{\mathsf{ind}} p[x, e] \equiv x$ and $F \models_{\mathsf{ind}} p[e, x] \equiv x$. Then in (13), one may also have z instead of $p[e, z]$. For example, in uni we had the non-recursive result z instead of $\mathsf{app}(\mathsf{nil}, z)$. Moreover we demand $m > k \geq 1$, but the order of the f-cases is again irrelevant and the rule may also be applied if z is not the *last* parameter of f.

We want to ensure that all occurrences of $f(t^*, e)$ in other algorithms g (that f is not dependent on) may be replaced by $f'(t^*)$. For the soundness of this transformation, similar to context moving, the accumulator z must not occur in conditions or in the subterms $r_1^*, \ldots, r_k^*$ or $r_1, \ldots, r_m$. Then for constructor ground terms u^*, the evaluation of $f(u^*, e)$ and of $f'(u^*)$ leads to the same cases $i_1, \ldots, i_d$ where $i_1, \ldots, i_{d-1} \in \{1, \ldots, k\}$ and $i_d \in \{k+1, \ldots, m\}$. For $1 \leq h \leq d$ let a_h be $r_{i_h}[r_{i_{h-1}}^*[\ldots[r_{i_1}^*[u^*]]\ldots]]$. Then the result of $f(u^*, e)$ is (15) and the result of $f'(u^*)$ is (16).

$$p[a_d, p[a_{d-1}, \ldots p[a_2, a_1]\ldots]] \tag{15}$$
$$p[p[\ldots p[p[a_d, a_{d-1}], a_{d-2}]\ldots a_2], a_1] \tag{16}$$

To ensure the equality of these two results, p must be associative. The following theorem summarizes our rule for context splitting.

Theorem 2 (Soundness of Context Splitting). *Let F be a functional program containing (13) and let F' result from F by adding the algorithm (14). Then for all data objects t^* and q, $f(t^*, e)$ evaluates to q in F iff $f'(t^*)$ evaluates to q in F', provided that the following requirements are fulfilled:*

(A) $z \notin \mathcal{V}(b_1) \cup \ldots \cup \mathcal{V}(b_m)$
(B) $z \notin \mathcal{V}(r_1^*) \cup \ldots \cup \mathcal{V}(r_k^*) \cup \mathcal{V}(r_1) \cup \ldots \cup \mathcal{V}(r_m)$
(C) $F \models_{ind} p[p[x_1, x_2], x_3] \equiv p[x_1, p[x_2, x_3]]$
(D) $F \models_{ind} p[x, e] \equiv x$ and $F \models_{ind} p[e, x] \equiv x$.

Proof. Note that evaluation of f is the same in F and F'. Moreover, Conditions (C) and (D) also hold for F'. We prove the (stronger) conjecture

$$f(t^*, t) \equiv_{F'} q \quad \text{iff} \quad p[f'(t^*), t] \equiv_{F'} q \tag{17}$$

for all constructor ground terms t^*, t, and q.

For the "only if"-direction of (17) we use induction on the length of $f(t^*, t)$'s evaluation. There must be a case i such that $b_i[t^*] \equiv_{F'}$ true and $b_j[t^*] \equiv_{F'}$ false for all $1 \le j < i$. If $i \ge k+1$, then we have $f(t^*, t) \equiv_{F'} p[r_i[t^*], t] \equiv_{F'} p[f'(t^*), t]$.

If $i \le k$, then $f(t^*, t) \equiv_{F'} f(r_i^*[t^*], p[r_i[t^*], t]) \equiv_{F'} p[f'(r_i^*[t^*]), p[r_i[t^*], t]]$ by the induction hypothesis. By (C), this is $\equiv_{F'}$-equal to $p[p[f'(r_i^*[t^*]), r_i[t^*]], t]$ which in turn is is $\equiv_{F'}$-equal to $p[f'(t^*), t]$. The "if"-direction of (17) is proved analogously (by induction w.r.t. the relation $\succ_{f'}$, where $u^* \succ_{f'} q^*$ holds for two tuples of constructor ground terms u^* and q^* iff evaluation of $f'(u^*)$ is defined and it leads to the evaluation of $f'(q^*)$).   □

Context splitting is only applied if there is a term $f(t^*, e)$ in some other algorithm g that f is not dependent on. In this case, the conditions (C) and (D) are checked by an underlying induction theorem prover (where usually associativity is even easier to prove than (left-)commutativity). Conditions (A) and (B) are just syntactic. In case of success, f' is generated and the term $f(t^*, e)$ in the algorithm g is replaced by $f'(t^*)$.

Similar to context moving, a variant of the above rule if often used in the *reverse* direction (*re-bracketing*, cf. e.g. [Coo66,DB76,BD77,Wan80,BW82,PP96]). Again, instead of directly reversing the technique, we modified and generalized it, e.g., by regarding several tail recursive and non-tail recursive cases. An algorithm where this general form of our rule is needed will be presented in Sect. 5 and several others can be found in [Gie99b]. Moreover, the next section also introduces important refinements which increase the applicability of context splitting considerably and which have no counterpart in the classical re-bracketing rules.

5   Pre-processing Transformations for Context Splitting

In examples where the context p is not yet in the right form, one can use suitable pre-processing transformations which in turn enable the application of context splitting. Regard the following imperative procedure for reversing lists.

$$\textbf{procedure } \mathsf{reverse}(l, z : \mathsf{list}) \Leftarrow$$
$$z := \mathsf{nil};$$
$$\textbf{while } l \neq \mathsf{nil } \textbf{ do } z := \mathsf{cons}(\mathsf{car}(l), z);$$
$$l := \mathsf{cdr}(l) \qquad\qquad \textbf{od}$$

By translating reverse into functional form one obtains

$$\textbf{function } \mathsf{reverse}(l : \mathsf{list}) : \mathsf{list} \Leftarrow \qquad \textbf{function } \mathsf{rev}(l, z : \mathsf{list}) : \mathsf{list} \Leftarrow$$
$$\mathsf{rev}(l, \mathsf{nil}) \qquad\qquad\qquad \textbf{if } l \neq \mathsf{nil } \textbf{ then } \mathsf{rev}(\mathsf{cdr}(l), \mathsf{cons}(\mathsf{car}(l), z))$$
$$\textbf{else } z.$$

In order to eliminate the accumulator z, we would like to apply context splitting. Here, the term p in (13) would be $\mathsf{cons}(x_1, x_2)$. But then x_1 would be a variable of type nat (instead of list as required) and hence, the associativity law is not even well typed.

Whenever p has the form $c(x_1, \ldots, x_1, x_2)$ for some constructor c, where x_1 is of the "wrong" type, then one may use the following reformulation of the algorithm. (Of course, here x_2 does not have to be the *last* argument of c.) The idea is to "lift" $x_1, \ldots, x_1$ to an object $\mathsf{lift}_c(x_1, \ldots, x_1)$ of type τ and to define a new function $c' : \tau \times \tau \to \tau$ such that $c'(\mathsf{lift}_c(x_1, \ldots, x_1), x_2) \equiv c(x_1, \ldots, x_1, x_2)$. Moreover, in order to split contexts afterwards, c' should be associative.

As a heuristic, we use the following construction for lift_c and c', provided that apart from c the data type τ just has a constant constructor c_{con}. The function $\mathsf{lift}_c(x_1, \ldots, x_n)$ should yield the term $c(x_1, \ldots, x_n, c_{con})$ and the function c' is defined by the following algorithm (where $d_1, \ldots, d_{n+1}$ are the selectors to c).

$$\textbf{function } c'(x, z : \tau) : \tau \Leftarrow$$
$$\textbf{if } x = c(d_1(x), \ldots, d_n(x), d_{n+1}(x)) \textbf{ then } c(d_1(x), \ldots, d_n(x), c'(d_{n+1}(x), z))$$
$$\textbf{else } z$$

Then $c'(\mathsf{lift}_c(x_1, \ldots, x_n), z) \equiv c(x_1, \ldots, x_n, z)$, c_{con} is a neutral argument for c', and c' is associative. So for rev, we obtain $\mathsf{lift}_{\mathsf{cons}}(x_1) \equiv \mathsf{cons}(x_1, \mathsf{nil})$ and

$$\textbf{function } \mathsf{cons}'(x, z : \mathsf{list}) : \mathsf{list} \Leftarrow$$
$$\textbf{if } x = \mathsf{cons}(\mathsf{car}(x), \mathsf{cdr}(x)) \textbf{ then } \mathsf{cons}(\mathsf{car}(x), \mathsf{cons}'(\mathsf{cdr}(x), z))$$
$$\textbf{else } z.$$

Note that in this example, cons' corresponds to the concatenation function app.

Thus, the term $\mathsf{cons}(\mathsf{car}(l), z)$ in the algorithm rev may be replaced by $\mathsf{cons}'(\mathsf{lift}_{\mathsf{cons}}(\mathsf{car}(l)), z)$, i.e., by $\mathsf{cons}'(\mathsf{cons}(\mathsf{car}(l), \mathsf{nil}), z)$. Now the rule for context splitting is applicable which yields

$$\textbf{function } \mathsf{reverse}(l : \mathsf{list}) : \mathsf{list} \Leftarrow \qquad \textbf{function } \mathsf{rev}'(l : \mathsf{list}) : \mathsf{list} \Leftarrow$$
$$\mathsf{rev}'(l) \qquad\qquad\qquad \textbf{if } l \neq \mathsf{nil } \textbf{ then } \mathsf{cons}'(\mathsf{rev}'(\mathsf{cdr}(l)), \mathsf{cons}(\mathsf{car}(l), \mathsf{nil}))$$
$$\textbf{else } \mathsf{nil}.$$

In contrast to the original versions of reverse and rev, these algorithms are well suited for verification.

Of course, there are also examples where the context p has the form $g(x_1, x_2)$ for some *algorithm* g (instead of a constructor c) and where x_1 has the "wrong" type. For instance, regard the following imperative procedure to filter all even elements out of a list l. It uses an auxiliary algorithm even and an algorithm $\mathsf{atend}(x, z)$ which inserts an element x at the end of a list z.

> **function** $\mathsf{atend}(x : \mathsf{nat}, z : \mathsf{list}) : \mathsf{list} \Leftarrow$
> **if** $z = \mathsf{nil}$ **then** $\mathsf{cons}(x, \mathsf{nil})$
> **else** $\mathsf{cons}(\mathsf{car}(z), \mathsf{atend}(x, \mathsf{cdr}(z)))$

Now the procedure filter reads as follows.

> **procedure** $\mathsf{filter}(l, z : \mathsf{list}) \Leftarrow$
> $z := \mathsf{nil};$
> **while** $l \neq \mathsf{nil}$ **do** **if** $\mathsf{even}(\mathsf{car}(l))$ **then** $z := \mathsf{atend}(\mathsf{car}(l), z);$
> $l := \mathsf{cdr}(l)$ **od**

Translating this procedure into functional algorithms yields

function $\mathsf{filter}(l : \mathsf{list}) : \mathsf{list} \Leftarrow$ **function** $\mathsf{fil}(l, z : \mathsf{list}) : \mathsf{list} \Leftarrow$
$\quad \mathsf{fil}(l, \mathsf{nil})$ **if** $l = \mathsf{nil}$ **then** z
                        if $\mathsf{even}(\mathsf{car}(l))$ **then** $\mathsf{fil}(\mathsf{cdr}(l), \mathsf{atend}(\mathsf{car}(l), z))$
                              else $\mathsf{fil}(\mathsf{cdr}(l), z)$.

To apply context splitting for fil, p would be $\mathsf{atend}(x_1, x_2)$ and thus, x_1 would be of type nat instead of list as required. While for constructors like cons, such a problem can be solved by the *lifting* technique described above, now the root of p is the algorithm atend. For such examples, the following *parameter enlargement* transformation often helps.

In the algorithm atend, outside of its own recursive argument the parameter x only occurs in the term $\mathsf{cons}(x, \mathsf{nil})$ and the value of $\mathsf{cons}(x, \mathsf{nil})$ does not change throughout the whole execution of atend (as the value of x does not change in any recursive call). Hence, the parameter x can be "enlarged" into a new parameter y which corresponds to the value of $\mathsf{cons}(x, \mathsf{nil})$. Thus, we result in the following algorithm atend', where $\mathsf{atend}'(\mathsf{cons}(x, \mathsf{nil}), z) \equiv \mathsf{atend}(x, z)$.

> **function** $\mathsf{atend}'(y, z : \mathsf{list}) : \mathsf{list} \Leftarrow$
> **if** $z = \mathsf{nil}$ **then** y
> **else** $\mathsf{cons}(\mathsf{car}(z), \mathsf{atend}'(y, \mathsf{cdr}(z)))$

In general, let $h(x^*, z^*)$ be a function where the parameters x^* are not changed in recursive calls and where x^* only occur within the terms $t_1, \ldots, t_m$ outside of their recursive calls in the algorithm h. If $\mathcal{V}(t_i) \subseteq \{x^*\}$ for all i and if the t_i only contain total functions (like constructors), then one may construct a new algorithm $h'(y_1, \ldots, y_m, z^*)$ by enlarging the parameters x^* into $y_1, \ldots, y_m$. The algorithm h' results from h by replacing all t_i by y_i, where the parameters y_i again remain unchanged in their recursive arguments. Then we have $h'(t_1, \ldots, t_m, z^*) \equiv h(x^*, z^*)$. Thus, in all algorithms f that h is not dependent on, we may replace any subterm $h(s^*, p^*)$ by $h'(t_1[x^*/s^*], \ldots, t_m[x^*/s^*], p^*)$. (The only restriction for this replacement is that all possibly undefined subterms of s^* must still occur in some $t_i[x^*/s^*]$.)

Hence, in the algorithm fil, the term atend(car(l), z) can be replaced by atend'(cons(car(l), nil), z). It turns out that atend'(l_1, l_2) concatenates the lists l_2 and l_1 (i.e., it corresponds to app(l_2, l_1)). Therefore, atend' is associative and thus, context splitting can be applied to fil now. This yields the following algorithms which are well suited for verification.

function filter(l : list) : list $\Leftarrow$ **function** fil'(l : list) : list $\Leftarrow$
   fil'(l)   **if** $l = $ nil   **then** nil
                             if even(car(l)) **then** atend'(fil'(cdr(l)), cons(car(l), nil))
                                   else   atend'(fil'(cdr(l)), nil)

Of course, by subsequent unfolding (or "symbolic evaluation") of atend', the algorithm fil' can be simplified to

$$\text{\textbf{function} \ fil'}(l : \text{list}) : \text{list} \Leftarrow$$
$$\text{\textbf{if} } l = \text{nil} \quad\quad \text{\textbf{then} nil}$$
$$\text{\textbf{if} even(car}(l)) \text{ \textbf{then} cons(car}(l), \text{fil'(cdr}(l)))$$
$$\text{\textbf{else} \ fil'(cdr}(l)).$$

Note that here we indeed needed a context splitting rule which can handle algorithms with *several* tail recursive cases. Thus, a direct reversal of the classical re-bracketing rules [BW82] would fail for both reverse and filter (since these rules are restricted to just one recursive case and moreover, they lack the concepts of lifting and of parameter enlargement).

The examples union, reverse, and filter show that context splitting can help in cases where context moving is not applicable. On the other hand for algorithms like plus, context moving is successful, but context splitting is not possible. So none of these two transformations subsumes the other and to obtain a powerful approach, we indeed need *both* of them. But there are also several algorithms where the verification problems can be solved by both context moving and splitting. For example, the algorithms resulting from mult by context moving or splitting only differ in the order of the arguments of $+$ in mult's first recursive case. Thus, both resulting algorithms are well suited for verification tasks.

6   Conclusion

We have presented a new transformational approach for the mechanized verification of imperative programs and tail recursive functions, which consists of the following transformations:

- *context moving* for left-commutative contexts of accumulators (Sect. 3)
- *context splitting* for (partly) associative contexts of accumulators (Sect. 4)
- *lifting* of arguments in order to enable context splitting (Sect. 5)
- *parameter enlargement* to enable context splitting (Sect. 5)

By our technique, functions that are hard to verify are automatically transformed into functions where verification is significantly easier. Hence, for many programs the invention of loop invariants or of generalizations is no longer required and an automated verification is possible by the existing induction theorem provers. As our transformations generate *equivalent* functions, this transformational verification approach is not restricted to partial correctness, but it can also be used to simplify total correctness and termination proofs [Gie95,Gie97,GWB98,BG99,AG00]. See [Gie99b] for a collection of examples that demonstrates the power of our approach. It shows that our transformation indeed simplifies the verification tasks substantially for many practically relevant algorithms from different areas of computer science (e.g., arithmetical algorithms or procedures for processing (possibly multidimensional) lists including algorithms for matrix multiplication and sorting algorithms like selection-, insertion-, and merge-sort, etc.). Based on the rules and heuristics presented, we implemented a system to perform such transformations automatically [Gie99a].

The field of mechanized verification and induction theorem proving represents a new application area for program transformation techniques. It turns out that our approach of transforming algorithms often seems to be superior to the classical solution of generalizing theorems. For instance, our technique automatically transforms all (first order) tail recursive functions treated in recent generalization techniques [IS97,IB99] into non-tail recursive ones whose verification is very simple. On the other hand, the techniques for finding generalizations are mostly semi-automatic (since they are guided by the system user who has to provide suitable lemmata). Obviously, by formulating the right lemmata (interactively), in principle generalization techniques can deal with almost every conjecture to be proved. But in particular for conjectures which involve *several* occurrences of a tail recursive function, finding suitable generalizations is often impossible for fully automatic techniques. Therefore, our approach represents a significant contribution for mechanized verification of imperative and tail recursive functional programs. Nevertheless, of course there also exist tail recursive algorithms where our automatic transformations are not applicable. For such examples, (interactive) generalizations are still required.

Further work will include an examination of other existing program transformation techniques in order to determine whether they can be modified into transformations suitable for an application in the program verification domain. Moreover, in future work the application area of program verification may also give rise to new transformations which have no counterpart at all in classical program transformations.

References

AK82.   J. Arsac and Y. Kodratoff. Some techniques for recursion removal from recursive functions. *ACM Trans. Prog. Languages Systems*, 4:295–322, 1982.

AG00.   T. Arts and J. Giesl. Termination of term rewriting using dependency pairs. *Theoretical Computer Science*, 2000. To appear.

Aub79.   R. Aubin. Mechanizing structural induction. *TCS*, 9:347–362, 1979.

BW82.   F. L. Bauer and H. Wössner. *Algorithmic Language and Program Development.* Springer, 1982.

BR95.   A. Bouhoula and M. Rusinowitch. Implicit induction in conditional theories. *Journal of Automated Reasoning,* 14:189–235, 1995.

BM79.   R. S. Boyer and J S. Moore. *A Computational Logic.* Academic Press, 1979.

BM98.   R. S. Boyer and J S. Moore. *A Computational Logic Handbook.* Academic Press, 2nd edition, 1998.

BG99.   J. Brauburger and J. Giesl. Approximating the domains of functional and imperative programs. *Science of Computer Programming,* 35:113–136, 1999.

BSH+93. A. Bundy, A. Stevens, F. van Harmelen, A. Ireland, and A. Smaill. Rippling: A heuristic for guiding inductive proofs. *Artif. Int.,* 62:185–253, 1993.

BD77.   R. M. Burstall and J. Darlington. A transformation system for developing recursive programs. *Journal of the ACM,* 24:44–67, 1977.

Coo66. D. Cooper. The equivalence of certain computations. *Comp. J.,* 9:45–52, 66.

DB76.   J. Darlington and R. M. Burstall. A system which automatically improves programs. *Acta Informatica,* 6:41–60, 1976.

Dij85. E. W. Dijkstra. Invariance and non-determinacy. In *Mathematical Logic and Programming Languages,* chapter 9, pages 157–165. Prentice-Hall, 1985.

Gie95. J. Giesl. Termination analysis for functional programs using term orderings. In *Proc. SAS' 95,* LNCS 983, pages 154–171, Glasgow, UK, 1995.

Gie97. J. Giesl. Termination of nested and mutually recursive algorithms. *Journal of Automated Reasoning,* 19:1–29, 1997.

GWB98. J. Giesl, C. Walther, and J. Brauburger. Termination analysis for functional programs. In Bibel and Schmitt, eds., *Automated Deduction – A Basis for Applications, Vol. III,* Applied Logic Series 10, pages 135–164. Kluwer, 1998.

Gie99a. J. Giesl. Mechanized verification of imperative and functional programs. Habilitation Thesis, TU Darmstadt, 1999.

Gie99b. J. Giesl. Context-moving transformations for function verification. Technical Report IBN 99/51, TU Darmstadt. Available from http://www.inferenzsysteme.informatik.tu-darmstadt.de/~giesl/ibn-99-51.ps

Gie99c. J. Giesl. Induction proofs with partial functions. *Journal of Automated Reasoning.* To appear. Preliminary version appeared as Technical Report IBN 98/48, TU Darmstadt. Available from http://www.inferenzsysteme.informatik.tu-darmstadt.de/~giesl/ibn-98-48.ps

HK92.   P. Harrison and H. Khoshnevisan. A new approach to recursion removal. *Theoretical Computer Science,* 93:91–113, 1992.

HBS92. J. Hesketh, A. Bundy, and A. Smaill. Using middle-out reasoning to control the synthesis of tail-recursive programs. In *Proc. CADE-11,* LNAI 607, pages 310–324, Saratoga Springs, NY, 1992.

Hoa69. C. A. R. Hoare. An axiomatic basis for computer programming. *Communications of the ACM,* 12:576–583, 1969.

IS97.   A. Ireland and J. Stark. On the automatic discovery of loop invariants. *4th NASA Langley Formal Methods Workshop,* NASA Conf. Publ. 3356, 1997.

IB99.   A. Ireland and A. Bundy. Automatic verification of functions with accumulating parameters. *Journal of Functional Programming,* 9:225-245, 1999.

KM87.   D. Kapur and D. R. Musser. Proof by consistency. *AI,* 31:125–158, 1987.

McC60. J. McCarthy. Recursive functions of symbolic expressions and their computation by machine. *Communications of the ACM,* 3, 1960.

MPS93. B. Möller, H. Partsch, and S. Schuman. *Formal Program Development.* LNCS 755, Springer, 1993.

Moo75.   J S. Moore. Introducing iteration into the Pure LISP theorem prover. *IEEE Transactions on Software Engineering*, 1:328–338, 1975.

Par90.   H. Partsch. *Specification and Transformation of Programs*. Springer, 1990.

PP96.   A. Pettorossi and M. Proietti. Rules and strategies for transforming functional and logic programs. *ACM Computing Surveys*, 28:360–414, 1996.

PP98.   A. Pettorossi and M. Proietti. Transformations of logic programs. *Handbook of Logic in AI and Logic Programming, Vol. 5*, Oxford University Pr., 1998.

RY76.   C. Reynolds and R. T. Yeh. Induction as the Basis for Program Verification. *IEEE Transactions on Software Engineering*, SE-2(4):244–252, 1976.

SI98.   J. Stark and A. Ireland. Invariant discovery via failed proof attempts. In *Proc. LOPSTR '98*, LNCS 1559, Manchester, UK, 1998.

Wal94.   C. Walther. Mathematical induction. *Handbook of Logic in Artificial Intelligence and Logic Programming, Vol. 2*. Oxford University Press, 1994.

Wan80.   M. Wand. Continuation-based program transformation strategies. *Journal of the ACM*, 27:164–180, 1980.

ZKK88.   H. Zhang, D. Kapur, and M. S. Krishnamoorthy. A mechanizable induction principle for equational specifications. *CADE-9*, LNCS 310, Argonne, 1988.

Constraint Logic Programming Applied to Model Checking

Laurent Fribourg

LSV, Ecole Normale Supérieure de Cachan & CNRS
61 av. Pdt. Wilson, 94235 Cachan, France
Laurent.Fribourg@lsv.ens-cachan.fr

Abstract. We review and discuss here some of the existing approaches based on CLP (*Constraint Logic Programming*) for verifying properties of various kinds of state-transition systems.

1 Introduction: Model Checking and Fixed-Point Engines

Model-checking is an automatic technique for verifying finite-state concurrent systems. Specifications are expressed in a certain temporal logic, and the concurrent system is modeled as a state-transition system [9]. There are several kinds of temporal logic, the most used in model-checking being PLTL (*Propositional Linear Temporal Logic*) [37], CTL (*Computation Tree Logic*) [8] and the mu-calculus [32]. Reachability analysis is a variant of model-checking consisting in characterizing all the reachable states of the system. This is useful for proving safety properties, i.e. verifying that something "bad" never happens to the system. More generally, model checking is the problem of finding the set of states in a state transition graph where a given formula (of the underlying temporal logic) is true. This mainly reduces to computing least fixed-point(s) or greatest fixed-point(s) for the temporal logic operators involved in the formula. Model-checking has been extended for treating infinite-state systems such as timed automata [1] or linear hybrid systems [27,22]. Logic Programming, and more generally CLP (*Constraint Logic Programming* [31]), has been recently used by several teams of researchers for constructing "engines" that compute fixed-points related to model-checking, and benefit from general techniques of program transformation. We review and discuss here some of the proposed approaches.

The plan of the paper is as follows. Section 2 explains how fixed-point engines have been developed for mu-calculus using tabled logic programming. Section 3 reports on an extension of mu-calculus for handling constraints over finite domains. CLP-based methods for analysing automata enriched with timing constraints, are reviewed in section 4, as well as methods for automata with integer constraints in section 5. Section 6 gives some experimental results obtained with CLP-based methods. The paper ends with a discussion in section 7.

A. Bossi (Ed.): LOPSTR'99, LNCS 1817, pp. 30–41, 2000.

2   Encoding Mu-Calculus in Tabled Logic Programming

This section is essentially borrowed from [40]. The modal mu-calculus [32] is an expressive temporal logic whose semantics is usually described over sets of states of labeled transition systems. The logic is encoded is an equational form, the syntax of which is given by the following grammar:

```
F ::= Z | tt | ff | F\/ F | F /\ F | diam(A, F) | box(A, F)
```

In the above, Z is a set of formula variables (encoded as Prolog atoms) and A is set of actions; tt and ff are propositional constants; \/ and /\ are standard logical connectives; and diam(A, F) (possibly after action A formula F holds) and box(A, F) (necessarily after action A formula F holds) are dual modal operators. Additionally, logical variables can be given defining equations of the form X :== mu(F) (least fixed-point) or X :== nu(F) (greatest fixed-point). For example, a basic property, the absence of deadlock, is expressed in this logic by a formula variable deadlock_free defined as:

```
deadlock_free ::= nu(box(-, deadlock_free) /\ diam(-, tt))
```

where '-' stands for any action. The formula states, essentially, that from every reachable state ((box(-,deadlock_free)) a transition is possible (diam(-,tt)).

The labeled transition system is a *finite-state automaton*, specified in terms of a set of facts trans(*Src*, *Act*, *Dest*), where *Src*, *Act*, and *Dest* are the source location, label and target location, respectively, of each transition. The semantics of the modal mu-calculus is specified declaratively in logic programming by providing a set of rules for each of the operators of the logic. For example, the semantics of \/ , diam, and mu are encoded as follows:

```
models(Loc_S, (F1 \/ F2))   :- models(Loc_S, F1).
models(Loc_S, (F1 \/ F2))   :- models(Loc_S, F2).

models(Loc_S, diam(A, F))   :- trans(Loc_S, A, Loc_T),
                                models(Loc_T, F).

models(Loc_S, Z)            :- Z :== mu(F),
                                models(Loc_S, F).
```

Consider the rule for diam. It states that a location Loc_S (of a process) satisfies a formula of the form diam(A, F) if Loc_S has an A transition to some location Loc_T and Loc_T satisfies F. Greatest fixed-point computations are encoded as negation of their dual least fixed-point. This encoding provides a sound method for model checking any modal mu-calculus formula that is alternation free [17]. An extension for implementing *full* modal mu-calculus was proposed in in [34].

The computation of fixed-points using the standard strategy of Prolog generally fails due to nontermination problems. The XSB tabled logic programming system developed at SUNY Stony Brook is an implementation of *tabled resolution* [49,7], which is integrated into Prolog-style SLD resolution (extended with negation-as-failure rule). Many programs that would loop infinitely in Prolog will terminate in XSB because XSB calls a predicate with the same arguments only once, whereas Prolog may call such a predicate infinitely often. For these terminating programs XSB efficiently computes the least model, which is the least fixed-point of the program rules understood as "equations" over sets of atoms.

By using XSB as a programmable fixed-point engine, one can construct an efficient model checker, called XMC, under 200 lines of code. XMC benefits from optimization techniques developed for deductive-database-style applications, such as literal reordering (see, e.g., [50]) and clause resolution factoring [11], as well as from source-code representational changes of process terms. These logic-based optimization techniques lead to considerable space and time reduction. Performance can be improved even further with XSB by *compiling* high-level specifications into low-level automata of a certain kind, using continuation-passing style [14].

3   Mu-Calculus for Automata with Finite Domains

In [43], Rauzy presents *Toupie*, a system implementing an extension of the propositional mu-calculus to finite domain constraints. *Toupie* encodes arithmetic relations over finite domains by means of *decision diagrams*, an extension to finite domains of Bryant's binary decision diagrams [4]. Decision diagrams (DD), as used in *Toupie*, admit a compact canonical coding. In order to solve systems of linear equations, i.e. to compute a DD that encodes all the solution of the system, *Toupie* uses the classical implicit enumeration/propagation technique [26]. The principle is to enumerate variables in the order of their indices, and to build the DD in a bottom-up way. The adopted propagation – the Waltz's filtering – consists in maintaining, for each variable a minimum and maximum value. Each time a variable domain is modified, this modification is propagated until a fixed-point is reached.

Rauzy mentions very good performances using general purpose constraint language *Toupie* with respect to specialized model checkers. These results are attributed to the use of extended decision diagrams instead of binary ones.

4   Reachability Analysis for Timed Automata

Timed automata [1] are finite-state automata enriched with a set of clocks, which are real-valued variables that increase continuously at the same rate with time. There are two kinds of transitions: *discrete* and *delay* transitions. Discrete transition are instantaneous transitions (as in the case of finite-state automata), which make the automaton switch from one location to another. Such transitions can be performed only if a certain relationship holds among the current values of the clocks (*guard*). When they are performed, these transitions update some of the clocks to 0. Discrete transitions are interleaved with delay transitions, which correspond to the evolution of time at a certain location. Time can increase continuously through delay-transitions as long as the *location invariant* (a specific constraint on clock values associated with each location) is not violated. We now review various CLP-based methods for performing reachability analysis of timed automata.

4.1 Tabled Resolution

This subsection is essentially borrowed from [16]. Timed automata are represented in [16] within a (tabled) logic programming framework. This requires the definition of two relations `inv/2` and `trans/5`:

1. `inv(L, Inv)` associates location names with location invariants.

2. `trans(L1, Act, Rho, RSL, L2)` represents a transition of the timed automaton such that L1, L2. Act, Rho, RSL are the source and target locations, the label of the transition, the transition conditions, and the set of clocks to be reset, respectively.

The implementation of reachability analysis is done using the integration of a library of polyhedra manipulations, as explained below. In the case of an ordinary finite-state labeled transition system, reachability can simply be computed using predicate `trans/3`, as follows:

```
reach(X,Y) :- trans(X,_,Y).
reach(X,Y) :- reach(X,Z), trans(Z,_,Y).
```

The relation `reach` can be naturally generalized using constraint representation to compute *forward reachability* in timed automata. The desired generalization of `reach` is attained in two steps. First, a state of a timed automaton is represented by a pair $\langle L, R \rangle$, where L is a location and R is a constraint representing a set of clock valuations. Secondly, the transition `trans/3` is redefined, with the help of `trans/5`, as follows:

```
trans((L1,R1), Act, (L2,R2)) :-              % discrete transition
       trans(L1,Act,Rho,RSL,L2),
       conjunction(R1,Rho,E1),
       reset(E1, RSL, E2),
       inv(L2,Inv),
       conjunction(E2, Inv, R2).
trans((L1,R1), epsilon, (L2,R2)) :-          % time successor
       time_succ(L1, R1, R2).
```

The predicate `reset(E1,RSL,E2)` computes a constraint E2 by projecting the constraint E1 on the surface generated by setting all the (clock) variables in RSL to zero. This can be implemented using a library of polyhedra manipulations. The predicate `time_succ(L,R1,R2)` computes the time successor of R1. This can be still computed using primitive of polyhedra manipulations [23]. R2 is computed by intersecting the resultant region with the location invariant L. Likewise, backward reachability can be defined through a `back_reach` predicate by essentially reversing the application of the `trans/3` relation.

4.2   Meta-Programming in CLP($\mathcal{R}$)

A similar solution has been developed by Urbina [52,51]. However, in contrast with [14], Urbina performs forward and backward fixed-point computation, without appealing to tabled resolution or to any special polyhedra manipulation library. Urbina uses just CLP($\mathcal{R}$) [24], its built-in real arithmetic solver and some of its meta-programming facilities (`assert`, `not`, `consistent`, `infer`, ...).

In a related work by Pontelli and Gupta [38], the simulation of timed automata is performed via the top-down operational semantics of CLP($\mathcal{R}$).

4.3   Revesz's Procedure

Another solution consists in using Revesz's bottom-up evaluation procedure instead of tabled resolution or meta-programming in CLP($\mathcal{R}$). Revesz has shown that bottom-up evaluation (with subsumption) terminates for a special class of logic programs with *gap-order constraints*. Gap-order constraints are inequalities of the form $X_1 \geq X_2 + c$ where X_1 and X_2 are variables and c a non-negative integer [44]. Originally in [44], the domain of variables was assumed to be $\mathcal{Z}$, but the procedure can be slightly modify in order to involve real-valued variables instead. The reachability problem can be easily encoded under the form of a logic program with constraints. For example, consider the timed automaton with three clocks X_1, X_2, X_3, represented in Figure 1. We assume that, initially: $X_1 = X_2 = X_3 = 0$. Beside transition in (resp. down) resets clocks X_1, X_2, X_3 (resp. X_3) to 0, and has *true* (resp. $1 \leq X_2 < 2$) as a guard. Location ℓ_1 (resp. ℓ_2) has $X_1 \leq 5 \wedge X_2 < 2$ (resp. $X_1 \leq 5$) as an invariant.

The reachability relation for this automaton can be encoded under the form of the following CLP program:

```
p(l0,Y1,Y2,Y3,T)        :- Y1=Y2=Y3=0.

p(l1,Y1',Y2',Y3',T')  :- Y1'=T,  Y2'=T,  Y3'=T,  T=<T',  T'=<Y1'+5,
                         T'<Y'+2,  p(l0,Y1,Y2,Y3,T).

p(l2,Y1',Y2',Y3',T')  :- Y1'=Y1,  Y2'=Y2,  Y3'=T,  T=<T',
                         Y2+1=<T,  T<Y2+2,  T'=<Y1'+5,
                         p(l1,Y1,Y2,Y3,T).
```

where T denotes a new clock variable which is never reset, and Y_i (resp. Y_i') is a variable standing for $T - X_i$ (resp. $T' - X_i'$). A further simple variable manipulation allows to transform this program into a program with only gap-order constraints, and the computation of the reachability space can be then computed using Revesz's procedure. (See [18] for details.)

5   Reachability Analysis for Automata with Integers

Automata with integers is another extended form of finite-state automata. They correspond to finite-state automata enriched with a set of integer-valued variables. A (discrete) transition can only be performed if a certain constraint over

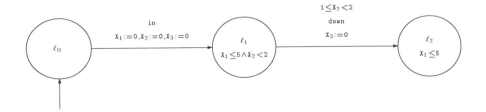

Fig. 1. A simple timed automaton

the values of these variables holds. The transition modifies the values of the variables according to a specified update relation.

5.1   Gap-Order Constraints.

As in the case of timed automata, it is easy to encode the reachability relation via a logic program with arithmetical constraints. When the guard and update relations all belong to the class of gap-order constraints, it is still possible to use Revesz's procedure in order to compute the set of reachable states. Otherwise, one may still use Revesz's procedure, but one has to approximate non-gap order constraints: typically, constraints of the form $X = Y + c$ are approximated under the form $X \geq Y + c$. What is then computed is still a fixed-point, but not necessarily the *least one*. However this may be sufficient to prove that some undesirable symbolic state is never reached [21].

5.2   Presburger Arithmetic

In [5] the fixed-point calculations associated with transitions of automata with integers are executed symbolically using a Presburger solver called the Omega library [39]. Convergence is guaranteed by using *abstract interpretation* techniques such as "widening" [10].

   In [19] a Presburger solver is similarly used in order to compute symbolically the reachable space of Petri nets, viewed as special forms of automata with integers. The fixed-point computation is optimized by integrating a method of "path decomposition" [20]. This method can be regarded, from a logic programming point of view, as a method of redundant derivation elimination [47,33,25,41], or, from a model-checking point of view, as a method of *partial order* [30] (a technique for combating the combinatorial explosion that results from interleaving concurrent independent transitions in all possible orders).

5.3   Real Arithmetic

An alternative proposed in [12] is to compute the least fixed-point of the reachability program via meta-programming facilities provided in SICStus Prolog via the CLP(Q,R) library [28]. Logic-based optimization techniques are also used, such as *magic set transformations* [42] or *local subsumption* [46]. Since they manipulate formulas over reals instead of integers, they add an extra abstraction for which in general a loss of precision is possible. Furthermore, in order to improve the termination of the procedure, it may be useful to appeal to classical (dynamic) techniques of approximations such as *widening* [10,22]. Note that Delzanno and Podelski do not only treat reachability problems, but general problems of CTL logic by exhibiting a connection between CTL properties (safety, liveness) and model-theoretic or denotational semantics of logic programs with constraints.

The reachability analysis of Petri nets along the lines of [19] is further studied in [2] using the constraint solver over reals built-in HyTech instead of a Presburger solver. As in [12] the manipulation of reals instead of integers entails *a priori* a loss of precision, but it is shown in [2] that the computation of least fixed-points is actually exact when it terminates.

6   Experimental Results

We now review some of the most significant results obtained when running the CLP-based systems mentioned above.

6.1   Finite-State Transition Systems

XMC. In [40], XMC system is said to have good memory usage on a well-known set of benchmarks, as compared to SPIN [29], but its speed appears uneven. The speed weakness of XMC is attributed to the absence of partial order optimization [30]. In [15] results from XMC as well as 4 other model checkers are given for detecting a livelock error of the i-protocol, a sophisticated sliding-window protocol consisting of about 300 lines of C code. XMC performs much better than all the other model checkers on this example (except Murφ which has comparable results, when the error is fixed). The success of XMC is attributed to the local, top-down nature of its model-checking algorithm. In [14] further comparisons are done with an optimizing compiler for XMC, and confirms the good performance of XMC over SPIN on the i-protocol example. On another example (leader election protocol) however, SPIN significantly outperforms XMC, again because of use of partial order reduction.

Toupie. In [43], Toupie is favourably compared with two specialized model checkers on Milner's scheduler example [36]. The difference of performance in favor of Toupie is attributed to the use of extended decision diagrams instead of binary ones.

6.2   Timed Automata

XMC/RT. The tabled-resolution-based XMC system, enriched with a constraint solver over reals is called XMC/RT, consists in 350 lines of Prolog code.

Preliminary experiments on two standard examples (Fisher's mutual exclusion protocol, bridge crossing system) indicate that performance of XMC/RT is comparable to HyTech.

GAP. A fully automatic proof of a fundamental property of a parametric real-time protocol (ABR conformance) is obtained for the first time in [18], using an implementation, called GAP, of Revesz's bottom-up evaluation procedure.

6.3   Automata with Integers

Presburger Arithmetic. Omega library-based system of [5] is experimented on two example programs (bakery and ticket algorithms), for which safety and liveness properties are proved. In [19] the Presburger-based system is used for performing a parametric analysis of safety properties: the deadlock-freeness analysis of a flexible manufacturing system is, e.g., achieved for the first time in a fully mechanical way.

Real Arithmetic. The SICStus-based system of [12] was experimented on several examples (among which the bakery and ticket algorithms). The execution times are about an order of magnitude shorter than those obtained in [5] using the Omega library for Presburger arithmetic.

In [2] experiments conducted with the real constraint solver of HyTech show a considerable performance improvement with respect to those obtained with Presburger solver of [19]. Besides, a deadlock is detected for the first time in a real-life protocol (PNCSA).

7   Discussion

Model-checking was originally designed for verifying finite-state transition systems. Only recently some extensions of the method were introduced in order to treat infinite-state systems.

When applied to the verification of finite-state systems, the stake of using constraint logic programming languages is (*a priori*) clear. The goal is to have a system written into a high-level language with declarative and flexible facilities while keeping good performance compared to specialized model checkers written in low-level code [40]. This goal seems to have been (partly) achieved by a system like XMC. However some qualifications should be made. First, the treated examples are often drawn out of simple sets of benchmarks. More experiments on real-life systems remain to be done. Second, in order to achieve comparable efficiency, some specialized optimizing or compiling techniques had sometimes to be introduced, which may compromise the initial objectives of flexibility and declarativeness. Third, CLP-based systems still cannot compete with specialized model-checkers on several examples, due to the lack of integration of partial order techniques.

As regards to infinite-state systems, the situation of CLP-based systems compared with specialized model-checkers is much less clear, mainly because the frontier between the two classes of systems is blurred. For example, should HyTech system be considered as a specialized model-checker or as a CLP-based one? On the one hand, HyTech is a specialized model-checker as it is written in C, and is designed to treat the class of so-called linear hybrid systems. On the other hand, it can be considered as a CLP-based system as it makes use of a library of convex real-valued constraints manipulation. The main difference between HyTech and a system like XMC/RT may just lie in the language in which they are written. In this context, all the methods are more or less at the same level, and may be called "constraint-based", as they necessarily appeal to symbolic manipulation of data. Now, to some extent, this observation also applies to *finite-state* systems model-checkers. For example, why should a system like Toupie be called "constraint-based" system, and not a specialized model-checker like SMV [35] which, still, relies basically also on (binary) decision diagrams for manipulating Boolean? Here again, the main distinctive feature may be the level of programming language in which the two systems are implemented.

Let us also mention an issue, which has received considerable attention from the model-checking community: the use of specialized data-structures for representing constraints. Binary Decision Diagrams (BDD) are thus considered in the model-checking community as a decisive breakthrough explaining the success of finite-state verification tools. One explanation for this success is that BDD provide a *canonical form* for boolean formulas that is often substantially more compact than conjunctive or disjunctive normal form, and very efficient algorithms have been developed for manipulating them [9]. Research in model-checking for infinite-state systems also exploits the use of such compact canonical forms for representing real-time constraints, such as "Difference Bounded Matrices" [13] or "Clock Difference Diagrams" [3] for timed automata, and "closed convex polyhedra" for linear hybrid systems [27,22]. How can such data structures be smoothly and efficiently implemented in the framework of high-level languages such as CLP? This question has not yet been treated, except in the work of [43] and the recent work of [16]. We believe that performances of CLP-based systems can benefit considerably from this integration. However it would contribute to blur further the border between classical model-checkers and CLP-based systems.

Finally, let us point out that several researchers have also addressed a slightly different but very interesting and related issue: the relationship between static analysis (instead of constraint solving) and model-checking [6,45,48].

References

1. R. Alur and D. Dill. "Automata for Modeling Real-Time Systems". *Proc. 17th ICALP*, LNCS 443, 1990, pp. 322–335.
2. B. Bérard and L. Fribourg. "Reachability Analysis of (Timed) Petri Nets Using Real Arithmetic". *CONCUR'99*, LNCS 1664, Springer-Verlag, 1999, pp. 178–193.

3. G. Behrmann, K.G. Larsen, J. Pearson, C. Weise and W. Yi. "Efficient Timed Reachability Analysis Using Clock Difference Diagrams". *CAV'99*, LNCS 1633, Springer-Verlag, 1999, pp. 341–353.

4. R. Bryant. "Graph Based Algorithms for Boolean Function Manipulation". *IEEE transactions on Computers* 35:8, 1986, pp. 677–691.

5. T. Bultan, R. Gerber and W. Pugh. "Symbolic Model Checking of Infinite-state Systems using Presburger Arithmetics". *CAV'97*, LNCS 1254, Springer-Verlag, 1997, pp. 400–411.

6. W. Charatonik and A. Podelski. "Set-Based Analysis of Reactive Infinite-State Systems". *TACAS'98*, LNCS 1384, Springer-Verlag, 1998, pp. 358-375.

7. W. Chen and D.S. Warren. "Tabled evaluation with delaying for general logic programs". *J. ACM* 43:1, 1996, pp. 20–74.

8. E.M. Clarke and E.A. Emerson. "Design and synthesis of synchronization skeletons using branching time temporal logic." *Logic of Programs Workshop*, LNCS 131, Springer-Verlag, 1981, pp. 52–71.

9. E. Clarke, O. Grumberg and D. Long. "Verification Tools for Finite-State Concurrent Systems". *REX school/symposium on A decade of concurrency: reflections and perspectives*, LNCS 803, Springer-Verlag, 1993.

10. P. Cousot and N. Halbwachs. "Automatic Discovery of Linear Restraints Among Variables of A Program". *POPL'78*, ACM Press, 1978, pp. 84–97.

11. S. Dawson, C.R. Ramakrishnan, I.V. Ramakrishnan and T. Swift. "Optimizing clause resolution: Beyond unification factoring". *Intl. Logic Programming Symp.*, MIT Press, 1995, pp. 194–208.

12. G. Delzanno and A. Podelski. "Model Checking in CLP". *TACAS'99*, LNCS 1579, Springer-Verlag, 1999, pp. 74-88.

13. D. Dill. "Timing Assumptions and Verification of Finite-State Concurrent Systems." *Automatic Verification Methods for Finite State Systems*, LNCS 407, Springer-Verlag, 1989, pp. 197–212.

14. Y. Dong and C.R. Ramakrishnan. "An Optimizing Compiler for Efficient model Checking". *FORTE/PSTV'99*, Beijing, 1999.

15. Y. Dong, X. Du, Y.S. Ramakrishna, C.R. Ramakrishnan, I.V. Ramakrishnan, S.A. Smolka, O. Sokolsky, E.W. Stark and D.S. Warren. "Fighting Livelock in the i-Protocol: A Comparative Study of Verification Tools". *TACAS'99*, LNCS 1579, Springer-Verlag, 1999, pp. 74–88.

16. X. Du, C.R. Ramakrishnan and S.A. Smolka. "Tabled Resolution + Constraints: A Recipe for Model Checking Real-Time Systems", 1999. (http://www.cs.sunysb.edu/ vicdu/)

17. E.A. Emerson and C.-L. Lei. "Efficient model checking in fragments of the propositional mu-calculus". *LICS'86*, 1986, pp. 267–278.

18. L. Fribourg. "A Closed-Form Evaluation for Extended Timed Automata". *Technical Report LSV-98-2*, CNRS & Ecole Normale Supérieure de Cachan, March 1998. (http://www.lsv.ens-cachan.fr/Publis/)

19. L. Fribourg and H. Olsén. "Proving Safety Properties of Infinite State Systems by Compilation into Presburger Arithmetic". *CONCUR'97*, LNCS 1243, Springer-Verlag, 1997, pp. 96–107.

20. L. Fribourg and H. Olsén. "A Decompositional Approach for Computing Least Fixed-Points of Datalog Programs with $\mathcal{Z}$-Counters". *Constraints: An International Journal*: 2, 1997, pp. 305–335.

21. L. Fribourg and J. Richardson. "Symbolic Verification with Gap-Order Constraints". *Proc. 6th Intl. Workshop on Logic Program Synthesis and Transformation (LOPSTR)*, LNCS 1207, 1996, pp. 20–37.

22. N. Halbwachs, Y.-E. Proy and P. Raymond. "Verification of Linear Hybrid Systems by means of Convex Approximations". *SAS'94*, LNCS, Springer-Verlag, 1994, pp. 223–237.

23. N. Halbwachs, Y.-E. Proy and P. Roumanoff. "Verification of Real-time Systems using Linear Relation Analysis". *Formal Methods in System Design* 11:2, 1997, pp. 157–185.

24. N. Heintze, J. Jaffar, S. Michaylov, P. Stuckey and R. Yap. *The CLP(R) Programmer's Manual Version 1.2*. 1992.

25. A.R Helm. "On the detection and elimination of redundant derivations during bottom-up execution". *North American Conf. on Logic Programming*, Cleveland, Ohio, 1989, pp.945–961.

26. P. van Hentenryck. *Constraint Satisfaction in Logic Programming*. Logic Programming Series. MIT Press, 1989.

27. T. Henzinger, P.-H. Ho and H. Wong-Toi. "A User Guide to HYTECH". *Proc. TACAS'95*, LNCS 1019, 1995, pp. 41–71.

28. C. Holzbaur. *OFAI CLP(Q,R), Manual Edition 1.3.3*. Technical Report TR-95-09, Austrian Research Institute for Artificial Intelligence, Vienna, 1995.

29. G.J. Holzmann and D. Peled. "The state of SPIN". *CAV'96*, LNCS 1102, Springer-Verlag, 1996, pp. 385–389.

30. G.J. Holzmann, D. Peled and V. Pratt, editors. *Partial-Order Methods in Verification (POMIV'96)*. DIMACS Series in Discrete Mathematics and Theoretical Computer Science, American Mathematical Society, 1996.

31. J. Jaffar and J.-L. Lassez. "Constraint Logic Programming". *POPL'87*, ACM Press, 1987, pp. 111–119.

32. D. Kozen. "Results on the propositional μ-calculus". *Theoretical Computer Science* 27, 1983, pp. 333–354.

33. J.-L. Lassez and M.J. Maher. "The denotational semantics of Horn clauses as a production system." *AAAI 83*, washington D.C., 1983, pp. 229–231.

34. X. Liu, C.R. Ramakrishnan and S.A. Smolka. "Fully local and efficient evaluation of alternating fixed points". *TACAS'98*, LNCS 1384, Springer-Verlag, 1998, pp. 5–19.

35. K.L. McMillan. *Symbolic Model-Checking: An Approach to the State Explosion Problem*. Kluwer Academic, 1993.

36. R. Milner. *Communication and Concurrency*. Prentice Hall, 1989.

37. A. Pnueli. "The temporal semantics of concurrent programs". *TCS 13*, 1981, pp. 45–60.

38. E. Pontelli and G. Gupta. "A Constraint-based Approach for Specification and Verification of Real-time Systems". *RTSS'97*. IEEE Computer Society, 1997.

39. W. Pugh. "A Practical Integer Algorithm for Exact Array Dependence Analysis". *C.ACM* 35:8, 1992, pp. 102–114.

40. Y.S. Ramakrishna, C.R. Ramakrishnan, I.V. Ramakrishnan, S.A. Smolka, T. Swift and D.S. Warren. "Efficient Model Checking Using Tabled Resolution". *CAV'97*, LNCS 1254, Springer-Verlag, 1997, pp. 143–154.

41. R. Ramakrishnan, Y. Sagiv, J.D. Ulmann and M.Y. Vardi. "Proof-Tree Transformation Theorems and their Application". *8th ACM Symp. on Principles of Database Systems*, Philadelphia, 1989, pp. 172–181.

42. R. Ramakrishnan, D. Srivastava and S. Sudarshan. "Efficient Bottom-up Evaluation of Logic Programs". *Computer Systems and Software Engineering: State-of-the-Art*, chapter 11. Kluwer Academic, 1992.

43. A. Rauzy. "Toupie: A Constraint Language for Model Checking". *Constraint Programming: Basics and Trends*, LNCS 910, Springer-Verlag, 1994, pp. 193–208.

44. P.Z. Revesz. "A Closed-Form Evaluation for Datalog Queries with Integer (Gap)-Order Constraints", *Theoretical Computer Science*, 1993, vol. 116, pp. 117-149.
45. D.A. Schmidt. "Data Flow Analysis is Model Checking of Abstract Interpretations". *POPL'98*, ACM Press, 1998.
46. D. Srivastava. "Subsumption and Indexing in Constraint Query Languages with Linear Arithmetic Constraints". *Annals of Mathematics and Artificial Intelligence* 8:3-4, 1993, pp. 315–343.
47. D. Srivastava and R. Ramakrishnan. "Pushing Constraints Selections". *11th ACM Symp. on Principles of Database Systems*, San Diego, 1992, pp. 301–315.
48. B. Steffen. "Data flow analysis as model checking". *TACS'91*, LNCS 526, Springer-Verlag, 1991.
49. H. Tamaki and T. Sato. "OLDT resolution with tabulation". *Intl. Conf. on Logic Programming*. MIT Press, 1986, pp. 84–98.
50. J.D. Ullman. *Principles of Data and Knowledge-base Systems*,vol.1 . Computer Science Press, Rockville, MD, 1988.
51. L. Urbina. "Analysis of Hybrid Systems in CLP($\mathcal{R}$)". *CP'96*, LNCS 1102, Springer-Verlag, 1996.
52. L. Urbina and G. Riedewald. "Simulation and Verification in Constraint Logic Programming". *2nd European Workshop on Real-Time and Hybrid Systems*, 1995, pp. 85–104.

On Dynamic Aspects of OOD Frameworks in Component-Based Software Development in Computational Logic

Juliana Küster Filipe[1]*, Kung-Kiu Lau[2], Mario Ornaghi[3], and Hirokazu Yatsu[4]

[1] Abt. Informationssysteme, Informatik, Technische Universität Braunschweig,
Postfach 3329, D-38023 Braunschweig, Germany
J.Kuester-Filipe@tu-bs.de
[2] Department of Computer Science, University of Manchester
Manchester M13 9PL, United Kingdom
kung-kiu@cs.man.ac.uk
[3] Dipartimento di Scienze dell'Informazione, Universita' degli studi di Milano
Via Comelico 39/41, 20135 Milano, Italy
ornaghi@dsi.unimi.it
[4] Information Technologies & Services Division
Technologies Research & Development
Nihon Unisys Ltd., 1-1-1 Toyosu, Koto-ku, Tokyo 135-8560, Japan
Hirokazu.Yatsu@unisys.co.jp

Abstract. In component-based software development, object-oriented design (OOD) frameworks are increasingly recognised as better units of reuse than objects. This is because OOD frameworks are groups of interacting objects, and as such they can better reflect practical systems in which objects tend to have more than one role in more than one context. In an earlier paper, we described a formal semantics of the static aspects of OOD frameworks in computational logic. In this paper, we make a preliminary attempt to extend this to the dynamic aspects.

1 Introduction

In [12,13] we present a formalisation of Object-Oriented Design (OOD) frameworks in component-based software development (CBD) in computational logic. Such frameworks are groups of (interacting) objects. For example, in the CBD methodology *Catalysis* [6], a driver may be represented as the OOD framework shown in Figure 1.[1]A driver is a person who drives a car, or in OOD terminology, a driver is a framework composed of a car object and a person object, linked by

Fig. 1. The Driver OOD framework.

a 'drives' association (or attribute).

---

* The first author was supported by the DFG under Eh 75/11-2 and partially by the EU under ESPRIT-IV WG 22704 ASPIRE.
[1] *Catalysis* uses the UML notation, see e.g. [18].

A. Bossi (Ed.): LOPSTR'99, LNCS 1817, pp. 42–61, 2000.

OOD frameworks are increasingly recognised as better units of reuse in software development than objects (see e.g. [9,15]). The reason for this is that in practical systems, objects tend to have more than one role in more than one context, and OOD frameworks can capture this, whereas existing OOD methods (e.g. Fusion [4] and Syntropy [5]) cannot. The latter use classes or objects as the basic unit of design or reuse, and are based on the traditional view of an object, as shown in Figure 2, which regards an object as a closed entity with one fixed role. On the other hand, OOD frameworks allow objects that play different

Fig. 2. Traditional view of an object.

roles in different frameworks to be composed by composing OOD frameworks. In *Catalysis*, for instance, this is depicted in Figure 3.

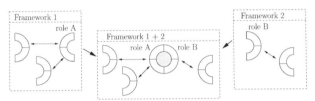

Fig. 3. Objects by composing OOD frameworks.

For example, a person can play the roles of a driver and of a guest at a motel simultaneously. These roles are shown separately in the PersonAsDriver and PersonAsGuest OOD frameworks in Figure 1. If we compose these two

Fig. 4. PersonAsDriver and PersonAsGuest OOD frameworks.

frameworks, then we get the PersonAsDriverGuest OOD framework as shown in Figure 1. In this OOD framework, a person object plays two roles, and is a

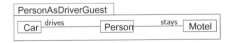

Fig. 5. PersonAsDriverGuest OOD framework.

composite object of the kind depicted in Figure 3.

OOD frameworks should play a crucial role in next-generation CDB methodologies. Our intention is to endow them with suitable (declarative) semantics for CBD in computational Logic.

2   Specification Frameworks

In [13,12] we describe the static semantics of OOD frameworks, i.e. one without time or state transitions. This semantics is based on *specification frameworks* (or *frameworks* for short), which we briefly describe in this section. In the next section, we will introduce classes and OOD frameworks.

A (*specification*) *framework* $\mathcal{F} = \langle \Sigma, X \rangle$ is defined in the context of first-order logic with identity. It is composed of a signature Σ (containing sort symbols, function declarations and relation declarations), and a finite or recursive set X of Σ-axioms. The main purpose of a framework is to axiomatise a problem domain and to reason about it. More specifically, a framework contains the ADT's and the concepts needed to build a (possibly, though not necessarily, object-oriented) model of the application at hand.

A framework is thus a (first-order) theory, and we choose its intended model to be a *reachable isoinitial model*, defined as follows:[2]

Definition 1. Let X be a set of Σ-axioms. A Σ-structure i is an *isoinitial model* of X iff, for every other model m of X, there is one isomorphic embedding $i : i \rightarrow m$.

A model i is *reachable* if its elements can be represented by ground terms.

We distinguish between *closed* and *open* frameworks. A framework $\mathcal{F} = \langle \Sigma, X \rangle$ is *closed* iff there is a reachable isoinitial model i of X. An *open* framework $\mathcal{F}(\Omega) = \langle \Sigma, X \rangle$ does not have an isoinitial model, since its axioms leave open the meaning of some symbols Ω of the signature, that we call *open* symbols. Non-open symbols are called *defined* symbols.

An open framework $\mathcal{F}(\Omega) = \langle \Sigma, X \rangle$ can be *closed*, i.e made into closed frameworks, by *instantiating* the symbols of Ω by new axioms, that fix their meaning. The new axioms are called *closure axioms*, and a set of closure axioms is called a *closure*. To guarantee that a closure works, i.e., it is consistent and gives rise to a closed framework, we use suitable *constraints* (see [13]) and we assume that a constraint satisfaction relation is defined, at least for closures of a suitable form. In this way, for a constrained open framework, every closure that satisfies the constraints gives rise to a closed framework.

In this paper, we will consider closure by *internalisation*, as defined in [13]. As shown in [13], internalisation can be used to implement constrained parameter passing, as well as to introduce *objects* as the closures of suitable open frameworks that represent *classes*.

Let $\mathcal{F}(\Omega) = \langle \Sigma + \Delta, X \rangle$ be an open framework with a subsignature Δ that does not contain symbols of Ω. A Δ-*internalisation* is a closure operation that may change the signature or add new axioms, as follows:

- *Sort closure*. The closure: CLOSE S BY s
  renames the open *sort* S by a sort s of Δ. No axioms are added.

---

[2] See [13] for a justification of this choice and [2,11] for a discussion of isoinitial theories.

- *Relation closure.* The operation: CLOSE r BY $\forall x \,.\, r(x) \leftrightarrow R(x)$
  introduces the explicit definition $\forall x \,.\, r(x) \leftrightarrow R(x)$ of the *relation* r as a
  new axiom. The declaration of r may contain only sorts of Δ, and $R(x)$ is a
  quantifier free Δ-formula.
- *Function closure.* The operation: CLOSE f BY $\forall x \,.\, y = f(x) \leftrightarrow F(x,y)$
  introduces the explicit definition $\forall x \,.\, y = f(x) \leftrightarrow F(x,y)$ of the *function*
  f as a new axiom. The declaration of f may contain only sorts of Δ, and
  $F(x,y)$ is a quantifier-free Δ-formula such that $X|\Delta \vdash \forall x \exists! y \,.\, F(x,y)$.[3]

For Δ-internalisation, constraints are a distinguished subset of the axioms.
Thus we represent an open constrained framework as $\mathcal{F}(\Omega) = \langle \Sigma + \Delta, X \cup Constr \rangle$, where $Constr$ is the (distinguished) set of constraints. A Δ-internalisation
of Ω is an internalisation of all the symbols of Ω. In general, it closes the open
symbols by a set Cl of explicit definitions. We say that the constraints are *satisfied* if

$$X|\Delta \cup Cl \vdash Constr.$$

Of course, if some open sort has been internalised, then we assume that the
corresponding renaming has been applied to Cl and to the constraints.

Example 1. The following framework imports the closed framework $\mathcal{NAT}$ of
natural numbers, and introduces two new symbols q and r.

Framework $\mathcal{NAT}(q : [Nat, Nat])$;

IMPORT: $\mathcal{NAT}$;

DECLS: $q, r : [Nat, Nat]$;

AXIOMS: $r(x,y) \leftrightarrow q(y,x)$;
               $r(x,y) \rightarrow x < y$;

CONSTRS: $q(x,y) \rightarrow x < y$.

In the first axiom, $q(x,y)$ is open (since it is declared as a parameter) and is
used to define $r(x,y)$. Since it is open, we need to consider suitable closures for
q. (Here we consider $\Sigma_{\mathcal{NAT}}$-closures, where $\Sigma_{\mathcal{NAT}}$ is the signature of $\mathcal{NAT}$.) To
avoid closures that are inconsistent with respect to the second axiom, we have
introduced the constraint $q(x,y) \rightarrow x < y$. The closure $q(x,y) \leftrightarrow y = s(s(x))$,
for example, of q satisfies the constraint $q(x,y) \rightarrow x < y$, which can be proved
using the closure itself and the axioms of $\mathcal{NAT}$.

3   Static Aspects of OOD Frameworks

As we have seen in Section 1, OOD frameworks are composite objects/classes.
Here, we define OOD frameworks and objects/classes in terms of specification
frameworks. Although it is based on [12,13], the material here is mostly new in
order that we can deal with dynamic aspects of OOD frameworks later on.

    When we build a class or an OOD framework, we start from a specification
framework $\mathcal{P} = \langle \Sigma_P, X_P \rangle$ that axiomatises the problem domain. For convenience, we will call $\mathcal{P}$ a *problem framework*.

---

[3] $X|\Delta$ is the restriction of X to the Δ-formulas.

Example 2. The Car class in Figures 1 and 1 can be defined in the context of a problem framework $\mathcal{CAR}$ that contains the data types for strings and integers, enumerated types to indicate (for example) the possible uses of cars, and so on. Thus it will contain data-type sorts (like Int for integers, Str for strings), data-type operations and predicates (like integer sum $+$, list concatenation $conc$, (overloaded) ordering $<$ on lists and strings), as well as sorts and operations from the problem domain, like the sort $Opts$ of possible optional features.

3.1   Classes

For simplicity, we will assume that our classes are based on a fixed closed problem framework $\mathcal{P} = \langle \Sigma_P, X_P \rangle$. As usual, a class is interpreted as the collection of objects that are instances of the class. A class has *attributes*, that represent dynamic properties of the objects of the class, and *actions*, that represent methods used for updating the values of the attributes of the objects of the class.[4]

Therefore, a problem signature Σ_P will be enriched by the special sort Act of possible *action states*, the special sort Obj of *object identities* (as well as a denumerable set of constants of sort Obj), and the special predicates $\triangleright : [Act]$ and $\odot : [Act]$. Intuitively, for an action a, $\triangleright a$ means that a is enabled, and $\odot a$ that it has just occurred. The intended meaning of the special symbols is fixed by the following special axioms:

- The axioms X_{Act}: $\exists! x : Act . (\triangleright x \wedge \odot x)$
    $\exists! x : Act . (\triangleright x \wedge \neg \odot x)$
    $\exists! x : Act . (\neg \triangleright x \wedge \odot x)$
    $\exists! x : Act . (\neg \triangleright x \wedge \neg \odot x)$

  This small theory has a (non-reachable) isoinitial model where the sort Act of action states contains exactly four elements, corresponding to the possible truth combinations of $\triangleright$ and $\odot$. This means that, at each time, for an action a there are exactly four possibilities: a may be currently enabled or not, and it may have just occurred (in the transition from the previous state) or not. At the dynamic level, this meaning is enforced by the conditions to be satisfied by $\mathcal{F}$-labelled event structures, in Definition 3.
- The axioms X_{Obj} that contains the axioms $\neg o = o'$, for every pair of distinct constants o and o' of sort Obj. The isoinitial model of X_{Obj} has the set of its constants as domain. Constants of sort Obj are called *object identities* and will be used to (uniquely) name objects (and framework instances, see later).

We will always assume that the signature and axioms of X_{Act} and X_{Obj} are understood.

Besides these axioms, class axioms may also (explicitly) contain:

- A set ATB of attribute declarations. An attribute declaration introduces a new function or relation symbol using sorts from Σ_P.

---

[4] Actions can also effect inter-object communication since an object may invoke actions in another object.

- A set ACT of action declarations. An action declaration has the form $a : A \rightarrow Act$, where the (possibly empty) arity A contains sorts of Σ_P.
- A set $Constr$ of attribute and action constraints, where an attribute constraint belongs to the language generated by $\Sigma_P + ATB$ (and contains at least one attribute), while an action constraint belongs to the language generated by $\Sigma_P + ATB + ACT$ (and contains at least one action).

Thus the signature of a class is $\Sigma_P + ATB + ACT$, where Σ_P contains the problem signature, the special sorts Act and Obj, the predicates $\triangleright$, $\odot$, and the object identities. The symbols of Σ_P are closed by their axioms, while $ATB + ACT$ are open.

Example 3. In the context of the problem framework $\mathcal{CAR}$, the class Car in Figures 1 and 1 can be (statically) specified as follows:

Class $\mathcal{CAR}$;

ATTRIBUTES: $.km : [\,] \rightarrow Int$;
$.option : [Opts]$;

ACTIONS: $.go : [Int] \rightarrow Act$;

CONSTRS: $.km \geq 0$;
$\forall x \,.\, (.km + x < 100000 \rightarrow \triangleright.go(x))$;
$\forall x, y \,.\, (\odot(.go(x)) \wedge \odot(.go(y)) \rightarrow x = y)$.

$.km$ and $.option$ are attributes, representing the odometer reading and the car's optional features respectively. At the class level, they are open. In a car object, they will be closed to indicate the (current) odometer reading and the optional features of the car.

$.go$ is an (open) action symbol. In the current state of a car object, $go(x)$ may be enabled or have just occurred, for suitable values of x.

$.km$ must have positive values, as stipulated by the first constraint. The second constraint says that $go(x)$ is always enabled if the final odometer reading does not exceed 100000, while the third one says that $go(x)$ cannot have occurred with different x and y at the same time.

The dynamic meaning of attributes and actions will be explained in the next section. Here we are concerned only with their static meaning, namely with the way of fixing them in a state. To this end, we will use suitable closure axioms that we call *state axioms*.

The closure of *attributes* is obtained through internalisation in $\mathcal{P}$, as explained in the previous section. An attribute closure will be indicated by $Cl(atb)$.

The closure of an *action* $a : A \rightarrow Act$ has the following general form:

$$\forall((\triangleright a(x) \leftrightarrow E(x)) \wedge (\odot a(x) \leftrightarrow H(x)))$$

where $E(x)$ and $H(x)$ are quantifier-free formulas that may contain symbols of Σ_P and attributes. A closure of all the actions will be denoted by $Cl(act)$.

We allow constraints on actions and attributes. Let *Constr* be such constraints. Then they must be proved by the closures of attributes and actions, i.e.:

$$X_P \cup X_{Act} \cup X_{Obj} \cup Cl(atb) \cup Cl(act) \vdash Constr. \tag{1}$$

The possible closures of a class by state axioms represents its possible objects. Moreover, each object has its own identity, represented by a unique name o of sort *Obj*, and its own language, obtained by prefixing attributes and actions by o. The closures $Cl(atb)$ and $Cl(act)$ for an object o, must be given in the language of o. Thus all the objects share the signature Σ_P, while different objects have disjoint attribute and action signatures. Constraint satisfaction (1) must be checked by each object, in its own language.

Example 4. An object *spider* of class $\mathcal{CAR}$ is given, for example, by the following state axioms:

NEW *spider* : $\mathcal{CAR}$;
CLOSE: *spider.km*   BY   *spider.km* = 25000;
          spider.option BY $\forall(spider.option(x) \leftrightarrow x = Airbag \vee x = AirCond)$;
          spider.go(x)   BY $\forall(\triangleright spider.go(x) \leftrightarrow x \leq 80000)$;
                                 $\forall(\odot spider.go(x) \leftrightarrow x = 12500)$.

Constraints are satisfied in the *spider* language because, in the context of the problem framework $\mathcal{CAR}$, we have:

$spider.km = 25000 \vdash spider.km \geq 0$;

$spider.km = 25000 \wedge \forall(\triangleright spider.go(x) \leftrightarrow x \leq 80000) \vdash$
$$\forall(spider.km + x < 100000 \rightarrow \triangleright spider.go(x));$$
$\forall(\odot spider.go(x) \leftrightarrow x = 12500) \vdash \forall(\odot spider.go(x) \wedge \odot spider.go(y) \rightarrow x = y)$;

State axioms can be updated, i.e. an object is a dynamic entity. As we will see in Section 4, updating is the result of actions.

3.2   OOD Frameworks

An OOD framework is a composition of many classes or simpler OOD frameworks, i.e., it is of the form $\mathcal{F} = comp(\mathcal{F}_1, \ldots, \mathcal{F}_k)$, where *comp* is a composition operation, and $\mathcal{F}_1, \ldots, \mathcal{F}_k$ are classes or sub-frameworks (of a lower nesting level, see below). $\mathcal{F}$ itself may have attributes and/or actions that are distinct from those in $\mathcal{F}_1, \ldots, \mathcal{F}_k$. We model $\mathcal{F}$ as a *container* which contains not only the classes in $\mathcal{F}_1, \ldots, \mathcal{F}_k$ but also a special class, that we call the *container class* of $\mathcal{F}$,[5] and (possibly) with its own attributes and actions.

Thus, whereas a class has objects as instances, an OOD framework $\mathcal{F}$ has *systems* of objects as instances, where each object is an instance of a class contained in $\mathcal{F}$, and objects can be created (and deleted) and updated dynamically.

---

[5] We will use the same name $\mathcal{F}$ to denote both the framework and its container class.

For simplicity, we will assume that all the classes contained in an OOD framework are based on the same problem framework $\mathcal{P}$. As stated in the previous section, $\mathcal{P}$ always contains the theory X_{act} of action states, and the theory X_{Obj} of object identities. Since $\mathcal{P}$ is always the same for a given OOD framework, we will assume that it is understood. For an OOD framework $\mathcal{F} = comp(\mathcal{F}_1, \ldots, \mathcal{F}_k)$, we need to distinguish between the (static) *framework language* and the associated (dynamic) *system languages*. The framework language is given by the languages of the contained classes. By contrast, the system language dynamically depends on the languages of the objects that belong to the system at any given time. We define the (static) framework language, (dynamic) system languages, and framework instances inductively, starting from frameworks of level 0.

An OOD framework of level 0 is a class $\mathcal{C}$, seen as a container of one class $\mathcal{C}$. Its static framework language contains Σ_P, the attributes and actions of $\mathcal{C}$, and the special *class predicate* $.C : [Obj]$, where $.C(x)$ is true if x is an object in the current system instance of class $\mathcal{C}$.

The system languages associated with a class $\mathcal{C}$ are defined through the instances of $\mathcal{C}$, as follows. For every identity $o : Obj$, we may have a system instance $o.\mathcal{C}$, with the following (system) language:

– For every attribute $.atb$ of $\mathcal{C}$, $o.atb$ is an attribute of $o.\mathcal{C}$.
– For every action $.act$ of $\mathcal{C}$, $o.act$ is an action of $o.\mathcal{C}$.
– $o.C : [Obj]$ is the special class predicate of the instance.

An instance $o.\mathcal{C}$ also has its *closure axioms*, which are a closure for $\mathcal{C}$ in the language renamed by prefixing the identity o to attributes and actions. $o.\mathcal{C}$ is an *object of class* $\mathcal{C}$ with *identity* o. If an instance $o.\mathcal{C}$ exists, then the special class predicate is closed by the axiom $o.C(x) \leftrightarrow x = o$.

As we can see, instances and their languages depend on the corresponding objects.

An OOD framework of level $(i + 1)$ is a framework $\mathcal{F} = comp(\mathcal{F}_1, \ldots, \mathcal{F}_n)$, where i is the maximum of the levels of $\mathcal{F}_1, \ldots, \mathcal{F}_n$. The framework language of $\mathcal{F}$ is the union of the languages of its classes, that are determined as follows:

– There is an indexed set of injective framework morphisms $h_j : \mathcal{F}_j \to \mathcal{F}$, for $1 \leq j \leq n$, where h_j is a signature morphism (possibly) renaming attributes and actions, and the h_j-translations of the constraints of $\mathcal{F}_j$ become constraints of $\mathcal{F}$. These morphisms depend on the kind of composition *comp*.
– The classes of $\mathcal{F}$ are the container class $\mathcal{F}$ and the (h_j images of the) classes of $\mathcal{F}_j$, for $1 \leq j \leq n$. Suitable renamings are applied by h_j (when necessary), to give a unique name to every class of $\mathcal{F}$.
– For every class $\mathcal{C}$ of $\mathcal{F}$, the predicate $.C : [Obj]$ is an attribute of $\mathcal{F}$ (the attribute $.F : [Obj]$ is always included).
– $\mathcal{F}$ may export only some of its classes; selective exporting, i.e., exporting of a selected subset of attributes and actions, is allowed. Non-exported symbols are said to be hidden. Thus we have a visible framework language that contains, at each level, only the part exported by the lower levels, and a full framework language that contains also the hidden parts.

– A framework may contain its own constraints, in the container class. Constraints can be given using only the visible language, while (part of) the full language will be used to define the system instances.

Example 5. Consider the frameworks of level 0 (i.e., classes) $\mathcal{CAR}$ (defined in Example 3), $\mathcal{PERSON}$ (defined below) and $\mathcal{SHOP}$ (sketched below).

Class $\mathcal{PERSON}$;

ATTRIBUTES:	$.name : [\,] \rightarrow Str$;
	$.pocket : [\,] \rightarrow Int$;
CONSTRS:	$.pocket \geq 0$.

Class $\mathcal{SHOP}$;

ATTRIBUTES:	...
ACTIONS:	...
CONSTRS:	...

We can compose $\mathcal{PERSON}$ and $\mathcal{SHOP}$ into a framework $\mathcal{CONSUMER}$ of level 1.

Framework $\mathcal{CONSUMER}$;

IMPORT:	$\mathcal{PERSON}$, $\mathcal{SHOP}$;
ATTRIBUTES:	$.shops : [Obj]$;
ACTIONS:	$.buy : [Int] \rightarrow Act$;
CONSTRS:	$.CONSUMER(x) \rightarrow .PERSON(x)$;
	$\triangleright .buy(x) \rightarrow .pocket \geq x$;
	$.shops(x) \rightarrow .SHOP(x)$.

The classes of $\mathcal{CONSUMER}$ are $\mathcal{PERSON}$, $\mathcal{SHOP}$ and $\mathcal{CONSUMER}$. The class predicates $.PERSON : [Obj]$, $.SHOP : [Obj]$ and $.CONSUMER : [Obj]$ are understood. The first constraint says that a consumer must be a person, i.e., $\mathcal{CONSUMER}$ is a subclass of $\mathcal{PERSON}$. Therefore it inherits the attributes and constraints of $\mathcal{PERSON}$.

We can compose $\mathcal{PERSON}$ and $\mathcal{CAR}$ into a framework $\mathcal{DRIVER}$ of level 1.

Framework $\mathcal{DRIVER}$;

IMPORT:	$\mathcal{PERSON}$, $\mathcal{CAR}$;
ATTRIBUTES:	$.maydrive : [Obj]$;
ACTIONS:	$.drives : [Obj, Int] \rightarrow Act$;
CONSTRS:	$.DRIVER(x) \rightarrow .PERSON(x)$;
	$.maydrive(c) \rightarrow .CAR(c)$;
	$\triangleright .drives(c, m) \rightarrow .maydrive(c)$;
	$\triangleright .drives(\hat{c}, m) \rightarrow \triangleright \hat{c}.go(m)$.

The classes of $\mathcal{DRIVER}$ are $\mathcal{PERSON}$, $\mathcal{CAR}$ and $\mathcal{DRIVER}$. A driver must be a person. In the fourth constraint $\hat{c}$ is a meta-variable standing for an object name, because it is used in $\hat{c}.go$. So it represents a family of axioms, one for each object identity.

Now we can compose $\mathcal{DRIVER}$ and $\mathcal{CONSUMER}$ into a framework $\mathcal{MALL}$ of level 2.

Framework $\mathcal{MALL}$;

IMPORT:	$\mathcal{DRIVER}$, $\mathcal{CONSUMER}$;
CONSTRS:	$\neg(.DRIVER(x) \wedge .CONSUMER(x))$.

The classes of $\mathcal{MALL}$ are $\mathcal{PERSON}$, $\mathcal{CAR}$, $\mathcal{SHOP}$, $\mathcal{DRIVER}$, $\mathcal{CONSUMER}$ and $\mathcal{MALL}$. By inheritance, drivers and consumers must be persons. By the framework constraint, a person cannot be a consumer and a driver at the same time.

Now we can define *framework instances*. Let $\mathcal{F}$ be a framework. A framework instance $f.\mathcal{F}$ is a closure of $\mathcal{F}$ that is built from a closure of the special class predicates of the framework. The special class predicate $f.F$ is closed by

$$f.F(x) \leftrightarrow x = f.$$

The intended meaning of a closure

$$f.C(x) \leftrightarrow x = o_1 \vee \ldots \vee x = o_k$$

is that the objects of class C contained in the instance $f.\mathcal{F}$ are $o_1, \ldots, o_k$.
More generally, a closure must satisfy the following meta-assumption:

$f.C(o)$ holds in the current closure of $f.\mathcal{F}$ if and only if the current closure contains a class instance $o.C$, and the language of $o.C$, together with the closure axioms of $o.C$, belong to the closure axioms of $f.\mathcal{F}$.

In this way, we obtain the system language and the corresponding closure axioms at a given state. Of course, closure axioms are assumed to satisfy all the constraints, those inherited by the constituent frameworks, and those stated in $\mathcal{F}$.

If a framework constraint H of a (possibly container) class C does not contain meta-variables, then the constraint instance $o.H$, to be satisfied by an instance $o.C$, is obtained simply by prefixing o to the (possible) attribute and action symbols in H. If it is a schema, i.e. it contains meta-variables for objects, then it has the form

$$Guard(\hat{x}_1, \ldots \hat{x}_n) \rightarrow H$$

where the formula[6] $Guard(x_1, \ldots x_n)$ is true in an instance $o.C$ for a finite set of objects, to be used to build the instances of the schema. For example, if in the current instance the formula $\triangleright.drives(c, m)$ is closed by

$$\triangleright Dustin.drives(c, m) \leftrightarrow (c = spider \wedge \ldots) \vee (c = spitfire \wedge \ldots)$$

then
$$\triangleright.drives(\hat{c}, m) \rightarrow \triangleright\hat{c}.go(m)$$

instantiates to
$$\triangleright Dustin.drives(spider, m) \rightarrow \triangleright spider.go(m)$$
$$\triangleright Dustin.drives(spitfire, m) \rightarrow \triangleright spitfire.go(m).$$

Thus, if a constraint of a class C is a (guarded) schema, then an instance of $o.C$ determines a finite set of constraints in the system language, that must be satisfied by the instance.

---

[6] With variables $x_1, \ldots x_n$ in place of the corresponding meta-variables.

We assume that $\mathcal{F}$ is consistent, i.e., there is at least one consistent closure for it. We can see that a consistent closure closes all the classes, i.e., it is a theory with an isoinitial model in the current system language.

We will not deal with consistency problems in this paper. We assume that we can build well constrained frameworks, and that there is a suitable way to test constraints when we compose frameworks. Constraint satisfaction and propagation should guarantee that consistency is preserved. The goal of this paper is to give a semantics for the dynamic behaviours of systems specified by frameworks. We conclude this section with an example.

Example 6. We give a system state for the framework $\mathcal{MALL}$, starting from the following closure of class predicates:

$$Maceys.MALL(x) \leftrightarrow x = Maceys$$
$$Maceys.CAR(x) \leftrightarrow x = spider \vee x = spitfire$$
$$Maceys.PERSON(x) \leftrightarrow x = Dustin \vee x = Ann$$
$$Maceys.DRIVER(x) \leftrightarrow x = Dustin$$
$$Maceys.CONSUMER(x) \leftrightarrow x = Ann$$

That is, in the mall *Maceys* there are two persons *Dustin* and *Ann* and two cars *spider* and *spitfire*. *Dustin* is a driver, and *Ann* a consumer. In this context, possible closure axioms for *Dustin* are:

$$Dustin.DRIVER(x) \leftrightarrow x = Dustin$$
$$Dustin.PERSON(x) \leftrightarrow x = Dustin$$
$$Dustin.name = \text{``Dustin Hoffman''}$$
$$Dustin.pocket = 0$$
$$Dustin.maydrive(x) \leftrightarrow x = spider$$
$$\triangleright Dustin.drives(x, m) \leftrightarrow x = spider \wedge m < 10000 \wedge \triangleright spider.go(m)$$
$$\forall x, y \,.\, \neg \odot Dustin.drives(x, y)$$

where, since *Dustin* inherits from $\mathcal{PERSON}$, it has to inherit the *PERSON* predicate, with closure $Dustin.Person(x) \leftrightarrow x = Dustin$. We omit, for conciseness, the complete closure. Note, however, that there may be many closures, as well as many instances of $\mathcal{MALL}$.

4 Dynamic Aspects of OOD Frameworks

In this section, we introduce dynamic aspects, i.e. time and state changes for systems of objects, by using OOD frameworks with temporal constraints. We interpret such frameworks as *event structures* [20,14], following the logic MDTL [10], an extension of the TROLL logic [8] for describing dynamic aspects of large object systems. For this purpose, in our formalisation, we need to make sure that the following property is guaranteed: for every class or subframework $\mathcal{C}$ of a framework $\mathcal{F}$, every closure of $\mathcal{F}$ and every object identity o, we can state whether a closure $o.\mathcal{C}$ belongs to the closure of $\mathcal{F}$, and, if it does, then it can be uniquely determined. Of course, if $\mathcal{C}$ is a basic class, then $o.\mathcal{C}$ is an object; and if $\mathcal{C}$ is a subframework, then $o.\mathcal{C}$ is a system of objects. If $o.\mathcal{C}$ belongs to a closure (for some $\mathcal{C}$), we will say that the closure contains the object o.

4.1   Labelled Event Structures

An event structure $E = \langle Ev, \rightarrow^*, \# \rangle$ consists of a set of *events* Ev equipped with two binary relations $\rightarrow^*$ and $\#$ for expressing *causal dependency* and *nondeterminism* respectively. The causal relation $\rightarrow^*$ implies a (partial) order among event occurrences. Intuitively, $e \rightarrow^* e'$ means that the occurrence of event e may *cause* the occurrence of event e'. The $\#$ relation expresses how the occurrence of certain events excludes the occurrences of others. The conflict relation also propagates over causality, i.e. if $e \# e' \rightarrow^* e''$ then $e \# e''$, for all $e, e', e'' \in Ev$. We will use $e \rightarrow e'$ for immediate causality (no other event in between). $e..e'$ will indicate a chain $e \rightarrow e_1 \rightarrow \cdots \rightarrow e_n \rightarrow e'$; the internal part $e_1 \rightarrow \cdots \rightarrow e_n$ may be empty; $e'' \in e..e'$ means that e'' belongs to the internal part. Finally, two events e and e' are *concurrent* if they are not in conflict $(\neg e \# e')$ and are not causally related $(\neg(e \rightarrow^* e' \vee e' \rightarrow^* e))$.

Now we interpret in a framework $\mathcal{F}$ the events of a structure $E = \langle Ev, \rightarrow^*, \# \rangle$, by labelling them by the closures of $\mathcal{F}$.

Definition 2. An $\mathcal{F}$-*labelling* of $E = \langle Ev, \rightarrow^*, \# \rangle$ is a partial function λ, with domain $dom(\lambda) \subseteq Ev$, that maps every event $e \in dom(\lambda)$ into a closure $\lambda(e)$ of $\mathcal{F}$, in such a way that, for every pair e, e' of concurrent events, the objects contained in $\lambda(e)$ are different from the ones contained in $\lambda(e')$.

The language of $\mathcal{F}$ is, so far, a first-order language. We assume that $\mathcal{F}$ has been built in a sound way, i.e., there is at least one closure, and each closure of $\mathcal{F}$ has an isoinitial model. Since a label $\lambda(e)$ is a closure of $\mathcal{F}$, it has an isoinitial model, that represents the state of the system described by $\mathcal{F}$ at event e. We will write $\lambda(e) \models H$, to indicate that a sentence H of the system language of $\lambda(e)$ is true in the isoinitial model of $\lambda(e)$. When a closure of $o.\mathcal{C}$ belongs to the closure $\lambda(e)$, the formulas H of the language of $o.\mathcal{C}$ have interpretation in the isoinitial model of $\lambda(e)$. With this in mind, we can define temporal $\mathcal{F}$-models using $\mathcal{F}$-labelled event structures.

Definition 3. Let $\mathcal{F}$ be a framework. An $\mathcal{F}$-*labelled event structure* is a pair $\langle E = \langle Ev, \rightarrow^*, \# \rangle, \lambda \rangle$, where E is an event structure, and λ is a $\mathcal{F}$-labelling of E such that: for every event $e \in dom(\lambda)$, every $o.\mathcal{C}$ that belongs to the closure $\lambda(e)$ and every ground action term t in the language of $o.\mathcal{C}$, if $\lambda(e) \models \odot t$, then there is an event $e' \in dom(\lambda)$, such that $e' \rightarrow e$, $o.\mathcal{C}$ belongs to $\lambda(e')$ and $\lambda(e') \models \triangleright t$.

The existence of an $e' \rightarrow e$ such that t is enabled in e' forces the intended meaning of $\triangleright t$ and $\odot t$: an action t must be enabled, in order to occur. That is, $\triangleright$ and *hocc* are not temporal operators, but their intended temporal meaning follows from the constraints that we impose on the class of possible $\mathcal{F}$-labelled event structures (according to the approach of [7]).

4.2   A Temporal Constraint Language

Now we define a temporal language for constraints, that is interpreted on our temporal models, namely $\mathcal{F}$-labelled event structures. In this language we distinguish between *framework* and *system* formulas.

Temporal framework formulas are built from the framework formulas defined in the previous section, that we will call *static formulas*.

Temporal formulas use the operators $\mathbf{U}$ (*until*) and $\mathbf{S}$ (*since*). Intuitively, $A\mathbf{U}B$ means that A has to hold from the next state, until B becomes true. $A\mathbf{S}B$ means that A has been true starting from a past state where B was true. In both cases, A is not obliged to hold in the current state. The set of temporal formulas of a framework $\mathcal{F}$ is the set of formulas generated from the static formulas of $\mathcal{F}$, by the previous temporal operators and by the usual logical connectives and quantifiers.

Formulas with the temporal operators $\mathbf{S}$ and $\mathbf{U}$ are called *temporal formulas*. Other temporal operators like *next* (X), *sometime in the future* (F), *always in the future* (G), *sometime in the past* (P), and *always in the past* (H) can be derived from $\mathbf{S}$ and $\mathbf{U}$ (cf. [7] for details).

The instances of a framework $\mathcal{F}$ are defined as in Section 3.2, because the closure axioms do not contain temporal operators. As before, each closure has an isoinitial model, that interprets the *static system formulas*, namely the system formulas defined in Section 3.2.

The *temporal system formulas* of a framework instance are built through the temporal operators, the logical connectives and the quantifiers, starting from the static system formulas.

A temporal framework $\mathcal{F}$ is one whose constraints may be temporal framework formulas. Temporal constraints cannot be interpreted in a single closure of $\mathcal{F}$. They have meaning only in the context of a temporal model, i.e., a $\mathcal{F}$-labelled event structure $M = \langle E = \langle Ev, \rightarrow^*, \# \rangle, \lambda \rangle$. At this level, static constraints are already satisfied, because the closures $\lambda(e)$ satisfy them by definition (of closure).

To interpret temporal constraints, we define the relation $M, e, v \models H$, which means that a system formula H, evaluated in a state e of an $\mathcal{F}$-labelled event structure M, is true at e for the valuation v of its (possible) free variables. v maps each $x : s$ of $dom(v)$ into a value $v(x) \in s^{\lambda(e)}$, where $s^{\lambda(e)}$ is the interpretation of the sort s in the isoinitial model of $\lambda(e)$. Since all the sort symbols belong to the signature Σ_P (see Section 3), their meaning is stated by the axioms $X_P \cup X_{Act} \cup X_{Obj}$, that is, we have constant domains. The constant domain $s^{\lambda(e)}$ will be indicated by s^P, to reflect that it does not depend on e and is fixed by the axioms for Σ_P. By $v[x/\alpha]$ we denote the valuation v' such that $dom(v') = dom(v) \cup x$, $v'(x) = \alpha$ and $v'(y) = v(y)$, for $y \neq x$ in $dom(v)$.

Definition 4. Let $\mathcal{F}$ be a framework and $M = \langle E = \langle Ev, \rightarrow^*, \# \rangle, \lambda \rangle$ be an $\mathcal{F}$-labelled event structure. Let e be an event in the domain $dom(\lambda)$, H be a formula that belongs to $L(\lambda(e))$, and v be an assignment of the free variables of H. Then $M, e, v \models H$ holds iff one of the following inductive clauses applies:

- *Basis.* H is a *static* formula true for the valuation v in the isoinitial model of $\lambda(e)$.

— *Step*. H is a *temporal* formula of the form AUB, ASB, $\neg A$, ..., and, according to the cases:[7]

$$M, e, v \models AUB \quad \text{iff there is } e..e' \text{ s.t. } M, e', v \models B \in L(\lambda(e'))$$
$$\text{and for } e'' \in e..e' \; M, e'', v \models A \in L(\lambda(e''))$$
$$M, e, v \models ASB \quad \text{iff there is } e'..e \text{ s.t. } M, e', v \models B \in L(\lambda(e'))$$
$$\text{and for } e'' \in e..e' \; M, e'', v \models A \in L(\lambda(e''))$$
$$M, e, v \models \neg A \quad \text{iff } M, e, v \not\models A$$
$$M, e, v \models A \wedge B \quad \text{iff } M, e, v \models A \text{ and } M, e, v \models B$$
$$M, e, v \models A \vee B \quad \text{iff } M, e, v \models A \text{ or } M, e, v \models B$$
$$M, e, v \models A \rightarrow B \quad \text{iff } M, e, v \models A \implies M, e, v \models B$$
$$M, e, v \models \forall x : s \,.\, A \text{ iff } M, e, v[x/\alpha] \models A \text{ for every } \alpha \in s^P$$
$$M, e, v \models \exists x : s \,.\, A \text{ iff } M, e, v[x/\alpha] \models A \text{ for at least one } \alpha \in s^P$$

As usual, if a formula H is closed, we omit the assignment and we simply write $M, e \models H$. Now, we consider the temporal constraints of a framework $\mathcal{F}$. As for static constraints, in every closure $\lambda(e)$, each temporal framework constraint instantiates to a corresponding system constraint, or a finite set of system constraints, if it is a (guarded) constraint schema.

Temporal constraint satisfaction is defined as follows. We say that a constraint H of a class $\mathcal{C}$ in a framework $\mathcal{F}$ is *satisfied* by a $\mathcal{F}$-labelled event structure M if, for every $e \in \lambda$, every instance $o.\mathcal{C}$ of $\lambda(e)$ and every instance H_o of H contained in $o.\mathcal{C}$, we have that $M, e \models H_o$.

We say that an $\mathcal{F}$-labelled event structure is a *model* of $\mathcal{F}$ if it satisfies the temporal constraints of $\mathcal{F}$.

4.3 Example: A *Catalysis* OOD Framework

To illustrate our formalisation of OOD frameworks, we now show how to specify an OOD framework in the style of the CBD methodology *Catalysis* [6].

Example 7. Consider the PersonAsEmployeeConsumer OOD framework in *Catalysis* depicted in Figure 6.

In PersonAsEmployeeConsumer, a person plays the role of an employee of a company. A person as an employee has an attribute *pocket* representing the amount of money he possesses, and two actions *receive_pay* and *work*. In this example, a person as an employee only works if he has less than £500 (precondition for *work*). A person only receives a payment if he has worked before (pre-condition for *receive_pay*). If a person receives a payment, the money in his pocket increases by the amount received.

In PersonAsEmployeeConsumer, a person also plays the role of a consumer. As a consumer, a person has an action $buy(p)$, where p represents the price of the item bought.

We have formalised the class $\mathcal{PERSON}$ in Example 5. Here, for conciseness, we will omit the attribute *.name*, and use only *.pocket*. Also in Example 5, we

---

[7] $M, e, v \models F \in L(\lambda(e'))$ abbreviates $F \in L(\lambda(e'))$ and $M, e, v \models F$.

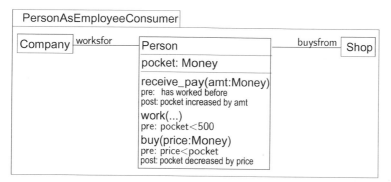

Fig. 6. PersonAsEmployeeConsumer OOD framework.

have formalised the class $\mathcal{CONSUMER}$, but without any temporal constraints. Now we add the following temporal constraint:

$$\odot.buy(p) \land Y(.pocket = n) \to .pocket = n - p.$$

This constraint says that, after buying an item, the money in the pocket of a consumer decreases by the amount of money spent.

The framework $\mathcal{EMPLOYEE}$ can be formalised as follows.

Framework $\mathcal{EMPLOYEE}$;

IMPORT: $\mathcal{PERSON}$

ACTIONS : $.receive\_pay : Int \to Act$;
                 $.work \quad : [\,] \to Act$;

CONSTRS: $\triangleright.receive\_pay(a) \to P \odot .work$;
                 $\odot.receive\_pay(a) \land Y(.pocket = n) \to .pocket = n + a$;
                 $\triangleright.work \to .pocket < £500.$

The first constraint states that if the action $receive\_pay$ is enabled, then sometime in the past (temporal operator P) the action $work$ must have occurred.

The second constraint says that the occurrence of action $receive\_pay(a)$ implies that if in the previous state (i.e., yesterday Y) the value of $pocket$ was n, then its current value is $n + a$.

The third constraint states that if the action $work$ is enabled (it might occur in the next state) then the value of $pocket$ must be less than £500.

Now we can build the framework $\mathcal{EMPLOYEECONSUMER}$:

Framework $\mathcal{EMPLOYEECONSUMER}$;

IMPORT: $\mathcal{EMPLOYEE}, \mathcal{CONSUMER}$
COMMON: $\mathcal{PERSON}$

ACTIONS : $.bePerson \quad : [\,] \to Act$;
                   $.beEmployee : [\,] \to Act$;
                   $.beConsumer : [\,] \to Act$;

CONSTRS: $.EmployeeConsumer(x) \rightarrow .Person(x)$

$\quad\quad\quad\quad (\triangleright self.bePerson \leftrightarrow self.Consumer(self) \vee self.Employee(self))$

$\quad\quad\quad\quad (\triangleright self.beEmployee \leftrightarrow \neg self.Employee(self) \wedge self.pocket < 500)$

$\quad\quad\quad\quad (\triangleright self.beConsumer \leftrightarrow \neg self.Consumer(self) \wedge self.pocket > 400)$

$\quad\quad\quad\quad (\odot self.bePerson \rightarrow \neg self.Consumer(self) \wedge \neg self.Employee(self))$

$\quad\quad\quad\quad (\odot self.beEmployee \rightarrow self.Employee(self))$

$\quad\quad\quad\quad (\odot self.beConsumer \rightarrow self.Consumer(self))$

Here *self* is a special meta-variable for objects with the usual meaning.

The first constraint says that the class EmployeeConsumer inherits from Person. However, nothing is said about Consumer and Employee. These roles can be assumed (by a person) dynamically, one at a time or both together.

The other constraints give the meaning of the actions to change the role of an object of class EmployeeConsumer. A Consumer or an Employee may always become a Person (the action *.bePerson* is enabled, second constraint). If he becomes a Person, then he is no longer a Consumer or an Employee (fifth constraint). The other constraints can be interpreted in a similar fashion.

Now for the framework $\mathcal{EMPLOYEECONSUMER}$, we can give an example of a model. Consider the event structure in Figure 7 for a person *Joe* who can play the roles of an employee and a consumer. In general, when we represent event

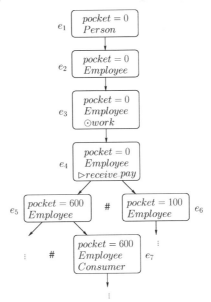

Fig. 7. Event structure for *Joe* as an employee and a consumer.

structures graphically, *boxes* denote events $\{e_1, e_2, \ldots\}$, *arrows* between boxes represent *causality*, and # denotes *conflict*. Event e_1 corresponds to the initial state. The occurrence of e_2 depends on the previous occurrence of e_1. The state of the object at a given event is written inside the box as a state formula. In Figure 7, for simplicity, the states are just indicated by the current value of *Joe*'s *pocket* and the current role(s) played by him.

In Figure 7, in state e_1, *Joe* starts as a simple person, with *Joe.pocket* $= 0$:

$$\lambda(e_1) = Joe.EmployeeConsumer(x) \leftrightarrow x = Joe$$
$$\neg Joe.Consumer(x)$$
$$\neg Joe.Employee(x)$$
$$Joe.Person(x) \leftrightarrow x = Joe$$
$$Joe.pocket = 0$$
$$\triangleright Joe.beEmployee \wedge \neg \odot Joe.beEmployee$$
$$\neg \triangleright Joe.beConsumer \wedge \neg \odot Joe.beConsumer$$

Since his pocket is 0, *Joe* may become an employee (constraint 3), but not a Consumer (constraint 4). No action has occurred, because there is no previous state where any action was enabled.

In the next state e_2, the action *Joe.beEmployee* has occurred, so *Joe* is now an Employee. It acquires the attributes of class Employee, and *Joe.work* is enabled. *Joe* works ($e_2 \rightarrow e_3$), but only in e_4 may he receive pay ($\triangleright receive\_pay(x) \leftrightarrow x < 800$).

$$\lambda(e_2) = Joe.EmployeeConsumer(x) \leftrightarrow x = Joe$$
$$\neg Joe.Consumer(x)$$
$$Joe.Employee(x) \leftrightarrow x = Joe$$
$$Joe.Person(x) \leftrightarrow x = Joe$$
$$Joe.pocket = 0$$
$$\triangleright Joe.work \wedge \neg \odot Joe.work$$
$$\neg \triangleright Joe.receive\_pay(x) \wedge \neg \odot Joe.receive\_pay(x)$$
$$\neg \triangleright Joe.beEmployee \wedge \odot Joe.beEmployee$$
$$\neg \triangleright Joe.beConsumer \wedge \neg \odot Joe.beConsumer$$

$$\lambda(e_3) = Joe.EmployeeConsumer(x) \leftrightarrow x = Joe$$
$$\neg Joe.Consumer(x)$$
$$Joe.Employee(x) \leftrightarrow x = Joe$$
$$Joe.Person(x) \leftrightarrow x = Joe$$
$$Joe.pocket = 0$$
$$\triangleright Joe.work \wedge \odot Joe.work$$
$$\neg \triangleright Joe.receive\_pay(x) \wedge \neg \odot Joe.receive\_pay(x)$$
$$\neg \triangleright Joe.beEmployee \wedge \neg \odot Joe.beEmployee$$
$$\neg \triangleright Joe.beConsumer \wedge \neg \odot Joe.beConsumer$$

$$\lambda(e_4) = Joe.EmployeeConsumer(x) \leftrightarrow x = Joe$$
$$\neg Joe.Consumer(x)$$
$$Joe.Employee(x) \leftrightarrow x = Joe$$
$$Joe.Person(x) \leftrightarrow x = Joe$$
$$Joe.pocket = 0$$
$$\triangleright Joe.work \wedge \neg \odot Joe.work$$
$$(\forall x . \triangleright Joe.receive\_pay(x) \leftrightarrow x < 800) \wedge$$
$$(\forall x . \neg \odot Joe.receive\_pay(x))$$

$$\neg \triangleright Joe.beEmployee \wedge \neg \odot Joe.beEmployee$$
$$\neg \triangleright Joe.beConsumer \wedge \neg \odot Joe.beConsumer$$

The next two states $e_4 \to e_5$ and $e_4 \to e_6$ are in conflict (only one of them may occur). In e_5 the pay is 600 and *Joe* may become a Consumer, whereas in e_6 the pay is 100, and he cannot become a Consumer.

$$\lambda(e_5) = \ldots$$
$$Joe.pocket = 600$$
$$(\forall x \,.\, \neg \triangleright Joe.receive\_pay(x))$$
$$\wedge(\forall x \,.\, \odot Joe.receive\_pay(x) \leftrightarrow x = 600)$$
$$\ldots$$
$$\triangleright Joe.beConsumer \wedge \neg \odot Joe.beConsumer$$

$$\lambda(e_6) = \ldots$$
$$Joe.pocket = 100$$
$$(\forall x \,.\, \neg \triangleright Joe.receive\_pay(x))$$
$$\wedge(\forall x \,.\, \odot Joe.receive\_pay(x) \leftrightarrow x = 100)$$
$$\ldots$$
$$\neg \triangleright Joe.beConsumer \wedge \neg \odot Joe.beConsumer$$

In Figure 7, we also show a state e_7 where *Joe.beConsumer* has occurred. In some states, some attributes change without any explicit action occurrence, because we allow specifications of open modules, where some other parts are not modelled. For example, the action *receive_pay* is enabled by *Joe*'s company, and it occurs through a bank, but the cooperations with those objects is left implicit.

Finally, it is easy to see that this event structure is indeed a model of the framework $\mathcal{EMPLOYEECONSUMER}$, since all the (system instances of the) temporal constraints of the framework are satisfied.

5   Conclusion

In this paper we have described our preliminary effort to formalise dynamic aspects of OOD frameworks. So far our formalisation of OOD frameworks does not deal with the dynamic aspects of framework composition. This is future work. Our eventual goal is a semantics for composing OOD frameworks with state transitions in the manner depicted in Figure 3.

Our work is closely related to TROLL [8], which is used for specifying large distributed/concurrent object systems, and to [3], which formalises an algebraic semantics for object model diagrams in OMT [19]. The main difference is that they take the traditional view of objects (Figure 2), whereas we adopt the multiple-role, more reusable approach (Figure 3). Another fundamental difference is that their semantics is based on initial theories, as opposed to isoinitial theories that we use. Initial semantics is convenient for defining computations at the operational level (a good example is Maude [16,17]), whereas isoinitial semantics is more suited to declarative semantics for specifications.

Overall, our approach is model-theoretic, whereas other approaches are mostly proof- or type-theoretic. For example, our model-theoretic characterisation of states and objects stands in contrast to the type-theoretic approach, e.g., [1]. Our model-theoretic approach also enables us to define a notion of correctness that is preserved through inheritance hierarchies, which is particularly suitable for component-based software development.

Acknowledgements. We wish to thank Don Sannella for his helpful comments and suggestions during our discussion at the workshop, and Alberto Pettorossi for pointing out important technical issues.

References

1. M. Abadi and L. Cardelli. *A Theory of Objects*. Springer-Verlag, 1996.
2. A. Bertoni, G. Mauri, and P. Miglioli. On the power of model theory in specifying abstract data types and in capturing their recursiveness. *Fundamenta Informaticae* **VI**(2):127–170, 1983.
3. R.H. Bourdeau and B.H.C. Cheng. A formal semantics for object model diagrams. *IEEE Trans. Soft. Eng.*, 21(10):799-821, 1995.
4. D. Coleman, P. Arnold, S. Bodoff, C. Dollin, H. Gilchrist, F. Hayes, and P. Jeremaes. *Object-Oriented Development: The Fusion Method*. Prentice-Hall, 1994.
5. S. Cook and J. Daniels. *Designing Object Systems*. Prentice-Hall, 1994.
6. D.F. D'Souza and A.C. Wills. *Objects, Components, and Frameworks with UML: The Catalysis Approach*. Addison-Wesley, October 1998.
7. H.-D. Ehrich, C. Caleiro, A. Sernadas, and G. Denker. Logics for specifying concurrent information systems. G. Saake and J. Chomicki, editors, *Logics for Databases and Information Systems*, pages 167–198, Kluwer Academic, 1998.
8. A. Grau, J. Küster Filipe, M. Kowsari, S. Eckstein, R. Pinger and H.-D. Ehrich. The TROLL approach to conceptual modelling: syntax, semantics and tools. In T.W. Ling, S. Ram and M.L. Leebook, editors, *Proc. 17th Int. Conference on Conceptual Modeling*, *LNCS* 1507:277-290, Springer, 1998.
9. R. Helm, I.M. Holland, and D. Gangopadhay. Contracts — Specifying behavioural compositions in OO systems. *Sigplan Notices* 25(10) (*Proc. ECOOP/OOPSLA 90*).
10. J. Küster Filipe. Fundamentals of a module logic for distributed object systems. *J. Functional and Logic Programming* 2000(3), 2000.
11. K.-K. Lau and M. Ornaghi. Isoinitial models for logic programs: A preliminary study. In J.L. Freire-Nistal, M. Falaschi, and M. Vilares-Ferro, editors, *Proceedings of the 1998 Joint Conference on Declarative Programming*, pages 443-455, A Coruña, Spain, July 1998.
12. K.-K. Lau and M. Ornaghi. On specification and correctness of OOD frameworks in computational logic. In A. Brogi and P. Hill, editors, *Proc. 1st Int. Workshop on Component-based Software Development in Computational Logic*, pages 59-75, September 1998, Pisa, Italy.
13. K.-K. Lau and M. Ornaghi. OOD frameworks in component-based software development in computational logic. In P. Flener, editor, *Proc. LOPSTR'98*, *LNCS* 1559:101-123, Springer-Verlag, 1999.
14. R. Loogen and U. Goltz. Modelling nondeterministic concurrent processes with event structures. *Fundamenta Informaticae* XIV(1):39–73, January 1991.
15. R. Mauth. A better foundation: development frameworks let you build an application with reusable objects. *BYTE* 21(9):40IS 10-13, September 1996.

16. Maude home page. http://maude.csl.sri.com/
17. J. Meseguer. Conditional rewriting logic as a unified model of concurrency. *Theoretical Computer Science*, 96:73–155, 1992.
18. R. Pooley and P. Stevens. *Using UML: Software Engineering with Objects and Components.* Addison-Wesley, 1999.
19. J. Rumbaugh, M. Blaha, W. Premerlani, F. Eddy, and W. Sorenson. *Object-Oriented Modeling and Design.* Prentice-Hall, 1991.
20. G. Winskel. Event structures. In W. Brauer, W. Reisig, and G. Rozenberg, editors, *Petri Nets: Applications and Relationships to Other Models of Concurrency, Advances in Petri Nets 1986, Part II, LNCS* 255:325–392, Springer, 1987.

Infinite State Model Checking by Abstract Interpretation and Program Specialisation

Michael Leuschel[1] and Thierry Massart[2]

[1] Department of Electronics and Computer Science
University of Southampton, e-mail: mal@ecs.soton.ac.uk
[2] Département d'Informatique
University of Brussels (ULB), e-mail: tmassart@ulb.ac.be

Abstract. We illustrate the use of logic programming techniques for finite model checking of CTL formulae. We present a technique for infinite state model checking of safety properties based upon logic program specialisation and analysis techniques. The power of the approach is illustrated on several examples. For that, the efficient tools LOGEN and ECCE are used. We discuss how this approach has to be extended to handle more complicated infinite state systems and to handle arbitrary CTL formulae.

1 Introduction

Recent years have seen dramatic growth [9] in the application of model checking [8,5] techniques to the validation and verification of correctness properties of hardware, and more recently software systems. One of the methods is to model a hardware or software system as a finite, labeled transition system (LTS) which is then exhaustively explored to decide whether a given temporal specification holds. Recently, there has been increasing interest in applying logic programming techniques to model checking. Table-based logic programming can be used as an efficient means of performing explicit model checking [35] and set-based logic program analysis for model checking is explored in [7].

However, despite the success of model checking, most systems must be substantially simplified (i.e., *abstracted*) and "considerable human guidance and ingenuity is generally required to transform the original problem to a form where the final push button automation can be applied" [36]. Furthermore, most *software* systems can conveniently be modelled by infinite state systems: as soon as some kind of recursion, dynamic or unbounded data structures come into play, an unbounded number of states can be reached and must be verified. In practice the number of possible states in implementations is always finite but may be so huge as to make any exhaustive approach futile. This probably explains why, contrary to the situation in hardware, verification in general and model checking in particular has had hardly any impact on standard software practice.

For these reasons, there has recently been considerable interest in *infinite model checking* (e.g., [3,39,32,12,2]). This, by its generally undecidable nature, is a daunting task, for which *abstraction* is the key issue [9]. Indeed, abstraction

A. Bossi (Ed.): LOPSTR'99, LNCS 1817, pp. 62–81, 2000.

allows one to approximate an infinite system (or a complicated finite one) by a (simple) finite one, and if proper care is taken the results obtained for the finite abstraction will be valid for the infinite system.

This research aims at exploring automatic means of building precise but tractable abstractions for infinite model checking (or model checking of finite, but very complex systems). We propose to do this by extending technology that has been developed to tackle similar problems in the context of automatic logic program analysis and specialisation. In essence, we:

- model a system to be verified as a logic program. This obviously includes finite LTS, but also allows to express systems with an infinite number of states. Note that this translations is often very straightforward, due to the built-in support of logic programming for non-determinism and unification.
- model the full temporal logic CTL as a logic program interpreter acting on the representation above. This interpreter will make use of the tight link that exists between the semantics of logic programs and least-fixed points.
- and then try to *automatically derive abstractions for infinite model checking through a combination of partial evaluation and abstract interpretation technology*. The tools LOGEN [19,26] and ECCE [25,27] are used successfully to automate the work.

The contribution of the paper is the development of a correct CTL interpreter in logic programming and its use as a sound basis for model checking of finite and infinite state systems via program analysis and specialisation in general and the tools LOGEN and ECCE in particular. This paper builds upon the initial insights and experiments in [14] where it was shown that abstraction-based partial deduction can be used as a powerful inversion tool.

In the following, we present the logic CTL [11] to express the properties we want to verify and its translation into a logic program. We discuss the validity of model checking infinite systems. We implement as logic programs, systems expressed as labeled transition systems, Petri nets, processes synchronised through shared variables, etc. We then show how existing technology for the specialisation and analysis of logic programs can be used to achieve some model checking tasks of infinite state systems. We present some successful experiments, but also shortcomings of the existing systems. We then give directions for further research to enable model checking of arbitrary CTL formulae on infinite state systems.

2   The Model-Checking of CTL in Logic Programming

2.1   CTL Syntax and Semantics

The temporal logic CTL (Computation Tree Logic) introduced by Clarke and Emerson in [11], allows to specify properties of specifications generally described as Kripke structures. The syntax and semantics for CTL are given below.

Given *Prop*, the set of *propositions*, the set of CTL formulae ϕ is inductively defined by the following grammar (where $p \in Prop$):

$$\phi := true \mid p \mid \neg\phi \mid \phi \wedge \phi \mid \forall \bigcirc \phi \mid \exists \bigcirc \phi \mid \forall\phi\mathcal{U}\phi \mid \exists\phi\mathcal{U}\phi$$

A CTL formula ϕ can be either true or false in a given state. For example, *true* is true in all states, $\neg true$ is false in all states, and p is true in all states which contain the elementary proposition p. The symbol $\bigcirc$ is the *nexttime* operator and $\mathcal{U}$ stands for *until*. $\forall \bigcirc \phi$ (resp. $\exists \bigcirc \phi$) intuitively means that ϕ holds in every (resp. some) immediate successor of the current program state. The formula $\forall \phi_1 \mathcal{U} \phi_2$ (resp. $\exists \phi_1 \mathcal{U} \phi_2$) intuitively means that for every (resp. some) computation path, there exists an initial prefix of the path such that ϕ_2 holds at the last state of the prefix and ϕ_1 holds at all other states along the prefix.

The semantics of CTL formulae is defined with respect to a Kripke structure (S, R, μ, s_0) with S being the set of states, $R (\subseteq S \times S)$ the transition relation, $\mu(S \to 2^{Prop})$ giving the propositions which are true in each state, and s_0 being the initial state. Figure 1a gives a graphical representation of a Kripke structure with 3 states s_0, s_1, s_2, where s_0 is the initial state. The propositions p, q, r "label" the states. Generally it is required that any state has at least one

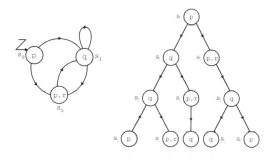

a   b

Fig. 1. Example of a Kripke structure.

outgoing vertex. From a Kripke structure, we can define an infinite transition tree as follows: the root of the tree is labelled by s_0. Any vertex labelled by s has one son labelled by s' for each vertex s' with a transition $s \to s'$ in the Kripke structure. For instance, the Kripke structure of Fig. 1a gives the prefix for the transition tree starting from s_0 given in Fig. 1b.

If the system is not directly specified by a Kripke structure but e.g. by a Petri net, the markings and transitions between them give resp. the states and transition relation of the Kripke structure.

The CTL semantics is defined on states s by:

- $s \models true$
- $s \models p$ *iff* $p \in P(s)$
- $s \models \neg \phi$ *iff* $\mathrm{not}(s \models \phi)$
- $s \models \phi_1 \wedge \phi_2$ *iff* $s \models \phi_1$ and $s \models \phi_2$
- $s \models \forall \bigcirc \phi$ *iff* for all state t such that $(s, t) \in R$, $t \models \phi$
- $s \models \exists \bigcirc \phi$ *iff* for some state t such that $(s, t) \in R$, $t \models \phi$
- $s \models \forall \phi_1 \mathcal{U} \phi_2$ *iff* for all path $(s_0, s_1, \ldots)$ of the system with $s = s_0, \exists i (i \geq 0 \wedge s_i \models \phi_2 \wedge \forall j (0 \leq j < i \to s_j \models \phi_1))$
- $s \models \exists \phi_1 \mathcal{U} \phi_2$ *iff* it exists a path $(s_0, s_1, \ldots)$ with $s = s_0$, such that $\exists i (i \geq 0 \wedge s_i \models \phi_2 \wedge \forall j (0 \leq j < i \to s_j \models \phi_1))$

If we look at the unfolding of the Kripke structure, starting from s_0 (Fig. 1b), we can see, for instance, that

- $s_0 \models \exists \bigcirc p$ since there exists a successor of s_0 (i.e. s_2) where p is true ($p \in \mu(s_2)$),
- $s_0 \not\models \forall \bigcirc p$ since in some successor of s_0, p does not hold.
- $s_0 \models \forall p \mathcal{U} q$ since the paths from s_0 either go to s_1 where q is true or to s_2 and then directly to s_1. In both cases, the paths go through states where p is true before reaching one state where q holds.

Since they are often used, the following abbreviations are defined

- $\forall \Diamond \phi \equiv \forall \text{ true } \mathcal{U} \phi$ i.e. for all paths, ϕ eventually holds,
- $\exists \Diamond \phi \equiv \exists \text{ true } \mathcal{U} \phi$ i.e. there exists a path where ϕ eventually holds,
- $\exists \Box \phi \equiv \neg \forall \Diamond (\neg \phi)$ i.e. there exists a path where ϕ always holds,
- $\forall \Box \phi \equiv \neg \exists \Diamond (\neg \phi)$ i.e. for all paths ϕ always holds.

E.g. $\forall \Box \phi$ states that ϕ is an invariant of the system, $\forall \Diamond \phi$ states that ϕ is unavoidable and $\exists \Diamond \phi$ states that ϕ may occur.

2.2   CTL as Fixed Point and Its Translation to Logic Programming

One starting point of this paper is that both the Kripke structure defining the system under consideration and the CTL specification can be easily defined using logic programs. This is obvious for the standard logic operators as well as for the CTL operators $\exists \bigcirc$. The following equality can be easily proved $\forall \bigcirc \phi \equiv \neg \exists \bigcirc \neg \phi$. Moreover, the operators $\exists \mathcal{U}$ and $\forall \mathcal{U}$ can be defined as fixpoint solutions [31]. Indeed, if you take the view that ϕ represents the set of states S where ϕ is valid, it can be proved that $\exists p \mathcal{U} q \equiv \mu Y = (q \vee (p \wedge \exists \bigcirc Y))$ where μ stands for the least fixpoint of the equation. Intuitively this equation tells that the set of states satisfying $\exists p \mathcal{U} q$ is the least one satisfying q or having a successor which satisfies this property.

$\exists \Diamond$ and $\forall \Box$ can be derived from what precedes. $\forall \bigcirc$ can be derived using the equivalence $\forall \bigcirc \phi \equiv \neg \exists \bigcirc \neg \phi$. Slightly more involved is the definition of the set of states which satisfy $\exists \Box \phi$. These states can be expressed as the solution of $\nu X = \phi \wedge \exists \bigcirc X$ where ν stands for the greatest fixpoint of the equation. Greatest fixpoint cannot be directly computed by logic programming systems, but the equation can be translated into $\exists \Box \phi \equiv \neg \Phi$ where the set Y of states which satisfy Φ is defined by $\mu Y = \neg \phi \vee \neg \exists \bigcirc \neg Y$. Finally, $\forall \Diamond \phi \equiv \neg \exists \Box \neg \phi$ and $\forall \phi_1 \mathcal{U} \phi_2 \equiv \neg(\exists \neg \phi_2 \mathcal{U}(\neg \phi_1 \wedge \neg \phi_2)) \wedge \neg \exists \Box \neg \phi_2$. This last equality says that a state satisfies $\forall \phi_1 \mathcal{U} \phi_2$ if it has no path where ϕ_2 is continuously false until a state where both ϕ_1 and ϕ_2 are false nor a path where ϕ_2 is continuously false.

We can see that we only use least fixpoint of monotonic equations. Moreover, the use of table-based Prolog (XSB Prolog) ensures proper handling of cycles.

For infinite state systems, the derivation of the fixpoints cannot generally be completed. However, by the monotonicity of all the used fixpoints, all derived implications belong indeed to the solution (no overapproximation).

Our CTL specification is independant of any model. It only supposes that the successors of a state s can be computed (through the predicate **trans**) and that the elementary proposition of any state s can be determined (through `prop`). In Fig. 2 we present a particular implementation of CTL as a (tabled) logic program. For example, it can be used to verify the mutual exclusion example from [8], simply by running it in XSB-Prolog. This follows similar lines as [35,28] where tabled logic programming is used as an (efficient) means of *finite* model checking. Nonetheless, our translation of CTL in this paper is expressed (more clearly) as a meta-interpreter and will be the starting point for the model checking of *infinite* state systems using program specialisation and analysis techniques.

```
/* A Model Checker for CTL fomulas written for XSB-Prolog */
sat(_E,true).
sat(_E,false) :- fail.
sat(E,p(P)) :- prop(E,P). /* elementary proposition */
sat(E,and(F,G)) :- sat(E,F), sat(E,G).
sat(E,or(F,_G)) :- sat(E,F).
sat(E,or(_F,G)) :- sat(E,G).
sat(E,not(F)) :- not(sat(E,F)).
sat(E,en(F)) :- trans(_Act,E,E2),sat(E2,F). /* exists next */
sat(E,an(F)) :- not(sat(E,en(not(F)))). /* always next */
sat(E,eu(F,G)) :- sat_eu(E,F,G).   /* exists until */
sat(E,au(F,G)) :- sat(E,not(eu(not(G),and(not(F),not(G))))),
                  sat_noteg(E,not(G)). /* always until */
sat(E,ef(F)) :- sat(E,eu(true,F)). /* exists future */
sat(E,af(F)) :- sat_noteg(E,not(F)). /* always future */
sat(E,eg(F)) :- not(sat_noteg(E,F)).   /* exists global */
                /* we want gfp -> negate lfp of negation */
sat(E,ag(F)) :- sat(E,not(ef(not(F)))).  /* always global */
:- table sat_eu/3. /* table to compute least-fixed point using XSB */
sat_eu(E,_F,G) :- sat(E,G).  /* exists until */
 sat_eu(E,F,G) :- sat(E,F), trans(_Act,E,E2), sat_eu(E2,F,G).
:- table sat_noteg/2. /* table to compute least-fixed point using XSB */
sat_noteg(E,F) :- sat(E,not(F)).
sat_noteg(E,F) :- not((trans(_Act,E,E2),not(sat_noteg(E2,F)))).
```

Fig. 2. CTL interpreter

Model Checking of Infinite Systems The infinite state system we handle are finitely branching. In fact, what is required is to be able, in a finite number of "steps", to look at all the succesors of a state. (In real-time systems a state can have an infinite number of direct successors, and model checking then requires more sophisticated symbolic methods.) We have to show that, using these infinite state systems, our CTL interpreter is correct wrt. the SLS-semantics [34]. This is because our analysis and specialisation might replace infinite failure by finite failure but do so only in accordance with the SLS-semantics.

Indeed, the only potential loops are linked with $\exists\mathcal{U}$ or $\forall\mathcal{U}$. In fact, we can notice that the computation is based on two fixpoint calculations; one is defined through `sat_eu` and the other through `sat_noteg`. If we look at `sat_eu` (the treatment of sat_noteg will pose similar problems), three cases may occur in the SLD-resolution:

- A path is found satisfying F *Until* G (success; no difference with SLDNF-semantics).
- It is found that no path satisfies F *Until* G, i.e. all the paths satisfy $\neg G\mathcal{U}(\neg F \vee \neg G)$ (finite failure; no difference with SLDNF-semantics)
- The resolution loops in an infinite path satisfying F. In this case the system will not reply if no means is given to detect this infinite path. However, wrt the SLS-semantics the answer is *no* (which is different from the SLDNF-semantics), which is the correct answer according to the CTL-semantics we have given earlier (no path satisfies the requested property).

3   The Systems Analysed

We illustrate our approach by analysing finite or simple but infinite states systems specified initially by LTS, Petri nets or parallel processes using shared variables. This section presents these systems.

3.1   Petri Net of a Simple Mutual Exclusion Problem

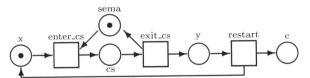

Fig. 3. Petri net with a single semaphore

Figure 3 models a single process which may enter a critical section (cs), the access to which is controlled by a semaphore (sema). This Petri net can be encoded directly as trans/3 facts for our CTL interpreter:

```
trans(enter_cs,[s(X),s(Sema),CritSec,Y,C],[X,Sema,s(CritSec),Y,C]).
trans(exit_cs, [X,Sema,s(CritSec),Y,C],[X,s(Sema),CritSec,s(Y),C]).
trans(restart,[X,Sema,CritSec,s(Y),C],[s(X),Sema,CritSec,Y,s(C)]).
```

3.2   Petri Net of a Manufacturing System

The manufacturing system in Fig. 4, used in [3], has been analysed. It models an automated manufacturing system with 4 machines, 2 robots, 2 buffers (x_{10} and x_{15}) and an assembly cell. The initial marking is such that $x_1 = p$ for some nonnegative parameter p. In [3], Bérard and Fribourg have used Hytech [17] to discover a potential deadlock when $p > 8$.

3.3   Producer/Consumer Processes with Shared Variables

The following is a simplified version of the producer/consumer example from [1], using a buffer of length 1. A state of the system is not only, as in the previous cases, a tuple of natural numbers but this time contains items (simple values) and lists of items. A "state" of the system is given by [A,Prod,In,Out,Buf,CR,B] where A is the list of items which remain to be produced, Prod the last item which has been produced, In the number of empty places in the buffer, Out the number of full places in the buffer, Buff the buffer and CR the last item which has been removed by the consumer. Finally B allows to check the items which remain to be consumed (and is initially a copy of A).

```
trans(prod, [[X|T],prod,In,Out,Buf,CR,B], [T,add(X),In,Out,Buf,CR,B]).
trans(add,  [A,add(X),1,0,Buf,CR,B], [A,prod,0,1,X,CR,B]).
trans(rem,  [A,PA,0,1,Buf,cons,B], [A,PA,1,0,Buf,rem(Buf),B]).
trans(cons, [A,PA,In,Out,Buf,rem(Buf),[Buf|B]], [A,PA,In,Out,Buf,cons,B]).
trans(err , [A,PA,In,Out,Buf,rem(Buf),[B2|B]],
            [err,err,err,err,err,err,err]) :- Buf\==B2.
```

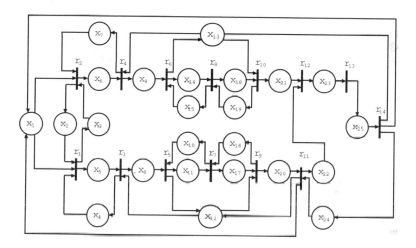

Fig. 4. Petri net representation of an automated manufacturing system with four machines, two robots, two buffers (x_{10}, x_{15}) and an assembly cell.

4   Infinite Model Checking of Safety Properties

Before attempting to verify any CTL formula, let us restrict our attention to checking safety properties, i.e., formulae of the form $s \models \forall\Box safe$. Model checking of such properties amounts to showing that there exists no trace which leads to an invalid state, i.e., exploiting the fact that $\forall\Box safe \equiv \neg\exists\Diamond(\neg safe)$.

Consider the Petri net in subsection 3.1. We first have to specify properties of interest by defining prop/2: prop([X,Sema,s(s(CritSec)),Y,C],unsafe).

Here, we have specified that a state is unsafe if two or more processes are in their critical section at the same time. Now, to check whether the above Petri net can reach an unsafe state for an initial marking with 1 token in the semaphore (sema), 0 tokens in the reset counter (c), no processes in the critical section (cs), no processes in the final place (y) and X processes in the initial place (x) we simply run the query: `sat([X,0,s(0),0,0],ef(p(unsafe)))`.

Unfortunately, this query does not terminate under Prolog or XSB-Prolog although the system does indeed satisfy the safety property for any value of X. Even if we try to prove the property just for a particular value of X (e.g., $X = s(0)$) neither Prolog nor XSB-Prolog [37] will terminate (even when adding moding or delay declarations). Indeed, the queries have infinitely failed SLD/SLG-trees with an infinite number of distinct call patterns (due to the counter c). Thus, according to the well-founded semantics, we have that the program indeed entails `not(sat([X,0,s(0),0,0],ef(p(unsafe))))`, but existing procedures are unable to establish this.

In the following, we will be able to prove this safety property by a *semantics-preserving program specialisation and analysis technique*, specialising the CTL interpreter for the query `sat([X,0,s(0),0,0],ef(p(unsafe)))` to the empty program (in a logically sound fashion). For this we will proceed in three phases:

1. specialise the full CTL interpreter for the particular property using an offline specialiser, so as to get rid of unneccesary complexities.
2. specialise the so obtained simplified interpreter using a full-fledged online specialiser so as to obtain a finite, and as precise as possible abstraction of the infinite state system for the property at hand.
3. use abstract interpretation to analyse this finite representation and determine whether the property is true, false, or undecided.

In the following we will describe and illustrate each of these phases.

4.1   Pre-compilation with LOGEN

The complete CTL interpreter of Fig. 2 is quite complex, and makes heavy usage of negation. The latter is difficult to handle by most current program analysis and specialisation tools. However, for the particular class of formulae we want to handle in this section we can get rid of the unnecessary complexity of full CTL by pre-compiling the interpreter for the formula to be checked. This task is best performed by an offline specialiser, such as the LOGEN system [19,26]. For instance, specialising Fig. 2 for the query `sat([Processes,0,s(0),0,0],ef(p(unsafe)))` yields the much simplified interpreter below, which contains no negation and where the Petri net has been compiled into the interpreter:

```
/* benchmark info: 1.17 ms */
/* atom specialised: sat([_264,0,s(0),0,0],ef(p(unsafe))) */
sat__0(B) :- sat_eu__1(B).
sat_eu__1([B,C,s(s(D)),E,F]).
sat_eu__1([s(G),s(H),I,J,K]) :- sat_eu__1([G,H,s(I),J,K]).
sat_eu__1([L,M,s(N),O,P]) :- sat_eu__1([L,s(M),N,s(O),P]).
sat_eu__1([Q,R,S,s(T),U]) :- sat_eu__1([s(Q),R,S,T,s(U)]).
```

This interpreter should now be called using the predicate `sat__0(P)` (which corresponds to calling `sat([P,0,s(0),0,0],ef(p(unsafe)))` in the original

program). Observe that LOGEN (and ECCE as well) concatenates two underscores and a unique identifier to existing predicate names.

The exact details of this compilation phase are not relevant for the present
article; all we need to know is that it terminates (actually it is also very efficient)
and that it is totally correct in the sense that it preserves the computed answers
and finite failure. In other words, the specialised program succeeds for a specialised query (e.g., sat_0(s(X))) with a computed answer θ (respectively finitely
fails) iff the original program does so for the corresponding original query (e.g.,
sat([s(X),0,s(0),0,0],ef(p(unsafe)))).

Observe that even this much simplified interpreter still does not terminate
under either SLD or tabled SLG resolution. Below, we will show how this interpreter can be analysed using automatic techniques and how we can show that
the encoded, infinite state Petri net obeys the safety property.

4.2   Online Partial Deduction with ECCE

The second phase of our model checking technique will perform online partial
deduction using the ECCE tool. It will construct a finite representation of the
infinite state space in the form of a specialised program. Below we present the
essential details of partial deduction and the essential details of the algorithm
used by ECCE.

The underlying technique of partial deduction is to construct finite but possibly incomplete SLD(NF)-trees (i.e. a SLD(NF)-tree which, in addition to success
and failure leaves, may also contain leaves where no literal has been selected for
a further derivation step). These incomplete SLD(NF)-trees are obtained by applying an unfolding rule, defined as follows.

Definition 1. *An* unfolding rule *is a function which, given a program P and a
goal G, returns a finite non-trivial[1] and possibly incomplete SLD(NF)-tree τ for
$P \cup \{G\}$. We also define leaves(τ) to be the atoms in the leaf goals of τ.*

Formally, the resultant of a branch of τ leading from the root G to a leaf goal
G_i via computed answer θ is the formula $G\theta \leftarrow G_i$. Partial deduction uses the
resultants for a given set of atoms $\mathcal{S}$ to construct the specialised program (and
for each atom in $\mathcal{S}$ a different specialised predicate definition will be generated).
Under the conditions stated in [29], namely *closedness* (all leaves are an instance
of an atom in $\mathcal{S}$) and *independence* (no two atoms in $\mathcal{S}$ have a common instance),
total correctness of the specialised program is guaranteed (i.e., as above we
preserve the computed answers and finite failure).

We now present a concrete partial deduction algorithm based upon [27]. This
algorithm structures the set S of atoms to be specialised as a *global tree* γ: i.e.,
a tree whose nodes are labeled by atoms and where A is a descendant of B if
specialising *label*(B) lead to the specialisation of *label*(A). It outputs a set of
atoms $\mathcal{A}$ which can be used to construct a totally correct specialisation of P

---

[1] A trivial SLD(NF)-tree is one in which no literal in the root has been selected for
resolution. Such trees are disallowed to obtain correct partial deductions.

for all instances of $\leftarrow Q$ (possibly using a renaming transformation to ensure independence).

Note that the algorithm below can be seen as a special kind of *forwards* abstract interpretation (see [24]), where each atom in γ actually denotes all its instances (i.e., the concretisations $\gamma(A)$ of an atom A are all the instances of A).

To ensure termination of our algorithm, we have to ensure that the unfolding rule U builds a finite SLD(NF)-tree. In addition, we have to guarantee that no infinite branches are built up in the global tree γ: If it looks like an infinite branch is being built up we have to abstract some of the atoms and restart the process. We thus also have to ensure that this abstraction process itself cannot be repeated infinitely often.

The following auxiliary concepts will help us to achieve this feat. First, to be able to perform a suitable generalisation we define:

Definition 2. *The* most specific generalisation *of a finite set of expressions S, also denoted by $msg(S)$, is the most specific expression M such that all expressions in S are instances of M.*

Algorithms for calculating the *msg* exist [21], and we have for example $msg(\{p(0, s(0)),\ p(0, s(s(0)))\}) = p(0, s(X))$. We also have the important property, that for every expression A, there are no infinite chains of strictly more general expressions. Now, to detect infinite branches, both in the global tree γ and the SLD(NF)-trees constructed by U, we will use the homeomorphic embedding relation derived from [18,20]. The following is the definition from [38]:

Definition 3. *The* (pure) homeomorphic embedding *relation $\trianglelefteq$ on expressions is inductively defined as follows (i.e. $\trianglelefteq$ is the least relation satisfying the rules):*

1. $X \trianglelefteq Y$ *for all variables X, Y*
2. $s \trianglelefteq f(t_1, \ldots, t_n)$ *if $s \trianglelefteq t_i$ for some i*
3. $f(s_1, \ldots, s_n) \trianglelefteq f(t_1, \ldots, t_n)$ *if $\forall i \in \{1, \ldots, n\} : s_i \trianglelefteq t_i$.*

(Notice that n is allowed to be 0 and we thus have $c \trianglelefteq c$ for all constant and proposition symbols). The intuition behind the above definition is that $A \trianglelefteq B$ iff A can be obtained from B by "striking out" certain parts, or said another way, the structure of A reappears within B. We have the important property ([18,20]) that $\trianglelefteq$ is a so-called well-quasi order on the set of expressions over a finite alphabet, i.e., for every infinite sequence $s_1, s_2, \ldots$ of expressions there exists $i < j$ such that $s_i \trianglelefteq s_j$.

Algorithm 4.1 (*partial deduction algorithm*)

Input: a program P and a goal $\leftarrow Q$
Output: a set of atoms $\mathcal{A}$ and a global tree γ
Initialisation: $\gamma :=$ a "global" tree with a single unmarked node, labelled by Q
repeat
    pick an unmarked leaf node L in γ
    if $\exists$ a marked variantof L in γ **then**   mark L
    else if $\exists$ ancestor W of L such that $label(W) \trianglelefteq label(L)$ **then**
    $label(W) := msg(L, W)$

```
     remove all descendants of W  and  unmark W
  else
     mark L
     for all A ∈ leaves(U(P, label(L))) do
        add a new unmarked C child of L to γ
        label(C) := A
        label(L → C) := a characteristic path i.e. a sequence of clauses in P which were
        resolved with
  until all nodes are marked
  output A := {label(A) | A ∈ γ}
```

In this algorithm, M is a variant of L iff for some θ_1, θ_2: $M\theta_1 = L$ and $L\theta_2 = M$. The notion of *characteristic path* is developped in [13,27].

The above algorithm is parametrised by an unfolding rule U. Upon termination of the algorithm the closedness condition of [29] is satisfied, i.e., it is ensured that *together* the atoms $\mathcal{A}$ with their SLD(NF)-trees form a *complete description* of all possible computations that can occur for all concrete instances $\leftarrow A\theta$ of the goal of interest.

Note that ECCE can also handle entire conjunctions of atoms [10] (instead of just single atoms), but this was not required for the experiments in this paper. By default, its control is also more refined in that it uses an extended $\trianglelefteq$ [27,22] and characteristic trees on top of syntactic structure to control abstraction [27].

4.3   Most Specific Version Abstract Interpretation

The task of the abstract interpretation phase will be to do the verification proper and try to infer whether the finite representation produced by the previous phase admits a solution. For this we will use an abstract interpretation method based on [30] which calculates so-called most specific versions of programs.

By $mgu^*(A, B)$ we denote a particular idempotent and relevant most general unifier of A and some B', obtained from B by renaming apart wrt A (i.e., so that B' and A have no variables in common). We also define the predicate-wise application msg^* of the msg: $msg^*(S) = \{msg(S_p) \mid p \in Pred(P)\}$, where S_p are all the atoms of S having p as predicate and $Pred(P)$ denotes the set of predicates occurring in the program P. In the following we define the well-known *non-ground* T_P operator (whose least fixed point gives the S-semantics [4]) along with an abstraction T_P^α of it.

Definition 4. *For a definite logic program P and a set of atoms $\mathcal{A}$ we define:* $T_P(\mathcal{A}) = \{H\theta_1 \dots \theta_n \mid H \leftarrow B_1, \dots, B_n \in P \wedge \theta_i = mgu^*(B_i\theta_1 \dots \theta_{i-1}, A_i)$ *with* $A_i \in \mathcal{A}\}$. *We also define* $T_P^\alpha(\mathcal{A}) = msg^*(T_P(\mathcal{A}))$.

One of the abstract interpretation methods of [30] can be seen as calculating $lfp(T_P^\alpha) = T_P^\alpha \uparrow^\infty (\emptyset)$ (this in turn can be seen as an abstract interpretation method which infers top level functors for every predicate). The idea is to initially proceed like T_P, but if we get two or more success patterns for the same predicate then we retain only one success pattern which covers them. $T_P^\alpha \uparrow^\infty (\emptyset)$ will always stabilise after a finite number of iterations and it will produce a safe approximation of the success set (i.e., any call which does not unify using mgu^* with an element of $T_P^\alpha \uparrow^\infty (\emptyset)$ will fail [finitely or infinitely]). In [30] more specific versions of clauses and programs are obtained in the following way (which preserves the least Herbrand model and the computed answers, but may replace infinite by finite failure):

Definition 5. *Let* $C = H \leftarrow B_1, \ldots, B_n$ *be a definite clause and* $\mathcal{A}$ *a set of atoms. We define:* $msv_{\mathcal{A}}(C) = \{C\theta_1 \ldots \theta_n \mid \theta_i = mgu^*(B_i\theta_1 \ldots \theta_{i-1}, A_i) \text{ with } A_i \in \mathcal{A}\}$. *The more specific version* $msv(P)$ *of a program* P *is then obtained by replacing every clause* $C \in P$ *by* $msv_{lfp(T_P^\alpha)}(C)$ *(note that* $msv_{lfp(T_P^\alpha)}(C)$ *contains at most 1 clause).*

Notably, the most specific version of a program without facts is the empty program! Also observe that the above described analysis works *backwards* (or bottom-up) from the facts to the query. It is thus an ideal complement to the forwards analysis that partial deduction performs. (Ideally one would like to perform the forwards and backwards analysis together [25]; generic algorithms for this exist [25,24] but they are not yet implemented.)

4.4 Putting It All Together

Let us now return to checking the earlier mentioned safety property $\neg\exists\Diamond(unsafe)$ of the Petri net of Fig. 3, meaning that it is *impossible* to reach a marking where two processes are in their critical section at the same time.

We have already compiled the formula $\exists\Diamond(unsafe)$ and our particular Petri net into the interpreter by LOGEN in Section 4.1.

Let us first attempt to prove that property for 2 processes. We thus apply ECCE to the compiled interpreter, specialising it for `sat__0([s(s(0)),0,s(0),0,0])` (i.e., an initial marking with 2 processes and 1 token in the semaphore). This yields the following specialised program (after a transformation time of 0.5 s):

```
sat__0([s(s(0)),0,s(0),0,0]) :- sat__0__1.
sat__0__1 :- sat_eu__1__2.
sat__0__1 :- sat_eu__1__3.
sat_eu__1__2 :- sat_eu__1__7(s(s(0)),s(0)).
sat_eu__1__2 :- sat_eu__1__3.
sat_eu__1__3 :- sat_eu__1__4.
sat_eu__1__4 :- sat_eu__1__5(s(s(0)),s(0)).
sat_eu__1__4 :- sat_eu__1__3.
sat_eu__1__5(A,s(B)) :- sat_eu__1__6(A,B).
sat_eu__1__5(s(A),B) :- sat_eu__1__5(A,s(B)).
sat_eu__1__6(A,B) :- sat_eu__1__5(s(A),B).
sat_eu__1__6(s(A),B) :- sat_eu__1__6(A,s(B)).
sat_eu__1__7(A,s(B)) :- sat_eu__1__8(A,B).
sat_eu__1__7(s(A),B) :- sat_eu__1__5(A,s(B)).
sat_eu__1__8(A,B) :- sat_eu__1__7(s(A),B).
sat_eu__1__8(s(A),B) :- sat_eu__1__8(A,s(B)).
```

As you can see ECCE always generates one clause (the first one, defining sat__0) which allows the specialised program to be used in the same way as the original one and then clauses for a renamed (two underscores and the number 1 are usually added to the predicate name) and filtered (only variables occuring in the query are left as arguments) version of the query (the clauses defining sat__0__1). As this program contains no facts, the most specific version transformation trivially produces:

```
sat__0([s(s(0)),0,s(0),0,0]) :- fail.
```

This establishes the safety property: $\exists\Diamond(unsafe)$ is false and there is no way that the system can reach a state where unsafe holds. As already mentioned, this task cannot be established by PROLOG or XSB-PROLOG [37] with tabling.

Similarly, one can prove the safety property *regardless* of the number of processes, i.e., for *any* number of tokens in the initial place (x). When we specialise the same compiled version of Fig. 2 for the query sat__0([X,0,s(0),0,0]) and then compute the most specific version we get the following (in similar transformation times):

```
sat__0([X,0,s(0),0,0]) :- fail.
```

There are now of course two important questions that arise:

1. How can we be sure that the above implies the safety property? In fact, if the safety property of the system in Fig. 3 is not satisfied, there must be a trace of finite length leading to an unsafe state. Hence, by completeness of SLD (and correctness of the CTL interpreter) we can deduce that there should have been a computed answer for the query: sat__0([X,0,s(0),0,0]). Now, as LOGEN, ECCE, and the most specific program technique all preserve (provided there are no bugs in the implementations of course) failure and the computed answers (cf. [29] and [30] respectively), and as the specialised program fails we can conclude that the safety property does hold.

Indeed, the specialised program produced by any of the 3 phases is totally correct: they do not remove any computed answer nor do they add any. So, in a sense there is no over-approximation or under-approximation! Approximations only come into play if we analyse the residual programs.

For instance, we can produce the following *safe over-approximation* of the success set: deduce that a call $p(\bar{t})$ fails if it unifies with no clause in the residual program (or just with a single clause $p(\bar{s}) \leftarrow fail$). For all other calls deduce that they potentially succeed. Similarly, we can extract a *safe under-approximation* of the success set: deduce that a call $p(\bar{t})$ succeeds if there is a fact $p(\bar{s}) \leftarrow$ in the residual program such that $p(\bar{t})$ is an instance of $p(\bar{s})$. Otherwise deduce that the call potentially fails.

2. How did the system achieve this (automatically) ? In essence, the *specialisation component* (ECCE) performed a symbolic traversal of the infinite state space, thereby producing a finite representation of it, on which the analysis component performed the verification of the specification. More precisely, the following ingredients of our system seem to be relevant or even vital:

 – the homeomorphic embedding $\trianglelefteq$ ensures that we build a finite representation of the state space. At the same time $\trianglelefteq$ is sufficiently powerful [23] to minimise unnecessary abstraction, increasing the chances of successful verification.

- characteristic trees ensure that we produce enough polyvariance to account for different behaviour of configurations. It further minimises the risk of unnecessary, harmful abstraction (cf. [27]).
- abstract interpretation performs the model checking proper on the finite representation obtained above.
- the abstract interpretation works backwards (from unsafe states towards initial states) while the partial deduction works forwards (from initial states to unsafe states). Our technique thus gives a combined backwards/forwards analysis (which should become even better by implementing the full integration of [25,24]).

4.5   Tackling the Manufacturing Petri Net Example

We applied the approach to the manufacturing system in subsection 3.2 and were able to prove absence of deadlocks for parameter values of e.g., 1,2,3. When leaving the parameter unspecified, the system did not establish an absence of deadlocks and produced a (large) residual program containing facts. And indeed, for parameter values ≥ 9 the system can actually deadlock. We are investigating whether a counter example can effectively be extracted from this residual program. The runtimes of our system compare favourably with HyTech [3].

5   Coping with More Complicated Formalisms

In principle, it is possible to extend our approach to verify larger, more complicated infinite systems. (Notice that larger systems have been approached with related techniques as a preprocessing phase [16]. However, their purpose is to reduce the state space rather than provide novel ways of reasoning.) As with all automatic specialisation tools, there are several points that need to be addressed: allow more generous unfolding and polyvariance (efficiency, both of the specialisation process and the specialised program, are less of an issue in model checking) to enable more precise residual programs and implement the full algorithm of [24] which allows for more fine grained abstraction and use BDD-like representations whenever possible. We elaborate on some of these issues below.

Also, in theory, we can apply the power of our approach, to systems specified in other formalisms such as the π-calculus (cf. the experiment in [15]) or processes with synchronisations, simply by writing an interpreter for these formalisms in logic programming.

Looking at the producer/consumer example presented in 3.3, we use the same interpreter for Petri nets as in Fig. 3 but for more complex states. An error occurs in the system of Subsection 3.3 when the next item consumed does not correspond to the one expected. To encode this as well as the possible initial states of our system, we add:

```
prop([err,err,err,err,err,err,err],unsafe).
err(A) :- sat([A,prod,1,0,vide,cons,A],ef(p(unsafe))).
```

Again, our 3-phased approach has achieved infinite model checking and has inferred err(A) :- fail., i.e. for *any* list of items, the safety property is verified.

However, things are not always that easy and problems do appear with more complicated systems.

Example 1. The following is a slightly more involved version of the produce-consume example from [1]. It still uses a buffer of length 1, but uses arithmetic operations to test whether the buffer contains any item to consume. Here, In (resp. Out) stands for the number of items which have been put in (resp. removed) from the buffer. (In the full version of [1], we have tests of the form $In < Out + N$, where N is the size of the buffer.)

```
trans(prod, [N,[X|T],prod,In,Out,Buf,CR,B], [N,T,add(X),In,Out,Buf,CR,B]).
trans(add,  [N,A,add(X),In,Out,Buf,CR,B],
            [N,A,prod,In1,Out,X,CR,B]) :- In < Out+1, In1 is In+1.
trans(rem,  [N,A,PA,In,Out,Buf,cons,B],
            [N,A,PA,In,Out1,Buf,rem(Buf),B]) :- In>Out, Out1 is Out+1.
trans(cons, [N,A,P,In,Out,Buf,rem(Buf),[Buf|B]],[N,A,P,In,Out,Buf,cons,B]).
trans(err , [N,A,PA,In,Out,Buf,rem(Buf),[B2|B]],
            [N,err,err,err,err,err,err]) :- Buf\==B2.
```

This example cannot be successfully verified by our current approach, due to its inability to detect simple inconsistencies. For example, neither ECCE nor the technique of [30] will detect that the conjunction X < 1, X > 1 cannot succeed. It should be possible to remedy this deficiency by adding CLP-techniques to ECCE and/or going to more sophisticated abstract domains as outlined in [24]. Similar extensions will probably be needed to handle real time systems [3,17].

Other problems do appear when we move to formalisms where the state representation gets more complex. For example, whereas for Petri nets a state was just a sequence of natural numbers, in CCS a state is an (arbitrarily complex) expression. As the following example shows, this leads to other difficulties.

Example 2. Take the following simple CCS specification of an agent P (where "a" and "$\bar{a}$" are complementary actions, "." denotes the action prefix, and "$|$" the parallel composition):

$P =_{Def} a.P|\bar{a}.P$

The transitional semantics of CCS tells us that the agent P can perform the action a and $\bar{a}$ respectively thanks to its left and right branch. Moreover, P can perform the invisible action τ (via the synchronization of a and $\bar{a}$) leading to a new expression $P|P$ which in turn can perform τ leading to $(P|P)|P$ (or $P|(P|P)$). One possible way to encode this system for use by our CTL interpreter is as follows:

```
trans(A,prefix(A,X),X).
trans(A,par(X,Y),par(X1,Y)) :- trans(A,X,X1).
```

```
trans(A,par(X,Y),par(X,Y1)) :- trans(A,Y,Y1).
trans(tau,par(X,Y),par(X1,Y1)) :- trans(A,X,X1),trans(bar(A),Y,Y1).
trans(A,agent(X),X1) :- agent(X,XDef),trans(A,XDef,X1).
agent(p, par( prefix(a,agent(p)), prefix(bar(a),agent(p))) ).
```

Having encoded the system, we may wonder whether we can use our approach to prove a very simple safety property: that in no reachable state we can perform an action b (this is indeed an infinite model checking task: the model checker FDR for CSP loops when given such a task). Unfortunately, the present system is incapable of doing so. The problem now is that, as explained above, the state agent(p) can lead to the state par(agent(p),agent(p)) (more precisely the call sat__0(agent(p)) can lead to sat__0(par(agent(p),agent(p)))). This means that when unfolding the interpreter, ECCE which will detect (and rightly so) a possible infinite sequence as agent(p) $\trianglelefteq$ par(agent(p),agent(p)). The only problem then is that it will compute the most specific generalisation of { agent(p) , par(agent(p),agent(p)) } which is a fresh variable X. In other words our approach loses all the information on the system and we cannot prove the safety property (as the unconstrained variable X can of course also represent prefix(b,X) which *can* perform the action b). So, while the $\trianglelefteq$ relation is quite refined, the most specific generalisation is rather crude and does not take the actual growth information into account. One solution is to generate (regular) types based upon homeomorphic embedding, as outlined in [24]. For this example we would need to generate something like the following type σ for the generalisation: $\sigma = $ agent(P) | par(σ,σ) .

6   Going Towards Full CTL

Let us now examine how we have to adapt our approach to handle more complicated CTL formulae.

Example 3. We can actually prove, using the current tools, the absence of deadlocks ($\forall\Box(\exists\bigcirc true)$) for our Petri net example from Sections 3.1 and 4.4. For this we first apply the LOGEN pre-compilation phase for the formula $\forall\Box(\exists\bigcirc true)$ (i.e., specialising the CTL interpreter for the query sat(X,ag(en(true)))):

```
sat__0(B) :- not((B = C, sat__1(C))).
sat__1(B) :- sat_eu__2(B).
sat_eu__2(B) :- not(( B = C,sat__3(C))).
sat_eu__2([s(D),s(E),F,G,H]) :- sat_eu__2([D,E,s(F),G,H]).
sat_eu__2([I,J,s(K),L,M]) :- sat_eu__2([I,s(J),K,s(L),M]).
sat_eu__2([N,O,P,s(Q),R]) :- sat_eu__2([s(N),O,P,Q,s(R)]).
sat__3([s(B),s(C),D,E,F]).
sat__3([G,H,s(I),J,K]).
sat__3([L,M,N,s(O),P]).
```

Observe that this program now contains negations and that both the ECCE system and the technique of [30] only provide a safe but rather crude treatment of negation (we will actually extend [30] slightly below).

Applying the ECCE partial deduction for the initial marking $\langle 1, 1, 0, 0, 0 \rangle$ (i.e., specialising sat__0([s(0),s(0),0,0,0])) now gives:

```
sat__0([s(0),s(0),0,0,0]) :- not(sat__1__2).
sat__0__1 :- not(sat__1__2).
sat__1__2 :- not(sat__3__3).        sat_eu__2__6 :- not(sat__3__7).
sat__1__2 :- sat_eu__2__4.          sat_eu__2__6 :- sat_eu__2__8.
sat__3__3.                          sat__3__7.
sat_eu__2__4 :- not(sat__3__5).     sat_eu__2__8 :- not(sat__3__9).
sat_eu__2__4 :- sat_eu__2__6.       sat_eu__2__8 :- sat_eu__2__4.
sat__3__5.                          sat__3__9.
```

Let us now compute the most specific version of this residual program. In order for the example to go through we actually have to extend [30] by adding a rudimentary treatment of negation by extracting, as explained in Section 4.4, a safe under-approximation of the success set from the residual program and using it to obtain a safe over-approximation of negated calls: we will (correctly) assume that $not(p(\bar{t})\theta)$ fails if there is a fact $p(\bar{t}) \leftarrow$ in the program. Otherwise, we assume that a negated call potentially succeeds. We then obtain:

```
sat__0([s(0),s(0),0,0,0]) :- not(sat__1__2).
sat__0__1 :- not(sat__1__2).
sat__1__2 :- fail.                  sat_eu__2__6 :- fail.
sat__3__3.                          sat__3__7.
sat_eu__2__4 :- fail.               sat_eu__2__8 :- fail.
sat__3__5.                          sat__3__9.
```

This already contains the information that our system satisfies the CTL formula, but re-applying ECCE once more makes this fully explicit:

```
sat__0([s(0),s(0),0,0,0]).
```

Similarly, we can try to prove the absence of deadlocks for *any* number of processes ≥ 1. For this we specialised for sat__0([s(A),s(0),0,0,0]) using ECCE 3 times (using a more agressive unfolding rule) interleaved with two (extended) most specific version computations, thereby obtaining:

```
sat__0([s(A),s(0),0,0,0]).
```

If we try to prove that absence of deadlocks holds for any number of processes even 0, by specialising the call sat__0([A,s(0),0,0,0]), we obtain after 4 iterations:

```
sat__0([A,s(0),0,0,0]) :- not(sat__1__2__2__2__2(A)).
sat__0__1(A) :- not(sat__1__2__2__2__2(A)).
sat__1__2__2__2__2(A) :- not(sat__3__5__4__3__3(A)).
sat__3__5__4__3__3(s(A)).
```

I.e. sat__1__2__2__2__2(A) is true for $A = 0$ and thus sat__0([A,s(0),0,0,0]) is false for $A = 0$ and we have identified the counter-example. We have also re-proven that for any value > 0 the property holds.

One can notice that, as the systems and properties get more complex, more and more iterations of ECCE and most specific version computations are required. For more complicated examples we will probably reach the limit of an approach working by *separate* phases and we will need the *fully integrated* techniques of [25,24] (there are certain properties which can only be proven by a fully integrated approach, see [25]). Also, for more complicated CTL-formulae, the above treatment of negation will be too rudimentary and we will need more refined under-approximations of the success set. Something along the lines of constructive negation, allowing to extract partial answers from a negated call, might also prove to be essential. All of this is subject of ongoing research.

7   Conclusion, Assessment, and Future Work

We have shown the usefulness of logic programming techniques for model checking. We have presented a complete interpreter for CTL formulae, implemented as a pure logic program (e.g., without the `tfindall` used in [35,28]) and we have shown it to be correct (under the SLS/well-founded semantics), even for infinite state systems. We have shown how this interpreter can be used for finite state model checking using tabling-based execution. We also have presented a particular technique for infinite state model checking of safety properties, using existing techniques for partial deduction and abstract interpretation, as implemented in the ECCE system. The idea was to reduce the interpreter, searching for unsafe states, to the empty program. We discussed how this approach has to be extended to handle more complicated infinite state systems and to handle arbitrary CTL formulae. We presented some succesfull examples but argue that more refined treatment of negation and more refined abstract domains will be required for the method to scale up to such systems and properties.

Of course, an important aspect of model checking of finite state systems is the complexity of the underlying algorithms. We have not touched upon this issue in the present paper, but plan to do so in future work. In future work, we will also strive to identify classes of problems and infinite state systems which can be precisely solved by our approach. First promising results, for coverability problems of unbounded Petri nets, have been obtained.

Another important issue arises when our model checking approach is incapable of establishing the desired property. In that case, one would like to assist the user by extracting a counter example from the residual program (if possible; due to the undecidability of most problems for infinite state systems we actually cannot be sure whether such a counter example exists). A naive solution is to run the residual program using some sophisticated computation mechanisms such as tabling, breadth-first, or iterative deepening.

References

1. K. Apt and E. Olderog. *Verification of Sequential and Concurrent Programs.* Springer-Verlag, 1991.

2. S. Bensalem, Y. Lakhnech, and S. Owre. Computing abstractions of infinite state systems compositionally and automatically. In *Proceedings of CAV'98*, LNCS, pages 319–331. Springer-Verlag, 1998.

3. B. Bérard and L. Fribourg. Reachability analysis of (timed) Petri nets using real arithmetic. In *Proceedings of Concur'99*, LNCS 1664, pages 178–193. Springer-Verlag, 1999. Extended version as Research Report LSV-99-3, Lab. Specification and Verification, ENS de Cachan, Cachan, France, Mar. 1999.

4. A. Bossi, M. Gabrielli, G. Levi, and M. Martelli. The s-semantics approach: Theory and applications. *The Journal of Logic Programming*, 19 & 20:149–198, May 1994.

5. R. Bryant. Symbolic boolean manipulation with ordered binary-decision diagrams. *ACM Computing Surveys*, 24(3):293–318, September 1992.

6. O. Burkart and J. Ezparza. More infinite results. In *Proceedings of Infinity'96*, 1996. Research Report MIP-9614, University of Passau.

7. W. Charatonik and A. Podelski. Set-based analysis of reactive infinite-state systems. In B. Steffen, editor, *Tools and Algorithms for the Construction and Analysis of Systems*, LNCS 1384, pages 358–375. Springer-Verlag, March 1998.

8. E. M. Clarke, E. A. Emerson, and A. P. Sistla. Automatic verification of finite-state concurrent systems using temporal logic specifications. *ACM Transactions on Programming Languages and Systems*, 8(2):244–263, 1986.

9. E. M. Clarke and J. M. Wing. Formal methods: State of the art and future directions. *ACM Computing Surveys*, 28(4):626–643, Dec. 1996.

10. D. De Schreye, R. Glück, J. Jørgensen, M. Leuschel, B. Martens, and M. H. Sørensen. Conjunctive partial deduction: Foundations, control, algorithms and experiments. *The Journal of Logic Programming*, 41(2 & 3):231–277, 1999.

11. E.M. Clarke and E.A. Emerson. Design and Synthesis of Synchronization Skeletons using Branching Time Temporal Logic. In D. Kozen, editor, *Proceedings of the Workshop on Logics of Programs*, LNCS 131, pages 52–71, Yorktown Heights, New York, May 1981. Springer-Verlag.

12. J. Ezparza. Decidability of model-checking for infinite-state concurrent systems. *Acta Informatica*, 34:85–107, 1997.

13. J. Gallagher and M. Bruynooghe. The derivation of an algorithm for program specialisation. *New Generation Computing*, 9(3 & 4):305–333, 1991.

14. R. Glück and M. Leuschel. Abstraction-based partial deduction for solving inverse problems – a transformational approach to software verification. In *Proceedings of PSI'99*, LNCS 1755, pages 93–100, Novosibirsk, Russia, 1999. Springer-Verlag.

15. P. Hartel, M. Butler, A. Currie, P. Henderson, M. Leuschel, A. Martin, A. Smith, U. Ultes-Nitsche, and B. Walters. Questions and Answers About Ten Formal Methods. Proceedings of FMICS'99, Trento, Italy, 1999.

16. J. Hatcliff, M. Dwyer, and S. Laubach. Staging analysis using abstraction-based program specialization. In C. Palamidessi, H. Glaser, and K. Meinke, editors, *Proceedings of ALP/PLILP'98*, LNCS 1490, pages 134–151. Springer-Verlag, 1998.

17. T. A. Henzinger and P.-H. Ho. HYTECH: The Cornell HYbrid TECHnology tool. *LNCS*, 999:265–293, 1995.

18. G. Higman. Ordering by divisibility in abstract algebras. *Proceedings of the London Mathematical Society*, 2:326–336, 1952.

19. J. Jørgensen and M. Leuschel. Efficiently generating efficient generating extensions in Prolog. In O. Danvy, R. Glück, and P. Thiemann, editors, *Proceedings of the 1996 Dagstuhl Seminar on Partial Evaluation*, LNCS 1110, pages 238–262, Schloß Dagstuhl, 1996. Springer-Verlag.

20. J. B. Kruskal. Well-quasi ordering, the tree theorem, and Vazsonyi's conjecture. *Transactions of the American Mathematical Society*, 95:210–225, 1960.

21. J.-L. Lassez, M. Maher, and K. Marriott. Unification revisited. In J. Minker, editor, *Foundations of Deductive Databases and Logic Programming*, pages 587–625. Morgan-Kaufmann, 1988.

22. M. Leuschel. Improving homeomorphic embedding for online termination. In P. Flener, editor, *Proceedings of LOPSTR'98*, LNCS 1559, pages 199–218, Manchester, UK, June 1998. Springer-Verlag.

23. M. Leuschel. On the power of homeomorphic embedding for online termination. In G. Levi, editor, Static Analysis. *Proceedings of SAS'98*, LNCS 1503, pages 230–245, Pisa, Italy, September 1998. Springer-Verlag.

24. M. Leuschel. Program specialisation and abstract interpretation reconciled. In J. Jaffar, editor, *Proceedings of JICSLP'98*, pages 220–234, Manchester, UK, June 1998. MIT Press.

25. M. Leuschel and D. De Schreye. Logic program specialisation: How to be more specific. In H. Kuchen and S. Swierstra, editors, *Proceedings of PLILP'96*, LNCS 1140, pages 137–151, Aachen, Germany, September 1996. Springer-Verlag.

26. M. Leuschel and J. Jørgensen. Efficient specialisation in Prolog using a handwritten compiler generator. Technical Report DSSE-TR-99-6, Department of Electronics and Computer Science, University of Southampton, September 1999.

27. M. Leuschel, B. Martens, and D. De Schreye. Controlling generalisation and polyvariance in partial deduction of normal logic programs. *ACM Transactions on Programming Languages and Systems*, 20(1):208–258, January 1998.

28. X. Liu, C. R. Ramakrishnan, and S. A. Smolka. Fully local and efficient evaluation of alternating fixed points. In B. Steffen, editor, *Proceedings of TACAS'98*, LNCS 1384, pages 5–19. Springer-Verlag, 1998.

29. J. W. Lloyd and J. C. Shepherdson. Partial evaluation in logic programming. *The Journal of Logic Programming*, 11(3& 4):217–242, 1991.

30. K. Marriott, L. Naish, and J.-L. Lassez. Most specific logic programs. *Annals of Mathematics and Artificial Intelligence*, 1:303–338, 1990.

31. K. L. McMillan. *Symbolic Model Checking*. PhD thesis, Boston, 1993.

32. F. Moller. Infinite results. In *Proceedings of CONCUR'96*, LNCS 1119, pages 195–216. Springer-Verlag, 1996.

33. U. Nitsche and P. Wolper. Relative liveness and behavior abstraction. In *Proceedings of PODC'97*, pages 45–52, Santa Barbara, California, 1997. ACM.

34. T. C. Przymusinksi. On the declarative and procedural semantics of logic programs. *Journal of Automated Reasoning*, 5(2):167–205, 1989.

35. Y. S. Ramakrishna, C. R. Ramakrishnan, I. V. Ramakrishnan, S. A. Smolka, T. Swift, and D. S. Warrend. Efficient model checking using tabled resolution. In *Proceedings of CAV'97*, LNCS. Springer-Verlag, 1997.

36. J. Rushby. Mechanized formal methods: Where next? In *Proceedings of FM'99*, LNCS 1708, pages 48–51, Toulouse, France, Sept. 1999. Springer-Verlag.

37. K. Sagonas, T. Swift, and D. S. Warren. XSB as an efficient deductive database engine. In *Proceedings of the ACM SIGMOD International Conference on the Management of Data*, pages 442–453, Minneapolis, Minnesota, May 1994. ACM.

38. M. H. Sørensen and R. Glück. An algorithm of generalization in positive supercompilation. In J. W. Lloyd, editor, *Proceedings of ILPS'95*, pages 465–479, Portland, USA, December 1995. MIT Press.

39. P. Wolper and B. Boigelot. Verifying systems with infinite but regular state spaces. *Proceedings of CAV'98*, LNCS 1427, pages 88–97. Springer-Verlag, 1998.

Mode Analysis Domains for Typed Logic Programs

Jan–Georg Smaus[1], Patricia M. Hill[2], and Andy King[3]

[1] INRIA-Rocquencourt, France,
jan.smaus@inria.fr
[2] University of Leeds, United Kingdom
hill@scs.leeds.ac.uk
[3] University of Kent at Canterbury, United Kingdom
a.m.king@ukc.ac.uk

Abstract. Precise mode information is important for compiler optimisations and in program development tools. Within the framework of abstract compilation, the precision of a mode analysis depends, in part, on the expressiveness of the abstract domain and its associated abstraction function. This paper considers abstract domains for polymorphically typed logic programs and shows how specialised domains may be constructed for each type in the program. These domains capture the degree of instantiation to a high level of precision. By providing a generic definition of abstract unification, the abstraction of a program using these domains is formalised. The domain construction procedure is fully implemented using the Gödel language and tested on a number of example programs to demonstrate the viability of the approach.

Note: Some proofs have been omitted for space reasons. They can be found in the full version of this paper [17].

1 Introduction

1.1 Background

Typed logic programming languages such as Mercury [19] and Gödel [10] use a *prescriptive* type system [15], which restricts the underlying syntax so that only meaningful expressions are allowed. This enables most typographical errors and inconsistencies in the knowledge representation to be detected at compile time. An increasing number of applications using typed languages are being developed.

Our notion of *modes* is, in contrast, a *descriptive* one [3,7]: Modes characterise the degree to which program variables are instantiated at certain program points. This information can be used to underpin optimisations such as the specialisation of unification and the removal of backtracking, and to support determinacy analysis [9]. When a mode analysis is formulated in terms of abstract interpretation, the program execution is traced using *descriptions* of data (the *abstract* domain) rather than *actual* data, and operations on these descriptions rather than operations on the actual data. The precision of a mode analysis depends, in part, on the expressiveness of the abstract domain.

A. Bossi (Ed.): LOPSTR'99, LNCS 1817, pp. 82–101, 2000.

1.2   Contribution

The main contribution of this paper is to describe a generic method of deriving precise abstract domains for mode analysis from the type declarations of a typed program. Each abstract domain is specialised for a particular type and characterises a set of possible modes for terms of that type. In particular it characterises the property of *termination*, well-known for lists as *nil*-termination.

The procedure for constructing such domains is implemented (in Gödel) for Gödel programs. By incorporating the constructed domains into a mode analyser, the viability of the approach is demonstrated.

The abstract domains are used in an *abstract compilation* [4] framework: A program is abstracted by replacing each unification with an abstract counterpart, and then the abstract program is evaluated by applying a standard operational semantics to it.

We believe that this work is the natural generalisation of [3,5] and takes the idea presented there to its limits: Our abstract domains provide the highest degree of precision that a generic domain construction should provide. Not only can this work be used directly for the mode analysis of typed logic programs, but it could be used as a basis for constructing (more pragmatic) domains as well as providing a unifying theory for other proposals.

The paper is organised as follows. Section 2 introduces three examples. Section 3 defines some syntax. Section 4 defines the concepts for terms and types that are used in the definition of abstract domains. Section 5 defines abstract domains and programs, and the relationship between concrete and abstract programs. Section 6 reports on experiments. Section 7 concludes.

2   Motivating and Illustrative Examples

We introduce three examples that we use throughout the paper. The syntax is that of the typed language Gödel [10], to avoid any confusion with the (untyped) language Prolog. Variables and (type) parameters begin with lower case letters; other alphabetic symbols begin with upper case letters. We use `Integer` (abbreviated as `Int`) to illustrate a type containing only constants $(1, 2, 3 \ldots)$.

Example 2.1. This is the usual list type. We give its declarations to illustrate the type description language of Gödel.

```
CONSTRUCTOR    List/1.
CONSTANT       Nil: List(u).
FUNCTION       Cons: u * List(u) -> List(u).
```

`List` is a (type) constructor; `u` is a type parameter; `Nil` is a constant of type `List(u)`; and `Cons` is the usual list constructor. We use the standard list notation $[\ldots | \ldots]$ where convenient. It is common to distinguish *nil-terminated* lists from *open* lists. For example, $[]$ and $[1, x, y]$ are nil-terminated, but $[1, 2|y]$ is open.

Previous approaches cannot deal with the following two examples [3,5,21].

Example 2.2. This example was invented to disprove a common point of criticism that "list flattening" cannot be realised in Gödel, that is terms such as [1, [2, 3]] cannot be defined, let alone flattened. The Nests module formalises nested lists by the type Nest(v). A trivial nest is constructed using function E, a complex nest by "nesting" a list of nests using function N. The declaration for N is remarkable in that the range type, Nest(v), is a proper sub"term" of the argument type List(Nest(v)).

```
IMPORT          Lists, Integers.
CONSTRUCTOR     Nest/1.
FUNCTION        E: v -> Nest(v);
                N: List(Nest(v)) -> Nest(v).
```

Example 2.3. A table is a data structure containing an ordered collection of nodes, each of which has two components, a key (of type String) and a value, of arbitrary type. We give part of the Tables module which is provided as a system module in Gödel.

```
IMPORT          Strings.
BASE            Balance.
CONSTRUCTOR     Table/1.
CONSTANT        Null: Table(u);
                LH, RH, EQ: Balance.
FUNCTION        Node: Table(u) * String * u * Balance * Table(u) -> Table(u).
```

Tables is implemented in Gödel as an AVL-tree [22]: A non-leaf node has a *key* argument, a *value* argument, arguments for the left and right subtrees, and an argument which represents balancing information.

3   Notation and Terminology

The set of polymorphic types is given by the term structure $T(\Sigma_\tau, U)$ where Σ_τ is a finite alphabet of **constructor** symbols which includes at least one **base** (constructor of arity 0), and U is a countably infinite set of **parameters** (type variables). We define the order $\prec$ on types as the order induced by some (for example lexicographical) order on constructor and parameter symbols, where parameter symbols come before constructor symbols. Parameters are denoted by u, v. A tuple of *distinct* parameters ordered with respect to $\prec$ is denoted by $\bar{u}$. Types are denoted by $\sigma, \rho, \tau, \phi, \omega$ and tuples of types by $\bar{\sigma}, \bar{\tau}$.

Let Σ_f be an alphabet of **function** (term constructor) symbols which includes at least one **constant** (function of arity 0) and let Σ_p be an alphabet of predicate symbols. Each symbol in Σ_f (resp. Σ_p) has its *type* as subscript. If $f_{\langle \tau_1 \dots \tau_n, \tau \rangle} \in \Sigma_f$ (resp. $p_{\langle \tau_1 \dots \tau_n \rangle} \in \Sigma_p$) then $\langle \tau_1, \dots, \tau_n \rangle \in T(\Sigma_\tau, U)^*$ and $\tau \in T(\Sigma_\tau, U) \setminus U$. If $f_{\langle \tau_1 \dots \tau_n, \tau \rangle} \in \Sigma_f$, then every parameter occurring in $\langle \tau_1, \dots, \tau_n \rangle$ must also occur in τ. This condition is called **transparency condition**. We call τ the **range type** of $f_{\langle \tau_1 \dots \tau_n, \tau \rangle}$ and $\{\tau_1 \dots \tau_n\}$ its **domain types**. A symbol is often written without its type if it is clear from the context. Terms and atoms are defined in the usual way [10,16]. In this terminology, if a term *has* a type σ, it also *has* every *instance* of σ.[1] If V is a countably infinite set of variables, then the triple $L = \langle \Sigma_p, \Sigma_f, V \rangle$ defines a **polymorphic many-sorted first order language** over $T(\Sigma_\tau, U)$. Variables are denoted by x, y; terms by t, r, s; tuples of *distinct* variables by $\bar{x}, \bar{y}$; and a tuple of terms by $\bar{t}$. The set of variables in a syntactic object o is denoted by $vars(o)$.

Programs are assumed to be in **normal form**. Thus a **literal** is an equation of the form $x =_{\langle u,u \rangle} y$ or $x =_{\langle u,u \rangle} f(\bar{y})$, where $f \in \Sigma_f$, or an atom $p(\bar{y})$, where $p \in \Sigma_p$. A **query** G is a conjunction of literals. A clause is a formula of the form $p(\bar{y}) \leftarrow G$. If S is a set of clauses, then the tuple $P = \langle L, S \rangle$ defines a **polymorphic many-sorted logic program**.

A **substitution** (denoted by Θ) is a mapping from variables to terms which is the identity almost everywhere. The **domain** of a substitution Θ is $dom(\Theta) = \{x \mid x\Theta \neq x\}$. The application of a substitution Θ to a term t is denoted as $t\Theta$. **Type substitutions** are defined analogously and denoted by Ψ.

4   The Structure of Terms and Types

An *abstract* term characterises the structure of a concrete term. It is clearly a crucial choice in the design of abstract domains *which* aspects of the concrete structure should be characterised [21,23]. In this paper we show how this choice can be based naturally on the information contained in the type subscripts of the function symbols in Σ_f. This information is formalised in this section. First we formalise the relationship between the range type of a function to its domain types. We then define *termination* of a term, as well as functions which extract certain subterms of a term. In the following, we assume a fixed polymorphic many-sorted first order language $L = \langle \Sigma_p, \Sigma_f, V \rangle$ over $T(\Sigma_\tau, U)$.

4.1   Relations between Types

Definition 4.1 (subterm type). A type σ is a **direct subterm type of** ϕ (denoted as $\sigma \lhd \phi$) if there is $f_{\langle \tau_1 \dots \tau_n, \tau \rangle} \in \Sigma_f$ and a type substitution Ψ such that $\tau\Psi = \phi$ and $\tau_i\Psi = \sigma$ for some $i \in \{1, \dots, n\}$. The transitive, reflexive closure of $\lhd$ is denoted as $\lhd^*$. If $\sigma \lhd^* \phi$, then σ is a **subterm type of** ϕ.

The relation $\lhd$ can be visualised as a *type graph* (similarly defined in [18,23]). The type graph for a type ϕ is a directed graph whose nodes are subterm types of ϕ. The node ϕ is called the *initial node*. There is an edge from σ_1 to σ_2 if and only if $\sigma_2 \lhd \sigma_1$.

Example 4.1. Figure 1 shows a type graph for each example in Sect. 2. The left hand type graph illustrates Ex. 2.1 where $u \lhd \text{List}(u)$ and $\text{List}(u) \lhd \text{List}(u)$. The other two type graphs illustrate Exs. 2.2 and 2.3, respectively.

---

[1]   For example, the term Nil has type List(u), List(Int), List(Nest(Int)) etc.

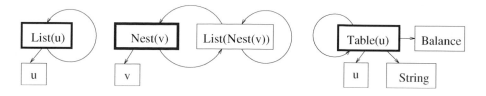

Fig. 1. Some type graphs, with initial node highlighted

A **simple type** is a type of the form $C(\bar{u})$, where $C \in \Sigma_\tau$. We impose the following two restrictions on the language.

Simple Range Condition: For all $f_{\langle \tau_1 \ldots \tau_n, \tau \rangle} \in \Sigma_f$, τ is a simple type.

Reflexive Condition: For all $C \in \Sigma_\tau$ and types $\sigma = C(\bar{\sigma}), \tau = C(\bar{\tau})$, if $\sigma \lhd^* \tau$, then σ is a sub"term" (in the syntactic sense) of τ.

The Simple Range Condition allows for the construction of an abstract domain for a type such as $\texttt{List}(\sigma)$ to be described independently of the type σ. In Mercury (and also in typed *functional* languages such as ML or Haskell), this condition is enforced by the syntax [19]. Being able to violate this condition can be regarded as an artefact of the Gödel syntax.

The Reflexive Condition ensures that, for a program and a given query, there are only finitely many types and hence, the abstract program has only finitely many abstract domains and the type graphs are always finite. It rules out, for example, a function symbol of the form $f_{\langle List(Int), List(u) \rangle}$ since this would imply that $\texttt{List}(\texttt{Int}) \lhd^* \texttt{List}(\texttt{u})$. We do not know of any real programs that violate the Reflexive Condition or the Simple Range Condition.

Definition 4.2 (recursive type and non-recursive subterm type). A type σ is a **recursive type** of ϕ (denoted as $\sigma \bowtie \phi$) if $\sigma \lhd^* \phi$ and $\phi \lhd^* \sigma$.

A type σ is a **non-recursive subterm type (NRS)** of ϕ if $\phi \ntrianglelefteq^* \sigma$ and there is a type τ such that $\sigma \lhd \tau$ and $\tau \bowtie \phi$. We write $\mathcal{N}(\phi) = \{\sigma \mid \sigma \text{ is an NRS of } \phi\}$. If $\mathcal{N}(\phi) = \{\sigma_1, \ldots, \sigma_m\}$ and $\sigma_j \prec \sigma_{j+1}$ for all $j \in \{1, \ldots, m-1\}$, we abuse notation and denote the *tuple* $\langle \sigma_1, \ldots, \sigma_m \rangle$ by $\mathcal{N}(\phi)$ as well.

It follows immediately from the definition that, for any types ϕ, σ, we have $\phi \bowtie \phi$ and, if $\sigma \in \mathcal{N}(\phi)$, then $\sigma \not\bowtie \phi$. Consider the type graph for ϕ. The recursive types of ϕ are all the types in the strongly connected component (SCC) containing ϕ. The non-recursive subterm types of ϕ are all the types σ not in the SCC but such that there is an edge from the SCC containing ϕ to σ.

Example 4.2. Consider again Ex. 4.1 and Fig. 1. Then $\texttt{List}(\texttt{u}) \bowtie \texttt{List}(\texttt{u})$, and this is non-trivial in that, in the type graph for $\texttt{List}(\texttt{u})$, there is an edge from $\texttt{List}(\texttt{u})$ to itself. Furthermore $\texttt{List}(\texttt{Nest}(\texttt{v})) \bowtie \texttt{Nest}(\texttt{v})$. Non-recursive subterm types of simple types are often parameters, as in $\mathcal{N}(\texttt{List}(\texttt{u})) = \langle \texttt{u} \rangle$ and

$\mathcal{N}(\texttt{Nest(v)}) = \langle \texttt{v} \rangle$. However, this is not always the case, since $\mathcal{N}(\texttt{Table(u)}) = \langle \texttt{u}, \texttt{Balance}, \texttt{String} \rangle$.

The following simple lemma is used in the proof of Lemma 4.2.

Lemma 4.1. Let ϕ, τ, σ be types so that $\sigma \lhd^* \tau \lhd^* \phi$ and $\sigma \bowtie \phi$. Then $\tau \bowtie \phi$.

Proof. Since $\sigma \bowtie \phi$, it follows that $\phi \lhd^* \sigma$. Thus, since $\sigma \lhd^* \tau$, it follows that $\phi \lhd^* \tau$. Furthermore $\tau \lhd^* \phi$, and therefore $\tau \bowtie \phi$. □

4.2 Traversing Concrete Terms

From now on, we shall often annotate a term t with a type ϕ by writing t^ϕ. The use of this notation *always* implies that the type of t must be an *instance* of ϕ. The annotation ϕ gives the (type) context in which t is used. If S is a set of terms, then S^ϕ denotes the set of terms in S, each annotated with ϕ.

Definition 4.3 (subterm). Let t^ϕ be a term where $t = f_{\langle \tau_1 \ldots \tau_n, \tau \rangle}(t_1, \ldots, t_n)$ and $\phi = \tau \Psi$. Then $t_i^{\tau_i \Psi}$ is a **subterm** of t^ϕ (denoted as $t_i^{\tau_i \Psi} \lhd t^\phi$) for each $i \in \{1, \ldots, n\}$. As in Def. 4.1, the transitive, reflexive closure of $\lhd$ is denoted by $\lhd^*$.

It can be seen that $s^\sigma \lhd^* t^\phi$ implies $\sigma \lhd^* \phi$. When the superscripts are ignored, the above is the usual definition of a subterm. The superscripts provide a uniform way of describing the "polymorphic type relationship" between a term and its subterms, which is independent of further instantiation.

Example 4.3. $\texttt{x}^\texttt{v}$ is a subterm of $\texttt{E(x)}^{\texttt{Nest(v)}}$, and $7^\texttt{v}$ is a subterm of $\texttt{E(7)}^{\texttt{Nest(v)}}$.

Definition 4.4 (recursive subterm). Let s^σ and t^τ be terms such that $s^\sigma \lhd^* t^\tau$, and ϕ a type such that $\sigma \bowtie \phi$ and $\tau \lhd^* \phi$. Then s^σ is a ϕ-**recursive subterm** of t^τ. If furthermore $\tau = \phi$, then s^σ is a **recursive subterm** of t^τ.

In particular, for every type ϕ, a variable is always a ϕ-recursive subterm of itself. The correspondence between subterms and subterm types can be illustrated by drawing the term as tree that resembles the corresponding type graph.

Example 4.4.
The term tree for $t = \texttt{N([E(7)])}^{\texttt{Nest(v)}}$ is given in Fig. 2 where the node for t is highlighted. Each box drawn with solid lines stands for a subterm. We can map this tree onto the type graph for $\texttt{Nest(v)}$ in Fig. 1 by replacing the sub-

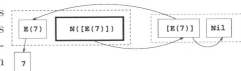

Fig. 2: Term tree for $\texttt{N([E(7)])}^{\texttt{Nest(v)}}$

graphs enclosed with dotted lines with corresponding nodes in the type graph. Thus the recursive subterms of t occur in the boxes corresponding to nodes in the SCC of $\texttt{Nest(v)}$. All subterms of t except $7^\texttt{v}$ are recursive subterms of t.

Note that $\mathrm{E}(7)^{\mathrm{Nest}(\mathrm{v})}$ is a $\mathrm{Nest}(\mathrm{v})$-recursive subterm of $[\mathrm{E}(7)]^{\mathrm{List}(\mathrm{Nest}(\mathrm{v}))}$ (in Def. 4.4, take $\sigma = \phi = \mathrm{Nest}(\mathrm{v})$ and $\tau = \mathrm{List}(\mathrm{Nest}(\mathrm{v}))$). However, $\mathrm{E}(7)^{\mathrm{u}}$ is not a recursive subterm of $[\mathrm{E}(7)]^{\mathrm{List}(\mathrm{u})}$. Thus whether or not a member of a list should be regarded as a recursive subterm of that list depends on the context.

We now define *termination* of a term. For a term t^ϕ, where ϕ is simple, termination means that no recursive subterm of t^ϕ is a variable.

Definition 4.5 (termination function $\mathcal{Z}$). Let t^τ be a term and ϕ be a type such that $\tau \bowtie \phi$. Define $\mathcal{Z}(t^\tau, \phi) = false$ if a ϕ-recursive subterm of t^τ is a variable, and *true* otherwise. For a set S^τ of terms define $\mathcal{Z}(S^\tau, \phi) = \bigwedge_{t \in S} \mathcal{Z}(t^\tau, \phi)$. We omit τ in the expression $\mathcal{Z}(t^\tau, \phi)$ whenever $\phi = \tau$. We say that t is **terminated** if τ is simple and $\mathcal{Z}(t, \tau) = true$, and t is **open** if it is not terminated.

Example 4.5. Any variable x is open. The term 7 has no variable subterm, so $\mathcal{Z}(7, \mathrm{Int}) = true$ and 7 is terminated. The term $[\mathrm{x}]^{\mathrm{List}(\mathrm{u})}$ has itself and $\mathrm{Nil}^{\mathrm{List}(\mathrm{u})}$ as recursive subterms, so $\mathcal{Z}([\mathrm{x}], \mathrm{List}(\mathrm{u})) = true$ and $[\mathrm{x}]$ is terminated. However, $[\mathrm{x}]^{\mathrm{List}(\mathrm{Nest}(\mathrm{v}))}$ has $\mathrm{x}^{\mathrm{Nest}(\mathrm{v})}$ as a $\mathrm{Nest}(\mathrm{v})$-recursive subterm, so $\mathcal{Z}([\mathrm{x}]^{\mathrm{List}(\mathrm{Nest}(\mathrm{v}))}, \mathrm{Nest}(\mathrm{v})) = false$. Furthermore, $\mathrm{N}([\mathrm{x}])^{\mathrm{Nest}(\mathrm{v})}$ has $\mathrm{x}^{\mathrm{Nest}(\mathrm{v})}$ as a recursive subterm, so $\mathcal{Z}(\mathrm{N}([\mathrm{x}]), \mathrm{Nest}(\mathrm{v})) = false$ and $\mathrm{N}([\mathrm{x}])$ is open.

The abstract domain should also characterise the instantiation of subterms of a term. We define functions which extract sets of subterms from a term.

Definition 4.6 (extractor $\mathcal{E}^\sigma$ for σ). Let t^τ be a term and ϕ, σ be types such that $\tau \bowtie \phi$ and $\sigma \in \mathcal{N}(\phi)$. Let R be the set of ϕ-recursive subterms of t^τ. Define

$$\mathcal{E}^\sigma(t^\tau, \phi) = vars(R) \cup \{s \mid r^\rho \in R \text{ and } s^\sigma \lhd r^\rho\}.$$

For a set S^τ of terms define $\mathcal{E}^\sigma(S^\tau, \phi) = \bigcup_{t \in S} \mathcal{E}^\sigma(t^\tau, \phi)$. As with $\mathcal{Z}$, we write $\mathcal{E}^\sigma(t^\tau, \tau)$ simply as $\mathcal{E}^\sigma(t, \tau)$.

Example 4.6. For $\mathrm{N}([\mathrm{E}(7)])$ of type $\mathrm{Nest}(\mathrm{Int})$, we have $\mathcal{E}^{\mathrm{v}}(\mathrm{N}([\mathrm{E}(7)]), \mathrm{Nest}(\mathrm{v})) = \{7\}$. The type $\mathrm{Table}(\mathrm{u})$ has three non-recursive subterm types u, $\mathrm{Balance}$ and String, and so there are three extractor functions: $\mathcal{E}^{\mathrm{u}}$, which extracts all value subterms; $\mathcal{E}^{\mathrm{Balance}}$, which extracts the argument containing balancing information; and $\mathcal{E}^{\mathrm{String}}$, which extracts all key subterms. Note that for a term t of type $\mathrm{Table}(\mathrm{String})$, both $\mathcal{E}^{\mathrm{String}}(t)$ and $\mathcal{E}^{\mathrm{u}}(t)$ would contain terms of type String.

Note that a priori, the extracted terms have no type annotation. This is because, in the proofs, we sometimes need to write an expression such as $\mathcal{E}^\sigma(\mathcal{E}^\rho(t, \tau)^{\rho\Psi}, \phi)$, which reads: first compute $\mathcal{E}^\rho(t, \tau)$, then annotate it with $\rho\Psi$, then pass it to $\mathcal{E}^\sigma$.

Note also that if t has a ϕ-recursive subterm which is a variable, then this variable is always extracted. Intuitively this is because this variable might later be instantiated to a term which has variable subterms of type σ. Thus the property "$\mathcal{E}^\sigma(t,\tau)$ does not contain variables" is closed under instantiation.

The following theorem shows that $\mathcal{Z}$ and $\mathcal{E}^\sigma$ can be expressed in terms of the immediate subterms of a term. This provides the basis for defining the abstraction of a (normal form) equation in a concrete program, which naturally involves a term and its immediate subterms.

Theorem 4.2. Let $t = f_{\langle \tau_1 \ldots \tau_n, \tau \rangle}(t_1, \ldots, t_n)$ be a term and $\sigma \in \mathcal{N}(\tau)$. Then

$$\mathcal{Z}(t,\tau) = \bigwedge_{\tau_i \bowtie \tau} \mathcal{Z}(t_i^{\tau_i}, \tau)$$

$$\mathcal{E}^\sigma(t,\tau) = \{t_i \mid \tau_i = \sigma\} \cup \bigcup_{\tau_i \bowtie \tau} \mathcal{E}^\sigma(t_i^{\tau_i}, \tau).$$

Proof. If for some $i \in \{1, \ldots, n\}$ where $\tau_i \bowtie \tau$, r^ρ is a τ-recursive subterm of $t_i^{\tau_i}$, then $\rho \bowtie \tau$ and $r^\rho \lhd^* t^\tau$. Thus r^ρ is a τ-recursive subterm of t^τ.

If r^ρ is a τ-recursive subterm of t^τ, then either $r^\rho = t^\tau$ or, for some $i \in \{1, \ldots, n\}$, $r^\rho \lhd^* t_i^{\tau_i}$. In the latter case, $\rho \lhd^* \tau_i$, $\tau_i \lhd \tau$ and $\rho \bowtie \tau$. Hence, by Lemma 4.1, $\tau_i \bowtie \tau$ so that r^ρ is a τ-recursive subterm of $t_i^{\tau_i}$.

Thus the τ-recursive subterms of t are t, together with the τ-recursive subterms of $t_i^{\tau_i}$, where $\tau_i \bowtie \tau$. The result then follows from Defs. 4.5 and 4.6.   □

Consider simple types ϕ, τ such that $\tau\Psi \bowtie \phi$ for some type substitution Ψ (for example $\phi = \mathtt{Nest(v)}$, $\tau = \mathtt{List(u)}$ and and $\Psi = \{\mathtt{u/Nest(v)}\}$). The following theorem relates ϕ with τ with respect to the termination and extractor functions.

Theorem 4.3 (Proof see [17]). Let ϕ and τ be simple types such that $\tau\Psi \bowtie \phi$ for some Ψ, let t be a term having a type which is an instance of $\tau\Psi$, and $\sigma \in \mathcal{N}(\phi)$. Then

$$\mathcal{Z}(t^{\tau\Psi}, \phi) = \mathcal{Z}(t,\tau) \wedge \bigwedge_{\substack{\rho \in \mathcal{N}(\tau) \\ \rho\Psi \bowtie \phi}} \mathcal{Z}(\mathcal{E}^\rho(t,\tau)^{\rho\Psi}, \phi) \tag{1}$$

$$\mathcal{E}^\sigma(t^{\tau\Psi}, \phi) = \bigcup_{\substack{\rho \in \mathcal{N}(\tau) \\ \rho\Psi = \sigma}} \mathcal{E}^\rho(t,\tau) \cup \bigcup_{\substack{\rho \in \mathcal{N}(\tau) \\ \rho\Psi \bowtie \phi}} \mathcal{E}^\sigma(\mathcal{E}^\rho(t,\tau)^{\rho\Psi}, \phi) \tag{2}$$

Example 4.7. First let $\phi = \tau = \mathtt{List(u)}$ and Ψ be the identity. Then by Def. 4.2 there is no ρ such that $\rho \in \mathcal{N}(\tau)$ and $\rho\Psi \bowtie \phi$. Therefore in both equations of Thm. 4.3, the right half of the right hand side is empty. Furthermore there is exactly one ρ such that $\rho\Psi = \sigma$, namely $\rho = \sigma$. Thus the equations read

$$\mathcal{Z}(t,\tau) = \mathcal{Z}(t,\tau) \tag{1}$$

$$\mathcal{E}^\sigma(t,\tau) = \mathcal{E}^\sigma(t,\tau) \tag{2}$$

Similarly, Thm. 4.3 reduces to a trivial statement for Ex. 2.3 and in fact for most types that are commonly used. However for Ex. 4.4, Thm. 4.3 says that

$$\mathcal{Z}([E(7)]^{\text{List(Nest(v))}}, \text{Nest}(v)) =$$
$$\mathcal{Z}([E(7)], \text{List}(u)) \wedge \mathcal{Z}(\mathcal{E}^u([E(7)], \text{List}(u)), \text{Nest}(v)) \quad (1)$$

$$\mathcal{E}^v([E(7)]^{\text{List(Nest(v))}}, \text{Nest}(v)) =$$
$$\emptyset \qquad\qquad \cup \mathcal{E}^v(\mathcal{E}^u([E(7)], \text{List}(u)), \text{Nest}(v)) \quad (2)$$

5   Abstract Terms and Abstract Programs

In this section, we first define the abstraction function for terms. Then we define termination and extractor functions for abstract terms. Finally, we define an abstract program and show how it approximates its concrete counterpart.

5.1   Abstraction of Terms

We first define an abstract domain for each type. Each abstract domain is a term structure, built using the constant symbols Bot, Any, Ter, Open, and the function symbols $C^{\mathcal{A}}$, for each $C \in \Sigma_\tau$.

Definition 5.1 (abstract domain). If ϕ is a parameter, define

$$\mathcal{D}_\phi = \{\text{Bot}, \text{Any}\}.$$

If $C(\bar{u})$ is a simple type with $\mathcal{N}(C(\bar{u})) = \langle \sigma_1, \dots, \sigma_m \rangle$ and $\phi = C(\bar{u})\Psi$ where Ψ is a type substitution, define

$$\mathcal{D}_\phi = \{C^{\mathcal{A}}(b_1, \dots, b_m, \text{Ter}) \mid b_j \in \mathcal{D}_{\sigma_j\Psi}\} \cup \{C^{\mathcal{A}}(\underbrace{\text{Any}, \dots, \text{Any}}_{m \text{ times}}, \text{Open}), \text{Any}\}.$$

$\mathcal{D}_\phi$ is the **abstract domain for** ϕ. If $b \in \mathcal{D}_\phi$, then b is an **abstract term for** ϕ.

In [17], it is proven that every domain is well-defined. We shall see later that if an abstract term $C^{\mathcal{A}}(b_1, \dots, b_m, \text{Ter})$ abstracts a term t, then each b_j corresponds to a non-recursive subterm type σ_j of $C(\bar{u})$. It characterises the degree of instantiation of the subterms extracted by $\mathcal{E}^{\sigma_j}$.

The termination flags Ter and Open in the last argument position of an abstract term are Boolean flags. The flag Ter abstracts the property of a term being terminated and Open that of being open. Note that for some types, for example Int, a term can be open only if it is a variable. In these cases, the termination flag can be omitted in the implementation (see Sect. 6).

Example 5.1. Consider the examples in Sect. 2 and Fig. 1.

$$\mathcal{D}_{\text{Int}} = \{\text{Int}^{\mathcal{A}}(\text{Ter}), \text{Int}^{\mathcal{A}}(\text{Open}), \text{Any}\}.$$

The following examples illustrate that Def. 5.1 is "parametric".

$$\mathcal{D}_{\texttt{List(Int)}} = \{\texttt{List}^{\mathcal{A}}(i,\texttt{Ter}) \mid i \in \mathcal{D}_{\texttt{Int}}\} \quad \cup \{\texttt{List}^{\mathcal{A}}(\texttt{Any},\texttt{Open}),\texttt{Any}\}$$
$$\mathcal{D}_{\texttt{List(String)}} = \{\texttt{List}^{\mathcal{A}}(i,\texttt{Ter}) \mid i \in \mathcal{D}_{\texttt{String}}\} \cup \{\texttt{List}^{\mathcal{A}}(\texttt{Any},\texttt{Open}),\texttt{Any}\}$$
$$\mathcal{D}_{\texttt{List(u)}} = \{\texttt{List}^{\mathcal{A}}(i,\texttt{Ter}) \mid i \in \mathcal{D}_{\texttt{u}}\} \quad \cup \{\texttt{List}^{\mathcal{A}}(\texttt{Any},\texttt{Open}),\texttt{Any}\}.$$

Some further examples are, assuming that $\texttt{u} \prec \texttt{Balance} \prec \texttt{String}$:

$$\mathcal{D}_{\texttt{Balance}} = \{\texttt{Balance}^{\mathcal{A}}(\texttt{Ter}), \texttt{Balance}^{\mathcal{A}}(\texttt{Open}), \texttt{Any}\}$$
$$\mathcal{D}_{\texttt{String}} = \{\texttt{String}^{\mathcal{A}}(\texttt{Ter}), \texttt{String}^{\mathcal{A}}(\texttt{Open}), \texttt{Any}\}$$
$$\mathcal{D}_{\texttt{Table(Int)}} = \{\texttt{Table}^{\mathcal{A}}(i,b,s,\texttt{Ter}) \mid i \in \mathcal{D}_{\texttt{Int}}, b \in \mathcal{D}_{\texttt{Balance}}, s \in \mathcal{D}_{\texttt{String}}\} \cup$$
$$\{\texttt{Table}^{\mathcal{A}}(\texttt{Any},\texttt{Any},\texttt{Any},\texttt{Open}), \texttt{Any}\}$$
$$\mathcal{D}_{\texttt{Nest(Int)}} = \{\texttt{Nest}^{\mathcal{A}}(i,\texttt{Ter}) \mid i \in \mathcal{D}_{\texttt{Int}}\} \cup \{\texttt{Nest}^{\mathcal{A}}(\texttt{Any},\texttt{Open}), \texttt{Any}\}.$$

We now define an order on abstract terms which has the usual interpretation that "smaller" stands for "more precise".

Definition 5.2 (order $<$ on abstract terms). For the termination flags define $\texttt{Ter} < \texttt{Open}$. For abstract terms, $<$ is defined as follows:

$$\texttt{Bot} < b \qquad \text{if } b \neq \texttt{Bot},$$
$$b < \texttt{Any} \qquad \text{if } b \neq \texttt{Any},$$
$$C^{\mathcal{A}}(b_1,\ldots,b_m,c) \leq C^{\mathcal{A}}(b_1',\ldots,b_m',c') \text{ if } c \leq c' \text{ and } b_j \leq b_j', j \in \{1,\ldots,m\}.$$

For a set S of abstract terms, let $\sqcup S$ denote the least upper bound of S.

We now define the abstraction function for terms. This definition needs an abstraction of *truth values* as an auxiliary construction.

Definition 5.3 (abstraction function α for terms). Let $\tau = C(\bar{u})$ and $\mathcal{N}(\tau) = \langle\sigma_1,\ldots,\sigma_m\rangle$. For the truth values define $\alpha(true) = \texttt{Ter}$ and $\alpha(false) = \texttt{Open}$. If S is a set of terms, define

$$\alpha(S) = \sqcup\{\alpha(t) \mid t \in S\},$$

where $\alpha(t)$ is defined as:

$$\texttt{Any} \qquad\qquad\qquad\qquad\qquad\qquad \text{if } t \text{ is a variable,}$$
$$C^{\mathcal{A}}(\alpha(\mathcal{E}^{\sigma_1}(t,\tau)),\ldots,\alpha(\mathcal{E}^{\sigma_m}(t,\tau)),\alpha(\mathcal{Z}(t,\tau))) \quad \text{if } t = f_{\langle\tau_1\ldots\tau_n,\tau\rangle}(t_1,\ldots,t_n).$$

Note that this definition is based on the fact that $\alpha(\emptyset) = \texttt{Bot}$. From this it follows that the abstraction of a constant $t = f_{\langle\tau\rangle}$ is $C^{\mathcal{A}}(\texttt{Bot},\ldots,\texttt{Bot},\texttt{Ter})$.

The least upper bound of a *set* of abstract terms gives a safe approximation for the instantiation of *all* corresponding concrete terms. *Safe* means that each concrete term is at least as instantiated as indicated by the least upper bound.

Example 5.2. We illustrate Def. 5.3.

$$\alpha(7) = \mathtt{Int}^{\mathcal{A}}(\mathtt{Ter}) \qquad\qquad (\tau = \mathtt{Int}, m = 0, n = 0)$$

$$\alpha(\mathtt{Nil})\qquad\qquad\qquad\qquad (\tau = \mathtt{List(u)}, \mathcal{N}(\tau) = \langle \mathtt{u}\rangle, n = 0)$$
$$\quad = \mathtt{List}^{\mathcal{A}}(\alpha(\emptyset), \alpha(\mathcal{Z}(\mathtt{Nil}, \tau)))$$
$$\quad = \mathtt{List}^{\mathcal{A}}(\mathtt{Bot}, \mathtt{Ter})$$

$$\alpha(\mathtt{Cons(7,Nil)})\qquad\qquad (\tau = \mathtt{List(u)}, \mathcal{N}(\tau) = \langle \mathtt{u}\rangle, n = 2)$$
$$\quad = \mathtt{List}^{\mathcal{A}}(\sqcup\{\alpha(7)\}, \alpha(\mathcal{Z}(\mathtt{Cons(7,Nil)}, \tau)))$$
$$\quad = \mathtt{List}^{\mathcal{A}}(\mathtt{Int}^{\mathcal{A}}(\mathtt{Ter}), \mathtt{Ter}).$$

The table below gives some further examples.

term	type	abstraction
x	u	Any
[7,x]	List(Int)	$\mathtt{List}^{\mathcal{A}}(\mathtt{Any}, \mathtt{Ter})$
[7|x]	List(Int)	$\mathtt{List}^{\mathcal{A}}(\mathtt{Any}, \mathtt{Open})$
E(7)	Nest(Int)	$\mathtt{Nest}^{\mathcal{A}}(\mathtt{Int}^{\mathcal{A}}(\mathtt{Ter}), \mathtt{Ter})$
[E(7)]	List(Nest(Int))	$\mathtt{List}^{\mathcal{A}}(\mathtt{Nest}^{\mathcal{A}}(\mathtt{Int}^{\mathcal{A}}(\mathtt{Ter}), \mathtt{Ter}), \mathtt{Ter})$
N([E(7)])	Nest(Int)	$\mathtt{Nest}^{\mathcal{A}}(\mathtt{Int}^{\mathcal{A}}(\mathtt{Ter}), \mathtt{Ter})$
N([E(7),x])	Nest(Int)	$\mathtt{Nest}^{\mathcal{A}}(\mathtt{Any}, \mathtt{Open})$

Note that there is no term of type Int whose abstraction is $\mathtt{Int}^{\mathcal{A}}(\mathtt{Open})$.

The following theorem show that the abstraction captures groundness.

Theorem 5.1 (Proof see [17]). Let S be a set of terms having the same type. Then a variable occurs in an element of S (that is S is non-ground) if and only if Any or Open occurs in $\alpha(S)$.

5.2   Traversing Abstract Terms

In order to define abstract unification and, in particular, the abstraction of an equation in a program, we require an abstract termination function and abstract extractors similar to those already defined for concrete terms. The type superscript annotation for concrete terms is also useful for abstract terms.

Definition 5.4 (abstract termination function and extractor for σ).
Let ϕ and $\tau = C(\bar{u})$ be simple types such that $\tau\Psi \bowtie \phi$ for some Ψ, and $\mathcal{N}(\tau) = \langle \sigma_1, \ldots, \sigma_m\rangle$. Let b be an abstract term for an instance of $\tau\Psi$.
1. Abstract termination function.

$$\mathcal{AZ}(b^{\tau\Psi}, \phi) = \mathtt{Open} \qquad\qquad \text{if } b = \mathtt{Any}$$
$$\mathcal{AZ}(b^{\tau\Psi}, \phi) = \mathtt{Ter} \qquad\qquad\ \text{if } b = \mathtt{Bot}$$
$$\mathcal{AZ}(b^{\tau\Psi}, \phi) = c \wedge \bigwedge_{\sigma_j\Psi\bowtie\phi} \mathcal{AZ}(b_j^{\sigma_j\Psi}, \phi) \qquad \text{if } b = C^{\mathcal{A}}(b_1, \ldots, b_m, c).$$

2. Abstract extractor for σ. Let $\sigma \in \mathcal{N}(\phi)$.

$$\mathcal{AE}^\sigma(b^{\tau\Psi}, \phi) = \mathsf{Any} \qquad\qquad\qquad\qquad \text{if } b = \mathsf{Any}$$
$$\mathcal{AE}^\sigma(b^{\tau\Psi}, \phi) = \mathsf{Bot} \qquad\qquad\qquad\qquad \text{if } b = \mathsf{Bot}$$
$$\mathcal{AE}^\sigma(b^{\tau\Psi}, \phi) = \sqcup(\{b_j \mid \sigma_j\Psi = \sigma\} \cup$$
$$\qquad\qquad \{\mathcal{AE}^\sigma(b_j^{\sigma_j\Psi}, \phi) \mid \sigma_j\Psi \bowtie \phi\}) \quad \text{if } b = C^{\mathcal{A}}(b_1, \ldots, b_m, c).$$

We omit the superscript $\tau\Psi$ in the expressions $\mathcal{AZ}(b^{\tau\Psi}, \phi)$ and $\mathcal{AE}^\sigma(b^{\tau\Psi}, \phi)$ whenever $\phi = \tau$ and Ψ is the identity. In this (very common) case, the abstract termination function is merely a *projection* onto the termination flag of an abstract term (or Open if the abstract term is Any). Similarly, the abstract extractor for σ is merely a projection onto the jth argument of an abstract term, where $\sigma = \sigma_j$. Note the similarity between the above definition and Thm. 4.2.

Example 5.3.

$$\mathcal{AZ}(\mathsf{List}^{\mathcal{A}}(\mathsf{Any}, \mathsf{Ter})^{\mathsf{List}(\mathsf{Nest}(v))}, \mathsf{Nest}(v)) = \mathsf{Ter} \wedge \mathcal{AZ}(\mathsf{Any}, \mathsf{Nest}(v)) = \mathsf{Open}.$$
$$\mathcal{AE}^{\mathsf{v}}(\mathsf{List}^{\mathcal{A}}(\mathsf{Any}, \mathsf{Ter})^{\mathsf{List}(\mathsf{Nest}(v))}, \mathsf{Nest}(v)) = \mathsf{Any}.$$
$$\mathcal{AZ}(\mathsf{List}^{\mathcal{A}}(\mathsf{Nest}^{\mathcal{A}}(\mathsf{Int}^{\mathcal{A}}(\mathsf{Ter}), \mathsf{Ter}), \mathsf{Ter})^{\mathsf{List}(\mathsf{Nest}(v))}, \mathsf{Nest}(v)) =$$
$$\mathsf{Ter} \wedge \mathcal{AZ}(\mathsf{Nest}^{\mathcal{A}}(\mathsf{Int}^{\mathcal{A}}(\mathsf{Ter}), \mathsf{Ter}), \mathsf{Nest}(v)) = \mathsf{Ter}.$$
$$\mathcal{AE}^{\mathsf{v}}(\mathsf{List}^{\mathcal{A}}(\mathsf{Nest}^{\mathcal{A}}(\mathsf{Int}^{\mathcal{A}}(\mathsf{Ter}), \mathsf{Ter}), \mathsf{Ter})^{\mathsf{List}(\mathsf{Nest}(v))}, \mathsf{Nest}(v)) =$$
$$\mathcal{AE}^{\mathsf{v}}(\mathsf{Nest}^{\mathcal{A}}(\mathsf{Int}^{\mathcal{A}}(\mathsf{Ter}), \mathsf{Ter}), \mathsf{Nest}(v)) = \mathsf{Int}^{\mathcal{A}}(\mathsf{Ter}).$$

The following theorem states the fundamental relationship between concrete and abstract termination functions and extractors.

Theorem 5.2. Let ϕ and $\tau = C(\bar{u})$ be simple types such that $\tau\Psi \bowtie \phi$ for some Ψ, and $\sigma \in \mathcal{N}(\phi)$. Let $t^{\tau\Psi}$ be a term. Then

$$\alpha(\mathcal{Z}(t^{\tau\Psi}, \phi)) = \mathcal{AZ}(\alpha(t)^{\tau\Psi}, \phi) \qquad\qquad (1)$$
$$\alpha(\mathcal{E}^\sigma(t^{\tau\Psi}, \phi)) = \mathcal{AE}^\sigma(\alpha(t)^{\tau\Psi}, \phi) \qquad\qquad (2)$$

Proof. We only show (2), as the proof for (1) is similar. The proof is by induction on the structure of t. First assume t is a variable x or a constant d. Here we omit the type superscripts because they are irrelevant.

$$\alpha(\mathcal{E}^\sigma(x, \phi)) = \sqcup\{\alpha(x)\} = \mathsf{Any} = \mathcal{AE}^\sigma(\mathsf{Any}, \phi) = \mathcal{AE}^\sigma(\alpha(x), \phi).$$

$$\alpha(\mathcal{E}^\sigma(d, \phi)) = \sqcup\, \emptyset = \mathsf{Bot} = \mathcal{AE}^\sigma(C^{\mathcal{A}}(\mathsf{Bot}, \ldots, \mathsf{Bot}, \mathsf{Ter}), \phi) = \mathcal{AE}^\sigma(\alpha(d), \phi).$$

Now assume t is a compound term. Let $\mathcal{N}(\tau) = \langle \sigma_1, \ldots, \sigma_m \rangle$. In the following sequences of equations, $*$ marks steps which use straightforward manipulations such as rearranging least upper bounds or applications of α to sets.

$$\mathcal{AE}^\sigma(\alpha(t)^{\tau\Psi}, \phi) = \quad\quad (\text{Def. 5.3})$$
$$\mathcal{AE}^\sigma(C^{\mathcal{A}}(\alpha(\mathcal{E}^{\sigma_1}(t, \tau)), \ldots, \alpha(\mathcal{E}^{\sigma_m}(t, \tau)), \alpha(\mathcal{Z}(t, \tau)))^{\tau\Psi}, \phi) = \quad\quad (\text{Def. 5.4})$$
$$\sqcup(\{\alpha(\mathcal{E}^{\sigma_j}(t, \tau)) \mid \sigma_j\Psi = \sigma\} \cup \{\mathcal{AE}^\sigma(\alpha(\mathcal{E}^{\sigma_j}(t, \phi))^{\sigma_j\Psi}, \phi) \mid \sigma_j\Psi \bowtie \phi\}) =$$
$$(* \ \& \ \text{hyp.})$$
$$\sqcup(\bigcup_{\sigma_j\Psi = \sigma} \{\alpha(\mathcal{E}^{\sigma_j}(t, \tau))\} \quad \cup \bigcup_{\sigma_j\Psi\bowtie\phi} \{\alpha(\mathcal{E}^\sigma(\mathcal{E}^{\sigma_j}(t, \tau)^{\sigma_j\Psi}, \phi))\}) =$$
$$(* \ \& \ \text{Thm. 4.3})$$
$$\alpha(\mathcal{E}^\sigma(t^{\tau\Psi}, \phi)).$$

$\square$

Example 5.4. This illustrates Thm. 5.2 for $\phi = \tau\Psi = \text{List}(u)$ and $\sigma = u$.

$$\alpha(\mathcal{Z}([7], \text{List}(u))) = \quad \text{Ter} \quad = \mathcal{AZ}(\text{List}^{\mathcal{A}}(\text{Int}^{\mathcal{A}}(\text{Ter}), \text{Ter}), \text{List}(u))$$
$$\alpha(\mathcal{E}^u([7], \text{List}(u))) = \text{Int}^{\mathcal{A}}(\text{Ter}) = \mathcal{AE}^u(\text{List}^{\mathcal{A}}(\text{Int}^{\mathcal{A}}(\text{Ter}), \text{Ter}), \text{List}(u)).$$

5.3 Abstract Compilation

We now show how the abstract domains can be used in the context of *abstract compilation*. We define an abstract program and show that it is a safe approximation of the concrete program with respect to the usual operational semantics.

In a (normal form) program, each unification is made explicit by an equation. We now define an abstraction of such an equation. For an equation of the form $x = f(y_1, \ldots, y_n)$, the abstraction is an atom of the form $f_{\text{dep}}(b, b_1, \ldots, b_n)$, where f_{dep} is a predicate defined in the abstract program.

Definition 5.5 (f_{dep})**.** Let $f_{\langle\tau_1\ldots\tau_n,\tau\rangle} \in \Sigma_f$ where $\tau = C(\bar{u})$ and $\mathcal{N}(\tau) = \langle\sigma_1, \ldots, \sigma_m\rangle$. Then $f_{\text{dep}}(b, b_1, \ldots, b_n)$ **holds** if

$$b = C^{\mathcal{A}}(a_1, \ldots, a_m, c) \quad \text{where}$$
$$a_j = \sqcup(\{b_i \mid \tau_i = \sigma_j\} \cup \{\mathcal{AE}^{\sigma_j}(b_i^{\tau_i}, \tau) \mid \tau_i\bowtie\tau\}) \quad\quad \text{for all } j\in\{1,\ldots,m\} \quad (1)$$
$$c = \bigwedge_{\tau_i\bowtie\tau} \mathcal{AZ}(b_i^{\tau_i}, \tau) \quad\quad (2)$$

Example 5.5. To give an idea of how Def. 5.5 translates into code, consider Cons. Assuming that $\text{Lub}(a, b, c)$ holds if $c = \sqcup\{a, b\}$, one clause for Cons_{dep} might be:

```
Cons_dep(List_a(c,Ter),b,List_a(a,Ter)) <-
  Lub(a,b,c).
```

The following theorem shows that f_{dep} correctly captures the dependency between $\alpha(f(t_1, \ldots, t_n))$ and $\alpha(t_1), \ldots, \alpha(t_n)$.

Theorem 5.3. If $t = f(t_1, \ldots, t_n)$ then $f_{\text{dep}}(\alpha(t), \alpha(t_1), \ldots, \alpha(t_n))$ holds.

Proof. Suppose $\mathcal{N}(\tau) = \langle \sigma_1, \ldots, \sigma_m \rangle$ and $\tau = C(\bar{u})$. By Def. 5.3

$$\alpha(t) = C^{\mathcal{A}}(\alpha(\mathcal{E}^{\sigma_1}(t,\tau)), \ldots, \alpha(\mathcal{E}^{\sigma_m}(t,\tau)), \alpha(\mathcal{Z}(t,\tau))).$$

We show that (1) in Def. 5.5 holds. For each $\sigma_j \in \mathcal{N}(\tau)$,

$$
\begin{aligned}
\alpha(&\mathcal{E}^{\sigma_j}(t,\tau)) \\
&= \alpha(\{t_i \mid \tau_i = \sigma_j\} \ \cup \bigcup_{\tau_i \bowtie \tau} \mathcal{E}^{\sigma_j}(t_i^{\tau_i}, \tau)) && \text{(Thm. 4.2)} \\
&= \sqcup(\{\alpha(t_i) \mid \tau_i = \sigma_j\} \cup \{\alpha(\mathcal{E}^{\sigma_j}(t_i^{\tau_i}, \tau)) \mid \tau_i \bowtie \tau\}) && \text{(moving } \alpha \text{ inwards)} \\
&= \sqcup(\{\alpha(t_i) \mid \tau_i = \sigma_j\} \cup \{\mathcal{A}\mathcal{E}^{\sigma_j}(\alpha(t_i)^{\tau_i}, \tau) \mid \tau_i \bowtie \tau\}) && \text{(Thm. 5.2)}.
\end{aligned}
$$

Equation (2) in Def. 5.5 is proven in a similar way. $\qquad\square$

Definition 5.6 (abstraction $\aleph$ of a program). For a normal form equation e define

$$\aleph(e) = \begin{cases} e & \text{if } e \text{ is of the form } x = y \\ f_{\text{dep}}(x, y_1, \ldots, y_n) & \text{if } e \text{ is of the form } x = f(y_1, \ldots, y_n). \end{cases}$$

For a normal form atom a and clause $K = h \leftarrow g_1 \wedge \cdots \wedge g_l$ define

$$
\begin{aligned}
\aleph(a) &= a \\
\aleph(K) &= \aleph(h) \leftarrow \aleph(g_1) \wedge \cdots \wedge \aleph(g_l).
\end{aligned}
$$

For a program $P = \langle L, S \rangle$ define

$$\aleph(P) = \{\aleph(K) \mid K \in S\} \cup \{f_{\text{dep}}(a, a_1, \ldots, a_n) \mid f_{\text{dep}}(a, a_1, \ldots, a_n) \text{ holds}\}.$$

Example 5.6. In the following we give the usual recursive clause for Append in normal form and its abstraction.

%concrete clause	%abstract clause
`Append(xs,ys,zs) <-`	`Append(xs,ys,zs) <-`
`  xs = [x|x1s] &`	`  Cons_dep(xs,x,x1s) &`
`  zs = [x|z1s] &`	`  Cons_dep(zs,x,z1s) &`
`  Append(x1s,ys,z1s) .`	`  Append(x1s,ys,z1s) .`

We now define the operational semantics of concrete and abstract programs. We assume a fixed language L and program $P = \langle L, S \rangle$, and a left-to-right computation rule. A *program state* is a tuple $\langle G, \Theta \rangle$ where G is a query and Θ a substitution. It is an initial state if Θ is empty. We write $C \in_{\approx} S$ if C is a renamed variant of a clause in S.

Definition 5.7 (reduces to). The relation $\xrightarrow{P}$ ("reduces to") between states is defined by the following rules:

$$\langle h_1 : \cdots : h_l, \Theta \rangle \xrightarrow{P} \quad \langle h_2 : \cdots : h_l, \Theta\Theta' \rangle$$
$$\text{if } h_1 \text{ is } `x = t' \text{ and } x\Theta\Theta' = t\Theta' \quad (1)$$

$$\langle h_1 : \cdots : h_l, \Theta \rangle \xrightarrow{P} \langle G : h_2 : \cdots : h_l, \Theta\Theta' \rangle$$
$$\text{if } h \leftarrow G \in_{\approx} S \text{ and } h\Theta\Theta' = h_1\Theta\Theta' \quad (2)$$

$\xrightarrow{P}{}^{j}$ for $j \geq 0$ and $\xrightarrow{P}{}^{*}$ are defined in the usual way. If for an initial query G,

$$\langle G, \emptyset \rangle \xrightarrow{P}{}^{*} \langle p(x_1, \ldots, x_n) : H, \Theta \rangle \xrightarrow{P}{}^{*} \langle H, \Theta' \rangle,$$

we call $p(x_1, \ldots, x_n)\Theta$ a *call pattern* and $p(x_1, \ldots, x_n)\Theta'$ an *answer pattern* for p.

Note that this notion of "reduces" with arbitrary unifier is considered in [13].

The next theorem shows that for all call and answer patterns, which may arise in a derivation of a concrete program, there are corresponding patterns in a derivation of the abstract program.

Theorem 5.4. Let H, H' be queries, Θ a substitution and $j \geq 0$. If $\langle H, \emptyset \rangle \xrightarrow{P}{}^{j}$ $\langle H', \Theta \rangle$, then $\langle \aleph(H), \emptyset \rangle \xrightarrow{\aleph(P)}{}^{j} \langle \aleph(H'), \Theta^{\alpha} \rangle$, where $\Theta^{\alpha} = \{x/\alpha(x\Theta) \mid x \in dom(\Theta)\}$.

Proof. By Def. 5.7, $\langle H, \emptyset \rangle \xrightarrow{P}{}^{j} \langle H', \Theta \rangle$ if and only if $\langle H, \Theta \rangle \xrightarrow{P}{}^{j} \langle H', \Theta \rangle$, and likewise for $\aleph(P)$. Therefore it is enough to show that for all $j \geq 0$

$$\langle H, \Theta \rangle \xrightarrow{P}{}^{j} \langle H', \Theta \rangle \quad \text{implies} \quad \langle \aleph(H), \Theta^{\alpha} \rangle \xrightarrow{\aleph(P)}{}^{j} \langle \aleph(H'), \Theta^{\alpha} \rangle. \quad (3)$$

The proof is by induction on j. The base case $j = 0$ holds since $\langle \aleph(H), \Theta^{\alpha} \rangle \xrightarrow{\aleph(P)}{}^{0}$ $\langle \aleph(H), \Theta^{\alpha} \rangle$. For the induction step, assume (3) holds for some $j \geq 0$. We show that for every query H''

$$\langle H, \Theta \rangle \xrightarrow{P}{}^{j+1} \langle H'', \Theta \rangle \quad \text{implies} \quad \langle \aleph(H), \Theta^{\alpha} \rangle \xrightarrow{\aleph(P)}{}^{j+1} \langle \aleph(H''), \Theta^{\alpha} \rangle.$$

If $\langle H, \Theta \rangle \xrightarrow{P}{}^{j+1} \langle H'', \Theta \rangle$ is *false*, the result is trivial. If $\langle H, \Theta \rangle \xrightarrow{P}{}^{j+1} \langle H'', \Theta \rangle$, then

$$\langle H, \Theta \rangle \qquad \xrightarrow{P}{}^{j} \langle H', \Theta \rangle \qquad \xrightarrow{P} \langle H'', \Theta \rangle \qquad \text{for some query } H', \text{ and}$$
$$\langle \aleph(H), \Theta^{\alpha} \rangle \xrightarrow{\aleph(P)}{}^{j} \langle \aleph(H'), \Theta^{\alpha} \rangle \qquad \text{by hypothesis.}$$

It only remains to be shown that $\langle \aleph(H'), \Theta^{\alpha} \rangle \xrightarrow{\aleph(P)} \langle \aleph(H''), \Theta^{\alpha} \rangle$. We distinguish whether Rule (1) or (2) of Def. 5.7 was used for the step $\langle H', \Theta \rangle \xrightarrow{P} \langle H'', \Theta \rangle$.

(1): $H' = h_1 : \cdots : h_l$ where h_1 is '$x = t$', and $t = y$ or $t = f(x_1, \ldots, x_n)$. In the first case $\aleph(h_1) = h_1$. Since $x\Theta = y\Theta$, it follows that $\{x/\alpha(x\Theta), y/\alpha(x\Theta)\} \subseteq \Theta^{\alpha}$ and therefore $x\Theta^{\alpha} = y\Theta^{\alpha}$. Thus $\langle \aleph(H'), \Theta^{\alpha} \rangle \xrightarrow{\aleph(P)} \langle \aleph(H''), \Theta^{\alpha} \rangle$ by Rule (1). In the second case $\aleph(h_1) = f_{\text{dep}}(x, x_1, \ldots, x_n)$. Since $x\Theta = f(x_1\Theta, \ldots, x_n\Theta)$,

$$\{x/\alpha(f(x_1\Theta, \ldots, x_n\Theta)), x_1/\alpha(x_1\Theta), \ldots, x_n/\alpha(x_n\Theta)\} \subseteq \Theta^{\alpha}.$$

Thus, by Thm. 5.3, $f_{\text{dep}}(x, x_1, \ldots, x_n)\,\Theta^{\alpha}$ holds so that $f_{\text{dep}}(x, x_1, \ldots, x_n)\Theta^{\alpha} \in \aleph(P)$ by Def. 5.6. Thus $\langle \aleph(H'), \Theta^{\alpha} \rangle \xrightarrow{\aleph(P)} \langle \aleph(H''), \Theta^{\alpha} \rangle$ by Rule (2).

(2): $H' = h_1 : \cdots : h_l$ where $h \leftarrow G \in_{\approx} S$ and $h\Theta = h_1\Theta$. By Def. 5.6, $\aleph(h_1 \leftarrow G) \in_{\approx} \aleph(P)$. Furthermore $\aleph(h)$ has the form $p(\bar{x})$, and $\aleph(h_1)$ has the form $p(\bar{y})$. Since $\bar{x}\Theta = \bar{y}\Theta$ it follows that $p(\bar{x})\,\Theta^{\alpha} = p(\bar{y})\,\Theta^{\alpha}$. $\qquad\square$

Table 1. Some call and answer patterns for Insert

Insert(Tab$^{\mathcal{A}}$(Int$^{\mathcal{A}}$, Bal$^{\mathcal{A}}$, Str$^{\mathcal{A}}$, Ter), Str$^{\mathcal{A}}$, Int$^{\mathcal{A}}$, Any)   *leads to answer pattern*
Insert(Tab$^{\mathcal{A}}$(Int$^{\mathcal{A}}$, Bal$^{\mathcal{A}}$, Str$^{\mathcal{A}}$, Ter), Str$^{\mathcal{A}}$, Int$^{\mathcal{A}}$, Tab$^{\mathcal{A}}$(Int$^{\mathcal{A}}$, Bal$^{\mathcal{A}}$, Str$^{\mathcal{A}}$, Ter)).

Insert(Tab$^{\mathcal{A}}$(Int$^{\mathcal{A}}$, Bal$^{\mathcal{A}}$, Str$^{\mathcal{A}}$, Ter), Str$^{\mathcal{A}}$, Any, Any)   *leads to answer pattern*
Insert(Tab$^{\mathcal{A}}$(Int$^{\mathcal{A}}$, Bal$^{\mathcal{A}}$, Str$^{\mathcal{A}}$, Ter), Str$^{\mathcal{A}}$, Any, Tab$^{\mathcal{A}}$(Any, Bal$^{\mathcal{A}}$, Str$^{\mathcal{A}}$, Ter)).

6   Implementation and Results

From now on we refer to the abstract domains defined in this paper as *typed domains*. We have implemented our mode analysis for object programs in Gödel. This implementation naturally falls into two stages: In the first stage, the language declarations are analysed in order to construct the typed domains, and the program clauses are abstracted. In the second stage, the abstract program is evaluated using standard abstract compilation techniques.

We have implemented the first stage in Gödel, using the Gödel meta-programming facilities. Gödel meta-programming is slow, but this first stage scales well, as the time for abstracting the clauses of a program is linear in their number. Analysing the type declarations is not a problem in practice. We have analysed contrived, complex type declarations within a couple of seconds.

The second stage was implemented in Prolog, so that an existing analyser could be used. Abstract programs produced by the first stage were transformed into Prolog. All call and answer patterns, which may arise in a derivation of an abstract program for a given query, are computed by the analyser. By Thm. 5.4, these patterns correspond to patterns in the derivation of the concrete program. For example a call p(Any, Int$^{\mathcal{A}}$(Ter)) in the abstract program indicates that there may be a call p(x,7) in the concrete program.

We now demonstrate the precision of the typed domain for Table(Int). The arguments of the predicate Insert represent: a table t, a key k, a value v, and a table obtained from t by inserting the node whose key is k and whose value is v. Table 1 shows some initial call patterns and the answer pattern that is inferred for each call pattern. For readability, we have used some abbreviations and omitted the termination flag for types Integer, Balance and String.

Clearly, inserting a ground node into a ground table gives a ground table. This can be inferred with the typed domains, but it could also be inferred using a domain which can only distinguish between ground and non-ground terms [4]. Now consider the insertion of a node with an *uninstantiated* value into a ground table. With typed domains, it can be inferred that the result is still a table but whose values may be uninstantiated.

We used a modified form of the analyser of [8] running on a Sun SPARC Ultra 170. The analysis times for the two example analyses using Insert were were 0.81 seconds and 2.03 seconds, respectively. Comparing this to an analysis using a domain which can only distinguish ground and non-ground terms, the times were 0.09 seconds and 1.57 seconds, respectively. Apart from `Tables`, we also analysed some small programs, namely `Append`, `Reverse`, `Flatten` (from the `Nests` module), `TreeToList`, `Qsort`, and `Nqueens`. For these, all analysis times were below 0.03 seconds and thus too small to be very meaningful.

Our experience is that the domain operations, namely to compute the least upper bound of two abstract terms, are indeed the bottleneck of the analysis. Therefore it is crucial to avoid performing these computations unnecessarily. Also one might compromise some of the precision of the analysis by considering widenings [6] for the sake of efficiency. In order to conduct more experiments, one would need a suite of bigger typed logic programs. A formal comparison between analyses for typed logic programs and untyped ones is of course difficult.

7   Discussion and Related Work

We have presented a general domain construction for mode analysis of typed logic programs. This analysis gives more accurate information than one based on a ground/non-ground domain [4]. For common examples (lists, binary trees), our formalism is simple and yields abstract domains that are comparable to the domains in [3]. The novelty is that the construction is described for arbitrary types. In contrast, in [3], an abstract domain for obtaining this degree of precision for, say, the types in the `Tables` module, would have to be hand-crafted.

The fundamental concepts of this work are *recursive type* and *non-recursive subterm type*, which are generalisations of ideas presented in [3] for lists. The resulting abstract domains are entirely in the spirit of [3,5] and we believe that they provide the highest degree of precision that a generic domain construction should provide. Even if type declarations that require the full generality of our formalism are rare, we think that our work is an important contribution because it helps to understand other, more ad-hoc and pragmatic domain constructions as instances of a general theory. One could always simplify or prune down our abstract domains for the sake of efficiency.

In its full generality the formalism is, admittedly, rather complex. This is mainly due to function declarations where the range type occurs again as a *proper* sub"term" of an argument type, such as the declaration of N in Ex. 2.2. This phenomenon occurs in the declarations for *rose trees* [14], that is, trees where the number of children of each node is not fixed. One should note that while the theory which allows for a domain construction for, say, `Nest(Int)` is conceptually complex, the computational complexity of the domain operations for `Nest(Int)` is lower than for, say, `List(List(List(Int)))`. In short, the complexity of the abstract domains depends on the complexity of the type declarations.

We have built on the ideas presented in [5] for untyped languages. Notably the title of [5] says that *type*, not *mode*, dependencies are derived. Even in an untyped language such as Prolog, one can define types as sets of terms given by some kind of "declaration", just as in a typed language [1]. In this case type analysis (that is, inferring that an argument is instantiated to a term *of a certain type*) is inseparable from mode analysis. It seems that [5] provides a straightforward domain construction for *arbitrary* types, but this is not the case. It is not specified what kind of "declarations" are implied, but the examples and theory suggest that all types are essentially lists and trees. The `Tables` and `Nests` examples given in Sect. 2 are not captured.

Recursive modes [21] characterise that the left spine, right spine, or both, of a term are instantiated. The authors admit that this may be considered an ad-hoc choice, but on the other hand, they present good experimental results. They do not assume a typed language and thus cannot exploit type declarations in order to provide a more generic concept of *recursive modes*, as we have done by the concept of *termination*.

A complex system for type analysis of Prolog is presented in [23]. As far as we can see, this system is not in a formal sense stronger or weaker that our mode analysis. The domain `Pat(Type)` used there is infinite, so that widenings have to be introduced to ensure finiteness, and "the design of widening operators is experimental in nature" [23]. In contrast, we exploit the type declarations to construct domains that are inherently finite and whose size is immediately dictated by the complexity of the type declarations.

Mercury [19] has a strong mode system based on *instantiation states*. These are assertions of how instantiated a term is. An instantiation state is similar to an abstract term. Indeed, given some type declarations, it is possible to define an instantiation state in Mercury syntax which, while not being exactly the same, is comparable in precision to an abstract term in our formalism. The difference is that for a given type, there are potentially infinitely many instantiation states.

The current Mercury implementation does not support instantiation states in their full generality, although a version supporting partially instantiated data-structures is being developed. Within the limits of the expressiveness of the mode system, Mercury does a combination of mode analysis and mode checking of modes declared by the user.

Even if instantiation states were supported in their full generality, the potentially infinite number of instantiation states means that mode inference must always be approximate. Since our abstract terms formalise what might be called a "reasonable" degree of precision, we believe that our proposal could serve as a basis for this approximation. One could envisage a Mercury implementation doing a combination of mode inference and checking, based on the set of modes which is expressible using our abstract domains. Hence our domains could also be used to *declare* modes.

The mode system in Mercury is based on [18], where the Simple Range Condition and the Reflexive Condition that we impose are not explicitly required. However, [18] does not define the type system precisely, instead referring to [15], whose formal results have been shown to be incorrect [16]. It is therefore difficult to assess whether that approach would work for programs which violate these conditions. We know of no real Gödel programs that violate either of the Simple Range or Reflexive Conditions. We have found that violating the Reflexive

100   J.–G. Smaus, P.M. Hill, and A. King

Condition raises fundamental questions about decidability in typed languages, which seem to be related to the concept of *polymorphic recursion* [11,12].

There is another potential application of our work. In Gödel, the delay declarations which state that a predicate is delayed until an argument (or a subterm of the argument) is ground or non-variable, cannot describe the behaviour of the Gödel system predicates precisely. We have observed that, typically, the degree of instantiation for a Gödel system predicate to run safely without delaying could be specified by an abstract term in our typed domains. Thus they could provide a good basis for declaring conditions for delaying.

Our approach may also be applicable to untyped languages, if we have information at hand that is similar to type declarations. Such information might be obtained by inferring declarations [2] or from declarations as comments [20]. Certainly our analysis would then regain aspects of *type* rather than *mode* inference, which it had lost by transferring the approach to typed languages.

Acknowledgements. We thank Tony Bowers, Henning Christiansen, Bart Demoen, Andrew Heaton, Fergus Henderson, Jonathan Martin and Lambert Meertens for helpful discussions and comments. Jan–Georg Smaus was supported by EPSRC Grant No. GR/K79635.

References

1. A. Aiken and T. K. Lakshman. Directional type checking of logic programs. In *SAS '94*, pages 43–60. Springer-Verlag, 1994.
2. H. Christiansen. Deriving declarations from programs. Technical report, Roskilde University, P.O.Box 260, DK-4000 Roskilde, 1997.
3. M. Codish and B. Demoen. Deriving polymorphic type dependencies for logic programs using multiple incarnations of Prop. In *SAS'94*, pages 281–297. Springer-Verlag, 1994.
4. M. Codish and B. Demoen. Analyzing logic programs using "PROP"-ositional logic programs and a Magic Wand. *Journal of Logic Programming*, 25(3):249–274, 1995.
5. M. Codish and V. Lagoon. Type dependencies for logic programs using ACI-unification. In *Israeli Symposium on Theory of Computing and Systems*, pages 136–145. IEEE Press, 1996.
6. P. Cousot and R. Cousot. Comparing the Galois connection and widening/narrowing approaches to abstract interpretation. In M. Bruynooghe and M. Wirsing, editors, *PLILP'92*, LNCS, pages 269–295. Springer-Verlag, 1992.
7. J. Gallagher, D. Boulanger, and H. Sağlam. Practical model-based static analysis for definite logic programs. In J. W. Lloyd, editor, *ILPS'95*, pages 351–365. MIT Press, 1995.
8. A.J. Heaton, P.M. Hill, and A.M. King. Analysing logic programs with delay for downward-closed properties. In N.E. Fuchs, editor, *LOPSTR'97*, LNCS. Springer-Verlag, 1997.
9. P.M. Hill and A. King. Determinacy and determinacy analysis. *Journal of Programming Languages*, 5(1):135–171, 1997.
10. P.M. Hill and J.W. Lloyd. *The Gödel Programming Language*. MIT Press, 1994.

11. S. Kahrs. Limits of ML-definability. In H. Kuchen and S. D. Swierstra, editors, *PLILP'96*, LNCS, pages 17–31. Springer-Verlag, 1996.

12. A. J. Kfoury, J. Tiuryn, and P. Urzyczyn. Type recursion in the presence of polymorphic recursion. *ACM Transactions on Programming Languages and Systems*, 15(2):290–311, 1993.

13. J. W. Lloyd. *Foundations of Logic Programming*. Springer-Verlag, 1987.

14. L. Meertens. First steps towards the theory of rose trees. CWI, Amsterdam; IFIP Working Group 2.1 working paper 592 ROM-25, 1988.

15. A. Mycroft and R. O'Keefe. A polymorphic type system for Prolog. *Artificial Intelligence*, 23:295–307, 1984.

16. F. Pfenning, editor. *Types in Logic Programming*, chapter 1. MIT Press, 1992.

17. J.-G. Smaus, P. M. Hill, and A. M. King. Mode analysis domains for typed logic programs. Technical Report 2000.06, School of Computer Studies, University of Leeds, 2000. © Springer-Verlag.

18. Z. Somogyi. A system of precise modes for logic programs. In *ICLP'87*, pages 769–787. MIT Press, 1987.

19. Z. Somogyi, F. Henderson, and T. Conway. The execution algorithm of Mercury, an efficient purely declarative logic programming language. *Journal of Logic Programming*, November 1996.

20. K. Stroetmann and T. Glaß. A semantics for types in Prolog: The type system of PAN version 2.0. Technical report, Siemens AG, München, Germany, 1995.

21. Jichang Tan and I-Peng Lin. Recursive modes for precise analysis of logic programs. In *ILPS'97*, pages 277–290. MIT Press, 1997.

22. M. van Emden. AVL tree insertion: A benchmark program biased towards Prolog. *Logic Programming Newsletter 2*, 1981.

23. P. Van Hentenryck, A. Cortesi, and B. Le Charlier. Type analysis of Prolog using type graphs. Technical Report CS-93-52, Brown University Box 1910, Providence, RI 02912, November 1993.

Author Index

Lecture Notes in Computer Science 1817
Edited by G. Goos, J. Hartmanis, and J. van Leeuwen

Berlin
Heidelberg
New York
Barcelona
Hong Kong
London
Milan
Paris
Singapore
Tokyo

Annalisa Bossi (Ed.)

Logic-Based Program Synthesis and Transformation

9th International Workshop, LOPSTR'99
Venice, Italy, September 22-24, 1999
Selected Papers

Series Editors

Gerhard Goos, Karlsruhe University, Germany
Juris Hartmanis, Cornell University, NY, USA
Jan van Leeuwen, Utrecht University, The Netherlands

Volume Editor

Annalisa Bossi
Università Ca' Foscari di Venezia
Dipartimento di Informatica
Via Torino 155, I-30172 Mestre-Venezia, Italy
E-mail: bossi@dsi.unive.it

Cataloging-in-Publication Data applied for

Die Deutsche Bibliothek - CIP-Einheitsaufnahme

Logic-based program synthesis and transformation : 9th international
workshop ; selected papers / LOPSTR '99, Venice, Italy, September 22 -
24, 1999. Annalisa Bossi (ed.). - Berlin ; Heidelberg ; New York ;
Barcelona ; Hong Kong ; London ; Milan ; Paris ; Singapore ; Tokyo :
Springer, 2000
    (Lecture notes in computer science ; Vol. 1817)
    ISBN 3-540-67628-7

CR Subject Classification (1998): F.3.1, D.1.1, D.1.6, I.2.2, F.4.1

ISSN 0302-9743
ISBN 3-540-67628-7 Springer-Verlag Berlin Heidelberg New York

Springer is a company in the BertelsmannSpringer publishing group.
© Springer-Verlag Berlin Heidelberg 2000
Printed in Germany

Typesetting: Camera-ready by author, data conversion by PTP-Berlin, Stefan Sossna
Printed on acid-free paper   SPIN: 10720327   06/3142   5 4 3 2 1 0

Preface

This volume contains the proceedings of the ninth international workshop on logic-based program synthesis and transformation (LOPSTR'99) which was held in Venice (Italy), September 22-24, 1999.

LOPSTR is the annual workshop and forum for researchers in the logic-based program development stream of computational logic. The main focus used to be on synthesis and transformation of logic programs, but the workshop is open to contributions on logic-based program development in any paradigm. Previous workshops were held in Manchester, UK (1991, 1992), Louvain-la-Neuve, Belgium (1993), Pisa, Italy (1994), Arnhem, The Netherlands (1995), Stockholm, Sweden (1996), Leuven, Belgium (1997), and Manchester, UK (1998).

LOPSTR is a real workshop in the sense that it is a friendly and lively forum for presenting recent and current research as well as discussing future trends. Formal proceedings of the workshop are produced only after the workshop and contain only those papers selected by the program committee after a second refereeing process.

The program committee of LOPSTR'99 accepted 20 extended abstracts for presentation at the workshop; then selected 14 papers for inclusion in the post-workshop proceedings. Selected papers cover all the main streams of LOPSTR's topics: synthesis, specialization, transformation, analysis, and verification. Verification, transformation, and specialization methods are applied to functional, constraint, logic, and imperative programming.

The invited speaker was Donald Sannella, of the University of Edinburgh, UK. He presented and compared various formalizations of the concept of "refinement step" used in the formal development of programs from algebraic specifications. Two tutorials were offered to the audience: Mireille Ducassé presented the B formal method for software development, Laurent Fribourg discussed some of the approaches based on constraint logic programming for verifying properties of state-transition systems. An extended abstract of the invited talk is included in this volume together with the two tutorial papers.

I would like to thank all the members of the program committee and all the referees for their careful work in the reviewing and selection process. Special thanks go to Pierre Flener, the chairman of LOPSTR'98, for his helpful advise and to the organizing committee for the effort they invested.

March 2000   Annalisa Bossi

Program Committee

Annalisa Bossi	University of Venice, Italy (program chair)
Yves Deville	Université Catholique de Louvain, Belgium
Mireille Ducassé	IRISA, Rennes, France
Sandro Etalle	Universiteit Maastricht, The Netherlands
Pierre Flener	Uppsala University, Sweden
Patricia Hill	University of Leeds, UK
Kung-Kiu Lau	University of Manchester, UK
Baudouin Le Charlier	University of Namur, Belgium
Michael Leuschel	University of Southampton, UK
Michael Lowry	NASA Ames, USA
Ali Mili	Institute for Software Research, USA
Lee Naish	Melbourne University, Australia
Alberto Pettorossi	University of Rome Tor Vergata, Italy
Dave Robertson	University of Edinburgh, UK

Organizing Committee

Agostino Cortesi (Univ. of Venice)
Nicoletta Cocco (Univ. of Venice)
Riccardo Focardi (Univ. of Venice)
Sabina Rossi (Univ. of Venice)

Referees

D. Basin	P. Hill	L. Naish
A. Bossi	I. Hnich	A. Pettorossi
M. Bugliesi	J.M. Howe	M. Proietti
N. Cocco	E. Jahier	J. Richardson
T. Conway	K.-K. Lau	O. Ridoux
A. Cortesi	H. Lehmann	D. Robertson
Y. Deville	B. Le Charlier	S. Rossi
M. Ducassé	M. Leuschel	J.-G. Smaus
S. Etalle	F. Levi	H. Søndergaard
P. Flener	M. Lowry	P. Stuckey
J. Gow	S. Mallet	S.-A. Tärnlund
A. Heaton	A. Mili	Z. Kiziltan

Sponsoring Institutions

ALP
Compulog
CNR
Cá Foscari University of Venice
Padova University

Table of Contents

Verification